CLARENDON LAW SERIES

Edited by

PAUL CRAIG

LNDC

(HUMN)
Fre
STA)

CLARENDON LAW SERIES

Administrative Law (5th edition)
PETER CANE

An Introduction to the Law of Trusts
(3rd edition)
SIMON GARDNER

Natural Law and Natural Rights
(2nd edition)
JOHN FINNIS

Introduction to Company Law
(2nd edition)
PAUL DAVIES

Employment Law (2nd edition)
HUGH COLLINS

The Conflict of Laws (2nd edition)
ADRIAN BRIGGS

International Law
VAUGHAN LOWE

Civil Liberties
CONOR GEARTY

Intellectual Property
MICHAEL SPENCE

Policies and Perceptions of Insurance
Law in the Twenty-First Century
(2nd edition)
MALCOLM CLARKE

Philosophy of Private Law
WILLIAM LUCY

Land Law
ELIZABETH COOKE

Law in Modern Society
DENIS GALLIGAN

An Introduction to Tort Law
(2nd edition)
TONY WEIR

Equity (2nd edition)
SARAH WORTHINGTON

Atiyah's Introduction to the Law
of Contract (6th edition)
STEPHEN A. SMITH, P.S. ATIYAH

Unjust Enrichment (2nd edition)
PETER BIRKS

An Introduction to Family Law
(2nd edition)
GILLIAN DOUGLAS

Criminal Justice
LUCIA ZEDNER

Contract Theory
STEPHEN A. SMITH

Public Law
ADAM TOMKINS

Personal Property Law (3rd edition)
MICHAEL BRIDGE

Law of Property (3rd edition)
F.H. LAWSON AND BERNARD RUDDEN

An Introduction to Constitutional Law
ERIC BARENDT

Resulting Trusts
ROBERT CHAMBERS

The Concept of Law (2nd edition)
H.L.A. HART

Legal Reasoning and Legal Theory
NEIL MACCORMICK

DISCRIMINATION LAW

SECOND EDITION

SANDRA FREDMAN, FBA

OXFORD
UNIVERSITY PRESS

OXFORD

UNIVERSITY PRESS

Great Clarendon Street, Oxford OX2 6DP

Oxford University Press is a department of the University of Oxford.
It furthers the University's objective of excellence in research, scholarship,
and education by publishing worldwide in

Oxford New York

Auckland Cape Town Dar es Salaam Hong Kong Karachi
Kuala Lumpur Madrid Melbourne Mexico City Nairobi
New Delhi Shanghai Taipei Toronto

With offices in

Argentina Austria Brazil Chile Czech Republic France Greece
Guatemala Hungary Italy Japan Poland Portugal Singapore
South Korea Switzerland Thailand Turkey Ukraine Vietnam

Oxford is a registered trade mark of Oxford University Press
in the UK and in certain other countries

Published in the United States
by Oxford University Press Inc., New York

First published 2002
Second edition published 2011

British Library Cataloguing in Publication Data
Data available

Library of Congress Cataloging in Publication Data
Data available

Typeset by SPI Publisher Services, Pondicherry, India
Printed in Great Britain
on acid-free paper by
Clays Ltd, St Ives plc

ISBN 978-0-19-958442-0 (Hbk.)
978-0-19-958443-7 (Pbk.)

1 3 5 7 9 10 8 6 4 2

This book is dedicated to Jem, Kim, and Dan, to Alan, and to my parents, Naomi and Mike

Preface to the Second Edition

In the ten years since this book first came out, much has changed and much has stayed the same. Increasingly sophisticated legal tools have emerged for addressing inequality; yet true equality remains elusive. Indeed, by paying more attention to inequalities, we are more aware of their scale. On the one hand, the legal landscape in the UK has been altered dramatically by the Equality Act 2010, which draws together the confusing plethora of anti-discrimination legislation which had grown piece-meal over the years. On the other hand, the social landscape is being ravaged by cuts to public services, making gains in the equality field appear increasingly fragile. Simultaneously, the legitimacy of human rights is being challenged in some political quarters.

As in the first edition, this book aims to contribute to the search for equality, not by providing answers, but by articulating the questions. The second edition deepens and extends the use of comparative law, drawing particularly on equality law in the USA, Canada, South Africa, and India. European Union law is also of central importance, as is that of the European Convention on Human Rights. Similar questions are asked across all these jurisdictions, and there is increasing cross-pollination of legal concepts. Comparative law sharpens our understanding of our own jurisdiction, enriches the debate as to the purposes of equality law, and suggests alternative means of accomplishing stated aims. At the same time, comparative law carries with it important challenges: equality must always be understood within the specific legal, social, and political context of a particular jurisdiction. The aim is therefore to find a conception of equality which is both generalizable and context sensitive.

I owe very special thanks to a great many people for their help and support in writing the second edition. Special thanks go to Bob Hepple, as ever, for his friendship and support over many years, to Paul Craig, as editor of the Clarendon series and colleague, and to my two research assistants, Natasa Mavronicola and Aaron Rathmell, for their sterling background research. I remain indebted too to the former editor of the series, the late Peter Birks, whose warmth, friendship, and unstinting support remain as vivid in memory as in life. As ever, I have benefited enormously from ongoing discussions with my students, both graduate and under-graduate, and with colleagues in Oxford, in India, in South Africa, and all over the world. I would also like to thank my publishers, OUP, and particularly Gwen Booth, Natasha Knight, Emma Hawes, and Joy Ruskin-Tompkins.

As ever, my deepest appreciation remains for my husband Alan, my children, Jem, Kim, and Dan, my mother Naomi, and my late father Mike. It is from them that I draw inspiration, energy, and hope for a future with fewer inequalities. I dedicate this book to them, with love beyond words.

Oxford

March 2011

Preface to the First Edition

Despite the widespread belief in equality, we live in a world which is marred by deep inequalities. As a white South African Jewish woman, an immigrant and member of an ethnic minority, I personally have experienced discrimination in many guises. I have been both a victim and, involuntarily, one of the perpetrator class. Growing up in a society twisted by the systematic racism of apartheid, with the scars of the Holocaust still fresh, and in a deeply sexist world, I discovered both the central value, and the elusiveness of equality. This book aims to contribute to the search for equality, not by providing answers, but by articulating the questions. It introduces the reader to the controversies we confront as soon as we try to translate our ideal of equality into legal form, and, more difficult still, into social and political reality. The book does not attempt to provide a single solution, but points to a range of possible responses, drawing on the experience of different jurisdictions, and locating the issues firmly within their appropriate historical and political frame. It is to be hoped that the reader will come away both with renewed faith in the ideal of equality, and with a heightened sensitivity to the problems to be faced.

There are a great many people to whom I owe very special thanks for their help and support in writing this book. My thanks are especially due to Peter Birks, as editor and colleague, who has been unstinting in his support for the project and the outcome. My special thanks too to Bob Hepple, not only for his detailed comments on this book, but also for the friendship and inspiration he has provided over many years. I could not have written this book without the formative input of Chris McCrudden, Mark Freedland, and Paul Davies, who have always been immensely generous in sharing their thoughts and ideas. I have also benefited enormously from ongoing discussions with many students and colleagues from all over the world. My two research assistants, Christopher Brothers and Suzanne Lambert, gave invaluable assistance in putting the final touches to the manuscript. I owe too a particular debt to the Arts and Humanities Research Board for their assistance in funding this project.

I dedicate this work to my husband Alan, to my children, Jem, Kim, and Dan, and to the hope that the world of their adulthood will be one with fewer inequalities than that of their childhood. I dedicate this book

too to my mother, Naomi Fredman, and to my late father, Mike Fredman, whose courage in facing illness and death have added a deep
poignancy to the process of writing it.

Sandra Fredman
September 2001

Contents

Table of Cases   xiii
Table of Legislation and Statutory Materials   xxvii
List of Abbreviations   xxxiii

1. **Equality: Concepts and Controversies**   1
   I   The Principle of Equality   4
   II   Competing Values: Liberty or Equality   33
   III   Conclusion   37

2. **Social Context and Legal Developments**   38
   I   Gender   38
   II   Race and Ethnicity   50
   III   Gypsies and Travellers   69
   IV   Religion and Belief   73
   V   Sexual Orientation   86
   VI   Gender Reassignment   93
   VII   Disability   95
   VIII   Age Discrimination   101
   IX   Conclusion   108

3. **The Scope of Discrimination Law**   109
   I   Grounds of Discrimination   110
   II   Scope of Discrimination Law   143
   III   Who is Bound?   148

4. **Legal Concepts: Direct, Indirect Discrimination, and Beyond**   153
   I   Equal Pay Legislation. The Shackled Giant   156
   II   Direct Discrimination   166
   III   Indirect Discrimination   177
   IV   Competing Priorities: Justifying Discrimination   190
   V   The Difficult Divide: The Role of Motive and Intention in Direct and Indirect Discrimination   203
   VI   Duty of Accommodation or Adjustment   214

VII   Equality as Proportionality   221
VIII   Equality as Dignity   227
IX   Positive Duties to Promote Equality   230
X   Conclusion   231

5. **Symmetry or Substance: Reverse Discrimination**   232
   I   Concepts of Equality and Reverse Discrimination   233
   II   Reverse Discrimination and the Law: Contrasting
        Jurisdictions   237
   III Aims and Effectiveness   259
   IV   Conclusion   278

6. **Rights and Remedies: The Limits of the Law**   279
   I   Adversarialism: The Narrow Reach of Adjudication   280
   II   Agency Enforcement   295
   III 'Fourth Generation' Equality: Positive Duties   299
   IV   Conclusion   335

   Index   337

Table of Cases

AL (Serbia) v Secretary of State for the Home Department [2008]
UKHL 42; [2008] 1 WLR 1434; [2008] 4 All ER 1127; [2008] HRLR 41;
[2008] UKHRR 917; 24 BHRC 738; [2008] Imm AR 729; [2008] INLR 471;
(2008) 152(26) SJLB 29 . . . . 126, 128, 133, 136
Abdulaziz, Cabales and Balkandali v United Kingdom (1985) 7 EHRR 471
(ECtHR) 126, 222
Abrahamsson v Fogelqvist (C–407/98) [2000] ECR I-5539; [2002]
ICR 932; [2000] IRLR 732 (ECJ) 244, 246
Action Travail des femmes v Canadian National Railway Co [1987] 1
SCR 1114; 40 DLR (4th) 193 268
Adarand v Pena, 515 US 200; 115 S Ct 2097 (1995) 234, 235, 250, 251, 269, 277
Ahmad v Inner London Education Authority [1978] QB 36;
[1977] 3 WLR 396; [1978] 1 All ER 574; [1977] ICR 490; 75 LGR 753 (CA) 12
Ahmad v United Kingdom (8160/78) (1982) 4 EHRR 126
(European Commission on Human Rights) 12
Albermarle v Moody, 422 US 405; 95 S Ct 2362 (1975) 192
Aldridge v British Telecommunications plc [1989] ICR 790;
[1990] IRLR 10 (EAT) 282
Allonby v Accrington and Rossendale College (C–256/01)
[2005] All ER (EC) 289; [2004] ECR I-873; [2004] 1 CMLR 35; [2004]
ICR 1328; [2004] IRLR 224; [2004] OPLR 83; [2004] Pens LR 199 (ECJ) 160
Andrews v Law Society of British Columbia [1989] 1 SCR 143 . . . . . . .22, 32, 132, 135
Anuj Garg v Hotel Association of India [2007] INSC 1226; AIR 2008
SC 663 (Indian Supreme Ct) 132
Archibald v Fife Council [2004] UKHL 32; [2004] 4 All ER 303; 2004
SC (HL) 117; 2004 SLT 942; 2004 SCLR 971; [2004] ICR 954; [2004]
IRLR 651; (2005) 82 BMLR 185; (2004) 101(31) LSG 25; (2004) 148
SJLB 826; 2004 GWD 23-505 216
Ashoka Kumar v Union of India, IA No 13 In Writ Petition (Civil) No
265 of 2006 276
Azmi v Kirklees MBC [2007] ICR 1154; [2007] IRLR 484; [2007]
ELR 339 (EAT) 195, 220

Badeck's Application (C–158/97) [2000] All ER (EC) 289; [2000] ECR I-1875;
[2001] 2 CMLR 6; [2000] CEC 218; [2000] IRLR 432 (ECJ) 243, 245
Baer v Alberta [2007] 2 SCR 673 129
Bahl v Law Society [2004] EWCA Civ 1070; [2004] IRLR 799;
(2004) 154 NLJ 1292; (2004) 148 SJLB 976 142
Barber v Guardian Royal Exchange Assurance Group (C–262/88)
[1991] 1 QB 344; [1991] 2 WLR 72; [1990] 2 All ER 660; [1990] ECR

I-1889; [1990] 2 CMLR 513; [1990] ICR 616; [1990] IRLR 240;
[1990] 1 PLR 103; (1990) 140 NLJ 925 (ECJ) 21
Barnes v Castle, 561 F 2d 983 (US Ct of Appeals (DC Cir, 1997)) 167
Belgian Linguistics Case (No 2) (A/6) (1979-80) 1 EHRR 252
(ECtHR) 127, 147, 222, 226, 258
Bellinger v Bellinger [2003] UKHL 21; [2003] 2 AC 467; [2003]
2 WLR 1174; [2003] 2 All ER 593; [2003] 1 FLR 1043; [2003] 2 FCR 1;
[2003] HRLR 22; [2003] UKHRR 679; 14 BHRC 127; (2003) 72 BMLR 147;
[2003] ACD 74; [2003] Fam Law 485; (2003) 153 NLJ 594;
(2003) 147 SJLB 472 94
Bilka-Kaufhaus GmbH v Weber von Hartz (170/84) [1986] ECR 1607;
[1986] 2 CMLR 701; [1987] ICR 110; [1986] IRLR 317 (ECJ) 164, 182, 193
Bowers v Hardwick, 478 US 186 (1986) 123, 124
Bowman v United Kingdom (24839/94) (1998) 26 EHRR 1; 4 BHRC 25;
[1998] HRCD 273 (ECtHR) 34
Bradford City Council v Arora [1991] 2 QB 507; [1991] 2 WLR 1377;
[1991] 3 All ER 545; [1991] ICR 226; [1991] IRLR 164 (CA) 292
Briheche v Ministre de L'Interieur (C-319/03) [2004] ECR I-8807; [2005]
1 CMLR 4; [2005] CEC 106 (ECJ) 242, 245, 246, 272
British Coal Corp v Smith [1996] 3 All ER 97; [1996] ICR 515;
[1996] IRLR 399; (1996) 93(25) LSG 28; (1996) 140 SJLB 134 (HL) 159
British Columbia Public Service Employee Relations Commission v
BCGEU [1997] CCL 8468 (Canadian Supreme Ct) 11, 213
British Gas plc v Sharma [1991] ICR 19; [1991] IRLR 101 (EAT) 290
Brookes v Canada Safeway Ltd (1989) 1 SCR 1219 170
Brown v Rentokil (C-394/96) [1998] All ER (EC) 791; [1998]
ECR I-4185; [1998] 2 CMLR 1049; [1998] CEC 829; [1998] ICR 790;
[1998] IRLR 445; [1998] 2 FLR 649; [1999] 1 FCR 49; (1999)
48 BMLR 126; [1998] Fam Law 597 (ECJ) 171
Buckley v United Kingdom (20348/92) (1997) 23 EHRR 101; [1997] 2
PLR 10; [1996] JPL 1018 (ECtHR) 71, 72
Bucley v Valeo, 424 US 1; 96 S Ct 612 (1976) 34
Bush v Vera, 517 US 952; 116 S Ct 1941 (1996) 251, 252

California Federal Savings and Loan Association v Guerra, 479
US 272; 107 S Ct 683 (1987) 175
Carson v United Kingdom (42184/05) (2010) 51 EHRR 13;
29 BHRC 22 (ECtHR) 225
Centrum voor Gelijkheid van Kansen en voor Racismebestrijding v
Firma Feryn NV (C-54/07) [2008] All ER (EC) 1127; [2008] ECR
I-5187; [2008] 3 CMLR 22; [2008] CEC 1032; [2008] ICR 1390;
[2008] IRLR 732 (ECJ) 286
Chapman v United Kingdom (27238/95) (2001) 33 EHRR 18;
10 BHRC 48 (ECtHR) 72
Chief Constable of West Yorkshire Police v Homer [2010]
EWCA Civ 419; [2010] ICR 987; [2010] IRLR 619; (2010) 107(19)
LSG 24; (2010) 154(17) SJLB 29 189

Chief Constable of West Yorkshire Police v Khan [2001] UKHL 48;
   [2001] 1 WLR 1947; [2001] 4 All ER 834; [2001] ICR 1065;
   [2001] IRLR 830; [2001] Emp LR 1399; (2001) 98(42) LSG 37;
   (2001) 145 SJLB 230 174
Chorlton v Lings (1868–69) LR 4 CP 374 (Ct of Common Pleas). 39
Christian Education South Africa v Minister of Education,
   2000 (4) SA 757 (CC); 2000 (10) BCLR 1051 (CC) (South African
   Constitutional Ct) 220
City of Richmond v JA Croson, 488 US 469; 109 S Ct 706 (1989) 250
Clark v TDG Ltd (t/a Novacold Ltd) [1999] 2 All ER 977; [1999]
   ICR 951; [1999] IRLR 318; [1999] Disc LR 240; (1999)
   48 BMLR 1 (CA) 172, 173
Coleman v Attridge Law (A Firm) (C–303/06) [2008] All ER
   (EC) 1105; [2008] ECR I-5603; [2008] 3 CMLR 27; [2008] CEC 986;
   [2008] ICR 1128; [2008] IRLR 722 (ECJ) 203, 209, 227, 229
Commission for Racial Equality v Amari Plastics [1982] QB 1194;
   [1982] 2 WLR 972; [1982] 2 All ER 499; [1982] ICR 304; [1982]
   Crim LR 152; (1982) 126 SJ 227 (CA) 296
Commission for Racial Equality v Dutton [1989] QB 783; [1989]
   2 WLR 17; [1989] 1 All ER 306; [1989] IRLR 8; (1989) 133 SJ 19 (CA). 71
Commission for Racial Equality v Prestige Group plc. *See* Prestige Group plc, Re
Commission of the European Communities v France (C–265/95)
   [1997] ECR I-6959 (ECJ). 242
Communist Party, 5 BVerfGE 85 (1956) 21
Connors v United Kingdom (66746/01) (2005) 40 EHRR 9; 16 BHRC 639;
   [2004] HLR 52; [2004] 4 PLR 16; [2004] NPC 86 (ECtHR). 72, 226
Copsey v WBB Devon Clays Ltd [2005] EWCA Civ 932; [2005]
   ICR 1789; [2005] IRLR 811; [2005] HRLR 32; (2005) 155 NLJ 1484 12
Corbiere v Canada (Minister of Indian and Northern Affairs) [1999] 2
   SCR 203 . . . . 128, 131, 137
Cossey v United Kingdom (10843/84) [1991] 2 FLR 492;
   [1993] 2 FCR 97; (1991) 13 EHRR 622; [1991] Fam Law 362. . . . . .89, 94
Costello-Roberts v United Kingdom (13134/87) [1994] 1 FCR 65;
   (1993) 19 EHRR 112; [1993] ECHR 16 (ECtHR) 149
Craig v Boren, 429 US 190; 97 S Ct 451 (1976) 121

DH v Czech Republic (57325/00) (2008) 47 EHRR 3;
   23 BHRC 526; [2008] ELR 17 (ECtHR) 127, 180, 184, 223, 226, 258
Da'Bell v National Society for the Prevention of Cruelty to Children
   (NSPCC) [2010] IRLR 19 (EAT). 293
Dawkins v Crown Suppliers (PSA) [1993] ICR 517; [1993] IRLR 284 (CA) 115
De Souza v Cobden [1891] 1 QB 687 (CA). 39
Deane v Ealing LBC [1993] ICR 329; [1993] IRLR 209 (EAT) 292
Defrenne v SA Belge de Navigation Aerienne (SABENA) (43/75)
   [1981] 1 All ER 122; [1976] ECR 455; [1976] 2 CMLR 98;
   [1976] ICR 547 (ECJ). 42, 43, 149, 160
Defrenne v SA Belge de Navigation Aerienne (SABENA) (No 2)
   (149/77) [1978] ECR 1365; [1978] 3 CMLR 312 (ECJ) 35

DeGraffenreid v General Motors Assembly Division, 413 F Supp 142
   (US Federal Ct of Appeals) 140, 142
Dekker v Stichting Vormingscentrum voor Jonge Volwassenen Plus
   (C–177/88) [1990] ECR I-1394; [1992] ICR 325; [1991] IRLR 27 (ECJ) 170
Doherty v Birmingham City Council [2008] UKHL 57;
   [2009] 1 AC 367; 2008] 3 WLR 636; [2009] 1 All ER 653;
   [2008] HRLR 47; [2008] UKHRR 1022; [2008] HLR 45;
   [2008] BLGR 695; [2009] 1 P & CR 11; [2008] 31 EG 89 (CS);
   (2008) 105(32) LSG 16; (2008) 152(31) SJLB 30; [2008] NPC 91 72
Dumfries and Galloway Council v North [2009] ICR 1363;
   [2009] IRLR 915 (EAT)... 159

EB v France (43546/02) [2008] 1 FLR 850; [2008] 1 FCR 235;
   (2008) 47 EHRR 21; 23 BHRC 741; [2008] Fam Law 393
   (ECtHR)..88, 125, 126, 127, 147
EFTA Surveillance Authority v Norway (E–1/02) [2003] 1 CMLR 23;
   [2003] IRLR 318 (EFTA Ct) 244
East African Asians v United Kingdom (1981) 3 EHRR 76
   (European Commission on Human Rights)............................ 229
Eaton v Brant County Board of Education [1997] 1 SCR 241................. 217
Egan v Canada [1995] 2 SCR 513................. 22, 128, 132, 137, 139, 222, 227
Eldridge v British Columbia [1997] 3 SCR 624.................... 215, 216, 217
Employment Division, Department of Human Resources of
   Oregon v Smith, 494 US 872 (1990)............................... 220

Farah v Commissioner for Police of the Metropolis [1998] QB 65;
   [1997] 2 WLR 824; [1997] 1 All ER 289; (1997) 9 Admin LR 601;
   (1996) 93(41) LSG 29; (1996) 140 SJLB 227 (CA)...................... 151
Fitzpatrick v Sterling Housing Association Ltd [2001] 1 AC 27;
   [1999] 3 WLR 1113; [1999] 4 All ER 705; [2000] 1 FLR 271;
   [1999] 2 FLR 1027; [2000] 1 FCR 21; [2000] UKHRR 25; 7 BHRC 200;
   (2000) 32 HLR 178; [2000] L & TR 44; [2000] Fam Law 14; [1999]
   EG 125 (CS); (1999) 96(43) LSG 3; [1999] NPC 127; (2000) 79
   P & CR D4 (HL).. 87
Foster v British Gas plc (C–188/89) [1991] 1 QB 405; [1991] 2
   WLR 258; [1990] 3 All ER 897; [1990] ECR I-3313; [1990] 2
   CMLR 833; [1991] ICR 84; [1990] IRLR 353 (ECJ) 150
Franks v Bowman Transportation Co, 424 US 747; 96 S Ct 1251 (1975)......... 248
Fretté v France (36515/97) [2003] 2 FLR 9; [2003] 2 FCR 39;
   (2004) 38 EHRR 21; [2003] Fam Law 636 (ECtHR)...................... 88
Frontiero v Richardson, 411 US 677; 93 S Ct 1764 (1973).................. 121
Fullilove v Klutznick, 448 US 448; 100 S Ct 2758 (1980) 248, 250

Gaygusuz v Austria (17371/90) (1997) 23 EHRR 364 (ECtHR).............. 127
Geduldig v Aiello, 417 US 484; 94 S Ct 2485 (1974)...................169, 170
General Electric Co v Gilbert, 429 US 125; 97 S Ct 401 (1976)............169, 170
Ghaidan v Godin-Mendoza [2004] UKHL 30; [2004] 2 AC 557;
   [2004] 3 WLR 113; [2004] 3 All ER 411; [2004] 2 FLR 600;
   [2004] 2 FCR 481; [2004] HRLR 31; [2004] UKHRR 827; 16 BHRC 671;

[2004] HLR 46; [2005] 1 P & CR 18; [2005] L & TR 3; [2004] 2 EGLR 132;
[2004] Fam Law 641; [2004] 27 EG 128 (C.S.); (2004) 101(27) LSG 30;
(2004) 154 NLJ 1013; (2004) 148 SJLB 792; [2004] NPC 100;
[2004] 2 P & CR DG17 ....87, 127, 131, 147
Gillespie v Northern Health and Social Services Board (C–342/93)
    [1996] All ER (EC) 284; [1996] ECR I-475; [1996] 2 CMLR 969;
    [1996] ICR 498; [1996] IRLR 214; (1996) 31 BMLR 65 (ECJ) 171
Glor v Switzerland (13444/04) 30 April 2009 (ECtHR)..................... 126
Goesart v Cleary, 335 US 464; 69 S Ct 198 (1948)........................ 121
Goodwin v United Kingdom (28957/95) [2002] IRLR 664;
    [2002] 2 FLR 487; [2002] 2 FCR 577; (2002) 35 EHRR 18;
    13 BHRC 120; (2002) 67 BMLR 199; [2002] Fam Law 738;
    (2002) 152 NLJ 1171 (ECtHR)....................................... 94
Gosselin v Quebec, 2002 SCC 84 (Canadian Supreme Ct)............. 24, 138, 230
Grant v South West Trains Ltd (C–249/96) [1998] All ER (EC) 193;
    [1998] ECR I-621; [1998] 1 CMLR 993; [1998] CEC 263;
    [1998] ICR 449; [1998] IRLR 206; [1998] 1 FLR 839; [1998] 1
    FCR 377; 3 BHRC 578; [1999] Pens LR 69; [1998] Fam Law 392;
    (1998) 162 JPN 266 (ECJ) 90, 115
Griggs v Duke Power Co, 401 US 424; 91
    S Ct 849 (1971).................................154, 177, 178, 179, 192
Grutter v Bollinger, 539 US 306 (2003) 252, 253, 254, 266, 267, 269

Handels- og Kontorfunktionaerernes Forbund i Danmark v Dansk
Arbejdsgiverforening, ex p Danfoss A/S (109/88) [1989]
    ECR 3199; [1991] 1 CMLR 8; [1991] ICR 74; [1989] IRLR 532 (ECJ)........ 181
Handels-og Kontorfunktionaerernes Forbund i Danmark (Union of
Clerical and Commercial Employees) (for Hertz) v Dansk Arbejdsgiverforening
(Danish Employers Association) (for Aldi Marked K/S) (C–179/88)
    [1990] ECR I-3979; [1992] ICR 332; [1991] IRLR 31 (ECJ)................ 171
Harksen v Lane NO [1997] ZACC 12; 1997 (11) BCLR 1489 (CC);
    1998 (1) SA 300 (CC) 129, 137, 138, 139
Hassam v Jacobs NO (CCT83/08) [2009] ZACC 19; 2009 (11)
BCLR 1148 (South African Constitutional Ct) 143
Hertz. *See* Handels-og Kontorfunktionaerernes Forbund i Danmark
(Union of Clerical and Commercial Employees) (for Hertz) v Dansk
Arbejdsgiverforening (Danish Employers Association) (for Aldi Marked K/S)
Heyday Case. *See* R (on the application of Age UK) v Secretary of State
for Business, Innovation and Skills
Hockenjos v Secretary of State for Social Security [2004] EWCA
    Civ 1749 [2005] Eu LR 305, [2005] IRLR 471; [2005] 1 FLR 1009;
    [2005] 1 FCR 286; [2005] Fam Law 464; (2005) 102(7) LSG 27 .... 195, 196
Hoffmann v Austria (A/255-C) [1994] 1 FCR 193; (1994) 17
    EHRR 293; [1994] Fam Law 673 (ECtHR)............................. 127
Hoffmann v South African Airways (CCT 17/00) [2000] ZACC 17;
    2001 (1) SA 1; 2000 (11) BCLR 1235; [2000] 12 BLLR 1365 (CC)........... 129
Hoyt v Florida, 368 US 57; 82 S Ct 159 (1961).......................... 121
Humphreys v Revenue and Customs Commissioners [2010]
    EWCA Civ 56; [2010] 1 FCR 630; [2010] UKHRR 497.................... 195

Indra Sawhney v Union of India, AIR 1993 SC 447 276
Inze v Austria (A/126) (1988) 10 EHRR 394 (ECtHR) 127

JH Walker v Hussain [1996] ICR 291; [1996] IRLR 11 (EAT) 115
James v Eastleigh BC [1990] 2 AC 751; [1990] 3 WLR 55; [1990] 2
    All ER 607; [1990] ICR 554; [1990] IRLR 288; (1991) 155 LG Rev
    205; (1990) 140 NLJ 926 (HL) 205, 206, 211, 237, 238
Janzen v Platy Enterprises Ltd [1989] 1 SCR 1252; 59 DLR (4th) 352 228
Jefferies v Harris County Community Action Association, 615 F
    2d 1025 (5th Cir 1980) (US Federal Ct of Appeals) 142
Jenkins v Kingsgate (Clothing Productions) Ltd (96/80) [1981] 1 WLR 972;
    [1981] ECR 911; [1981] 2 CMLR 24; [1981] ICR 592; [1981] IRLR 228;
    (1981) 125 SJ 442 (ECJ) 164
Jepson v The Labour Party [1996] IRLR 116 (IT) 240
Johnson v California, 125 S Ct 1141 (2005) (US Supreme Ct) 9, 119
Johnson v Santa Clara, 480 US 616; 107 S Ct 1442 (1987) 248
Judge v Marsh, 649 F Supp 770 (1986) (US District Ct,
    District of Columbia) 142

Kalanke v Freie und Hansestadt Bremen (C–450/93) [1996]
    All ER (EC) 66; [1995] ECR I–3051; [1996] 1 CMLR 175; [1996]
    CEC 208; [1996] ICR 314; [1995] IRLR 660 (ECJ) 242, 243, 261, 263
Karner v Austria (40016/98) [2003] 2 FLR 623; [2004] 2 FCR 563;
    (2004) 38 EHRR 24; 14 BHRC 674; [2003] Fam Law 724 (ECtHR) 88, 225
Khosa and Mahlaule v Minister for Social Development, 2004 (6)
    BCLR 569 (South African Constitutional Ct) 29, 132, 135
Kjeldsen v Denmark (A/23) (1979-80) 1 EHRR 711 (ECtHR) 126
Konttinen v Finland (1996) 87 DR 68 (European Commission of
    Human Rights) 12
Korematsu v United States, 323 US 214; 65 S Ct 193 (1944) 119, 249
Kücükdeveci v Swedex GmbH & Co KG (C–555/07) [2010]
    All ER (EC) 867; [2010] 2 CMLR 33; [2011] CEC 3; [2010]
    IRLR 346 (ECJ) 115, 150, 151, 200
Kuddas v Chief Constable of Leicestershire [2001] UKHL 29; [2002] AC 122;
    [2001] 2 WLR 1789; [2001] 3 All ER 193; (2001) 3 LGLR 45; [2001] Po LR
    181; (2001) 98(28) LSG 43; (2001) 151 NLJ 936; (2001) 145 SJLB 166 292

L v Birmingham City Council [2007] UKHL 27; [2008] 1 AC 95; [2007] 3
    WLR 112; [2007] 3 All ER 957; [2007] HRLR 32; [2008] UKHRR 346;
    [2007] HLR 44; [2008] BLGR 273; (2007) 10 CCL Rep 505; [2007]
    LS Law Medical 472; (2007) 96 BMLR 1; (2007) 104(27) LSG 29;
    (2007) 157 NLJ 938; (2007) 151 SJLB 860; [2007] NPC 75 . . . . 149, 305
Ladele v Islington LBC [2009] EWCA Civ 1357; [2010] 1 WLR 955;
    [2010] PTSR 982; [2010] ICR 532; [2010] IRLR 211; [2010] BLGR 690 188
Larbi-Odam v Member of the Executive Council for Education
    (North-West Province) (CCT2/97) [1997] ZACC 16; 1997 (12)
    BCLR 1655; 1998 (1) SA 745 135
Law v Canada [1999] 1 SCR 497 (Canadian Supreme Ct) 19, 24

Lawrence v Regent Office Care (C–320/00) [2002] ECR I-7325;
[2002] 3 CMLR 27; [2003] ICR 1092; [2002] IRLR 822; [2002]
Emp LR 1248 (ECJ) 160
Lawrence v Texas, 539 US 558; 123 S Ct 247 .... 10, 123
League of United Latin American Citizens v Perry, 548 US 399 (2006) 252
Leverton v Clwyd CC [1989] AC 706; [1989] 2 WLR 47;
[1989] 1 All ER 78; [1989] 1 CMLR 574; [1989] ICR 33;
[1989] IRLR 28; (1988) 138 NLJ Rep. 366; (1989) 133 SJ 45 (HL) 158
Lochner v New York, 198 US 45; 25 S Ct 539 (1905) 35
Lommers v Minister van Landbouw, Natuurbeheer en Visserij
(C–476/99) [2002] ECR I-2891; [2004] 2 CMLR 49; [2002]
IRLR 430 (ECJ) 246, 247, 272
Loving v Virginia, 388 US 1; 87 S Ct 1817 (1967). 119

M v Secretary of State for Work and Pensions [2006] UKHL 11; [2006] 2
AC 91; [2006] 2 WLR 637; [2006] 4 All ER 929; [2006] 2 FLR 56;
[2006] 1 FCR 497; [2006] HRLR 19; [2006] UKHRR 799; 21 BHRC
254; [2006] Fam Law 524; (2006) 150 SJLB 363 89
MEC for Education: Kwazulu-Natal v Pillay (CCT 51/06)
[2007] ZACC 21; 2008 (1) SA 474 (CC); 2008 (2) BCLR 99 (CC) 221
McLaughlin v Florida, 379 US 184; 85 S Ct 283 (1964) 119
Malcolm v Lewisham LBC [2008] UKHL 43; [2008] 1 AC 1399; [2008] 3
WLR 194; [2008] 4 All ER 525; [2008] IRLR 700; [2008] HLR 41;
[2008] BLGR 549; (2008) 11 CCL Rep 573; (2008) 102 BMLR 170;
[2008] 2 P & CR 18; [2008] L & TR 29; [2008] 26 EG 117 (CS);
(2008) 105(26) LSG 23; (2008) 152(26) SJLB 29; [2008] NPC 76 .... 172, 173
Mandla (Sewa Singh) v Dowell Lee [1983] 2 AC 548; [1983] 2 WLR 620;
[1983] 1 All ER 1062; [1983] ICR 385; [1983] IRLR 209; (1983) 127
SJ 242 (HL) 14, 62, 84, 115, 182, 212
Mangold v Helm (C–144/04) [2006] All ER (EC) 383; [2005] ECR I-9981;
[2006] 1 CMLR 43; [2006] CEC 372; [2006] IRLR 143 (ECJ) 115, 151
Marckx v Belgium (A/31) (1979–80) 2 EHRR 330 (ECtHR) 222
Marleasing SA v La Comercial Internacional de Alimentacion SA
(C–106/89) [1990] ECR I-4135; [1993] BCC 421; [1992] 1 CMLR 305 (ECJ). ... 150
Marschall v Land Nordrhein-Westfalen (C–409/95) [1997] All ER (EC) 865;
[1997] ECR I-6363; [1998] 1 CMLR 547; [1998] CEC 152; [2001] ICR 45;
[1998] IRLR 39 (ECJ) 242, 243, 247, 261
Marshall v Southampton and South West Hampshire AHA
(152/84) [1986] QB 401; [1986] 2 WLR 780; [1986] 2 All ER 584;
[1986] ECR 723; [1986] 1 CMLR 688; [1986] ICR 335;
[1986] IRLR 140, (1986) 83 LSG 1720; (1986) 130 SJ 340 (ECJ) 150
Marshall v Southampton and South West Hampshire AHA (No 2)
(C–271/91) [1994] QB 126; [1993] 3 WLR 1054; [1993] 4 All ER 586;
[1993] ECR I-4367; [1993] 3 CMLR 293; [1993] ICR 893;
[1993] IRLR 445 (ECJ) 293
Massachusetts Board of Retirement v Murgia, 427 US 307 120
Mata Estevez v Spain (56501/00) Reports of Judgments and Decisions
2001-VI, p 311 (ECtHR) 88

Michael M v Superior Court, Sonoma Cty, 450 US 464;
    101 S Ct 1200 (1981) 121
Miller v Johnson, 515 US 900; 115 S Ct 2475 (1995). 251
Minister of Finance v Van Heerden, 2004 (6) 121 (CC); 2004 (11)
    BCLR 1125 (South African Constitutional Ct) 256, 272, 274
Minister of Home Affairs v Fourie (CCT 60/04); [2005] ZACC 19;
    2006 (3) BCLR 355 (CC); 2006 (1) SA 524 (CC) (South African
    Constitutional Ct) 90
Ministry of Defence v Meredith [1995] IRLR 539 (EAT) 292
Miron v Trudel [1995] 2 SCR 418 130
Murphy v An Bord Telecom Eireann (157/86) [1988] ECR 673;
    [1988] 1 CMLR 879; [1988] ICR 445; [1988] IRLR 267 (ECJ) 163

Naz Foundation v Government of NCT of Delhi, WP(C) No 7455/2001, 2
    July 2009 (Delhi High Ct) 129, 130, 133, 138
Nelson v Tyne and Wear Passenger Transport Executive
    [1978] ICR 1183; (1978) 122 SJ 642 (EAT) 290
Nolte v Landesversicherungsanstalt Hannover (C–317/93)
    [1996] All E.R. (E.C.) 212; [1995] E.C.R. I-4625;
    [1996] I.R.L.R. 225 (ECJ) 193
Noone v North West Thames RHA (No 2) [1988] ICR 813;
    [1988] IRLR 530 (CA) 290

O'Flynn v Adjudication Officer (C–237/94) [1996] All ER (EC) 541;
    [1996] ECR I-2617; [1996] 3 CMLR 103; [1998] ICR 608;
    (1997) 33 BMLR 54 (ECJ) 187, 212
Ojutiku v Manpower Services Commission [1982] ICR 661;
    [1982] IRLR 418; (1982) 79 LSG 920 (CA). 182, 192
O'Leary v Punch Retail Unreported 29 August 2000
    (Westminster County Ct) 71
Ontario Human Rights Commission v Simpsons-Sears [1985]
    2 SCR 53 . . . . 154, 215, 222
Orr v Orr, 440 US 268; 99 S Ct 1102 (1979). 121

P v S and Cornwall CC (C–13/94) [1996] All ER (EC) 397;
    [1996] ECR I-2143; [1996] 2 CMLR 247; [1996] CEC 574;
    [1996] ICR 795; [1996] IRLR 347; [1996] 2 FLR 347;
    [1997] 2 FCR 180; [1996] Fam Law 609 (ECJ) 93, 111, 115
Palmer v Thompson, 403 US 217, 91 S Ct 1940 (1971) 10
Parents Involved in Community Schools v Seattle School Dist
    No 1, 551 US 701; 127 S Ct 2738 (2007). 253, 254, 260, 267
Perera v Civil Service Commission (No 2) [1983] ICR 428;
    [1983] IRLR 166 (CA) 179
Petrovic v Austria (20458/92) (2001) 33 EHRR 14; 4 BHRC 232;
    [1998] HRCD 366 (ECtHR). 147
Plessy v Ferguson, 163 US 537; 16 S Ct 1138 (1896) 119
Porcelli v Strathclyde RC, 1986 SC 137; [1986] ICR 564 (Ct of Session). 228
Powers v Ohio, 499 US 400 (1991) 9

President of the Republic of South Africa v Hugo, CCT 11/96
(18 April 1997); 1997 (4) SA 1 (CC) (South African
Constitutional Ct) 23, 227
Prestige Group plc, Re [1984] 1 WLR 335; [1984] ICR 473;
[1984] IRLR 166; (1984) 81 LSG 134; (1984) 128 SJ 131 (HL) 296
Price v Civil Service Commission [1977] 1 WLR 1417; [1978] 1
All ER 1228; [1978] ICR 27; [1977] IRLR 291; (1977) 12 ITR 482;
(1977) 121 SJ 558 (EAT) 14, 181
Price v Rhondda UDC [1923] 1 Ch 372 (Ch D) 40
Prince v President of the Law Society of the Cape of Good Hope (CCT 36/00)
[2002] ZACC 1; 2002 (2) SA 794 (South African Constitutional Ct) 220

R v Birmingham City Council, ex p Equal Opportunities Commission [1989]
AC 1155; [1989] 2 WLR 520; [1989] 1 All ER 769; [1989] IRLR 173;
87 LGR 557; (1989) 86(15) LSG 36; (1989) 139 NLJ 292; (1989)
133 SJ 322 (HL) 204, 205
R v Commission for Racial Equality, ex p Hillingdon
LBC [1982] AC 779; [1982] 3 WLR 159; [1982] IRLR 424;
80 LGR 737; (1982) 126 SJ 449 (HL) 296
R v East Berkshire HA, ex p Walsh [1985] QB 152; [1984] 3 WLR 818;
[1984] 3 All ER 425; [1984] ICR 743; [1984] IRLR 278 (CA) 289
R v Entry Clearance Officer (Bombay), ex p Amin [1983] 2 AC 818;
[1983] 3 WLR 258; [1983] 2 All ER 864 (HL) 151
R v Harrald (1871-72) LR 7 QB 361 (Ct of QB) 39
R v Kapp, 2008 SCC 41 (Canadian
Supreme Ct) 24, 138, 230, 257, 270, 271, 273, 275
R v Keegstra (1996) 61 CCC (3d) 1 (Canadian Supreme Ct) 34
R v R (Rape: Marital Exemption) [1992] 1 AC 599; [1991] 3 WLR 767;
[1991] 4 All ER 481; (1992) 94 Cr App R 216; (1991) 155 JP 989;
[1992] 1 FLR 217; [1992] Crim LR 207; [1992] Fam Law 108; (1991) 155
JPN 752; (1991) 141 NLJ 1481; (1991) 135 SJLB 181 (HL) 39
R v Secretary of State for Employment, ex p Equal Opportunities Commission
[1995] 1 AC 1; [1994] 2 WLR 409; [1994] 1 All ER 910; [1995] 1 CMLR 391;
[1994] ICR 317; [1994] IRLR 176; 92 LGR 360; [1994] COD 301; (1994) 91(18)
LSG 43; (1994) 144 NLJ 358; (1994) 138 SJLB 84 (HL) 182, 193, 288
R v Secretary of State for Employment, ex p Seymour-Smith
(No 1) [1997] 1 WLR 473; [1997] 2 All ER 273; [1997] 2 CMLR 904;
[1997] ICR 371; [1997] IRLR 315; (1997) 147 NLJ 414 (HL) 185, 186
R v Secretary of State for Employment, ex p Seymour-Smith
(C–167/97) [1999] 2 AC 554; [1999] 3 WLR 460; [1999] All ER (EC) 97;
[1999] ECR I-623, [1999] 2 CMLR 273; [1999] CEC 79; [1999] ICR 447;
[1999] IRLR 253 (ECJ) 165, 193, 194
R v Secretary of State for Employment, ex p Seymour-Smith
(No 2) [2000] 1 WLR 435; [2000] 1 All ER 857; [2000] 1
CMLR 770; [2000] ICR 244; [2000] IRLR 263; (2000) 97(9) LSG 40 (HL) 194
R v Secretary of State for the Home Department, ex p Fire
Brigades Union [1995] 2 AC 513; [1995] 2 WLR 464; [1995] 2
All ER 244; (1995) 7 Admin LR 473; [1995] PIQR P228;
(1995) 145 NLJ 521; (1995) 139 SJLB 109 (HL) 7

RAV v City of St Paul, Minn, 505 US 377; 112 S Ct 2538 (1992). 34
R (on the application of A) v Secretary of State for Health
  [2009] EWCA Civ 225; [2010] 1 WLR 279; [2009] PTSR 1680;
  [2010] 1 All ER 87; (2009) 12 CCL Rep. 213; [2009] LS Law Medical 282 66
R (on the application of Age UK) v Secretary of State for Business,
  Innovation and Skills [2009] EWHC 2336 (Admin); [2010] 1
  CMLR 21; [2010] ICR 260; [2009] IRLR 1017; [2009] Pens LR 333;
  [2010] ACD 6; (2009) 106(39) LSG 22; (2009) 159 NLJ 1401; (2009)
  153(37) SJLB 36 . . . . 107, 201, 202
R (on the application of Amicus) v Secretary of State for
  Trade and Industry [2004] EWHC 860 (Admin); [2007] ICR 1176;
  [2004] IRLR 430; [2004] ELR 311; [2004] Pens LR 261. 85
R (on the application of Baker) v Secretary of State for Communities
  and Local Government, Bromley LBC [2008] EWCA Civ 141;
  [2009] PTSR 809; [2008] BLGR 239; [2008] 2 P & CR 6; [2008]
  JPL 1469; [2008] ACD 62; (2008) 105(10) LSG 27; (2008) 152(10)
  SJLB 31; [2008] NPC 26 . . . . 71, 308, 309
R (on the application of Boyejo) v Barnet LBC [2009] EWHC 3261
  (Admin); (2010) 13 CCL Rep 72. 327
R (on the application of Brown) v Secretary of State for Work and
  Pensions [2008] EWHC 3158 (Admin); [2009] PTSR 1506 309
R (on the application of Carson) v Secretary of State for Work and
  Pensions [2005] UKHL 37; [2006] 1 AC 173; [2005] 2 WLR 1369;
  [2005] 4 All ER 545; [2005] HRLR 23; [2005] UKHRR 1185;
  18 BHRC 677 . . . . 24, 127, 128, 133, 137
R (on the application of E) v JFS Governing Body [2009] UKSC 15; [2010] 2
  AC 728; [2010] 2 WLR 153; [2010] PTSR 147; [2010] 1 All ER 319; [2010]
  IRLR 136; 27 BHRC 656; [2010] ELR 26; (2010) 160 NLJ 29; (2009) 153(48)
  SJLB 32 . . . . 117, 190, 205, 207, 208, 209, 210, 211, 213
R (on the application of Elias) v Secretary of State for Defence
  [2006] EWCA Civ 1293; [2006] 1 WLR 3213;
  [2006] IRLR 934 . . . . 194, 195, 196, 307, 327
R (on the application of Gillan) v Commissioner of Police of the
  Metropolis [2006] UKHL 12; [2006] 2 AC 307; [2006] 2
  WLR 537; [2006] 4 All ER 1041; [2006] 2 Cr App R 36;
  [2006] HRLR 18; [2006] UKHRR 740; 21 BHRC 202; [2006]
  Po LR 26; [2006] Crim LR 752; (2006) 150 SJLB 366 177
R (on the application of Harris) v Haringey LBC [2010]
  EWCA Civ 703; [2010] B.L.G.R. 713; [2010] J.P.L. 1635;
  [2010] N.P.C. 72 327
R (on the application of Isaacs) v Secretary of State for Communities and Local Gov-
  ernment [2009] EWHC 557 (Admin) 327
R (on the application of Kaur) v Ealing LBC [2008]
  EWHC 2062 (Admin) 240
R (on the application of Limbuela) v Secretary of State for the
  Home Department [2005] UKHL 66; [2006] 1 AC 396; [2005] 3
  WLR 1014; [2007] 1 All ER 951; [2006] HRLR 4; [2006] HLR 10;
  (2006) 9 CCL Rep 30; (2005) 102(46) LSG 25; (2005)
  149 SJLB 1354 (HL) 66

R (on the application of M) v Secretary of State for Work and
Pensions [2008] UKHL 63; [2009] 1 AC 311; [2008] 3 WLR 1023;
[2009] PTSR 336; [2009] 2 All ER 556; [2009] HRLR 5; [2009]
UKHRR 117; 26 BHRC 587 . . . . 126, 128, 133, 134, 136
R (on the application of McCarthy) v Basildon DC [2009] EWCA Civ 13; [2009] BLGR
1013; [2009] JPL 1074; [2009] 4 EG 117 (CS); [2009] NPC 10 72
R (on the application of Meany) v Harlow DC [2009]
EWHC 559 (Admin) 308, 327
R (on the application of RJM) v Secretary of State for Work and Pensions.
See R (on the application of M) v Secretary of State for Work and Pensions
R (on the application of Reynolds) v Secretary of State for
Work and Pensions [2005] UKHL 37 137
R (on the application of SB) v Governors of Denbigh High School. *See* R (on the
application of Williamson) v Secretary of State for Education and Employment
R (on the application of Tekle) v Secretary of State for the
Home Department [2008] EWHC 3064 (Admin); [2009] 2 All ER 193 66
R (on the application of the European Roma Rights Centre) v Immigration
Officer, Prague Airport [2004] UKHL 55; [2005] 2 AC 1; [2005] 2 WLR 1;
[2005] 1 All ER 527; [2005] IRLR 115; [2005] HRLR 4; [2005] UKHRR
530; 18 BHRC 1; [2005] Imm AR 100; [2005] INLR 182; (2004) 154 NLJ
1893; (2005) 149 SJLB 26. . . . . 176, 196, 197, 204
R (on the application of Williamson) v Secretary of State for Education
and Employment [2006] UKHL 15; [2005] 2 AC 246; [2005] 2 WLR 590;
[2005] 2 All ER 1; [2005] 2 FLR 374; [2005] 1 FCR 498; [2005] HRLR 14;
[2005] UKHRR 339; 19 BHRC 99; [2005] ELR 291; [2005] Fam Law 456;
(2005) 102(16) LSG 27; (2005) 155 NLJ 324; (2005) 149 SJLB 266 220
Redcar and Cleveland BC v Bainbridge [2008] EWCA Civ 885; [2009]
ICR 133; [2008] IRLR 776 . . . . 162, 163
Reed v Reed, 404 US 71; 92 S Ct 251 (1971) 121
Rees v United Kingdom (A/106) [1987] 2 FLR 111; [1993] 2 FCR 49;
(1987) 9 EHRR 56; [1987] Fam Law 157 . . . . 89, 94
Regents of the University of California v Bakke, 438 US 265
(1978) 234, 250, 253, 254, 260, 265, 266
Reynolds. *See* R (on the application of Carson) v Secretary of State for
Work and Pensions
Ricci v DeStefano, 129 S Ct 2658 (2009). 226, 262
Richmond v JA Crosan Co, 488 US 469 (1989) 270
Rinner-Kuhn v FWW Spezial-Gebaudereinigung GmbH & Co KG
(171/88) [1989] ECR 2743; [1993] 2 CMLR 932; [1989] IRLR 493 (ECJ). 193
Roberts v Hopwood [1925] AC 578 (HL) 40
Romer v Evans, 517 US 620; 116 S Ct 1620 (1996) 124
Rutherford v Secretary for State and Industry [2006] UKHL 19; [2006]
4 All ER 577; [2006] ICR 785; [2006] IRLR 551; (2006) 103(20)
LSG 24; (2006) 150 SJLB 604 . . . . 115, 185, 186

SEIU, Local 204 v Ontario (Attorney General), 151 DLR (4th) 273
(Ontario Ct of Justice) 161
SL v Austria (45330/99) (2003) 37 EHRR 39 (ECtHR). 126, 127

St Helens MBC v Derbyshire [2007] UKHL 16; [2007] 3 All ER 81;
[2007] ICR 841; [2007] IRLR 540; (2007) 104(19) LSG 26; (2007)
157 NLJ 635; (2007) 151 SJLB 573. 174
Salgueiro da Silva Mouta v Portugal (33290/96) [2001] 1 FCR 653;
(2001) 31 EHRR 47; 2001 Fam LR 2 (ECtHR) 87, 126
San Antonio Independent School District v Rodriguez, 411 US 959
(1973) 121, 130, 136, 138
Scanlon v Redcar & Cleveland BC (2010) EOR. 293
Schnorbus v Land Hessen (C–79/99) [2000] ECR I-10997; [2001] 1
CMLR 40 (ECJ) 212
Schönheit v Stadt Frankfurt am Main (C–4/02) [2003] ECR I-12575;
[2006] 1 CMLR 51; [2004] IRLR 983; [2004] Pens LR 43 (ECJ) 165
Science Research Council v Nassé [1980] AC 1028; [1979] 3 WLR 762;
[1979] 3 All ER 673; [1979] ICR 921; [1979] IRLR 465; (1979)
123 SJ 768 (HL) 296
Scullard v Knowles [1996] ICR 399; [1996] IRLR 344 (EAT) 160
Sejdić v Bosnia and Herzegovina (27996/06) 28 BHRC 201 (ECtHR) 146, 147
Shamoon v Chief Constable of the Royal Ulster Constabulary [2003]
UKHL 11; [2003] 2 All ER 26; [2003] NI 174; [2003] ICR 337;
[2003] IRLR 285; (2003) 147 SJLB 268. 210
Shaw v Hunt, 517 US 899; 116 S Ct 1894 (1996) 251
Shaw v Reno, 509 US 630; 113 S Ct 2816 (1993). 251
Sheffield (Kristina) v United Kingdom (22985/93) [1998] 2 FLR 928;
[1998] 3 FCR 141; (1999) 27 EHRR 163; 5 BHRC 83; [1998]
HRCD 758; [1998] Fam Law 731 (ECtHR). 94
Short v Poole Corp [1926] Ch 66 (CA) 40
Smith v Avdel Systems Ltd (C–408/92) [1995] All ER (EC) 132;
[1994] ECR I-4435; [1995] 3 CMLR 543; [1995] ICR 596; [1994]
IRLR 602 (ECJ) 21, 168
Smith and Grady v United Kingdom (33985/96) [1999] IRLR 734;
(2000) 29 EHRR 493; (1999) 11 Admin LR 879 (ECtHR) 87
South Tyneside MBC v Anderson [2007] EWCA Civ 654; [2007]
ICR 1581; [2007] IRLR 715; [2008] BLGR 507; (2007)
151 SJLB 892 (CA) 159
Stec v United Kingdom (65731/01) (2006) 43 EHRR 47;
20 BHRC 348 (ECtHR) 147, 258
Stedman v United Kingdom (29107/95) (1997) 23 EHRR
CD168 (European Commission on Human Rights) 12
Steel v Union of Post Office Workers [1978] 1 WLR 64; [1978] 2
All ER 504; [1978] ICR 181; [1977] IRLR 288; (1978) 75 LSG 341;
(1977) 121 SJ 575 (EAT) 192
Stewart v Cleveland Guest (Engineering) Ltd [1996] ICR 535; [1994]
IRLR 440 (EAT) 9, 167
Sutherland v United Kingdom (25186/94) (1996) 22 EHRR CD182;
(1997) 24 EHRR CD22 (European Commission on Human Rights) 86

Thlimmenos v Greece (34369/97) (2001) 31 EHRR 15; 9 BHRC 12
(ECtHR). 223, 226
Trans World Airlines, Inc v Hardison, 432 US 63 (1977). 220

Turley v Allders Department Stores Ltd [1980] ICR 66; [1980]
IRLR 4 (EAT).. 169

United States v Carlene Products Co, 304 US 144; 58 S Ct 778
(1938)..32, 95, 134, 135
United States v Hays, 5 US 737; 115 S Ct 2431 (1995).................... 251
United States v Paradise, 480 US 149; 107 S Ct 1053 (1988)................ 248
United States v Virginia, 518 US 515; 116 S Ct 2264 (1996)..............121, 256
United States Airways v Barnett, 535 US 391 (2002)...................216, 219
United Steelworkers v Weber, 443 US 193; 99 S Ct 2721 (1979).............. 248

Vento v Chief Constable of West Yorkshire Police (No 2) [2003]
IRLR 102 (CA)... 293
Von Colson v Land Nordrhein-Westfahlen (14/83) [1984] ECR
1891; [1986] 2 CMLR 430 (ECJ)................................. 150
Vriend v Alberta [1998] 1 SCR 493; 156 DLR (4th) 385; [1998]
4 BHRC 140... 22

Wards Cove v Atonio, 490 US 642; 109 S Ct 2115 (1989)................184, 192
Washington v Davis, 426 US 229; 96 S Ct 2040 (1976).................... 224
Webb v EMO Air Cargo (UK) Ltd [1992] 2 All ER 43;
[1992] 1 CMLR 793; [1992] ICR 445; [1992] IRLR 116; (1992)
89(10) LSG 33; (1992) 142 NLJ 16; (1992) 136 SJLB 32 (CA).............. 170
Webb v EMO Air Cargo (UK) Ltd (C–32/93) [1994] QB 718;
[1994] 3 WLR 941; [1994] 4 All ER 115; [1994] ECR I-3567;
[1994] 2 CMLR 729; [1994] ICR 770; [1994] IRLR 482; (1994)
144 NLJ 1278 (ECJ)... 170
Wilkinson v Kitzinger [2006] EWHC 2022 (Fam); [2007] 1 FLR
295; [2007] 1 FCR 183; [2006] HRLR 36; [2007] UKHRR 164;
[2006] Fam Law 1030; (2006) 103(33) LSG 25 90
Wygant v Jackson Board of Education, 476 US 267; 106 S Ct 1842
(1986)..234, 249, 254, 268

X, Y and Z v United Kingdom (21830/93) [1997] 2 FLR 892;
[1997] 3 FCR 341; (1997) 24 EHRR 143; (1998) 39 BMLR 128;
[1997] Fam Law 605; (1997) 94(17) LSG 25 94

YL v Birmingham City Council. *See* L v Birmingham City Council

Table of Legislation
and Statutory Materials

Act of Supremacy 1559 75
Acts of Uniformity 1549 75
Additional Paternity Leave
    Regulations 2010
    (SI 2010/1055) 44
Additional Statutory Paternity Pay
    Regulations 2010
    (SI 2010/1056) 44
Aliens Act 1905 78
Aliens Order 1920 78
Aliens Restriction (Amendment)
    Act 1919 78
Americans with Disabilities Act
    1990 (US) 214, 219
    § 12112(b)(5)(A). 215
Anti-Terrorism, Crime and Security Act
    s 23. 10
Asylum and Immigration Act 1996
    s 8. 64
Canadian Charter of Rights and
    Freedoms. . . 22, 112, 125, 130, 135,
                      215, 260
    s 15. . . . . .128, 154
    s 15(1). 24, 125, 222
    s 15(2). 257, 260, 270, 273
Caravan Sites Act 1968 69
Catholic Relief Act 1829 76
Child Poverty Act 2010 309
Civil Partnership Act 2004 . . . . . . 89, 90
    s 71. 89
    s 75. 89
    s 79. 89
Civil Rights Act 1964 (US) 177
    Title VII 215, 224, 226, 248, 262
    § 703(a)(1) 215
    § 2000e-2 192
    § 2000e-2(a)(1) 215
    § 2000e-2(k)(1)(A)(i) 178
    § 2000e-2(k)(1)(C) 178
Civil Rights Act 1991 (US) 178
    § 105 192

Commonwealth Immigrants
    Act 1968 229
Commonwealth Immigration
    Act 1962 . . . . 54, 55
Council Directive 76/207/EEC Equal
    Treatment Directive 150, 156,
                        241, 292
    art 2(4) 241
    art 6 293
    art 7 174
Council Directive 79/7/EEC on
    Equal Treatment for
    Social Security 43
Council Directive 86/378/EEC on
    Equal Treatment in Social
    Security Schemes. 43
Council Directive 92/85/EEC
    Pregnant Workers Directive . . . 171
    art 11(3) 171
Council Directive 94/33/EC on the
    Protection of Young People at
    Work. 101
Council Directive 96/34/EC on
    Parental Leave 44
Council Directive 97/80/EC
    Burden of Proof
    Directive 43, 179, 286
    art 2(2) 179
Council Directive 98/52/EC Extension of
    Burden of Proof Directive 286
Council Directive 2000/43/EC
    Race Directive 62, 63, 72, 110,
          116, 144, 130, 166, 179,
                  188, 228, 286
    recital 8 286
    recital 12 144
    recital 13 63
    art 2(1)(a) 166
    art 2(2)(b) 179, 191
    art 2(3) 22, 228
    art 3(1) 144

art 3(1)(e)—(h) 63
art 3(2) 63
art 5 .63, 241
art 8 286
art 9 174
art 10 286
art 13 63
Council Directive 2000/78/EC
    Employment Directive . . 84, 91, 97,
        105, 106, 110, 116, 144, 145,
        150, 151, 166, 179, 188, 199
    preamble 91
    preamble recital 22. 91
    art 2(2)(a) 166
    art 2(2)(b) 191
    art 6 . . . . .106, 199
    art 6(1) 199
    art 7(1) 241
    art 11 174
Council Directive 2002/73/EC on
    Equal Treatment for Men and Women
    art 6 174
Council Directive 2003/9/EC
    Reception Directive 66
Council Directive 2004/38/EC on
    Freedom of Movement of Workers
    art 39 187
Council Directive 2004/113/EC
    on Equal Treatment for Men
    and Women 43, 145
Council Directive 2006/54/EC
    Recast Equal Treatment
    Directive 150, 161
    art 2(1)(a) 166
    art 2(1)(b) 191
    art 2(1)(c) 22
    art 2(2)(a) 22
    art 2(4) 244, 245, 247
    art 3 241
Crime and Disorder Act 1998. 63
    s 28(1)(a). 63
    s 28(1)(b). 63
Criminal Justice and Public
    Order Act 1994 86
    s 77. 69
Disabilities Act 1990 (US) 95
    s 2(a)(7). 96
Disability Discrimination Act 1995 97,
        114, 143, 214, 216

s 3A(6) 214
s 8(1)(c). 290
s 8(4). 293
s 8(5). 290
s 4. 114
s 49A 312
ss 49A—49D 302
s 49B. 304
s 56. 286
Disability Discrimination Act (US). . . .216
Disability Rights Commission
    Act 1999
    s 12. 287
Disabled Persons (Employment)
    Act 1944 97
Education Act 1996
    s 375(3). 83
Employment Act 2010
    s 212(5). 91
Employment Equality (Age)
    Regulations 2006
    (SI 2006/714) 106
    reg 30 . . . . 106, 201, 202
    reg 31 . . . . .107, 202
    Sch 6 paras 5—6 . . . . 106, 201
Employment Equality (Religion or Belief)
    Regulations 2003
    (SI 2003/1660) 84
Employment Equality (Sexual
    Orientation) Regulations 2003
    (SI 2003/1661) 91
Employment Equity Act 1986
    (Canada) 301, 330
    s 2. 15
Employment Equity Act 1995
    (Canada) 331
Employment Tribunals Act 1996 285
Equal Pay Act 1970 . . . . 6, 42, 156,
        163, 164, 174, 281
    s 1(3). 164
    s 21. 295
    s 40. 146
    s 61. 146
    s 84. 146
    s 101. 146
Equality Act 2006
    s 2(2). 299
    s 16. . . . . .297, 298
    s 20(2). 296

s 20(4). 296
s 23. 298
s 24(2). 299
s 24(3). 299
s 24A(4) 286
s 28. 287
s 30. . . . . .285, 288
s 31. 327
Sch 2 paras 2–5 . . . . .297, 298
Sch 2 para 3 296
Sch 2 paras 6—8 296
Sch 2 paras 9—14 . . . . .297, 298
Sch 2 para 17. . . . . .297, 298
Equality Act 2010 . . . . . 7, 8, 22, 61, 62,
      84, 85, 91, 106, 107, 110, 116,
    145, 152, 155, 161, 165, 166, 170,
    173, 174, 176, 179, 180, 187, 191,
    201, 202, 210, 214, 215, 217, 218,
    219, 228, 229, 238, 240, 285, 286,
    287, 288, 290, 292, 302, 305, 311,
               312, 313, 315
Pt 4. 218
Pt 5 Ch 3. 156
s 1. .7, 8, 302
s 4. . . . . .110, 170
ss 4—12 116
s 6(1). 98
s 7. 93
s 11 237
s 12 237
s 13 . . . . .166, 173, 202, 214
s 13(1). 229
s 13(3). 215, 238
s 13(6)(b). 176, 238
s 14. 143
s 15. . . . . .173, 174, 202, 214
s 16. 93
s 17. 170
s 18. 170
s 19. 180
s 19(1). 179
s 19(2)(b). 188
a 19(2)(d). 191
s 20. . . . . .98, 214
s 23. 173
s 24(1). 229
s 26. . . . . .22, 228
s 27. 228
s 27(1)(a). 175

s 28. 107
s 29(6). 152
s 29(8). 84, 91, 116
s 31(4). 152
s 33(6). 84, 91, 116
s 36. 218
s 39. 218
ss 64—80 156
s 69. . . . . .159, 164
s 69(1)(a). 164
s 69(1)(b). 165
s 69(2). 165
s 69(3). 166
ss 70—71 161
s 79. 158
s 84. 107
s 85(10). 93
s 104. 240
s 114. 287
s 114(7). 288
s 114(8). 288
s 119(4). 293
s 119(5). 292
s 124(2)(c) 290
s 124(4). 292
s 124(5). 292
s 124(6). 293
s 124(7). 290
s 136. 287
s 138. 286
s 149. . . . . 8, 62, 108, 302
s 149(1). 312
s 149(3). 313
s 149(3)(c). 315
s 149(5). 314
s 149(6). 129, 314
s 150. 305
s 156. 326
s 158. 238
s 159. 209
s 193. 239
s 202. 91
Sch 3 para 24. 95
Sch 4 218
Sch 8 Pt 2 218
Sch 9 Pt 1 198
Sch 9 para 2 . . . . 85, 92
Sch 9 para 3 85
Sch 9 paras 8—9 . . . . .106, 201

Sch 9 para 11. . . . . .107, 202
Sch 26 para 13. 286
EU Charter of Fundamental
    Rights 2000 . . . . . . .20, 23, 33, 110,
                                     112, 113
art 1 20
art 21 110
art 35 23
European Communities Act 1972 42
European Convention on Human
    Rights 7, 63, 94, 97, 110, 111,
                   112, 125, 128, 130, 137,
                   143, 146, 147, 148, 197, 224
art 3 .66, 229
art 8 . . . . 71, 87, 89, 94, 147
art 9 85
art 10 84
art 12 . . . . 89, 94
art 14 . . . . . 85, 87, 89, 110, 125, 126,
                127, 128, 133, 136, 138, 146,
                147, 148, 155, 195, 198, 222,
                                226, 258, 289
Protocol 1 art 3 148
Protocol 12 . . . .126, 147, 148, 197, 224
art 1(1) 147, 148
art 1(2) 148
European Social Charter 72
Fair Employment (Northern
    Ireland) Act 1989 . . . . . 15, 301, 328
s 49. 114
s 55. 301
Fair Employment and Treatment
    (Northern Ireland) Order 1998
    (SI 1998/3162)
Pt VII 301, 328
art 4(1) 15
art 13 324
art 44 286
art 55 329
arts 55—68 328
Framework Convention for the Protection
    of National
    Minorities 72
Gender Equality Act (Iceland) 304
Gender Mainstreaming Act 2007
    (Belgium) 303
Gender Recognition Act 2004 94
s 2(1). 94

German Basic Law 20
art 1(1) 20
German Civil Code 200
Housing and Regeneration
    Act 2008 s 318 72
Human Fertilisation and
    Embryology Act 2008 s 42 89
Human Rights Act (Canada) 331
Human Rights Act 1998. . . . . 7, 87, 149,
                152, 280, 283, 289, 304, 305
s 6(5). 149
Human Rights Code 1981
    (Ontario) 215, 222
s 4(1)(g). 215
s 10. 215
ILO Convention No 3 1919 43
Immigration, Asylum and
    Nationality Act 2006 64
Immigration Rules 1980 (UK) 222
Indian Constitution 129, 276
art 15 . . . . .129, 132
art 15(1) 129
art 15(4) 276
art 16(4) 276
art 340(1) 276
art 341(1) 276
art 342(2) 276
Industrial Tribunals (Constitution and
    Rules of Procedure) Regulations 1993
    (SI 1993/2687)
Sch 1 para 12. 283
Intermodal Surface Transportation
    Efficiency Act 1991 (US) 335
International Convention on the
    Elimination of Race Discrimination
    art 2(2) 258
International Covenant on Civil and
    Political Rights. 97
International Covenant on Social,
    Economic and Cultural Rights 309
    art 2 309
Law on Equal Treatment of Men and
    Women (Netherlands)
    art 5 247
Local Government Act 1988 s 28 87
Local Government Act 2003
    Sch 8(1) para 1. 87
Marriage Act 1949. 94

s 5B 94
Maternity and Parental Leave etc
   Regulations 1999 (SI 1999/3312)
   regs 13—14 44
Matrimonial Causes Act 1973 . . . . 89, 93, 94
Municipal Franchise Act 1869 39
National Minimum Wage
   Act 1998 . . . . 107, 202
National Minimum Wage Act
   Regulations 1999 (SI 1999/584)
   reg 13 102
Northern Ireland Act 1998
   s 75 . . . . 302, 306, 308, 310, 322,
               323, 324, 328, 330
   Sch 9 . . . . 306, 322, 323
Paternity and Adoption Leave
   Regulations 2002
   (SI 2002/2788) 44
Pay Equity Act 1990 (Ontario) 301, 318
   Pt IV 326
   s 3(1) 304
   s 25(2) 326
Pregnancy Discrimination
   Act (US) 170, 175
   § 2000e(k) 170
Prevention of Terrorism Act 2005 . . . 10
Public Law 109-59 (US) 278, 335
Public Order Act 1986
   Pt 3A 85
   ss 17—22 63
   s 23 63
Race Relations Act 1976 . . . . . . 6, 61, 62,
      63, 71, 83, 113, 115, 117, 151,
      179, 191, 216, 238, 291, 302
   s 1(1)(b) 179
   s 2 174
   s 3 61
   s 3(1) 114
   s 19B 62
   s 19B(2)(a) 62
   s 35 240
   ss 37—38 238
   ss 48—62 295
   s 56(1)(c) 290
   s 56(4) 290
   s 57(3) 292
   s 57(4) 293
   s 65 286
   s 66 287

s 71 . . . . 62, 302
   Sch 1A 304
Race Relations Act 1976 (Statutory
   Duties) Order 2001
   (SI 2001/3458) 310
Race Relations Act 1976 (Statutory
   Duties) Order 2004 (SI 2004/3125)
   art 3 310
Racial and Religious Hatred
   Act 2006 85
Religious Character of Schools
   (Designation Procedure) Regulations
   1998
   (SI 1998/2535) 83
Rent Act 1977 87
School Standards and Framework
   Act 1998
   s 69(3) 83
   s 70 82
   s 71 83
   Sch 20 82
Sex Discrimination Act 1975 . . . . . 6, 42,
      61, 113, 174, 179, 184, 191,
      216, 238, 281, 292
   s 1(1)(b) 179, 191
   s 1(1)(b)(i) 261
   ss 1—3 114
   s 4(1)(a) 174
   s 42A 240
   s 47(3) 238
   ss 47—48 238
   s 49 238
   ss 57—61 295
   s 64 284
   s 65(1)(c) 290
   s 65(3) 290
   s 66 293
   s 66(3) 292
   s 74 286
   s 75(1) 287
   s 76A 304
   ss 76A—76C 302
Sex Discrimination and Equal Pay
   (Miscellaneous Amendments)
   Regulations 1996 (SI 1996/438)
   reg 2(4) 292
Sex Discrimination and Equal
   Pay (Remedies) Regulations
   1993 (SI 1993/2798) 293

Sexual Offences Act 1956 s 12(1) 86
Sexual Offences Act 1967 s 1 86
Sexual Offences Act 2003
    Sch 7 para 1. 86
Sexual Offences (Amendment)
    Act 2000 86
Small Business Act (US)
    § 4a. 334
    § 8(a). 335
    §§ 631 et seq 277
    § 637(a)(5). 277
    § 637(a)(6)(A) 277
Small Business Regulations (US) . . . 278
    § 124.103(b). 277
    § 124.103(b)(3). 277
    § 124.103(c). 277
    § 124.104. 277
    § 124.105. 277
South African Constitution 20, 22,
        110, 112, 125, 129, 137, 198,
                225, 227, 272
    s 1. 20
    s 9. 125
    s 9(1). 129
    s 9(2). 256, 274
    s 9(3). 110, 136
    s 36(1). 20, 226
    s 39(1). 20
    s 39(2). 20
Surface Transportation and
    Uniform Relocation
    Assistance Act 1987 (US) 335
Surface Transportation Assistance
    Act 1982 (US) 335
Transportation Equity Act for the
    21st Century Act (US) 278, 335

Transportation Equity Act for the
    21st Century Regulations (US). . . .278
    § 26.67(a). 278
    § 26.67(b) 278
    § 26.67(d) 278
Treaty of Amsterdam 62, 90, 114, 150
    art 13 . . . . .84, 116
Treaty of Lisbon 20, 114
    art 19 116
    art 157. . . . . .43, 150
Treaty of Rome 227
    art 13 62
    art 119. . . . . .42, 114,
                        149, 156
    art 141. . . . . 43, 114, 149
    art 141(4). 241, 245
    art 157. 114
    art 157(4) 241, 245, 246
Treaty on European Union 241
UN Convention on the Elimination
    of Discrimination Against
    Women 141, 258
UN Convention on the Rights of
    Persons with Disabilities
    2006 . . . . 98, 99
US Constitution 112, 119
    Fifth Amendment, Equal
        Protection Clause. 123, 124
    Fourteenth Amendment. . . . 112, 118,
                120, 123, 124, 135, 270
University Test Act 1870 77
Voting Rights Act 1965 (US) 251
    § 1973(b). 252
Warm Homes and Energy Conservation
    Act 2000 309
    s 2. 310

List of Abbreviations

AC	Appeal Cases
ACAS	Advisory, Conciliation and Arbitration Service
AIR	All India Reporter
All ER	All England Reports
BCLR	Butterworths Constitutional Law Reports (South Africa)
BHRC	Butterworths Human Rights Cases
BVerfGE	Bundesverfassungsgerichtsentscheidungen (German Federal Constitutional Court Reports)
CCC	Canadian Criminal Cases
CEDAW	Convention on the Elimination of Discrimination Against Women
CERD	International Convention on the Elimination of Race Discrimination
CFR	Code of Federal Regulations (USA)
CHRC	Canadian Human Rights Commission
CLP	Current Legal Problems
CMLR	Common Market Law Reports
CRE	Commission for Racial Equality
DBE	Disadvantaged Business Enterprise (USA)
DDA	Disability Discrimination Act 1995
DLR	Dominion Law Reports (Canada)
DRA	default retirement age
DRC	Disability Rights Commission
EA 2010	Equality Act 2010
EAT	Employment Appeal Tribunal
ECHR	European Convention on Human Rights
ECtHR	European Court of Human Rights
ECJ	European Court of Justice
ECR	European Court Reports
ECRI	European Commission against Racism and Intolerance
EFTA	European Free Trade Association
EGGE	Expert Group on Gender and Employment (EU)
EHRC	Equality and Human Rights Commission
EHRLR	European Human Rights Law Review
EHRR	European Human Rights Reports
EJIL	European Journal of International Law

EOC	Equal Opportunities Commission
EOR	Equal Opportunities Review
EqPA	Equal Pay Act 1970
EWCA	England and Wales Court of Appeal
FETO	Fair Employment and Treatment (Northern Ireland) Order 1998
GDI	Gender-related Development Index
GDP	gross domestic product
HDI	Human Development Index
HRA	Human Rights Act 1998
ICR	Industrial Case Reports
ILJ	Industrial Law Journal
ILO	International Labour Organization
IRLR	Industrial Relations Law Reports
ISH	Index of Social Health
LGB	lesbian, gay, and bisexual
LQR	Law Quarterly Review
MLR	Modern Law Review
NGO	non-governmental organization
NUJS L Rev	National University of Juridical Studies Law Review (India)
OBC	other backward class (India)
OFCCP	Office of Federal Contract Compliance Programs (USA)
OJLS	Oxford Journal of Legal Studies
OMC	open method of coordination
PEO	Pay Equity Office (Canada)
PL	Public Law
RRA	Race Relations Act 1976
SBA	Small Business Administration (USA)
SCC	Supreme Court of Canada
SCR	Supreme Court Reports (Canada)
SC/ST	Scheduled Castes and Scheduled Tribes (India)
SDA	Sex Discrimination Act 1975
SWC	Status of Women Canada
TEA-21	Transportation Equity Act for the 21st Century (USA)
UKHL	UK House of Lords
UKSC	UK Supreme Court
USC	US Code
WLR	Weekly Law Reports

I

Equality: Concepts and Controversies

... to labour in the face of the majestic equality of the law, which forbids the rich as well as the poor to sleep under bridges, to beg in the streets, and to steal bread.

Anatole France (1897)[1]

We hold these truths to be sacred and undeniable, that all men are created equal and independent, that from that equal creation they derive rights inherent and inalienable, among which are the preservation of life, and liberty, and the pursuit of happiness.

Thomas Jefferson (c 1775)[2]

Equality as an ideal shines brightly in the galaxy of liberal aspirations. Nor is it just an ideal. Attempts to capture it in legal form are numerous and often grand: all human rights documents, both international and domestic, include an equality guarantee, and this is bolstered in many jurisdictions with statutory provisions. This suggests that we all have an intuitive grasp of the meaning of equality and what it entails. Yet the more closely we examine it, the more its meaning shifts. Is equality captured by the familiar aphorism that likes should be treated alike? This appears both morally irrefutable and straightforward. But the initial logic fades as soon as we begin to ask further questions. When can we say that one person is so 'like' another that they should be treated alike? For centuries it was openly asserted that women were not 'like' men and therefore deserved fewer rights, and this remains true in some countries in the world. The same apparent logic was used to deny rights to black people, slaves, and Jews; and still more recently to people on account of their age, disability, or sexual orientation. It is still current in respect of non-citizens.

[1] A France, *Le Lys rouge* (Calmann-Lévy, 1927), p 106.
[2] 'Rough Draft' of the American Declaration of Independence in J P Boyd (ed), *Papers of Thomas Jefferson*, vol 1 (Princeton University Press, 1950), p 423.

And even if we can agree on whether two individuals are relevantly alike, we may still have doubts as to whether they should always be treated alike. Experience has shown that equal treatment can in practice perpetuate inequalities. As Anatole France graphically depicts in the above quotation, a law which appears equal on its face bears far more heavily on the poor than the rich. A rule which requires a high level of formal education as a precondition for employment, will, although applied equally to all, have the effect of excluding many who have suffered educational disadvantage, often a residue of racial discrimination or slavery. A rule which requires full-time working as a prerequisite for training, pension, or promotion opportunities will operate to exclude many of those with primary responsibility for children, the vast majority of whom are still women. A rule which requires all employees or pupils to dress according to Christian traditions and take religious holidays according to the Christian calendar will perpetuate the exclusion of religious minorities.

How do we explain then how equal treatment can in effect lead to inequality, while unequal treatment might be necessary in order to achieve equality? The apparent paradox can be understood if we accept that equality can be formulated in different ways, depending on which underlying conception is chosen. Equality of treatment is predicated on the principle that justice inheres in consistency; hence likes should be treated alike. But this in turn is based on a purely abstract view of justice, which does not take into account existing distributions of wealth and power. Consistency in treatment of two individuals who appear alike but in fact differ in terms of access to power, opportunities, or material benefits, results in unequal outcomes. An alternative conception of equality, therefore, is based on a more substantive view of justice, which concentrates on correcting maldistribution. Such a principle would lead to a focus on equality of results, requiring unequal treatment if necessary to achieve an equal impact. Alternatively, the focus could lie on facilitating personal self-fulfilment, by equalizing opportunities. A notion of equality which stresses equal opportunities is consistent with inequality of treatment *and* inequality of results. Unequal treatment might be necessary to equalize the opportunities of all individuals, but once opportunities are equal, different choices and capacities might lead to inequality of results. More recently, equality has been linked to dignity.

The choice between different conceptions of equality is not one of logic but of values or policy. Equality could aim to achieve the redistributive goal of alleviating disadvantage, the liberal goal of treating all with equal concern and respect, the neo-liberal goal of market or contractual equality, and the political goal of access to decision-making processes. It is striking that, despite the widespread adherence to the ideal of equality, there is so little agreement on its meaning and aims.

Also complex is the relationship between equality and difference. It is an easy step to assume that 'difference' means inequality and inequality is synonymous with inferiority. This assumes a conceptual framework based on a set of dichotomies: reason and emotion, soul and body, good and bad, equal and different. In this schema, deriving from Aristotle, the second part of the pair is inferior to the first. Difference is characterized as the negative partner, legitimating detrimental treatment of those who are different. Yet in a plural society such as that in modern Britain, difference and diversity should be regarded as positive attributes. Equality, far from suppressing difference, should accommodate and even celebrate it. Nor is difference necessarily an all-or-nothing concept. As Young argues:

> To say that there are differences among groups does not imply that there are not overlapping experiences, or that two groups have nothing in common. The assumption that real differences in affinity, culture, or privilege imply oppositional categorisation must be challenged. Different groups are always similar in some respects, and always potentially share some attributes, experiences and goals.[3]

The above discussion has assumed that equality is the prime value in society. But equality may well conflict with other basic social values, such as liberty from State interference, including freedom of speech and thought. How then do we decide which takes priority? Should individuals be able to assert their freedom of speech rights in order to protect their rights to make racist comments? Or to produce pornographic material which degrades and stigmatizes women? Should an unborn foetus be entitled to claim a right to life to defeat the claims of the mother to reproductive freedom? On a different scale are the conflicts between equality and utilitarian or economic goals. Should equality be defeasible on the grounds that its achievement is too costly, either for the State or for private individuals?

For law-makers, facing the task of translating abstract notions into law, these questions are particularly complex. Legal formulations of equality must be coherent and comprehensible; and, equally importantly, they

---

[3] I M Young, *Justice and the Politics of Difference* (Princeton University Press, 1990), p 171.

must contain mechanisms for making equality effective. But traditional enforcement and compliance mechanisms are often inappropriate in the equality context. Civil rights are normally enforceable in adversarial proceedings initiated by one party to the dispute and carrying a financial remedy. Yet a right to equality might be an empty promise if it requires each individual victim of discrimination to conduct proceedings against a particular defendant, particularly if the defendant is her employer, the factual and legal issues complex, and the remedy limited to compensation. A wholehearted commitment to equality might well require far more imaginative legal structures, including not just prohibitions of discriminatory behaviour or practices, but positive duties to promote equality. Indeed, closer attention to the causes of inequalities in society point to the need to institute broader social programmes, such as the provision of targeted training and childcare, the modification of working hours, and the alteration of premises to accommodate disability. Even so, at the end of the day, we may also have to acknowledge the limits of the role traditional legal provisions and processes can play in bringing about social change.

The aim of this chapter is to examine in more detail some of these basic controversies. Chapter Two, recognizing that equality is ultimately highly sensitive to the society which it affects, examines the historical, social, and legal context in respect of each of the main groups to which anti-discrimination law applies in Britain. Chapter Three examines the scope of discrimination law. Chapter Four uses the discussion thus far to assess the actual legal tools used in discrimination law. Chapter Five focuses on one of the most contested aspects of discrimination law, namely reverse discrimination, and Chapter Six considers the role of legal processes and remedies.

I THE PRINCIPLE OF EQUALITY

(1) BACKGROUND AND DEVELOPMENT

Equality as an ideal is a relatively modern construct. Classical and mediaeval societies were not founded on a principle of equality. Instead, society was ordered in hierarchical form, with entitlements and duties determined by birth or status rather than by virtue of an individual's inherent worth as a human being. Indeed, thinkers from Aristotle to Aquinas found no difficulty in justifying the subordination of women and slaves on grounds of their inherent inferiority, their lack of rationality, and their need for supervision and guidance from free male householders.

It was only with the advent of mercantile capitalism and the loosening bonds of feudalism that equality began to emerge as an organizing social principle. Greater economic freedom of individuals to pursue trade within a free market was accompanied by greater political freedom as Parliament gained power from the monarchy. It was in this hot-house climate of change and expectation that liberal ideology blossomed. John Locke, writing in 1690 captured the spirit of the age in his well-known aphorism: 'Men [are] by Nature all free, equal and independent.'[4] Politically, this meant increasing challenges to the authority of the monarch. Its economic manifestation was in the principle of freedom of contract. Freedom of contract was premised on the notion of equal parties, an abstract contractual equality which was oblivious to market reality.

Yet even then the promise of equality was ambiguous and exclusive. Indeed, a glance at the legal framework in the centuries following Locke reveals a landscape pockmarked with inequalities. Numerous groups, including women, slaves, religious minorities, black people, gypsies, and the unpropertied classes were excluded from the promise of liberal equality. Exclusion was achieved by the apparently logical argument that the basic rights to liberty and equality only inhered in individuals by virtue of their rationality. The concept of rationality could then be easily manipulated in an exclusive way. Women, slaves, and others were characterized as irrational and emotional and therefore not entitled to the equal rights due to rational beings.[5] Thus the newly ascendant equality principle coexisted with continued and unchallenged relations of domination. Slavery was not outlawed; colonialism flourished and women were denied basic rights such as the franchise, property owner-ship, and rights over their own children.[6] Locke himself saw no incon-sistency between his lofty proclamation of equality and his description of the family as 'a Master... with all these subordinate Relations of Wife, Children, Servants and Slaves'.[7]

Nevertheless, the ideology of equality and freedom gave feminists and other disadvantaged groups the necessary vocabulary to argue for the emancipation of all. 'If all men are born free, why are women born

---

[4] John Locke, *Two Treatises of Government* (ed P Laslett) (Cambridge University Press, 1988), 'The Second Treatise', para 95.
[5] S Fredman, *Women and the Law* (Clarendon Press, 1997), ch 1.
[6] See Fredman, above n 5, chs 1 and 2.
[7] Locke, above n 4, 'Second Treatise', para 86.

slaves?' asked Mary Astell in 1700.[8] It was as a focus for political activism, rather than as a legal concept, that equality began to emerge as a real force for combating sex discrimination and racism. But since the groups claiming equality inevitably lacked political power, progress was painfully slow. Three main phases in the development of a legal principle of equality can be discerned. The first required the dismantling of formal legal impediments, such as slavery and the exclusion of married women from property rights, rights over their own children, and the suffrage. It was well into the twentieth century before the major impediments were removed.[9] Women in Britain only achieved equal suffrage as recently as 1928. Although equality before the law was a major achievement, it soon became clear that it was far from sufficient to achieve genuine equality. Women and members of racial or ethnic minorities were actively discriminated against, in the labour market, in housing, in social security, and on the streets. Women were routinely paid on separate and lower scales than men doing the same work; black people were subjected to prejudice and exclusion. A new impetus was needed, in the form of legal prohibitions on discrimination or unequal treatment whether by public or private actors. This heralded the second stage, that of anti-discrimination legislation. Beginning in 1965, with the first weak and ineffectual race discrimination statute, this phase saw the introduction of statutory restrictions on discrimination in employment, education, and services. The domestic legislation—the Equal Pay Act 1970, the Sex Discrimination Act 1975, and the Race Relations Act 1976—were complemented and strengthened by sex discrimination legislation from the European Community. In 1995, a similar statutory framework was created to deal with discrimination on grounds of disability. Notably, however, because of the absence of a written constitution and a bill of rights, there was no fundamental right to equality.

These laws have played an important role. But their limits have also become apparent. By the beginning of the new millennium, it was clear that three decades of anti-discrimination legislation had not been able to address deep-seated discriminatory structures. There remained a yawning gap between the pay of women and men; disabled people and ethnic minorities still experienced unacceptably high levels of unemployment; and high levels of homophobia, including homophobic bullying at school continued. Particularly disturbing was the finding of institutional

[8] M Astell, 'Reflections upon Marriage' in M Astell and B Hill, *The First English Feminist* (Gower, 1986).
[9] On women, see Fredman, above n 5, ch 2.

racism in the Metropolitan police service, a body which should be combating racism.[10] Equally problematic was the exclusion from current legislation both of significant groups and important areas of activity. It was these limitations which provoked a reconsideration of equality laws. Prompted by EU directives passed in 2000, legislation was introduced to prohibit discrimination on grounds of religion and belief, sexual orientation, and age. Further new grounds have been incorporated from the European Convention on Human Rights as part of the Human Rights Act 1998. In addition, the damning indictment of racism in the police forces produced legislation prohibiting discrimination across all public functions, not just employment, education, and services.

At the same time, sustained campaigning has meant that we have now taken the first tentative steps into a new phase of equality laws, which brings with it a movement from negative prohibitions on discrimination to positive duties to promote equality. Following pioneering legislation in Northern Ireland imposing positive equality duties, legislation in 2000 imposed similar proactive duties in relation to racial equality in Britain, which were in turn extended to disability and then gender. At the same time, in the EU, there has been a strong emphasis on gender 'mainstreaming', which requires decision-making bodies to consider the impact of all their decisions on gender equality, rather than regarding gender discrimination as a side issue.

These developments are now harmonized in the Equality Act (EA) 2010, which Hepple has called the fifth generation of equality and anti-discrimination laws.[11] The EA 2010 extends protection to nine 'protected characteristics', namely, age, disability, gender reassignment, race, religion or belief, sex, sexual orientation, marriage or civil partnership, and pregnancy and maternity. It also extends protection to public functions exercised by private bodies. The positive duty similarly incorporates all the protected characteristics, except for marriage and civil partnership. Furthermore, in an important recognition of the interaction between socio-economic disadvantage and discrimination, the Act imposes a duty in respect of socio-economic inequalities.[12]

---

[10] Home Office, 'Report of the MacPherson Inquiry' (Cmd 4262, 24 February 1999).

[11] B Hepple, 'The Aims of Equality Law' [2008] 61 CLP 1–22.

[12] EA 2010, s 1. Although this provision is part of the legislation, the Coalition Government which came to power in the election following the enactment of the legislation has stated that it will not bring it into effect. The legality of refusing to bring duly enacted legislation into effect is dubious: see *R v Home Secretary, ex p Fire Brigades Union* [1995] 2 AC 513 (HL).

These developments are, however, still in their infancy. Positive duties are generally timid, focusing more on changes in procedure than progress in substance. The public sector equality duty in the EA 2010 only requires a public body to 'have due regard to the need to' eliminate unlawful discrimination or promote equality of opportunity on the specified grounds.[13] It is not under a duty to take steps to do so. In relation to socio-economic inequalities, the duty is even more timid. Here public bodies are only required to 'have due regard to the *desirability*' of exercising strategic functions in a way which reduces socio-economic disadvantage.[14] Even in this form, the Coalition Government which came to power in the election following the enactment of the legislation, has stated that it will not bring it into effect.

It is against this background that we can begin to dissect the meaning of the concept of equality. In the following section, I consider more closely different notions of equality, considering first formal equality or equality as consistency, and then turning to different types of substantive equality, including equality of opportunity and equality of results. The second section is concerned with more substantive bases for equality, the most important being dignity, restitution, redistribution, and participative democracy. In the final section, I consider two important competitors with equality, namely liberty and market concerns.

(II) TREATING LIKES ALIKE

The basic Aristotelian principle that likes should be treated alike continues to form the basis of our ideas about equality. Its enduring strength lies in its resonance with our instinctive idea that fairness requires consistent treatment. The State should not arbitrarily differentiate between individuals: hence everyone should be equal before the law. This principle has therefore played a crucial role in dismantling express legal prohibitions in relation to particular identity groups. Similarly, 'likes should be treated alike' entails that everyone should be treated according to her merits as an individual in her own right. However, equality in this sense raises at least four sets of problems. The first concerns the threshold question of when two individuals are relevantly alike. Not every distinction is discriminatory. Governments and individuals classify people into groups for a wide variety of reasons and many of them are legitimate. It is quite legitimate to distinguish between high-income and low-income groups for taxation

---

[13] EA 2010, s 149.　　[14] Ibid, s 1 (emphasis added).

reasons. Similarly, it is quite legitimate to distinguish between people with families and people without in the allocation of council housing. On the other hand, as we have seen, for many years it was thought to be legitimate to distinguish women from men, blacks from whites. What sort of distinctions, therefore, should be outlawed by the law as illegitimate and unacceptable? One of the biggest leaps in twentieth-century struggles for equality has been the recognition that characteristics based on race, sex, colour, or ethnic origin should not in themselves constitute relevant differences justifying inferior treatment. In other areas, such as sexual orientation, this recognition has still not been fully achieved. This question is explored further in Chapter Three.

The second difficulty is that equality in this sense is merely a relative principle. It requires only that two similarly situated individuals be treated alike. In other words, fairness is a matter of consistency. There is no substantive underpinning: as long as two similarly situated people are treated the same, there is no difference in principle between treating them equally badly, and treating them equally well. For example, equal pay laws are of no benefit to a low paid woman if the only similarly situated male comparator is equally badly paid. In a case in the UK, the claimant argued that she had been discriminated against on grounds of her sex when her employer required her to work in areas of the workplace where fellow male employees displayed pictures of naked and semi naked women which she found offensive. The tribunal rejected her claim. It held that a man might have found the display as offensive as she did, and the employers 'would have treated a man just as badly whether he was complaining about the display of nude women or nude men'. There was, therefore, no question of less favourable treatment of the employee on the ground of her sex. This finding was upheld on appeal.[15] This can be contrasted with the conception of equality used in a recent case in the US involving racial segregation of prisoners.[16] The prison authority argued that this should not be regarded as discriminatory because all races were 'equally segregated'. The US Supreme Court emphatically rejected the argument that equality could be satisfied by 'neutrality' of this sort. Citing a previous case the Court stated. 'It is axiomatic that racial classifications do not become legitimate on the assumption that all persons suffer them in equal degree.'[17]

[15] *Stewart v Cleveland Guest (Engineering) Ltd* [1996] ICR 535.
[16] *Johnson v California* 125 S Ct 1141 (2005) (US Supreme Court).
[17] *Powers v Ohio* 499 US 400, 410 (1991).

Even more problematically, the absence of substantive underpinning means that a claim of equal treatment can be met by removing a benefit from the relatively privileged group (levelling down). In a famous US case, the city of Jackson in Mississippi was ordered to desegregate its four 'whites only' swimming pools, together with the single 'blacks only' pool. Instead, it decided to close down all its public swimming pools.[18] It was held that identical treatment had been applied to both whites and blacks and that therefore there was no breach of the equality guarantee. A similar response was seen more recently in the UK in relation to legislation giving the authorities the power to detain non-UK nationals indefinitely without trial if they were suspected of international terrorism.[19] The House of Lords struck down the legislation on the grounds, inter alia, that it applied only to non-UK nationals and not to UK nationals who might also be suspected of international terrorism. This left open the possibility of enacting similar legislation extending the powers to include UK nationals. Indeed, the government speedily enacted the Prevention of Terrorism Act 2005, which gave it power to issue orders curtailing the liberty (again without trial) of any individual suspected of involvement in terrorism-related activity, whether they were UK or foreign nationals. Equality as consistency was satisfied by intruding equally on the liberty of all.[20] It was partially because of the risk of levelling down of this sort that the majority of the US Supreme Court steered clear of the equality principle when it finally decided to strike down legislation criminalizing homosexuality. *Lawrence v Texas* concerned a Texas statute forbidding two persons of the same sex to engage in specified sexual intimacies.[21] Rather than relying on a breach of equality, the majority of the US Supreme Court found that the statute constituted a breach of due process. As Kennedy J put it:

Were we to hold the statute invalid under the Equal Protection Clause some might question whether a prohibition would be valid if drawn differently, say, to prohibit the conduct both between same-sex and different-sex participants.[22]

The third drawback of equality as consistency is the need to find a comparator. Inconsistent treatment can only be demonstrated by finding

---

[18] *Palmer v Thompson* 403 US 217, 91 S Ct 1940 (1971).

[19] *A v Secretary of State for the Home Office* [2004] UKHL 56 (HL), Anti-Terrorism, Crime and Security Act 2001, s 23.

[20] S Fredman, 'From Deference to Democracy: The Role of Equality under the Human Rights Act 1998' (2006) 122 LQR 53–81 at 53.

[21] *Lawrence v Texas* 123 S Ct 2472 (US Supreme Court).

[22] Ibid at 575.

a similarly situated person who does not share the characteristic in question (such as race or sex) and who has been treated more favourably than the complainant. The underlying assumption is that, once these characteristics are disregarded, individuals can be treated entirely on their merit. This in turn assumes that individuals can be considered in the abstract, apart from their colour, religion, ethnic origins, gender, or other such characteristic. Yet an individual's social, economic, and political situation is still heavily determined by these very characteristics. Even more fundamentally, each individual is constituted partly by group affinities,[23] whether it be her sense of identity, history, affinity with others, mode of reasoning, or expression of feelings. This is true of both the subject of discrimination and the comparator. Thus, the basic premise, namely that there exists a 'universal individual', is deeply deceptive. Instead, the apparently abstract comparator is clothed with the attributes of the dominant gender, culture, religion, ethnicity, or sexuality. It is not a coincidence that, when we talk of ethnicity, we generally refer to ethnic minorities, rather than ethnic majorities, attributing a 'normality' to the dominant culture rather than its own ethnic specificity.

The result of the assumption of a 'universal individual' is therefore to create powerful conformist pressures. In feminist literature this has been dubbed the 'male norm'. Equality as consistency requires an answer to the question: 'Equal to whom?' The answer is, inevitably, 'equal to a man'. In the powerful words of Catherine MacKinnon:

Concealed is the substantive way in which man has become the measure of all things. Under the sameness standard, women are measured according to our correspondence with man. . . . Gender neutrality is thus simply the male standard.[24]

This problem was graphically illustrated in a Canadian case, in which a woman forest firefighter was dismissed for narrowly failing to pass a fitness test based on an aerobic standard demonstrably based on male physiology. Far from accepting a female norm of measurement, the Canadian Court of Appeals held that to apply a different standard for women would be creating reverse discrimination, unfairly discriminating against men. Fortunately, the Canadian Supreme Court reversed.[25]

---

[23] Young, above n 3, at p 45.

[24] C MacKinnon, *Feminism Unmodified* (Harvard University Press, 1987), p 34.

[25] *British Columbia Public Service Employee Relations Commission v BCGEU* [1997] CCL 8468 (Canadian Supreme Court).

The problem has been even more acute in respect of pregnancy rights. On a strict view of equality as consistency, there is simply no appropriate male comparator and therefore no equality right arises. This difficulty was initially overcome by the unsatisfactory mechanism of comparing the treatment received by a pregnant woman with that of an ill man. It was only when the court could move beyond the idea of equality as consistency and therefore beyond the need for a male comparator that real progress could be made.[26] But this problem continues to dog discrimination legislation. In the area of equal pay, job segregation means that a low paid woman will frequently be unable to find a male comparator doing equivalent work in her establishment. A nursery nurse or a cleaner or a secretary is likely to find herself in an all-female workforce; or in an establishment where the only men are in managerial positions and therefore not useful comparators.[27]

The assimilationist tendency has also been problematic in the context of religion and ethnicity. This is demonstrated well in the European Court of Human Rights in the case of *Ahmad v the United Kingdom*,[28] in which a devout Muslim claimed he was forced to resign his teaching post after his employer insisted that his attendance at a nearby mosque for Friday prayers was inconsistent with his full-time contract. The European Commission declared the application inadmissible on the basis of a particularly narrow conception of equality. Relying on the proposition that since all minorities had to conform to the norms of the majority religion, the Commission found that the applicant had not proved 'less favourable treatment'. Instead of requiring some accommodation of difference, it deemed it sufficient to observe that 'in most countries, only the religious holidays of the majority of the population are celebrated as public holidays'.[29] This means that the only way to maintain religious practices which clash with majority expectations might be to resign one's post.[30] Parekh puts it starkly:

The choice before the minorities is simple. If they wish to become part of and be treated like the rest of the community, they should think and live like the latter;

---

[26] See further S Fredman, 'A Difference with Distinction: Pregnancy and Parenthood Reassessed' (1994) 110 LQR 106.

[27] See further Fredman, above n 5, pp 234 ff.

[28] *Ahmad v ILEA*, Application no 8160/78 (1982) 4 EHRR 126 (European Commission).

[29] Ibid at para 28.

[30] *Konttinen v Finland* (1996) 87 DR 68 (European Commission of Human Rights) at 75; *Stedman v United Kingdom* 23 EHRR CD 168 (European Commission of Human Rights); reluctantly accepted by the Court of Appeal in *Copsey v WBB Devon Clays Ltd* [2005] EWCA Civ 932 (CA).

if instead they insist on retaining their separate cultures, they should not complain if they are treated differently.[31]

The fourth problematic aspect of equality as consistency is its treatment of difference. Only 'likes' qualify for equal treatment; there is no requirement that people be treated appropriately according to their difference. Thus if a woman is doing work of less value than a comparable man, it may be appropriate to pay her less. But the equality as consistency principle does not require that she be paid proportionately to the difference in the value of her work. Similarly, cultural and religious difference might require positive measures which value difference in order to achieve genuine equality. Conversely, formal equality assumes that the aim is identical treatment. Yet, as we have seen, where there is antecedent inequality, 'like' treatment may in practice entrench difference. Thus unequal treatment may be necessary to achieve genuine equality. As Sen has argued: 'Equal consideration for all may demand very unequal treatment in favour of the disadvantaged.'[32]

Finally, equality as consistency is intensely individualist. Of course, the major contribution of equality has been its insistence that an individual be treated according to her own qualities or merits, and not on the basis of negative stereotypes attributed to her because of her race or sex. However, in rejecting the negative effects of taking group-based characteristics into account, the principle of equality has assumed that all aspects of group membership should be disregarded. Yet, as we have seen, cultural, religious, and ethnic group membership is an important aspect of an individual's identity. Diverse individual identities may be enriching and desired. This demonstrates that the problem is not the diversity of characteristics, but the detrimental treatment attached to it. Thus the aim should not be to eliminate difference, but to prohibit the detriment attached to such difference, preferably by adjusting existing norms to accommodate difference.

An equally problematic aspect of this individualism is the emphasis on individual fault as the only legitimate basis for imposing liability. The correlative of treating a person only on the basis of his or her 'merit', is the principle that an individual should only be liable for damage for which he or she is responsible. This in turn means that only a respondent who can be proved to have treated the complainant less favourably

---

[31] B Parekh, 'Integrating Minorities' in T Blackstone, B Parekh, and P Sanders, *Race Relations in Britain* (Routledge, 1998), p 2.
[32] A Sen, *Inequality Re-examined* (Oxford University Press, 1992).

on grounds of her race can be held liable for compensation. Yet sexism, racism, and other forms of discrimination extend far beyond individual acts of prejudice. Such prejudices are frequently embedded in the structure of society, and cannot be attributed clearly to any one person.

While formal equality or equality of treatment has a role to play, particularly in eradicating personal prejudice, it is clear from the above that it needs to be allied to a more substantive approach. It is to these we now turn.

(III) EQUALITY OF RESULTS

On this view, the equality principle goes beyond a demand for consistent treatment of likes, and requires instead that the result be equal. The strength of this notion of equality lies in its recognition that apparently identical treatment can in practice reinforce inequality because of past or ongoing discrimination. Thus if there has been race discrimination in the provision of education for black children, a requirement of literacy as a precondition for voting rights will, although applied equally to all, in effect exclude a significant proportion of black people. Similarly, given that many women have their children in their early twenties, an upper age limit of 28 for entry into the civil service, although applied to both men and women, will in effect exclude more women than men.[33] This description shows too that the aim of equality of results is different from that of equality as consistency. Equality of results is primarily concerned with achieving a fairer distribution of benefits; while formal equality is based on a notion of procedural fairness stemming from consistent treatment.

However, a closer look at the notion of equality of results demonstrates some worrying ambiguities. Results or impact can be used in at least three different ways. The first focuses on the impact on the individual. Has the apparently equal treatment had a detrimental impact on this individual because of her race, sex, or other irrelevant characteristic? On this version, the aim is not to achieve equality of results but to obtain a remedy for the individual. Take for example the case of the school which prohibited the wearing of head coverings.[34] The result was to exclude an observant Sikh boy. The removal of the rule meant that the boy was no longer barred, and the discriminatory impact on him was

---

[33] *Price v Civil Service Commission* [1978] ICR 27 (EAT).
[34] *Mandla v Lee* [1983] 2 AC 548 (HL).

remedied. The dismantling of this particular obstacle would not, however, lead to a proportionate representation of Sikhs at the school.

The second way in which equality of results is used focuses not on the results to the individual, but to the group. However, its aim is diagnostic, demonstrating the existence of obstacles to entry rather than prescribing an outcome pattern. Underlying this approach is the presumption that in a non-discriminatory environment, a fair spread of members of different sexes, races, or religions would be found in any particular body, be it a workforce, an educational establishment, or a decision-making body. The absence of one group, or its concentration in less lucrative or important areas, is taken as a sign that discrimination is probably taking place. But this is only a presumption. If no exclusionary criterion or obstacle can be proved, then it is assumed that the maldistribution is due to other factors, such as personal preference. Alternatively, if there is such a criterion, but it can be justified by the needs of the job, the presumption of discrimination is displaced. For example, a glance at the statistics shows that there are almost no women airline pilots. This inequality of results raises a presumption of discrimination. If it can be shown that women are excluded because it is believed that they will not make good pilots, then the inequality of results has been diagnostic of discrimination. But if it is shown that they are excluded because there are not enough well-trained women, then it could be argued, relying on this conception of equality, that despite the inequality of results, there is no discrimination.

The third and strongest meaning of 'equality of results' requires an equal outcome, that is that the spread of women or minorities in a category should reflect their proportions in the workforce or the population as a whole. Thus there is no need for proof of an intervening 'discriminatory' factor to trigger action. The mere fact of under-representation is discriminatory; and action should be aimed at achieving an equal outcome. Thus, as will be seen in later chapters, several jurisdictions have introduced legislation with the explicit aim of increasing the representation of minorities or women in employment or public office.[35] This notion of equality of results is at its most controversial when it goes beyond the removal of exclusionary criteria and requires the achievement of an equal outcome by preferential treatment of the under-represented group. The reconciliation of reverse discrimination with the principle of equality is considered in detail in Chapter Five. But

---

[35] Fair Employment and Treatment (Northern Ireland) Order 1998, art 4(1); Fair Employment Act 1989; Canadian Employment Equity Act 1995, s 2.

equality of results need not be achieved through openly preferential treatment. It could be achieved through encouragement, training, and other such measures. It is notable that even here, the notion of equality is not fully in focus: it is usually not equality but proportionality, fairness, or balance which is required.

There is a sense in which equality of results is a strategically straight-forward goal, since results are relatively easily quantifiable. However, the focus on results might itself be misleading. This is because monitoring of results does not necessitate any fundamental re-examination of the structures that perpetuate discrimination. A change in the colour or gender composition of a grade or sector, while to some extent positive, might reflect only an increasingly successful assimilationist policy. Thus women who achieve these positions might have done so by conforming to 'male' working patterns, contracting out their childcare obligations to other women, who remain as underpaid and undervalued as ever. Members of ethnic minorities who achieve these positions may be those who had assimilated, whether voluntarily or because of absence of available options, in terms of dress, religious observance, or language. Similarly, the increase in numbers of women or black people doing certain types of jobs might coincide with a decrease in the pay or status of the job in question. Such a pattern has been clearly demonstrated in catering. Here, in an apparently positive move towards equality of results, women have increased their share of management jobs dramatic-ally. Yet on closer inspection, it is found that the newly feminized managerial positions are relatively low paid (sometimes even less than the national average pay). Thus quantifiable change might only partially reflect qualitative change. There is a danger too that a focus on equality of results pays too little attention to the equally important duty to accommodate diversity by adapting existing structures.

Nor is it always entirely clear which 'results' are relevant. It is tempting to focus entirely on goods or benefits, whether jobs, places at schools or universities, or, more radically, income. However, while distributive justice is one concern of anti-discrimination law, it is not the only one. Other aspects of identity can be affected by prejudice and institutional discrimination. This is usefully illuminated by the distinc-tion, drawn by Nancy Fraser and others, between redistribution and recognition in relation to equality.[36] Redistribution refers to material

---

[36] N Fraser and A Honneth, *Redistribution or Recognition* (Verso, 2003); S Fredman, 'Redistribution And Recognition: Reconciling Inequalities' (2007) 23 South African Journal of Human Rights 214; S Liebenberg, 'Needs, Rights and Transformation: Adjudicating

inequality. Recognition is more complex. Drawing on the concept originally developed by Hegel, recognition refers to the central importance of inter-personal affirmation to our sense of who we are. Identity is shaped through the ways in which others recognize us, and we recognize others. Misrecognition or recognition inequalities arise through denigration, humiliation, and failure to value individuals. In many ways, in fact, recognition inequality covers the familiar ground of discrimination law: addressing prejudice in all its forms, including racism, sexism, and homophobia as well as violence. However, because recognition is difficult to measure and monitor, a focus on results might not capture the full range of harms caused by discrimination.

Also challenging for a theory of results is the question of participation, or representation, in representative bodies. Given that democratically elected representatives are not expected to mirror exactly the interests of the identity group to which they belong, a more sophisticated theory is necessary to explain the application of distributive justice to political representation. This is particularly so in the light of the fact that the interests of an identity group are not necessarily homogeneous or easily identifiable. This is discussed further in Chapter Five.

Even if we are clear as to which results we should focus on, we still need to determine what equality of results should entail. Should the results reflect the spread of all the identity groups in the population as a whole? This may be relatively easy to envisage in relation to gender or race. We might plausibly aim to achieve a balanced workforce, with parity between women and men in all grades. But are we aiming to achieve a workforce, educational institution, or representative body which exactly reflects the population in relation to age, disability, religion or belief, and sexual orientation? The way out of this conundrum is to reiterate that the harm of discrimination is not limited to distributive harms, but extends also to recognition harms, or harms to an individual's self-esteem. For some protected characteristics, recognition harms are more important than redistributive harms: sexual orientation may well fall into this category. Thus equality of results, while providing a welcome antidote to equality of treatment, can be seen to be at best a partial framework for situating anti-discrimination law.

Social Rights', Center For Human Rights And Global Justice Working Paper, Economic And Social Rights Series; J Fudge, 'The Canadian Charter of Rights: Recognition, Redistribution, and the Imperialism of the Courts' in T Campbell, KD Ewing, and A Tomkins (eds), *Sceptical Essays on Human Rights* (Oxford University Press, 2001).

(IV) EQUALITY OF OPPORTUNITY

An increasingly popular alternative to both equality as consistency and equality of results is the notion of equality of opportunity. This notion steers a middle ground between formal equality and equality of results. Proponents of this view recognize that equal treatment against a background of past and structural discrimination can perpetuate disadvantage. Using the graphic metaphor of competitors in a race, it is argued that true equality cannot be achieved if individuals begin the race from different starting points. However, according to this approach, to focus entirely on equality of results is to go too far in subordinating the right to individual treatment to a utilitarian emphasis on outcomes. Once individuals enjoy equality of opportunity, the problem of institutional discrimination has been overcome, and fairness demands that they be treated on the basis of their individual qualities, without regard to sex or race. This model therefore specifically rejects policies which aim to correct imbalances in the workforce by quotas or targets the aim of which is one of equality of outcome. Instead, an equal opportunities approach aims to equalize the starting point rather than the end result. Once all have equal opportunities, they should be judged on individual merit.

However, the metaphor of equal starting points is deceptively simple. What measures are required to ensure that individuals are genuinely able to compete equally? Williams distinguishes between a procedural and a substantive sense of equal opportunities. On a procedural view, equality of opportunity requires the removal of obstacles to the advancement of women or minorities, but does not guarantee that this will lead to greater substantive fairness in the result.[37] For example, the abolition of word-of-mouth recruitment or non-job-related selection criteria removes procedural obstacles and so opens up more opportunities. But this does not guarantee that more women or minorities will in fact be in a position to take advantage of those opportunities. Those who lack the requisite qualifications as a result of past discrimination will still be unable to meet job-related criteria; women with childcare responsibilities will still not find it easier to take on paid work. In the famous words of US President Lyndon Johnson, it is 'not enough to open the gates of

---

[37] B Williams, 'The Idea of Equality' in P Laslett and W G Runciman (eds), *Philosophy, Politics and Society Second Series* (Blackwell, 1965), p 110 and see J Waldron in S Guest and A Milne (eds), *Equality and Discrimination* (F Steiner Verlag, 1985), p 97.

opportunity. All our citizens must have the ability to walk through those gates.'[38]

A substantive sense of equality of opportunity, by contrast, requires measures to be taken to ensure that persons from all sections of society have a genuinely equal chance of satisfying the criteria for access to a particular social good.[39] This requires positive measures such as education and training, and family-friendly measures. It may go even further, and challenge the criteria for access, since existing criteria of merit may themselves reflect and reinforce existing patterns of disadvantage. For example, criteria which stress a continuous work history would reflect a view that experience out of the paid labour force is of little value to a future job. Women who have left the paid workforce to bring up children would thereby be subject to detriment. As Hepple argues, one is not supplying genuine equality of opportunity if one applies an unchallenged criterion of merit to people who have been deprived of the opportunity to acquire 'merit'.[40]

In practice, equality of opportunity is rarely used in its substantive sense when framing equality laws. Thus equality of opportunity, like equality of results, remains at most a partial basis for grounding anti-discrimination laws.

(v) DIGNITY

The limitations of formal equality have led courts, policy-makers, and theorists to search for a more substantive core to the notion of equality. The foremost candidate has been the notion of dignity. The primacy of individual dignity and worth as a foundation for equality rights has been clearly articulated in a number of jurisdictions, both in constitutional or statutory documents and by courts. Particularly vocal in this regard has been the Supreme Court of Canada, which has located dignity at the centre of the equality principle.

Equality means that our society cannot tolerate legislative distinctions that treat certain people as second class citizens, that demean them, that treat them as less capable for no good reason, or that otherwise offend fundamental human dignity.[41]

---

[38] Lyndon B Johnson, Address at Howard University (4 June 1965) cited in A Thernstrom 'Voting Rights, Another Affirmative Action Mess' (1996) 43 UCLA L Rev 2031 n 22.

[39] Williams, above n 19, at pp 125–6.

[40] B Hepple, 'Discrimination and Equality of Opportunity—Northern Irish Lessons' (1990) 10 OJLS 408 at 411.

[41] *Law v Canada* [1999] 1 SCR 497 (Canadian Supreme Court), para 51.

In other jurisdictions, dignity is a central pillar of the constitutional text itself. This is particularly true in South Africa. Addressing directly the history of humiliation and degradation to which the previous apartheid regime was dedicated, section 1 of the Constitution states that, amongst other things, the new South African State is founded on the values of 'human dignity, the achievement of equality, and the advancement of human rights and freedoms'. The general limitation clause in the South African Constitution also states emphatically that a right entrenched by the Constitution can only be limited to the extent that the limitation is 'reasonable and justifiable in an open and democratic society based on human dignity, autonomy and freedom'.[42] Every court, when interpreting human rights, must do so in a way which promotes the values of human dignity, equality, and freedom.[43] Similarly, the German Basic Law, also strongly influenced by recent history, provides in its first and absolutely entrenched article, that human dignity is unassailable and that it is the duty of all State authority to respect and protect it.[44] In the EU Charter of Fundamental Rights,[45] dignity plays a particularly central role. Not only is dignity mentioned in the preamble. In addition the Charter includes a specific right to dignity, stating in Article 1: 'Human dignity is inviolable. It must be respected and promoted.'

Certainly, there is much that makes dignity an intuitively appealing concept. Most importantly, dignity replaces rationality as a trigger for the equality right. As we have seen, linking equality to rationality has been used to deny access to the equality right; in particular to women, who were portrayed as lacking the prerequisite rationality. The crucial advance represented by substituting dignity for rationality is that dignity is seen to be inherent in the humanity of all people. According to Ackermann, dignity connotes 'innate, priceless and indefeasible human worth'.[46] The value attached to individuals simply by virtue of their humanity logically connotes that all are entitled to equal concern and respect. As the German Constitutional Court put it: 'Since all persons are entitled to human dignity and freedom and to that extent are equal,

---

[42] South African Constitution, s 36(1).

[43] Ibid, s 39(1) and (2).

[44] Basic Law for the Federal Republic of Germany (Grundgesetz, GG), Art 1(1).

[45] Charter of Fundamental Human Rights proclaimed in Nice in December 2000 is now incorporated into the Lisbon Treaty (subject, however, to an 'opt-out' by the UK).

[46] Ibid, p 8.

the principle of equal treatment is an obvious postulate for free democracy'.[47]

There are also several concrete ways in which the dignity value influences the development of the equality principle. First, dignity creates a substantive underpinning to the equality principle. This makes it impossible to argue that the principle of equality is satisfied by 'equally bad' treatment or by removing a benefit from the advantaged group and thereby 'levelling down'. Equality based on dignity must enhance rather than diminish the status of individuals. The importance of this can be seen by comparing the experience in the EU and South Africa over the question of equalizing pension ages. The lower pension age of 60 for women, as against 65 for men, has been contested in both jurisdictions as discriminatory against men. Although older women remain among the poorest in both Europe and South Africa, increasing unemployment for male workers above 50 has meant that access to pension rights at an earlier age is of growing importance to men. In a case brought initially to the UK courts, and subsequently, under EU law, to the European Court of Justice (ECJ), this claim of discrimination was upheld.[48] However, pension funds, claiming that the cost would be exorbitant, reacted by instituting policies to raise women's pension age to that of men over time. This strategy has been upheld in further litigation before the ECJ.[49] The result is that poor women are worse off, and poor men are no better off.[50] In South Africa, by contrast, when litigation was contemplated on the same issue, the risk of levelling down could be averted by reference to the substantive content of equality, including dignity. Litigation was, in the event, rendered unnecessary by the welcome intervention by political authorities in the form of legislative change. Even here, however, a substantive view was taken. In providing for age equalization for State old-age grants, there was no question of increasing women's pension age. Instead, the Social Assistance Amendment Bill passed in 2008, to be phased in over some years, opens the way for men aged 60 to 64 years to apply for the old-age grant, potentially benefitting over 450,000 men.

The second way in which the dignity value influences equality relates to the coverage of equality laws. In many human rights documents, the

---

[47] *Communist Party*, 5 BVerfGE 85 (1956). (I am indebted to Mr Justice L W H Ackermann for drawing my attention to this quote.)

[48] *Barber v Guardian Royal Exchange Assurance Group* [1990] IRLR 240 (ECJ).

[49] Case C-408/92 *Smith v Avdel Systems Ltd* [1994] ECR I-4435 (ECJ).

[50] S Fredman, 'The Poverty of Equality: Pensions and the ECJ' [1996] 25 ILJ 91–109.

list of groups who are protected against unlawful discrimination may be
expanded by courts. The dignity concept allows such expansion to take
place in a principled manner. For example, the Canadian Supreme
Court has held that the decision as to whether the equality guarantee
in the Canadian Charter of Rights prevents discrimination on a ground
not specifically enumerated should be decided by considering the primary mission of the equality guarantee. This mission, according to
L'Heureux-Dubé J, is 'the promotion of a society in which all are secure
in the knowledge that they are recognized at law as human beings
equally deserving of concern, respect and consideration'.[51] On this
view, a person or group has been discriminated against when a legislative
distinction makes them feel that they are less worthy of recognition or
value as human beings, as members of society.[52] Similarly, the question
of whether differentiation on a ground not specified in the South
African Constitution amounts to discrimination is answered by considering whether the differentiation is based on attributes or characteristics
which objectively have the potential to impair the fundamental dignity
of persons as human beings.[53]

Dignity has also been valuable in underscoring the role of equality in
situations in which there is no obvious comparator, making it impossible
to demonstrate that the demand of formal equality that likes should be
treated alike has been breached. This has been particularly salient in
relation to sexual harassment. Because sexual harassment is uniquely
bound up with sex, there is no easy answer to the question of whether
the harasser would have treated a man in the same manner. Substantive
equality does not require a comparator in the same way: it simply
prohibits sexual harassment because it is inconsistent with respect for
a woman's basic dignity and humanity. Dignity was expressly introduced into the statutory definition of sexual harassment by EU law, and
has now been incorporated into domestic law through the EA 2010.
Thus harassment is defined as unwanted conduct which has the purpose
or effect of violating the dignity of another person, or creating an
intimidating, hostile, degrading, humiliating, or offensive environment.[54] Moreover, it applies across a wide range of characteristics,

---

[51] *Andrews v Law Society of British Columbia* [1989] 1 SCR 143 at 171.

[52] *Egan v Canada* [1995] 2 SCR 513 at 545 (para 39); *Vriend v Alberta* [1998] 1 SCR 493, 156 DLR (4th) 385, [1998] 4 BHRC 140 at 185 (para 182).

[53] *Harksen v Lane NO & Others* [1997] ZACC 12 (CC).

[54] EA 2010, s 26; European Parliament and Council Directive 2006/54/EC, Art 2(1)(c) and Art 2(2)(a); for the similarly worded definition of racial harassment see Council Directive 2000/43/EC, Art 2(3). See also Chapter Four.

including age, disability, gender reassignment, race, religion or belief, sex, and sexual orientation (but not pregnancy and maternity or marriage and civil partnership). Dignity has played a similar role in the EU Charter of Fundamental Rights, particularly in relation to age discrimination. Thus under Article 35 of the EU Charter: 'The Union recognises and respects the rights of the elderly to lead a life in dignity and independence and to participate in social and cultural life.'

Dignity clearly has a central role to play in relation to equality. There has indeed been a temptation to regard equality as reducible to dignity. However, dignity also has its difficulties. As a start, the concept itself is open to different interpretations, and even opposite results.[55] This can be seen in one of the first decisions of the South African Constitutional Court on equality, the *Hugo* case.[56] The case concerned the pardon issued by President Mandela to all women prisoners who were mothers of young children. The pardon was challenged by a male prisoner, the sole carer of his young children, on the basis that it discriminated on grounds of gender. The court rejected the case. According to Goldstone J, 'The Presidential Act might have denied fathers an opportunity it afforded mothers, but it could not be said to have fundamentally impaired their rights of dignity or sense of equal worth.'[57] By contrast, for Kriegler J, it was the assumption that women are the primary childcarers which constituted an assault on their dignity. As he put it in his dissent:

One of the ways in which one accords equal dignity and respect to persons is by seeking to protect the basic choices they make about their own identities. Reliance on the generalisation that women are the primary care givers is harmful in its tendency to cramp and stunt the efforts of both men and women to form their identities freely...[58]

Secondly, there is a risk that dignity comes to be regarded as an independent element in discrimination law, requiring a claimant to prove not just that she has been disadvantaged, but that this signifies lack of respect of her as a person. This danger has been floridly demonstrated in the Supreme Court of Canada, in which the court held that proof of disadvantage on grounds of an enumerated characteristic would not in itself be discriminatory if the claimant could not prove in addition

---

[55] See D Feldman, 'Human Dignity as a Legal Value' [1999] PL (Winter) 682; C McCrudden, 'Human dignity and judicial interpretation of human rights' [2008] EJIL 655.

[56] *President of the Republic of South Africa v Hugo* (CCT 11/96) [1997] ZACC 4 (South African Constitutional Court).

[57] Ibid, para 47.

[58] Ibid, para 80.

that this disadvantage signified that society regarded her of less value than others.[59] Thus in *Gosselin*,[60] welfare beneficiaries under 30 received significantly lower benefit than those over 30 unless they participated in a designated work activity or education programme. In practice, there was a considerable shortfall in places available. As a result, many young people, including the claimant, experienced real poverty. She claimed that this constituted age discrimination, in breach of the equality guarantee in section 15(1) of the Canadian Charter. However, the majority held that 'the provision of different initial amounts of monetary support to each of the two groups does not indicate that one group's dignity was prized above the other's'.[61] It therefore rejected her claim. In a remarkably similar response, in the House of Lords in the UK case of *Reynolds*, Lord Rodgers stated:

> There is no doubt that the relevant regulations, endorsed by Parliament, deliberately gave less to those under 25. But this was not because the policy-makers were treating people under 25 years of age as less valuable members of society.[62]

This problem has now been recognized by the Canadian Court. In an important case in 2010, *R v Kapp*,[63] it acknowledged that

> several difficulties have arisen from the attempt . . . to employ human dignity as a legal test. There can be no doubt that human dignity is an essential value underlying the s. 15 equality guarantee. In fact, the protection of all of the rights guaranteed by the Charter has as its lodestar the promotion of human dignity. . . . But as critics have pointed out, human dignity is an abstract and subjective notion that . . . has . . . proven to be an additional burden on equality claimants, rather than the philosophical enhancement it was intended to be.[64]

A third problem with exclusive reliance on dignity is that, as Hepple puts it, it is not sufficiently sensitive to conflicts with individual liberty and autonomy.[65] The difficulty arises where an individual chooses to act in a way which conflicts with the State's view of individual dignity. For example, when the practice of 'dwarf-throwing' was banned in France, an individual argued that this deprived him, not only of his source of income, but his possibility of achieving fame. Given that health and

---

[59] *Law v Canada* above n 41; *Gosselin v Quebec* 2002 [SCC] 84 (Canadian Supreme Court).
[60] *Gosselin v Quebec* above n 59.
[61] Ibid, para 61 (per McLachlin J).
[62] [2005] UKHL 37 at para 45.
[63] *R v Kapp* 2008 SCC 41 (Supreme Court of Canada).
[64] Ibid, paras 21, 22.
[65] Hepple above n 11, p 11.

safety conditions could be assured, was the prohibition a means to protect his dignity and common humanity, or was it an infringement on his autonomy?[66] Hepple argues that instead of an intrusive paternalistic model, equality law should advance a 'stewardship' model, whereby the State is entitled to express value judgements about what is good for individuals, but should then leave it to those individuals to make up their own minds. On this basis, rather than 'treating dignity as an overarching or superior value', the question should be whether the State's action was a proportionate means of achieving a legitimate end.[67]

These difficulties can be avoided by regarding dignity as an aspect of equality rather than attempting to reduce equality to a single notion of dignity. It will be argued below that dignity should be regarded as one facet of a multi-dimensional notion of equality, which also comprises disadvantage, accommodation of difference, and participation.

(VI) SUBSTANTIVE EQUALITY: A FOUR–DIMENSIONAL CONCEPT

It is clear therefore that substantive equality resists capture by a single principle, whether it be equality of results, equality of opportunity, or dignity. I argue instead that equality should be seen as a multi-dimensional concept, pursuing four overlapping aims.[68] First, it aims to break the cycle of disadvantage associated with status or out-groups. This reflects the redistributive dimension of equality. Secondly, it aims to promote respect for dignity and worth, thereby redressing stigma, stereotyping, humiliation, and violence because of membership of an identity group. This reflects a recognition dimension. Thirdly, it should not exact conformity as a price of equality. Instead, it should accommodate difference and aim to achieve structural change. This captures the transformative dimension. Finally, substantive equality should facilitate full participation in society, both socially and politically. This is the participative dimension. Each of these, together with the challenges they represent, is outlined below. For ease of reference, the grounds of discrimination are referred to as 'status' or 'protected characteristics'. These generally refer to gender, race, disability, sexual orientation, religion and belief, age, and nationality, but, as will be seen in Chapter

---

[66] Cited in D Feldman, 'Human Dignity as a Legal Value' [1999] PL 682, 701–2.

[67] Hepple, above n 11, p 12.

[68] S Fredman, *The Future of Equality in Great Britain* (Working Paper No 5, Equal Opportunities Commission, Manchester, 2002).

Three, could encompass a range of other types of status. Because an asymmetric approach is advocated, however, it may not be that all status groups are the target of intervention. Only those which suffer disadvantage, stigma, or exclusion may be in issue. These are sometimes referred to as 'out-groups'.

(a) The redistributive dimension: breaking the cycle of disadvantage

Unlike formal equality, substantive equality is expressly asymmetric, recognizing that it is not so much an individual's status or group identity which is the problem, but the detrimental consequences attached to that status. Thus instead of aiming to treat everyone alike, regardless of status, substantive equality focuses on the group which has suffered disadvantage: women rather than men, black people rather than whites, people with disabilities rather than able-bodied, or gay people, rather than heterosexuals. Indeed, as will be seen in Chapter Two, disadvantage is disproportionately concentrated among these groups. Women, ethnic minorities, people of colour, and disabled people tend to be amongst the lowest earners, to experience the highest rates of unemployment, and to predominate among those living in poverty or social exclusion. The first aim of substantive equality is therefore to correct the cycle of disadvantage experienced because of status or other protected characteristic.

Targeting disadvantage rather than aiming at neutrality has several advantages. Most importantly, it makes it possible to reconcile affirmative action with the goal of equality. Although apparently breaching the principle of equal treatment, affirmative action in reality advances substantive equality by taking steps to redress the disadvantage. In addition, it allows us to show the links between distributive inequalities, which have traditionally been regarded as the terrain of the welfare state or socio-economic rights, and discrimination law. The power of substantive equality is its ability to address disadvantage as well as prejudice within one concept.

However, focusing on disadvantage also carries with it some important challenges. The most important is to specify the nature of disadvantage. Disadvantage is most easily understood in the context of redistribution of resources and benefits, addressing under-representation in jobs, underpayment for work of equal value, or limitations on access to credit, property, or similar resources. However, this facet of substantive equality should not be confined to a distributive paradigm. Young argues forcefully that the distributive paradigm, which defines social justice as the morally proper distribution of social benefits and burdens among society's members,[69] has been given a distorted significance in theories of justice. Because it focuses on the allocation of material goods, the distributive paradigm ignores social structures such as decision-making power, the division of labour and culture, or the symbolic meanings attached to people, actions, and things.[70] Power itself, in her view, is not appropriately defined as a distributive benefit, because this makes power appear to be a possession rather than a relationship. Instead, she argues, the focus should be on domination, or structures which exclude people from participating in determining their actions. Crucially, domination need not be attributable to the actions of any particular individual, but produces constraints which are the intended or unintended product of actions of many people.[71] Thus disadvantage should encompass more than maldistribution of resources. It needs also to take on board the constraints which power structures impose on individuals because of their status. For example, women who are trapped in the private sphere will suffer disadvantage in this sense even if they live in affluent households.

Disadvantage can also be understood as a deprivation of genuine opportunities to pursue one's own valued choices. This draws on the insights of the 'capabilities' theory developed by Amartya Sen[72] and Martha Nussbaum.[73] Starting from the premise that each individual should be able to be and do what she values, this theory stresses the importance of considering the extent to which people are actually able to exercise their choices, rather than simply having the formal right to do so. It may not be feasible for a person to achieve the goals she values due to social, economic, or physical constraints, as well as due to political interference.[74] 'What people can achieve is influenced by economic opportunities, political liberties, social powers and the enabling conditions of good health, basic education, and the encouragement and cultivation of initiatives.'[75] Thus it is not enough to treat everyone equally, since the same treatment of individuals with very different constraints can replicate disadvantage. The redistributive dimension of equality therefore aims to redress disadvantage by removing obstacles to genuine choice.

[69] Young, above n 3, p 16.
[70] Ibid.
[71] Ibid, pp 31–2.
[72] A Sen, *Development as Freedom* (Oxford University Press, 1999).
[73] M Nussbaum, *Women and Human Development* (Cambridge University Press, 2000).
[74] Ibid, pp 90–1.
[75] Sen, above n 72, p 5.

The capabilities approach is richer than equality of results, because it incorporates individual autonomy and the differing needs of differently situated individuals. It is also more difficult to measure. Choice itself can be problematic, since people often adapt their choices to their circumstances. Moreover, there are clearly circumstances in which the concern is not solely to increase the range of feasible options but to address the disadvantage attached to the circumstances a person actually finds herself in, even if she has chosen to be there. For example, the terms and conditions of work for part-time workers need to be improved, even if women have chosen to do such work.

The difficulties in defining disadvantage are alleviated by the multi-dimensional notion of equality, which means that not all the issues need to be dealt with in one concept. Thus the notion of disadvantage need not be stretched to addressing under-representation in decision-making, which is better dealt with as an aspect of the participative dimension of equality. Similarly, the need to value individuals regardless of capabilities or choice is better dealt with under the recognition dimension, to which we now turn.

(b) The recognition dimension: respect and dignity

Even in its most expansive sense, disadvantage does not cover all the wrongs associated with inequality. Stigma, stereotyping, humiliation, and violence on grounds of gender, race, disability, sexual orientation, or other status can be experienced regardless of relative disadvantage. Thus the second main aim of substantive equality should be to promote respect for the equal dignity and worth of all. This is the dimension of equality which speaks to our basic humanity. Equality attaches to all individuals, not because of their merit, or their rationality, or their citizenship or membership of any particular group, but because of their humanity. Individuals should not be humiliated or degraded through racism, sexism, violence, or other status-based prejudice.

What of the charge that dignity is so vague as to be malleable in the hands of courts?[76] McCrudden argues that 'instead of providing a basis for principled decision-making, dignity seems open to significant judicial manipulation, increasing rather than decreasing judicial discretion'.[77] However, as Carozza responds, the fact of disagreement as to the meaning of dignity does not constitute a reason for discarding the concept, but instead for engaging in continued discussion to determine

---

[76] McCrudden, above n 55.   [77] Ibid.

its meaning.[78] For our purposes the most useful approach to under-standing dignity is through the concept of 'recognition', discussed above. In addition, locating dignity as one dimension of a multi-faceted notion of equality permits us to buttress it in such a way as to utilise its strengths while addressing its weaknesses. Thus the inclusion of dignity in the concept of equality addresses basic recognition ills including harassment and prejudice. It also makes it impossible to argue that equality is compatible with levelling down. Particularly important is its role in resolving conflicts between different grounds of discrimina-tion, such as those which arise between religion, on the one hand, and gender and sexual orientation, on the other. In the name of religious freedom, it can never be acceptable to denigrate the dignity of other individuals, for example because they are women or gay.

Dignity has also been criticized on the grounds that it focuses on individuals as if they were separate and abstracted from their social context. This can be avoided by the interaction between dignity and the other dimensions of equality. Recognition is centrally about mutuality of esteem. In similar vein, the German Constitutional Court has stressed that dignity does not connote

an isolated sovereign individual; [but instead] . . . a relationship between individ-ual and community in the sense of a person's dependence on and commitment to the community, without infringing on a person's individual value.[79]

Locating dignity as one of several dimensions of equality also enables us to see that dignity is not a separate and additional element to socio-economic disadvantage in an equality claim. Socio-economic disadvan-tage is itself an assault on an individual's basic humanity. Unlike the Canadian jurisprudence referred to above, these two dimensions of equality should pull together rather than against each other. This was highlighted in the South African case of *Khosa*,[80] which concerned a legislative measure which confined the right to child benefit and old-age pensions to South African citizens, to the exclusion of permanent residents. In striking down this measure as a breach of equality, Mok-goro J emphasized that the consequences of exclusion were not only socio-economic. In addition, the exclusion of permanent residents had a

---

[78] PG Carozza, 'Human dignity and judicial interpretation of human rights: a reply' [2008] EJIL 931–44.

[79] BVerfGE 4, 7, 15 (1954).

[80] *Khosa and Mahlaule v Minister for Social Development* 2004 (6) BCLR 569 (South African Constitutional Court).

strong stigmatizing effect, creating the impression that they were inferior to citizens and less worthy of social assistance. Permanent residents
were in effect 'relegated to the margins of society and deprived of what
may be essential to enable them to enjoy other rights vested in them
under the Constitution'.[81]

(c) The transformative dimension: accommodating difference and structural change

Under a formal equality approach, gender, race, ethnicity, or other
status are regarded as irrelevant. This presupposes that it is both
desirable and possible to abstract an individual from these aspects of
her identity and treat her entirely on 'merit'. By contrast, substantive
equality recognizes that these characteristics can be valued aspects of an
individual's identity. The problem is not so much difference per se, but
the detriment which is attached to difference. The third aim of substantive equality should therefore be to respect and accommodate difference,
removing the detriment but not the difference itself. This in turn means
that existing social structures must be changed to accommodate difference, rather than requiring members of out-groups to conform to the
dominant norm. Substantive equality is therefore potentially transformative. For example, working hours have always been patterned on the
assumption that childcare takes place outside the labour market. Women
who wish to participate in the paid labour market must conform to this
paradigm, either by forgoing having children, or leaving their children
with paid childcarers or family members. Substantive equality aims to
change such institutions so that participative parenting is possible for
both mothers and fathers in the labour market. Similarly, the built
environment must be adapted to accommodate the needs of disabled
people, and dress codes and holidays must accommodate ethnic and
religious minorities.

As with the other facets of substantive equality, accommodating
difference raises challenges. The first is pragmatic. How much should
employers or the State be expected to spend in order to accommodate
difference? Duties of accommodation often include caveats, requiring
only such action as is reasonable or practicable. In framing such caveats,
however, it should be borne in mind that the question is not about how
much to spend, but who should bear the cost. It is misleading to argue
that it is too costly to accommodate difference, since the cost is incurred

---

[81] Ibid, para 77.

in any event. The status quo, without legal intervention, requires the out-group to bear the full cost: women bear the cost of child-bearing and childcare; disabled people bear the cost of disability; and ethnic minorities bear the cost of their own cultural or religious commitments. Whatever cost is not borne by employers or the State is left on the shoulders of those who are least able to bear it. At the same time, little notice is taken of the fact that society does bear the cost of the specific characteristics of dominant groups, be they male, able-bodied, or in the ethnic majority. Thus working time, the built environment, or religious or cultural holidays and dress already cater for the dominant groups. Substantive equality aims to redistribute these costs in ways which are fairer to all.

The second challenge for this facet of equality is more principled. At what point is it unreasonable or even wrong to accommodate difference, or tolerate minority cultures? Many of these dilemmas arise in respect of religion. Should polygamy be accommodated? Should exclusion of gays or women? Should burkas be permitted? Female mutilation? How does this compare with minority approaches to religious festivals, dietary laws, ritual slaughter of animals? What about minority views which are racist? Here again, resolution of these difficult dilemmas is facilitated by the multi-faceted approach to equality. Thus the transformative dimension must coexist with the recognition dimension. Practices which compromise the basic dignity and humanity of individuals cannot be acceptable in order to accommodate difference. Sexism, racism, and homophobia would all fall into this category. There may of course be complex debates as to whether particular cultural or religious practices do breach the recognition dimension, particularly if their adherents believe they do not. However, the multi-dimensional structure gives a framework within which such debates can occur. Moreover, it is possible to formulate a notion of dignity which is not wholly culturally relative: although its meaning can be the subject of ongoing debate, it remains rooted in the recognition of all individuals due to their basic humanity.

(d) The participative dimension: social inclusion and political voice

The fourth dimension of substantive equality relates to participation. Given that past discrimination or other social mechanisms have blocked the avenues for political participation by particular minorities, equality laws are needed both to compensate for this absence of political voice and to open up the channels for greater participation in the future. Indeed, one of the key contributions of the US Supreme Court has been its recognition of the role of equality in compensating for absence of political power. Thus in one of the most famous footnotes in history, the US Supreme Court stated that judicial intervention under the equality guarantee was particularly necessary because of the way in which 'prejudice against discrete and insular minorities... tends seriously to curtail the operation of those political processes ordinarily to be relied upon to protect minorities'.[82] Building on this approach, John Hart Ely has developed his 'representation–reinforcing' theory of judicial review in relation to groups 'to whose needs and wishes elected officials have no apparent interest in attending'.[83] Similarly, the Supreme Court of Canada in *Andrews v Law Society*[84] held that the equality guarantee should extend to non-citizens for the very reason that, lacking in political power, they were vulnerable to having their interests overlooked and their rights to equal concern and respect violated.

Participation is not, however, confined to political participation. Participation also refers to the importance of community in the life of individuals. Rather than the universal, abstract individual of formal equality, substantive equality recognizes that individuals are essentially social. To be fully human includes the ability to participate on equal terms in community and society more generally. The importance of participation is highlighted in different ways by different theorists. Thus, as we have seen, Young argues that the focus of theories of justice should be on structures which exclude people from participating in determining their actions.[85] For Young, therefore, social equality refers both to the distribution of social goods, and to the full participation and inclusion of everyone in major social institutions.[86] Fraser puts particular emphasis on participation, regarding parity of participation as the normative core of her conception of justice, encompassing both redistribution and recognition without reducing either one to the other.[87] Collins, in searching for a justification for departure from the equal treatment principle, develops the concept of social inclusion as central to his notion of substantive equality. Like Young and Fraser, Collins's conception includes but goes beyond distribution of material goods.

---

[82] *United States v Carolene Products Company* 304 US 144 (1938) at 152 n 4 (per Stone J).
[83] JH Ely, *Democracy and Distrust: A Theory of Judicial Review* (Harvard University Press, 1980), p 46.
[84] *Andrews v Law Society (British Columbia)* [1989] 1 SCR 143.
[85] Young, above n 3, pp 31–2.
[86] Ibid, p 173.
[87] Fraser and Honneth, above n 36, pp 36–7.

Although . . . social inclusion shares with equality a concern with the distributive allocations to groups and individuals in a society, its more fundamental objective is the outcome of social cohesion. Social inclusion is a theory of how society can be integrated and harmonious. At its simplest, the theory is that if everyone participates fully in society, they are less likely to become alienated from the community and will conform to its social rules and laws.[88]

He sees the goal of social inclusion as having the potential to provide a vital ingredient in a more coherent account of the aims of anti-discrimination law. A further alternative characterization is that of solidarity, a value which is also expressed in the EU Charter of Fundamental Rights. Barnard argues that solidarity requires not just the removal of obstacles to participation, but also active measures to integrate individuals into society.[89]

The participative dimension in equality law plays itself out in several practical ways. For old people, for example, the ability to participate in the life of the community is a central demand. To achieve equal participation therefore requires attention to be paid to such issues as sufficiency of transport, accessibility of community activities, and possibilities of voluntary work. This too has implications for the public–private divide, requiring equal participation in both family and public life for both men and women.

II COMPETING VALUES:
LIBERTY OR EQUALITY

Even when agreement is reached on a specific conception or set of conceptions of equality as a basis for a legislative formulation of equality, it is still necessary to consider whether and in what circumstances, other, non-equality-based values should trump equality concerns. Two related rivals with equality will be considered here: liberty and economic or market concerns.

(I) LIBERTY

Possibly the most serious rival for priority with equality is freedom or liberty. Indeed, Isaiah Berlin in his famous work characterized liberty and equality as the two major but frequently conflicting values.

---

[88] H Collins, 'Discrimination, Equality and Social Inclusion' [2003] 66 MLR 16 at 24.
[89] C Barnard in C Barnard, S Deakin, and G Morris (eds), *The Future of Labour law: Liber Amicorum Sir Bob Hepple* (Hart Publishing, 2004).

Both liberty and equality are among the primary goals pursued by human beings through many centuries; but total liberty for wolves is death to the lambs, total liberty of the powerful, the gifted is not compatible with the rights to a decent existence of the weak and the less gifted.[90]

Closer examination shows, however, that, just as equality can be interpreted in many differing ways, so can liberty. Liberty could, at one extreme, mean simply licence; but this is hardly a plausible interpretation, since that would prohibit even laws against murder and theft. Instead, liberty is normally allied with a substantive value, such as speech.[91] Moreover, the extent of conflict between equality and liberty depends in part on which conception of equality is chosen. Thus a laissez-faire egalitarian might find no conflict between liberty and equality: individuals should be equally free from State interference in order to pursue their own goals, and their fate depends on their own abilities, initiative, and luck.[92] Dworkin, by contrast, argues for a much stronger conception of equality, but nevertheless formulates a principle of liberty which, far from conflicting with equality, is a crucial ingredient. Equality of resources, on his argument, can only be achieved if each individual is not only free to make choices but must also take responsibility for those choices based on the cost of their decisions to other people.[93]

Nevertheless, the practical experience of equality laws demonstrates clear potential for conflict between liberty and equality. Thus courts have had to decide whether prohibitions on racist speech should be struck down as infringing freedom of speech, or upheld as promoting racial equality. While courts in the US have upheld the freedom of speech value, Canadian courts have upheld the equality value.[94] Similarly, a statute restricting expenditure on political campaigns could be construed as unduly restricting liberty. Alternatively, it could be seen as legitimately promoting the egalitarian aim of ensuring that the political voice of richer individuals did not drown out that of poorer people.[95] Particularly complex is the relationship of liberty to substantive equality based on socio-economic rights. Thus minimum wages

---

[90] I Berlin, *Four Essays on Liberty* (Oxford University Press, Oxford, 1969).

[91] R Dworkin *Sovereign Virtue* (Harvard University Press, 2000) p 127.

[92] Ibid, p 131.

[93] Ibid, p 122.

[94] *RAV v City of St Paul, Minn* 505 US 377, 112 S Ct 2538 (1992); cf *R v Keegstra* (1996) 61 CCC (3d) 1 (Supreme Court of Canada).

[95] *Buckley v Valeo* 424 US 1, 96 S Ct 612 (1976); *Bowman v UK* (1998) 26 EHRR 1.

and maximum hours laws could be struck down because they undermine individual freedom of contract or upheld because they promote
substantive equality.[96]

(II) BUSINESS- OR MARKET-ORIENTED CONCERNS

Apart from the conflict with fundamental liberties, the major modern
rival for priority with equality is that of business- or market-oriented
concerns. In most jurisdictions, statutes and case law have specifically
permitted individuals or States to defend incursions on equality on the
grounds that this is justified as a pursuit of business needs or State
macroeconomic policies. The question then concerns the weight to be
given to each of these concerns. Can a policy or business interest
displace equality simply because it is convenient or strategic, or must
it be demonstrably necessary to achieve the business needs in question?
The formulation and application of the so-called justification test has
been a central concern in numerous cases.

A particularly important symbiotic relationship between equality and
economic concerns has developed at EU level. The European Economic
Community was initially established with the primary purpose of creating a common market in goods, services, and labour. At most it was
envisaged that social policy at Community level was to have the sole
purpose of creating a European-wide labour market.[97] Yet such market-
based aims were seen as necessitating at the very least, a principle of
equal pay for equal work for men and women. If some Member States
were permitted to pay women less for the same work as men, it was
thought, those Member States would achieve an unfair competitive
advantage over others. This was particularly important for France,
which already had equal pay laws in place. It is striking, however, that
equality could not be kept in so subservient a position. Within two
decades, it was acknowledged, particularly by the ECJ, that the sex
equality provisions also had their basis in the fundamental human
right to equality.[98] The most recent anti-discrimination provisions at
EU level now place economic and social concerns side by side.

It is notable that little attention has been paid to why business needs
should trump equality. One plausible justification is that of liberty itself:

---

[96] *Lochner v New York* 198 US 45, 25 S Ct 539 (1905).
[97] See eg W Streeck, 'From Market Making to State Building' in S Leibfried and
P Pierson (eds), *European Social Policy: Between Fragmentation and Integration* (Brookings
Institution, 1995), p 397.
[98] Case 149/77 *Defrenne v Sabena* (*Defrenne No 2*) [1978] ECR 1365 (ECJ).

the liberty of employers or other powerful actors to pursue their own interests should not, on this view, be infringed. During the 1980s and the early 1990s, this view was in the ascendant, owing to the political dominance of a neo-liberal laissez-faire ideology. This blatant preference for liberty over equality is often softened by the assertion that the good of the individual business will further the good of all, even if it subordinates particular equality rights (such as the right of a woman to equal pay with a man doing work of equal value). In an attempt to counteract the power of this ideology, the more mellow final years of the twentieth century saw an attempt to a create convergence between the two notions. Thus it has been argued that, far from detracting from market concerns, equality laws are demonstrably capable of serving economic and particularly efficiency-based ends.[99] Indeed, in the EU, possibly the most striking characteristic of the past fifteen years has been the convergence, at least at the level of rhetoric, between fundamental rights justifications and labour market justifications for equal opportunities. This convergence is crucially related to the shift in the labour market objectives of the EU from market creation to job creation.[100] Crucially, the high rates of unemployment among women were identified as one of the areas of concern. The result is that the impetus for gender equality has been seen through an 'economic prism', which characterizes the disadvantaged position of women in the labour market as a source of economic inefficiency, and therefore includes sex equality within its strategy to achieve economic competitiveness.[101]

Of course, there is always the danger that instead of a genuine and mutually reinforcing coincidence of aims, the rhetoric of convergence has merely obscured the extent to which market concerns have stunted the growth of a truly rights-based equality principle. When the court holds the balance between the equality value and that of market or business concerns, the weight given to the various values becomes crucial. A bias towards business needs would yield a test which allowed mere convenience to justify an infringement on equality, whereas a greater (although not absolute) commitment to equality would require that it be limited only to the extent strictly necessary to achieve the stated aim. For example, if an employer wishes to justify paying female

---

[99] See S Deakin, 'Labour Law as Market Regulation' in P Davies et al (eds), *European Community Labour Law: Principles and Perspectives* (Clarendon Press, 1996); S Deakin and F Wilkinson, 'Rights vs Efficiency?' (1994) 23 ILJ 289.

[100] See M R Freedland, 'Employment Policy' in P Davies, A Lyon-Caen, S Sciarra, and S Simitis, *European Community Labour Law* (Clarendon Press, 1996), pp 275 ff.

[101] See S Duncan, 'Obstacles to a Successful Equal Opportunities Policy in the EU' (1996) 3:4 European Journal of Women's Studies 399–422.

part-time workers less than male full-timers doing the same job, a lenient standard would allow him or her simply to assert that part-timers are less valuable, or that it is more profitable to pay them less. A strict standard would require that the employer prove that there is no less discriminatory alternative to achieving the stated aim of increased profits or creating a more productive workforce.

III CONCLUSION

This chapter has examined some of the major conceptual issues surrounding the equality principle. It has considered differing conceptions of the equality principle and proposed a four-dimensional solution, as well as sketching out possible limitations and complexities. The next chapter, recognizing that equality cannot be considered in the abstract but must be understood in its historical and political context, turns to a consideration of the causes and patterns of inequality.

2

Social Context and Legal Developments

Anti-discrimination law is necessarily a response to particular manifestations of inequality, which are themselves deeply embedded in the historical and political context of a given society. Discrimination laws are only effective if they are moulded to deal with the types of inequalities which have developed in the society to which they refer. The legal framework has in turn developed and changed in response to a variety of influences, including political and social forces, EU and domestic law, and wider ranging human rights obligations. The result is a complex and interlocking set of factors, both legal and social, which continue to evolve in a dialectic fashion. This chapter aims to trace the evolution of these factors. It focuses on the major groupings which form the context of modern anti-discrimination law. These are gender, race and ethnicity, religion and belief , sexual orientation, transsexuality, disability, and age. Gypsies and Travellers are included as a separate sub-heading as they raise issues of their own. In each case, the historical context, legislative developments, and current inequalities are considered, within an overall framework which addresses the major challenges and dilemmas facing law and policy-makers.

I GENDER

(I) HISTORICAL CONTEXT

The development of gender equality in any real sense is disturbingly recent.[1] Until well into the twentieth century, women were legally subordinate to men in a host of different ways. This was especially true of marriage. Under the common law, known as 'coverture', marriage constituted of a legal obliteration of women's identity. 'The very being or legal existence of the wife is suspended during the marriage or

---

[1] This section is drawn substantially from S Fredman, *Women and the Law* (Clarendon Press, 1997), ch 2.

at least incorporated and consolidated into that of the husband under whose wing, protection and cover she performs everything',[2] wrote Blackstone in 1809. A married woman was a perpetual legal minor: her husband had near-absolute control over her property as well as her person. She had no right to custody of their children and no right to testamentary freedom. Substantial levels of violence perpetrated against wives were condoned, initially explicitly through the husband's legal power of 'domestic chastisement', and later, tacitly, even when this power had come to be doubted. Nor was a married woman entitled to refuse consent to sexual intercourse with her husband. Indeed, it was not until the last decades of the twentieth century that rape in marriage was recognized as a crime.[3] Not surprisingly, John Stuart Mill described the law of marriage as 'the only legal bondage known to our law'.[4]

Nor was marriage the only source of women's inequality. Until well into the twentieth century, women were barred from political participation. Women's continued subordination was reconciled with prevailing ideals of equality by characterizing women as irrational, temperamentally unsuited to political life and by nature consigned to the home. Rejecting a proposal to extend the suffrage to women in 1892, Asquith justified his position to Parliament by arguing that '[Women's] natural sphere is not the turmoil and dust of politics but the circle of social and domestic life.'[5] The refusal of nineteenth-century legislatures to accept women as equal citizens was supported by an intransigent judiciary.[6] Legislation granting women the municipal franchise in 1869[7] was immediately interpreted by the judges to exclude married women. On marriage, it was held, a woman's 'existence was merged with that of her husband', and therefore she could not vote.[8] Even when the right to vote at local level was established, judges moved quickly to hold that this did not include the right to stand for election. 'By the common law of England, women are not in general deemed capable of exercising public functions' and therefore only express words of a statute could change this.[9]

---

[2] W Blackstone, *Commentaries on the Law of England* (15th edn, T Cadell & W Davies, 1809), book I, ch XV, p 430.
[3] *R v R* [1991] 4 All ER 481 (HL).
[4] J S Mill, *The Subjection of Women* (Wordsworth Classics, 1996), p 135.
[5] Parliamentary Debates (series 4) vol 3, col 1513 (27 April 1892).
[6] *Chorlton v Lings* [1864] LR 4 CP 374.
[7] Municipal Franchise Act 1869.
[8] *R v Harrald* [1872] LR VII QB 361.
[9] *De Souza v Cobden* [1891] 1 QB 687 (CA) at 691.

Within the workforce, women were similarly disadvantaged. Women have always participated in the workforce. But it was assumed without question that women should be paid at a lower rate than men, even when they were engaged on identical work.[10] Again, this was justified by the well-worn myths that a woman's natural role was in the home; that she should depend on her husband for subsistence; that she did not have to support a family; or that she was less productive than a man. Again, the courts were active proponents of such discrimination. When Poplar Borough Council instituted equal pay for men and women on the lowest grade, the House of Lords struck down the policy as irrational. In its view, the council had allowed itself to be guided by 'some eccentric principles of socialistic philanthropy, or by a feminist ambition to secure the equality of the sexes in the matter of wages in the world of labour'.[11] An attempt by women teachers to enlist the aid of the courts to strike down the widespread policy of dismissing women teachers on marriage was met by a similar rebuff.

It would in my view be pressing public policy to intolerable lengths to hold that it was outraged by this Authority expressing a preference for unmarried women over married women as teachers, in view of the fact that the services of the latter are frequently... liable to be interrupted by absences extending over several months.[12]

This view was later endorsed by the Court of Appeal, which accepted the argument by the education authority that the duty of the married woman was primarily to look after her domestic concerns.[13]

As well as low pay for like work, job segregation was endemic. Women were formally excluded from important spheres of work, including medicine and law, until the late nineteenth century. In addition women workers were often physically segregated from men, in separate rooms or floors; and possibilities for training or promotion were minimal. These patterns were often reinforced by trade unions, whose male membership perceived that equal pay for women would constitute a threat to the legitimacy of their demand for a 'family wage'; and that permitting women to compete for 'male' jobs might undercut their own position. It was only when trade unions came to the view that equal pay

---

[10] See Fredman, above n 1, pp 107 ff.
[11] *Roberts v Hopwood* [1925] AC 578 (HL) at 591 (per Lord Atkinson).
[12] *Price v Rhondda UDC* [1923] 1 Ch 372 at 379.
[13] *Short v Poole Corp* [1926] Ch 26 (CA).

for women would in fact prevent cheap substitution of female labour that it was decided to support the campaign for equal pay.

(II) LEGISLATIVE DEVELOPMENT

The battle for juridical equality was a long and painful one. It was only in the late nineteenth century, and then at an excruciatingly slow pace, that these legal disabilities were gradually dismantled. Thus genuine progress towards formal equality in property rights between husband and wife was only clearly evident after 1882, a process which was not complete until 1935. Similarly, the father's absolute rights to custody of the children were only fully reversed in 1925. Most glaring in its contradiction of liberalism's promise of equality was the refusal to extend political rights to women. Women were not permitted to vote in national elections until 1918, and even then, a minimum voting age of 30 was imposed. True equality was not fully conceded until 1928, when the minimum voting age for men and women was equalized at 21. Even then, women were still barred from the House of Lords, in which formal equality was not achieved until as recently as 1963.

Juridical equality was not, however, the end of the struggle. It was with deep disappointment that feminists and women's rights campaigners realized that lifting legal impediments was not sufficient to dislodge the deeply ingrained patterns of prejudice and disadvantage suffered by women. The radical shake-up of the First World War, when women were of necessity precipitated into male jobs, was not sufficient to dislodge these deep-seated patterns. After the war, pay differentials between men and women were institutionalized across the public and private sectors. In the civil service, women's pay was pegged at a maximum of 80 per cent of that of men; and statutory instruments prescribing pay in the police forces and teaching profession prescribed similar discrepancies for men and women doing the same work. Returning veterans were given priority over jobs, and women were forced back into domestic work and other menial work by fierce polemical campaigns directed against women accused of taking men's jobs. An attempt to provide for equal pay in the teaching profession was vetoed by Churchill in 1944.

After the Second World War, women became a far more visible part of the workforce; helped by increasing availability of contraception, falling family sizes, and rapidly advancing technology creating electrical appliances to assist with domestic work. But job segregation and pay disparities persisted. Women were still dismissed on marriage in many occupations until well into the post-war period; and the practice of paying women less than men for performing the same work was widespread and officially endorsed. For example, women civil servants were paid on separate and lower pay scales than men doing the same work until 1962.[14] Jobs were highly segregated with women clustered in low paid, low status 'women's work'.

Equality before the law was clearly not sufficient. Legislation was necessary to ban discrimination against women, both by private and public actors. But it was not until 1970 that legislation with real impact was introduced. This took the form of the Equal Pay Act 1970, which provided for the right to equal pay for equal work for men and women. It was complemented by the Sex Discrimination Act 1975 (SDA), which prohibited discrimination on grounds of sex or marriage in employment more generally, including recruitment, promotion, and training. The SDA also made it unlawful to discriminate in education and the provision of services. The SDA was particularly innovative in its inclusion of the concept of indirect discrimination, transplanted from its origins in the US.[15]

It was at this time too that the UK became a member of the European Economic Community (now the European Union).[16] In one sense, this was a surprising source of women's rights. At its inception in 1957, the EU was conceived of primarily as creating a common market, where competition was undistorted by domestic tariffs and restrictions. Protection of social rights was regarded as a matter for Member States rather than the Community. Nevertheless, France, which already had an equal pay law, successfully argued that it would be placed at an unfair competitive disadvantage if other Member States were permitted to pay women less for the same work. It was for this, primarily economic, reason that a right to equal pay for equal work for men and women was included in Article 119 of the Treaty of Rome.

In practice, however, Article 119 lay dormant until the mid-1970s, when it was ignited by a remarkable campaign by women at European level. A test case brought on behalf of a Belgian air stewardess, Gabrielle Defrenne, led to the landmark decision of *Defrenne v Sabena*,[17] in which the European Court of Justice (ECJ) held that Article 119 was a source

---

[14] See Fredman, above n 1, p 134.

[15] See Chapter Four.

[16] European Communities Act 1972. The European Economic Community is henceforth referred to as the European Union (EU).

[17] Case 43/75 *Defrenne v Sabena* [1976] ECR 455 (ECJ).

of rights which could be enforced in courts in Member States even if there was no domestic legislation to this effect. Equally important was the Court's assertion in *Defrenne* that social aims of the EU were on a par with its economic aims. The Community, it stated, 'is not merely an economic union, but is at the same time intended...to ensure social progress and seek the constant improvement of the living and working conditions of their peoples'.[18] Subsequently known as Article 141, the provisions on gender equality have been deepened and expanded including a series of directives on equal pay, equal treatment, social security, burden of proof, pregnancy and parenthood, and other relevant areas. Article 141 now appears as Article 157 in the most recent treaty—the Lisbon Treaty—which came into force in December 2009.

The interaction between EU law and domestic law in the UK has worked in both directions, creating a dynamic interplay between the two regimes. Unlike the SDA, EU law on equal treatment did not originally include the concepts of direct and indirect discrimination. Instead, these concepts were gradually developed by the ECJ until they were finally incorporated into positive law in 1997.[19] Similarly, unlike the SDA which included education and the provision of goods, facilities, and services to the public, the scope of EU law was limited to issues relevant to the creation of a common market, namely employment, vocational training, and social security.[20] It was not until 2006 that sex discrimination law at EU level was extended to access to and supply of goods and services.[21]

Important strides have also been made in two other areas: first, the recognition of harassment as a species of sex discrimination;[22] and secondly, the development of protection in relation to pregnancy and parenting. Until well into the twentieth century, the assumption that paid work was incompatible with child-bearing was reinforced by legal and social security provisions permitting and even mandating dismissal of women on grounds of pregnancy.[23] Although as early as 1919, an International Labour Organization (ILO) Convention required signatories to provide maternity leave and protection against dismissal,[24] it was not until the mid-1970s that the UK began to protect pregnant

---

[18] Ibid, para 10.
[19] Council Directive 97/80/EC.
[20] Council Directive 79/7EEC; Council Directive 86/378/EEC.
[21] Council Directive 2004/113/EC.
[22] See Chapter Four.
[23] Fredman, above n 1, pp 181–2.
[24] ILO Convention No 3 (1919).

workers. The framework of protection, both for pregnancy and maternity, has now been progressively improved, primarily as a result of impetus from the EU.[25] Mothers with the requisite qualifications now receive a maximum of 52 weeks' maternity leave, of which up to 39 weeks are paid. However, while pregnancy and maternity rights are an essential precondition for equality for women in the workplace, they may reinforce women's primary responsibility for childcare unless matched by equivalent rights and responsibilities for fathers. Parallel provision for parental and paternity rights has been far slower in coming. It was not until 1996 that the provisions on parental leave were introduced at EU level,[26] but these remain weak and underdeveloped.[27] A token gesture towards paternity leave was introduced in 2002, giving a mere two weeks' paternity leave to a partner of a woman who has had a baby.[28] A more substantive development is the right to transfer maternity leave to a father or partner. Applicable to babies born or adopted from April 2011, these provisions entitle a mother to transfer up to six months' leave to the father or her partner or civil partner. If this is during the paid portion of her leave, fathers or partners receive the same rate of statutory maternity pay as the mother would have received.[29] Thus far, there has been little take-up of paternity rights, a pattern which is consistent across the vast majority of EU Member States. A primary reason is the fact that parental leave is unpaid, or, if paid, attracts compensation at too low a level to create sufficient incentives for fathers. Added to this are cultural expectations, which militate against fathers staying at home to look after children.[30]

---

[25] See Chapter Four.

[26] Council Directive 96/34/EC; Maternity and Parental Leave etc Regulations 1999 (SI 1999/3312), regs 13–14.

[27] Parents with one year's continuous service can take parental leave of 13 weeks per child or 18 weeks where the child is entitled to disability living allowance. Parental leave is unpaid.

[28] Paternity and Adoption Leave Regulations 2002 (SI 2002/2788); the right is only available to employees with 26 weeks' continuous employment at 14 weeks before the expected birth of the child. Pay is the lower of 90 per cent of average weekly earnings, or £124.88 as of 4 April 2010. The same rights apply in cases of adoption.

[29] Additional Paternity Leave Regulations 2010 (SI 2010/1055); Additional Statutory Paternity Pay Regulations 2010 (SI 2010/1056). Partners must fulfil the same eligibility requirements as for paternity leave.

[30] S Fredman, *Making Equality Effective: The Role of Proactive Measures* (European Network of Legal Experts in the Field of Gender Equality, 2010).

(III) CURRENT INEQUALITIES

This panoply of legal protection has not, however, eradicated the deep-seated inequalities between men and women. Although the effect of the equal pay legislation was initially dramatic,[31] the momentum was quickly exhausted. In fact, while some express inequalities might have diminished, new and different manifestations have appeared. In the UK and throughout the EU, women are entering the paid labour force in increasing numbers.[32] But they are not necessarily entering on equal terms. This is because women's primary responsibility for childcare has remained unchanged. Women are now both homeworkers and breadwinners, constantly traversing the boundary between unpaid and paid work. This has partly been facilitated by the changing labour market, with a new emphasis on flexible working. Flexible working may seem the ideal forum for combining family responsibilities and paid work. However, the reason why employers tend to introduce flexible working is not to achieve 'family friendly' outcomes, but to reduce labour costs by adjusting labour inputs to meet fluctuations in demand. The best opportunities for pay, training, promotion, job security, and employment-related benefits are still found in full-time working. The result is that women with young children tend to congregate in poorly paid, low status, part-time work, a pattern which has a lasting effect on their lifetime earnings. This is exacerbated by the UK's long hours' culture. The greater rewards open to men working long hours simply reinforce the gendered patterns of paid work and childcare.[33]

These patterns are clearly evident from the statistics. In 2009 in Britain, according to official figures, the gap between the median average hourly pay of full-time men and women, excluding overtime, was still as much as 12.2 per cent.[34] But this figure vastly understates the true extent of the pay gap. There are several reasons for this. First, official

---

[31] The average hourly pay of women rose from 61.8 per cent of that of men in 1970, to 74.2 per cent in 1977.

[32] The female employment rate grew from 54.4 to 58.3 per cent between 2002 and 2007; over the same period the employment rate of men increased from 70.3 to 72.5 per cent.

[33] S Fredman, 'Women at Work: The Broken Promise of Flexicurity' (2004) 33 ILJ 299.

[34] Except where otherwise indicated, the figures in this section are taken from Ceri Holdsworth, 'Patterns of Pay: Results of the Annual Survey of Hours and Earnings 1997 to 2009' (Office for National Statistics, published 26 February 2010, available at: <http://www.statistics.gov.uk/cci/article.asp?ID=2370>).

usage has shifted to the median instead of the customary mean.[35] Reverting to the mean reveals a significantly higher gap, namely 16.4 per cent in 2009. Secondly, the figure excludes overtime. Yet full-time male employees consistently earn a greater proportion of additional payments than their female counterparts. In 2009, for example, male employees earned £40 additional payments per week, accounting for 6.2 per cent of their total mean gross weekly earnings. For women, by contrast, additional payments amounted to £16, or just 3.2 per cent of their pay. This figure was particularly striking in the financial services sector, where a recent inquiry revealed that female full-time employees received on average only one-fifth of the annual incentive pay of men working full time in the sector. Since bonuses constitute such a large proportion of the overall pay in the sector, this, together with a high level of job segregation, meant that in 2009 women working full time in the finance sector earned 55 per cent less per year than men working full time.[36]

Thirdly, and particularly problematic, these figures leave part-time workers out of account. Part-time work lags well behind full-time work so far as pay is concerned. In 2009, part-time women workers' median hourly earnings excluding overtime were a mere 69 per cent of those for all full-time workers, a figure which had scarcely changed since 1997, when it was 68.4 per cent.[37] Yet the number of women working part time has grown rapidly over the past three decades. As many as 40 per cent of all working women now work part time, and two-thirds of women will work part time at some stage in their working lives.[38] Finally, the overall figure masks wide differences in the gender pay gap in respect of different types of jobs. In 2008, the mean gap between male and female pay in the group with the lowest median gross weekly pay, 'sales and customer service occupations', was 5.8 per cent. For 'managers and senior officials', who enjoy the highest median gross weekly earnings, this figure was as high as 26.6 per cent.[39] Taking all these factors into account yields a very different picture. If we focus on annual gross

---

[35] The mean (average) of male pay is higher than the median because of the effect of some very highly paid men. It was argued that this distorts the figures.

[36] Equality and Human Rights Commission, *Financial Services Inquiry: Sex Discrimination and Gender Pay Gap Report of the Equality and Human Rights Commission* (2009).

[37] Holdsworth, above n 34, figure 3 and accompanying text.

[38] S Connolly and M Gregory, 'The Part-Time Pay Penalty: Earnings Trajectories of British Women', Oxford Economic Papers, Vol 61, Issue suppl. 1, pp 176–197 (2009).

[39] C Dobbs, 'Patterns of Pay: Results of the Annual Survey of Hours and Earnings, 1997 to 2008', (2009) 3:3 Economic & Labour Market Review (March).

earnings, irrespective of hours, we find that the gender pay gap across the economy as a whole is a massive 40 per cent.[40]

It is not just inequality of pay that affects women. Women predominate amongst the lowest paid in the workforce. Almost two-thirds (64.3 per cent) of jobs under the minimum wage are held by women,[41] and women constitute as many as 80 per cent of workers in low paying sectors such as childcare, hairdressing, office work, and social care.[42] Moreover, the effects of low pay, interrupted working lives, and job segregation stretch well beyond women's working lives. Only 30 per cent of women reaching state pension age are entitled to a full basic state pension, compared with 85 per cent of men.[43] Inequality is particularly stark in relation to private or occupational pension income, since women tend to work in occupations without access to such benefits. The result is a significant gap: in 2007–8, single men received £76 a week on average from this source, compared with £51 for single women.[44] Indeed, around 70 per cent of the female pensioner population has no private pension at all.[45]

The causes of the pay gap are complex. Occupational segregation is a major factor. Women are still concentrated in lower paying occupations, with nearly two-thirds of women employed in 12 occupation groups, most of which are related to women's traditional roles in the family— caring, cashiering, catering, cleaning, and clerical occupations. They are also over-represented in teaching, health associate professionals (including nurses), and 'functional' management (financial managers, marketing and sales managers, and personnel managers).[46] For example, in Great Britain, women comprise 79 per cent of those involved in health and social work and 73 per cent of those working in education; while in the UK as a whole, 90 per cent of nurses and 96 per cent of school midday assistants are women.[47] It is a sad reflection on our society that these jobs are poorly paid relative to their demands in terms of skill, effort, responsibility, and contribution to society. By contrast, 92 per cent of those involved in skilled trades in Great Britain are male, as are

---

[40] H Metcalf and H Rolfe, *Employment and Earnings in the Finance Sector: A Gender Analysis*, Research Report 17 (Equality and Human Rights Commission, 2009), pp 44–6.
[41] Low Pay Commission, 'National Minimum Wage Report 2009', p 15.
[42] Ibid.
[43] M Sargeant, 'Gender Equality and the Pensions Acts 2007–2008' (2009) 38 ILJ 143–8.
[44] Department for Work and Pensions, *The Pensioners' Income Series* (2007–8), p 26.
[45] Sargeant, above n 43.
[46] Women and Work Commission, *Shaping a Fairer Future* (2006), para 8.
[47] Equal Opportunities Commission, *Facts about Women and Men in Great Britain 2006*.

90 per cent of those involved in construction; and 70 per cent of management consultants, actuaries, economists, and statisticians.[48] Other structural factors include the gender skills gap, particularly for older women, because there is less access to training in the lower paid sectors where more women than men tend to work.[49] But most important is the fact that women remain primarily responsible for childcare. Taking time out of the labour market; amassing less experience; limitations in respect of travel to work; and part-time work, all extract a severe wage penalty.

This pattern is consistent throughout the EU. Figures from 2007 show that across the EU women earn on average 17.4 per cent less than men. The pay gap[50] exceeds 25 per cent in two countries (Estonia and Austria). In only five countries is it below 10 per cent (Italy, Malta, Poland, Slovenia, and Belgium).[51] As in Britain, women's disadvantaged position in the labour market increases the risk that they will be exposed to poverty, particularly for those aged over 65.[52] Again, as in Britain, labour markets continue to be highly segregated. Women still cluster in women's only jobs, or predominate in the low levels of mixed jobs. In 2005, almost 36 per cent of women in work in the EU were employed in just six of the 130 standard occupational categories.[53] Although Nordic and Scandinavian countries have experienced relatively fast de-segregation, most Mediterranean countries, together with a few East European ones, have actually experienced an increase in segregation.[54] Moreover, women throughout the EU predominate among part-time workers. In 2007, the percentage of women employees working part time was

---

[48] Ibid.

[49] Women and Work Commission, above n 46, para 3–27; and see 'Closing the Gender Skills Gap: A National Skills Forum Report on Women, Skills and Productivity', available at: <http://www.policyconnect.org.uk/fckimages/Closing%20the%20Gender%20Skills%20Gap.pdf>.

[50] Defined as the difference between men's and women's average gross hourly earnings as a percentage of men's average gross hourly earnings.

[51] All figures are taken from *Equality Between Women And Men—2009*, Report from the Commission to the European Parliament, the Council, the European Economic and Social Committee and the Committee of the Regions (COM(2009) 77 final).

[52] Ibid.

[53] Eurostat, 2008, p 59.

[54] Francesca Bettio and Alina Verashchagina, *Gender Segregation in the Labour Market: Root Causes, Implications and Policy Responses in the EU*, European Commission's Expert Group on Gender and Employment (EGGE), European Commission Directorate-General for Employment, Social Affairs and Equal Opportunities (March 2009). The figures in this section are taken from *Report on Equality between Women and Men 2008*, European Commission Directorate-General for Employment, Social Affairs and Equal Opportunities (2008), p 8.

31.2 per cent in the EU while the corresponding figure for men was 7.7 per cent. The share of female part-timers exceeded 30 per cent in France, Ireland, Denmark, and Luxembourg; 40 per cent in Sweden, Belgium, Austria, the UK, and Germany, and even reached 75 per cent in the Netherlands.[55]

Economic disadvantage is not the only manifestation of continuing sexism in society. Violence, so well chronicled by John Stuart Mill two centuries ago, continues to stalk too many women's lives, whether in the home, at work, or in the street. As a recent report put it, 'violence against women has no boundaries, in terms of wealth, geography, race, religion, disability, age or sexual orientation'.[56] Violence against women manifests itself in many ways: it ranges from domestic abuse, rape, and sexual violence to female genital mutilation, forced and child marriage, and honour crimes, and includes human trafficking and sexual exploitation, sexual harassment, and prostitution. The figures paint a grim picture. At least three million women suffer violence each year in the UK;[57] one in four women are subjected to domestic violence in their lifetime, and each week two women are murdered by their partners or ex partners. As many as 80,000 women suffer rape and attempted rape every year, over half at the hands of current or former partners or boyfriends. But in only a minuscule of cases is the rapist caught and convicted. Only about 15 per cent come to the attention of the police, and of these, a mere 6 per cent lead to the rapist being caught and convicted. Honour crimes, forced and child marriage, and female genital mutilation continue to blight many women's lives.

At the same time, women are seriously under-represented in most of the areas of influence in society. Thus, in 2009, they formed only 19.6 per cent of MPs at Westminster, a figure which puts the UK 61st in the world league table.[58] In the Parliament elected in May 2010, a mere 22 per cent of MPs were women and there were only four women in a cabinet of 23. Compared to this, the figures for the Scottish Parliament (35 per cent) and the Welsh Assembly (47 per cent) look rosy indeed. In the EU as a

---

[55] *Equality Between Women And Men—2009*, above n 51.

[56] Equality and Human Rights Commission, *Breaking the Silence on Violence Against Women* (November 2009).

[57] Figures from this section are taken from Equality and Human Rights Commission, *Breaking the Silence on Violence Against Women*, ibid; Home Office (Office for Criminal Justice Reform), *Consultation Paper: Convicting Rapists and Protecting Victims—Justice for Victims of Rape 2006*.

[58] Inter-Parliamentary Union, 'Women in National Parliaments' (28 February 2010, available at: <http://www.ipu.org/wmn-e/classif.htm>).

whole, only about 24 per cent of national MPs and 35 per cent of MEPs are women.[59] The judiciary is even more male dominated. In 2010, fewer than 15 per cent of High Court and circuit judges were women. There was only one woman judge in the Supreme Court, and three in the Court of Appeal.[60] A similar pattern is evident in management, where the boardroom remains essentially a male preserve. In the UK, there are still 22 companies in the FTSE 100 that have all-male boards,[61] while in the EU as a whole, women comprise only 3 per cent of directors of top quoted company boards.[62]

II RACE AND ETHNICITY

(I) CHALLENGES AND DILEMMAS

Race relations in Britain have been similarly marked by deep-seated and institutionalized inequalities. However, this history differs from that of gender discrimination. Indeed, the complex interaction of race, nationality, religion, and culture makes for a tangle of forces which do not yield to a straightforward narrative. While religious discord had been a feature of British history for many years, Britain came into the twentieth century with a fixed self-image as a homogeneous, white Christian society. By contrast, by the end of the century, Britain's ethnic diversity was no longer contestable. However, equality remains illusory. The Equalities Review estimated that it might be decades before parity would be reached; and on some significant measures, it may never be eliminated.[63]

This complex picture of ethnic diversity and differential disadvantage prompts an equally sophisticated explanation. As a start, the concept of 'race' itself is highly problematic. Attempts to supply a physiological or evolutionary content to the notion of 'race' are themselves an invitation to racism. Under the guise of 'scientific knowledge', such theories have almost invariably been used to justify exclusion, subordination, or even extermination of some 'racial' groups by others. It is therefore increasingly recognized that race is itself a social construct, reflecting

---

[59] *Equality Between Men and Women—2009*, above n 51.
[60] *Statistics—Women Judges in Post*, as at April 2009, Judiciary of England and Wales (available at: <http://www.judiciary.gov.uk/publications-and-reports/statistics/judges/gender-statistics>).
[61] Women and Work Commission, *Shaping a Fairer Future* (2009), p 5.
[62] *Equality between Men and Women—2009*, above n 51.
[63] Equalities Review, pp 24–5 (available at: <http://www.theequalitiesreview.org.uk>.

ideological attempts to legitimate domination, and heavily based on social and historical context. As Stuart Hall argues,

'Black' is essentially a politically and culturally constructed category, which cannot be grounded in a set of fixed transcultural or transcendental racial categories and which therefore has no guarantees in Nature. What this brings into play is the recognition of the immense diversity and differentiation of the historical and cultural experiences of black subjects.[64]

Racism is, therefore, not about objective characteristics, but about relationships of domination and subordination, about hatred of the 'Other' in defence of 'Self', perpetrated and apparently legitimated through images of the 'Other' as inferior, abhorrent, even sub-human.

Because racism is based on a polarization of opposites: 'we' and 'they'; 'white' and 'black'; 'Self' and 'Other', it also has the effect of assuming that there is a uniform, undifferentiated 'Other'. This has several consequences. First, racism is insensitive to diversity between groups. Thus it is common to refer to 'ethnic minorities' as a homogeneous group, without noting the many differences between these groups described below. Moreover, the dominant group is considered 'normal' or natural, rather than one ethnicity among others. Second, the assumption of an undifferentiated 'Other' assumes that a group has a fixed essence, and that individuals can be wholly defined by their membership of their group. This in turn makes it easy to stereotype individuals, often linking their group identity to denigratory ascriptions. It also ignores the fact that many people have several different overlapping and intersecting sources of identity. Third, such essentialism creates a rigid and static view of group identity, described from the outside. It ignores both the voices of those within the group, and the constant, dynamic evolution of culture and ethnicity.

In the first energetic drive against racism it was of fundamental importance to stress the unity of oppressed peoples rather than their diversity. Thus 'blackness' became a political epithet rather than a description of individual characteristics. Assertions of differential ethnicity were thought to represent a strategy of 'divide and rule'. However, the diversity of cultural and socio-economic experiences among Britain's minorities has made it essential to reconsider the strategic value of an analysis based wholly on a black–white dichotomy. Modood has demonstrated how such an analysis negates the specificity of different

---

[64] Hall, 'New Ethnicities' in J Donald and A Rattansi (eds), *Race Culture and Difference* (Open University, 1992), p 254.

experiences of oppression. South Asian Muslims, he argues, are victims of a distinctive kind of racism, based on antithetical images of Islam. By contrast, Caribbeans suffer from a different set of stereotypes. It is therefore more appropriate to speak not of racism but of multiple racisms.[65] Moreover, contemporary racism cannot be understood simply as prejudice against individuals on the grounds of their colour. Besides 'colour-racism', Modood argues, there is a developing set of 'cultural racisms', which 'use cultural difference to vilify or demand cultural assimilation from groups who also suffer colour racism'.[66]

The fragmentation of the political concept of 'blackness' is a crucial step towards framing a more sophisticated legal framework. However, there remains an overarching commonality of experience of racism. This is harshly demonstrated by the pervasiveness of racist attacks to which all ethnic groups are vulnerable. The concept of racism therefore needs to be retained because it captures the underlying power relationship, a relationship where power is premised entirely on arbitrary assumptions of superiority.

At the same time, the discourse in the 1990s shifted towards one which stressed identity politics and multiculturalism. As Parekh put it, the demand for recognition goes 'far beyond the familiar plea for toleration'. It goes further and demands respect for difference, not as a pathological deviation, but 'as equally valid or worthy'.[67] Multiculturalism raises complex challenges for modern societies. It is not about minorities, because this assumes that the majority culture is 'right' or 'normal'. Instead, multiculturalism is about the 'proper terms of the relationship between different cultural communities'.[68] At the same time, the diversity of cultural values and practices should not weaken the centripetal force of society itself. During the 1990s, there was much optimism about the possibility of achieving a society with strong common values and a diversity of cultures. However, in the wake of the attack on the World Trade Center in New York and the terrorist bombings in London, commentators from both the left and the right

---

[65] R Bhavnani, *Black Women in the Labour Market: A Research Review* (EOC Research Series, 1994); T Modood, 'Ethnic Diversity and Disadvantage' in Modood et al, *Ethnic Minorities in Britain: Diversity and Disadvantage*, The Fourth National Survey of Ethnic Minorities in Britain (Policy Studies Institute, 1997), p 353.

[66] Ibid, p 353.

[67] B Parekh, *Rethinking Multiculturalism* (Palgrave, 2000), p 13.

[68] Ibid, p 13; see also B Parekh, *The Future of Multi-Ethnic Britain* (Profile Books, 2000); W Kymlicka, *Multicultural Citizenship* (Oxford University Press, 1995).

argued that multiculturalism was divisive and even dangerous.[69] Multiculturalism does not, however, necessarily entail division and separation. Parekh's approach, as outlined above, was about interaction rather than segregation, an injunction which should not be overshadowed by recent events. If these complex issues are to be dealt with effectively, a correspondingly sensitive and sophisticated legal framework is required.

The following section traces the transition to a multi-ethnic society and sketches current patterns of disadvantage. It will be seen that explanations for persistent disadvantage are complex. This raises particular challenges for the structure of discrimination law, the development of which is set out in the subsequent section.

(II) HISTORICAL CONTEXT

Even at the beginning of the twentieth century, Britain's view of itself as a white, Christian society was deceptive. There had always been small internal minorities, many of whom suffered prejudice and legal disabilities. Moreover, slavery was an accepted reality in eighteenth-century Britain. Black men and women were sold openly at auctions and the use of black slaves as domestic servants was fashionable and widespread. In 1770, there were between 14,000 and 20,000 black slaves in London alone.[70] Slavery was not formally abolished in both England and the colonies until 1833.

But the major factor shaping current patterns of ethnicity were the waves of migration to Britain from its ex-colonies in the post-war period.[71] The full political independence of Britain's colonies after the Second World War coincided with the urgent need for reconstruction of the battered British economy, which had lost many of its own workers in the war. Policies of active recruitment were instituted in many former colonies, particularly in the Caribbean, where systematic underdevelopment of the local economy had created a pool of desperate workers. In particular, faced with grinding poverty at home, people from the Caribbean flocked to the 'economic magnet, which lured so many of us to the

---

[69] N Meer and T Modood, 'The Multicultural State We're In: Muslims, "Multiculture" and the "Civic Re-balancing" of British Multiculturalism' (2009) 57 Political Studies 473–97.

[70] For a valuable discussion, see B Hepple, *Race, Jobs and the Law in Britain* (2nd edn, Penguin Books, 1970), pp 59–62.

[71] For a useful brief synopsis, see H Goulbourne, *Race Relations in Britain Since 1945* (Macmillan Press, 1998), ch 2.

Mother Country in the late forties and fifties'.[72] They were joined by increasing numbers of people from Africa, including significant numbers of East African Indians. Even greater numbers came from India after independence and the break-up of colonial India in 1947. In addition, Ireland, starved of capital to develop its own domestic economy, remained a ready source of cheap labour for Britain.

However, life in the 'Mother Country' was far from a panacea for the new migrants.[73] Migrants were overwhelmingly in manual work, confined to a limited number of industries and often trapped in jobs below their level of qualification. Racial prejudice was widespread: there was overt refusal by some employers to employ 'coloured' workers and employment opportunities were often available only in areas in which there were insufficient white workers to fill the posts. It was not uncommon for private landlords overtly to exclude blacks or Asians from private tenancies; mortgages were frequently only available on exorbitant terms; and very few migrants were in council housing. This left migrant families with little choice but to live in the worst available private rented housing in slum areas, with inevitably detrimental consequences for schooling and health. Disadvantage proved to be persistent: by 1974, minority groups were still disproportionately concentrated in semi-skilled and unskilled work, and very few had succeeded in obtaining professional or managerial jobs, despite being qualified for the job. Express discrimination continued; and ethnic minorities continued to live in inner-city areas, with poor amenities.

Although there were no express legal prohibitions, as was the case for women, issues of race and colour were dealt with by manipulating immigration rules. At first, citizenship rights were generous. In 1949, the colonial notion of the 'British subject' was replaced by the inclusive notion of 'citizen of the United Kingdom and Colonies'. This meant that post-war economic migrants arrived with immediate citizenship rights. However, by the early 1960s, the need for labour had abated and policy-makers became more concerned with keeping jobs for local people. The response took the form of a rapid retreat from an inclusive notion of citizenship. Beginning with the Commonwealth Immigration Act 1962, immigration controls were progressively tightened. Although ostensibly neutral, these regulations were widely perceived as being primarily aimed at restricting the entry of black and Asian people.

---

[72] B Bryan, S Dadzie, and S Scafe, *The Heart of the Race: Black Women's Lives in Britain* (Virago, 1985), p 16.
[73] The information in this section is taken from Modood et al, above n 65, ch 10.

This in turn signalled a sea change in patterns of migration. Until 1961, there had been a constant ebb and flow of migration. Single men or women had come to Britain to work temporarily as migrant workers, retaining strong ties with their families and communities and often sending remittances back to their home country. Paradoxically, it was the policy of tightening up on immigration control which transformed temporary movements to and from home countries into a process of settlement. The announcement in 1961 of the Commonwealth Immigrants Act led to a rapid increase in migrants, hoping to enter Britain before the ban came into force in 1962.[74] In the expectation that the option of temporary settlement would no longer be available, an inflow of families and dependants began, weakening the links with home countries. By 1981, the gate had clanged shut on new migration from the Caribbean and Indian sub-continent. Only families of men settled in Britain before 1973 were permitted to settle in Britain. In the meanwhile, the migrants of the 1960s have become the settled ethnic populations of the twenty-first century.

(III) CURRENT INEQUALITIES

Notably, the census continues to group individuals according to their country of origin. In 2001, about 2 per cent of the population identified themselves as 'Indian'; 1.5 per cent as 'Pakistani'; 0.5 per cent each as 'Bangladeshi' and 'Chinese'; and 1 per cent each as 'Black African', 'Black Caribbean', and 'mixed background'. About 88 per cent identified themselves as 'White British'.[75] While patterns of inequality persist, it is now abundantly clear that differences between minority groups can be as striking as those between minority and majority groups. For some groups, the downgrading effect of migration has finally been overcome, and these groups have reached pre-migration levels. Thus Platt finds that by the time of the census in 2001, Black Caribbeans, Indians, and white migrants had all obtained upward mobility relative to white non-migrants also from working class backgrounds. Indeed, the British-born

---

[74] H Ansari, *The Infidel Within: British Muslims since 1800* (C Hurst & Co, 2004), p 158.
[75] Information in the following paragraphs is taken from Lucinda Platt, *Poverty and Ethnicity in the UK* (Joseph Rowntree Institute, Policy Press, 2007); P Kenway and G Palmer, *Poverty Among Ethnic Groups: How and Why Does it Differ?* (New Policy Institute, Joseph Rowntree Foundation, 2009); L Platt, *Migration and Social Mobility: The Life Chances of Britain's Minority Ethnic Communities* (Policy Press, 2005); Equalities Review, above n 63.

children of migrants from these groups were more likely to have reached the professional and managerial classes than their White British equivalents.[76] However, upward mobility is not shared by all. The Equality and Human Rights Commission's (EHRC) first Triennial Review, completed in 2010, found that among working-age people, Indian people are more likely to be in the professional/managerial class (51 per cent) and Pakistani and Bangladeshi people (28 per cent) less likely to be so than white people (42 per cent).[77]

For many, the route to upward mobility has been through education. A recent study found that British-born ethnic minorities have higher average levels of education than comparable groups of British-born whites.[78] The Equalities Review in 2007 found that the children of Indian families outperform virtually all groups other than children of Chinese heritage at the GCSE.[79] This is reflected in their later lives: Indian men now have a significant pay advantage over white men.[80] Moreover, until the recession of 2009, the differential between employment rates of whites and ethnic minorities had been falling steadily, although there were some worrying signs that the recession was hitting some groups harder than others.[81]

However, relatively greater mobility does not necessarily translate into absolutely greater proportions in the higher classes. This is because minorities are disproportionately represented among lower socio-economic classes from the start.[82] Child poverty rates for Black Caribbeans and Indians are between 26 and 27 per cent, whereas the average across the population is one-fifth. The same is true for income poverty, where ethnic minorities are still over-represented. Platt shows that 30 per cent of Black Africans[83] live in income poverty, while the rate for whites is 16 per cent. Risks of higher poverty among ethnic minorities are only partially explained by other factors known to carry

---

[76] Platt, ibid, p 35; see also Equalities Review, above n 63.

[77] EHRC, *How Fair is Britain?*, Part II, p 50. The figures refer to people in classes 1–7 of the NS-SEC (National Statistics Socio-economic classification). Class 8 (unemployed) is excluded.

[78] C Dustmann and N Theodoropoulos, 'Ethnic Minority Immigrants and Their Children in Britain' (2010) Oxford Economic Papers 1–25.

[79] Public examinations taken by pupils in their 11th year at school. *Fairness and Freedom: the Final Report of the Equalities Review* (2007), p 55.

[80] L Platt, *Pay Gaps: The Position of Ethnic Minority Women and Men* (Equal Opportunities Commission, 2006), p 6.

[81] Dustmann and Theodoropoulos, above n 78.

[82] I am grateful to Lucinda Platt for her helpful explanations in this section.

[83] Figures for upward mobility of Black Africans are not available.

a high risk of poverty, namely, a higher incidence of lone parent families, large families, or families without work.[84]

But by far the most disadvantaged groups consist of Bangladeshis and Pakistani groups. As Berthoud put it in 1997 'Name any group whose poverty causes national concern—pensioners, disabled people, one-parent families, the unemployed—Pakistanis and Bangladeshis were poorer.'[85] Little has changed since then. Over half of all Bangladeshis live in income poverty and as many as two-thirds of Bangladeshi children.[86] Not far behind are the Pakistani community, around half of whom live in income poverty. Some of these differences can be explained by the fact that household sizes amongst these groups tend to be substantially higher than among their white contemporaries. Rates of sickness and disability also tend to be much higher in Bangladeshi households than others. Moreover, families of Pakistani or Bangladeshi origin are still disproportionately located in deprived areas, with more than two in three Bangladeshis and more than half of all Pakistanis living in areas in the bottom decile for deprivation. However, this does not account for the whole discrepancy. The remaining 'ethnic penalty' remains a clear factor in the ongoing disadvantage of these groups. This is particularly evident in relation to employment, with employment rates of Bangladeshis as much as 31.4 per cent behind those of comparable whites, while Pakistanis lagged by 23.4 per cent. Bangladeshi men experience particularly low rates of pay.[87] Nor do levels of educational achievement account for these discrepancies. Unlike other groups, for whom the path to upward mobility has been education, 'not even higher levels of qualifications can bring them the same occupational rewards as their white counterparts'.[88] Of particular concern is the fact that the low level of geographical and social mobility among these groups, especially those of Bangladeshi origin, suggests that this concentration of disadvantage will persist into the near future.[89]

It is essential in the analysis of race to consider gender, which intersects with class, ethnic origin, and religion to produce an increasingly complex pattern. We have already seen that women of all ethnicities earn

[84] L Platt, *Ethnicity and Child Poverty Research Report No 576* (Department for Work and Pensions, 2009).

[85] R Berthoud, 'Income and Standards of Living' in Modood et al, above n 65, p 180.

[86] Figures refer to pooled averages up to 2008.

[87] L Platt, *Pay Gaps: The Position of Ethnic Minority Women and Men* (Equal Opportunities Commission, 2006), pp 8–9.

[88] Platt, above n 75, p 34.

[89] Ibid, p 34.

substantially less than men, but there are important ethnic variations. Indeed, the weekly earnings of full-time ethnic minority women were found in 1994 to be higher than those of white women; and this remained true in 2005. Both Caribbean and Indian women have lower pay gaps when compared to white men than those experienced by white women.[90] Nevertheless, their pay is still on average substantially less than white men.[91] Like all women, they face a 'glass ceiling'. Only 9 per cent of Black Caribbean women are in top managerial positions, compared to 19 per cent of White British men and 11 per cent of White British women.[92] Nor are things necessarily improving. Whereas newly migrant Black Caribbean women were significantly more successful in the labour market than White British women, the employment probability for female British-born Black Caribbeans is now 4.8 percentage points lower than of their British-born white peers.[93]

On the other hand, the most severe intersectional disadvantage is experienced by Bangladeshi and Pakistani women. As well as the cumulative effect of their gender, ethnicity, and, for some, their religion, Bangladeshi and Pakistani women are likely to have three other disadvantaging characteristics—having young children, lower educational qualifications, and living in an area with relatively high unemployment rates.[94] It might be tempting to argue that these discrepancies are a matter of individual choice. For example, much of the employment discrepancy between Bangladeshi and other groups is due to the very low employment participation of Bangladeshi women. Indeed, the probability of employment among Bangladeshi women is 46.9 per cent lower than those of their white counterparts.[95] The primary reason given by most economically inactive women in these communities is that they do not want to work because they are looking after home and family.[96] However, it is not sufficient to regard their position as solely a matter of choice and therefore beyond the scope of discrimination law. A recent

[90] Platt, above n 80, p 7.
[91] Ibid, pp 14–15.
[92] Equal Opportunities Commission, *Moving On Up? Bangladeshi, Pakistani and Black Caribbean Women and Work. Early Findings from the EOC's Investigation in England* (2006).
[93] Dustmann and Theodoropoulosy, above n 78.
[94] Equalities Review, above n 63.
[95] Dustmann and Theodoropoulosy, above n 78.
[96] The Equalities Review, above n 63, found that this was the reason given by 72 per cent of economically inactive Bangladeshi women and 63 per cent of economically inactive Pakistani women: p 70.

study found that younger generations of women in these communities have invested a good deal in their education and would choose, with the support of their families, to enter the paid labour force.

Despite this, Pakistani and Bangladeshi women graduates are five times more likely to be unemployed than their white counterparts. When they do find work, they earn well below their qualification level. The highest pay gap relative to white men is suffered by Pakistani women. Their average full-time earnings are as much as 28 per cent lower than that of white men, a gap which is more than double that experienced by Caribbean and Indian women and substantially larger than that experienced by white women. Barriers to advancement are often specifically related to their gender and ethnicity. Many report that they have experienced stereotypical attitudes, such as that Asian women would not pursue their careers after marriage, or related to their dress or religious beliefs. Workplace culture is alien and can be hostile, especially when it entails long hours or time away from home or drinking with colleagues and clients. While these issues affect all women, they may be particularly burdensome for women from Pakistani and Bangladeshi communities, who tend to have larger families and may, for religious or cultural reasons, prefer not to socialize in these ways.[97]

It is also crucial to recognize the extent to which the statistics obscure class divisions internal to groups. Thus some individuals in all these groups have succeeded, while others remain disadvantaged. This in turn raises the question as to what is the aim of equality. Is it ultimately to reproduce within ethnic groups the pattern of advantage and disadvantage found in white groups, the assumption being that any divergence is a result of discrimination? Or is it to reduce the total sum of disadvantage, amongst whites as much as amongst others?

Socio-economic factors are not, however, the only measure of discrimination. Ethnic minorities are still seriously under-represented in public life. After the election in May 2010, a mere 26 out of 649 MPs were black or Asian. In 2009, there were only three black and Asian ethnic minority High Court judges; and only one Chief Constable came from one of these minorities.[98] In addition, there is a disturbing persistence of violence, harassment, and prejudice on the grounds of race and ethnicity. It is estimated that there were as many as 207,000 racially motivated incidents in 2007–8, up from 184,000 in the previous year.

---

[97] *Moving On Up?*, above n 92.
[98] Government Equalities Office, *A Fairer Future* (April 2009).

Only about a quarter of these are reported to the police.[99] A Home Office study in 1997 found that perpetrators of racial harassment are of all ages and sexes, including young children and pensioners, with a disturbingly high proportion of racial incidents attributed to young people. Particularly worrying was the finding that the views of the perpetrators were often shared by the wider communities to which they belonged, with a high level of racism found in children of primary and even pre-school age.[100]

Perhaps of greatest concern is the lack of confidence in the police. A significant number of people have experienced racial harassment at the hands of the police themselves, and even more believe that the police have not responded appropriately to complaints of racial violence or harassment. These issues were forced to the surface by the case of Stephen Lawrence, the victim of a racist assault and murder. Police failure to investigate the murder properly and to prosecute the perpetrators triggered allegations of racism. This in turn led to the establishment of what has been labelled a 'watershed' inquiry, led by MacPherson. The Report of the Inquiry[101] took a crucial step forward in recognizing that racism can extend beyond individual acts of prejudice to the institutional culture and organization of the police itself. Institutional racism was defined as the

collective failure of an organisation to provide an appropriate and professional service to people because of their colour, culture, or ethnic origin. It can be seen or detected in process, attitudes and behaviour which amount to discrimination through unwitting prejudice, ignorance, thoughtlessness and racist stereotyping which disadvantage minority ethnic people.[102]

It persists because of organizational failure to recognize and address its existence. Such 'institutional racism' was found to be endemic in the broader culture and structure of both the police and other agencies.[103]

Yet little has changed in the ten years since the publication of the MacPherson Report. Black people make up between 2–3 per cent of the population, yet constituted 15 per cent of those who were stopped

---

[99] J Riley, D Cassidy, and J Becker, *Statistics on Race and the Criminal Justice System 2007/8: A Ministry of Justice publication under Section 95 of the Criminal Justice Act 1991* (Ministry of Justice, 2009).

[100] R Sibbit, *The Perpetrators of Racial Harassment and Racial Violence*, Home Office Research Study 176 (Home Office, 1997).

[101] Home Office, 'Report of the MacPherson Inquiry' (Cmd 4262, 24 February 1999).

[102] Ibid, para 6.34.

[103] Ibid, para 6.34.

by the police in 2008–9.[104] Home Office statistics for 2007–8 showed that there were nearly eight times more stops and searches of black people per head of population than of white people, and twice as many stops and searches of Asian people.[105] This has been a consistent pattern over at least a decade of monitoring. According to the EHRC, racial discrimination is a significant reason why black and Asian people are more likely to be stopped and searched than white people.[106] A similar pattern can be detected in the criminal justice system as a whole. There were 3.8 times more arrests of black people per head of population than of white people in 2007–8, a similar figure to that in the previous year. Black people are more likely than white people to receive a custodial sentence, and are over-represented in the prison system: the proportion of black prisoners relative to the population was 6.8 per 1,000 population compared to 1.3 per 1,000 for white persons in 2007–8.

(iv) legislative developments

In the meanwhile, anti-discrimination legislation has been developing increasingly sophisticated tools to address the issue. Prior to 1965, there was no legal protection against discrimination, racial or otherwise. Judge-made common law never recognized racial discrimination as a distinct legal wrong;[107] nor were judges prepared to develop the common law in this direction. Racial discrimination, although on several occasions declared to be 'deplorable', was simply not considered as contrary to public policy.[108] At the legislative level, considerable reluctance was similarly evident: the years from 1950 to 1965 saw the failure of at least ten attempts to persuade Parliament to legislate against race discrimination. The legislation that did finally emerge, in 1965 and 1968, was weak and ultimately ineffective.[109]

Renewed impetus for change led to the enactment of the Race Relations Act 1976 (RRA), which remained the central legislative source of protection against discrimination on grounds of race, colour, nationality, and ethnic or national origins until the Equality Act (EA) 2010.[110] Following the model of the SDA, the RRA included both direct and

---

[104] *How Fair is Britain?*, above n 77, Part II, p 134.
[105] Riley, Cassidy, and Becker, above n 99.
[106] EHRC, *Stop and Think: A Critical Review of Stop and Search Powers in England and Wales* (2010).
[107] Hepple, above n 70, p 144.
[108] *Re Lysaght, Hill v Royal College of Surgeons* [1965] 3 WLR 391 at 402.
[109] Hepple, above n 70.
[110] RRA 1976, s 3.

indirect discrimination and covered employment, education, and goods, facilities, and services available to the public. It differed from the SDA in that no division was drawn between pay and non-pay issues. Notably, it did not cover discrimination on the grounds of religion or belief. Only if a religious group could also be characterized as an ethnic minority would its members gain protection under the Act.[111]

Further momentum came from the damning indictment of the Mac-Pherson Report, which prompted two significant extensions to the scope of the RRA in 2000. First, it became unlawful for public authorities to discriminate in any of their functions, not just employment, education, or goods, facilities, and services.[112] Private bodies carrying out functions of a public nature were also included.[113] Secondly, and particularly innovative, was the introduction of a proactive duty. Rather than relying only on complaints of discrimination, the Act required public authorities to take the initiative in respect of eliminating unlawful discrimination, and promoting equality of opportunity and good race relations.[114] At the same time, the content of the duty was relatively mild. Authorities do not have to take steps to achieve these goals, but merely to 'pay due regard' to the need to do so. This duty became the model for subsequent duties in relation to gender and disability, and was further extended in the EA 2010 to the other grounds of discrimination.[115]

At EU level, while gender discrimination was part of the EU agenda from the beginning, race discrimination was surprisingly late in coming. It was not until the Treaty of Amsterdam in 1998 that the EU was given the competence to legislate on matters of, inter alia, racial or ethnic origin.[116] This was quickly followed by the Race Directive.[117] The Directive covers both direct and indirect discrimination. It is also innovative in introducing the concept of harassment as a species of discrimination. Particularly noteworthy is the scope of coverage of the Directive. Whereas previous EU discrimination provisions had been confined to employment and vocational training, the Race Directive extends to social protection, including social security and healthcare, social advantages, education, and access to and supply of goods and

---

[111] *Mandla v Dowell Lee* [1983] 2 AC 548 (HL).
[112] RRA 1976, s 19B.
[113] RRA 1976, s 19B(2)(a).
[114] RRA 1976, s 71; now EA 2010, s 149.
[115] See Chapter Six.
[116] Treaty of Rome (Consolidated Version), Art 13.
[117] Council Directive 2000/43/EC.

services which are available to the public, including housing.[118] Notably too, the Directive specifies that the principle of equal treatment does not prevent a Member State from maintaining or adopting specific measures to prevent or compensate for disadvantages linked to racial or ethnic origin.[119] It also requires Member States to establish an equality body.[120]

Unlike the RRA, and the European Convention on Human Rights (ECHR), the Race Directive does not include nationality as a ground of discrimination. EU law already contains a strong principle of non-discrimination on grounds of nationality in respect of EU nationals. However, the situation of third country nationals is more complex. The Directive itself states expressly that it does not cover difference of treatment based on nationality, and is without prejudice to provisions and conditions relating to entry and residence of third country nationals and stateless persons and to any treatment which arises from their legal status.[121] Although third country nationals are protected against discrimination on grounds of race or ethnic origin, this prohibition does not cover differences of treatment based on nationality.[122]

There is also some intervention on the part of criminal law. The Crime and Disorder Act 1998 introduced a set of new offences to deal with racially aggravated violence, and this was extended in 2001 to religiously motivated violence. An offence is racially or religiously aggravated if the offender demonstrates hostility based on the victim's membership or presumed membership of a racial or religious group, or the offence is motivated (wholly or partly) by hostility towards members of a racial or religious group based on their membership of that group.[123] Sentences for these offences are higher than for those of the non-racially aggravated equivalent offences. There is also an offence of stirring up racial hatred by using threatening, abusive, or insulting words or behaviour or in written material. The offence is not limited to intentional behaviour; it can also occur if racial hatred is likely to be stirred up by that behaviour.[124] It extends too to being in possession of racially inflammatory material.[125]

---

[118] Ibid, Art 3(1)(e)–(h).   [119] Ibid, Art 5.
[120] Ibid, Art 13.   [121] Ibid, Art 3(2).
[122] Ibid, preamble para 13.
[123] Crime and Disorder Act 1998, s 28(1)(a) and (b).
[124] Public Order Act 1986, ss 17–22.   [125] Ibid, s 23.

(v) IMMIGRANTS AND ASYLUM SEEKERS

By the mid-1990s, migration from outside the EU was again on the increase. However, this was primarily prompted by skills shortages, and subject to strict controls. In 2006, a points system was put in place to permit the entry of skilled and highly skilled workers, while at the same time severely limiting low-skilled immigration. This has been accompanied by a tightening up of sanctions against illegal working in the UK. Legislation originally introduced in 1997[126] and strengthened in 2006[127] puts the onus on employers effectively to police the system. Those who knowingly employ an adult who is not legally entitled to work in the UK can be subjected to an unlimited fine and a prison sentence of up to two years. All employers must make specified checks; failure to do so might lead to a civil penalty of up to £10,000 per worker if the latter turns out to be illegal. Ignorance of the workers' status is no excuse. Enforcement has been vociferous. In the first few months after introduction of the new rules in February 2008, there were 137 prosecutions or penalty notices leading to fines totalling £500,000. This was ten times more than in 2007 and double the total for the previous decade. There is a clear danger that this might lead to racial prejudice if employers stereotype certain ethnic groups as being more likely to be illegal than others.

For citizens of the EU, the picture is very different. With the entry in 1972 of the UK into the EEC came an endorsement of the principle of free movement of labour within the EU. Freedom of internal migration within the EU contrasts strikingly with the strictness with which the boundaries of 'Fortress EU' are policed. Although the early decades of membership did not lead to large movements of EU workers, this changed with the accession to the EU of eight new members in Central and Eastern Europe (the 'A8'). The decision to allow workers from these countries free access to the UK labour market from May 2004 triggered a rapid inflow of Polish citizens. Between 2003 and 2009, the Polish-born population of the UK soared from 75,000 to 503,000, with Poles becoming one of the largest non-UK-born groups in the UK.[128]

---

[126] Asylum and Immigration Act 1996, s 8.

[127] Immigration, Asylum and Nationality Act 2006.

[128] Data from this section are taken from Office for National Statistics, 'Polish People in the UK' (March 2010, available at: <http://www.statistics.gov.uk/cci/nugget.asp?id=2369>); Home Office, UK Border Agency, *Accession Monitoring Report: 2004–2009* (available at: <http://webarchive.nationalarchives.gov.uk/20100422120657/http://www.ukba.homeoffice.gov.uk/sitecontent/documents/aboutus/reports/accession_monitoring_report/report-19/may04-mar09?view=Binary>); B Anderson, M Ruhs,

Notably, post-enlargement migrants have a very high employment rate, and very few claim state benefits.[129] Moreover, the absence of any control on migration has made it possible for migrants to come to the UK on a temporary or seasonable basis. Of the million migrant workers from the A8 who arrived in the UK from 2004, about half had already left by 2008. Among Polish people in particular, immigration peaked in 2007, and since then emigration has increased. This in turn supports the hypothesis that lower barriers to mobility do not lead to uncontrolled influxes, but to a lower incidence of permanent migration.[130]

The positive experience of internal EU migration has not, however, translated into any relaxation of the severity of control over aspiring migration from outside the EU. Many hundreds of thousands of people seeking refuge or a better life in the UK are routinely subjected to a harsh and complex system of screening. Each year, tens of thousands of applications for asylum are received, the vast majority of which are from Africa and Asia. Although the number has now dropped significantly, from a peak of 80,000 in 2000, there were still as many as 31,315 in 2008. To be recognized as a refugee, asylum seekers must be unable to return to their own country because they have a well-founded fear of persecution. Flight from poverty or the dream of a better life are not acceptable reasons. However, attempts to separate eligible from ineligible claims for asylum have led to a complex and often unworkable bureaucracy, riddled with inefficiency and inadequately resourced. In July 2006, the Home Secretary announced a backlog or 'legacy' of between 400,000 and 450,000 unresolved asylum cases. Only half of these had been concluded by September 2009; and the effort involved led to backlogs elsewhere. This, allied with a wave of suspicion and prejudice bordering on xenophobia, has meant that hundreds of thousands of aspirant entrants are consigned to many years of uncertainty, stigma, and destitution. During this time, they are prohibited from working. Many are detained pending deportation. Nearly 1,000 children a year are detained in immigration detention centres, spending

---

B Rogaly, and S Spencer, 'Fair Enough: Central and Eastern European Migrants in Low Wage Employment in the UK' (Centre for Migration Studies (COMPAS), 2006); M Ruhs, 'Greasing the Wheels of the Flexible Labour Market', Working Paper No 38 (Centre for Migration Studies (COMPAS), 2006).

[129] Ibid.

[130] N Pollard, M Latorre, and D Sriskandaraja, *Floodgates or Turnstiles? Post-EU Enlargement Migration Flows to and from the UK* (IPPR, 2008).

on average over a fortnight in detention. It is not uncommon for children to be detained for up to 61 days.[131]

More recently, asylum seekers have turned to the developing human rights regime rather than discrimination law for assistance. The results have been mixed. In a seminal case, the House of Lords held that provisions which withdrew support from asylum seekers in circumstances in which they had no option but destitution constituted a breach of the right not to be subjected to cruel and inhuman treatment or punishment.[132] Moreover, the denial of the right to work can interfere with the right to respect for one's private life.[133] Such interference cannot justify long delays deliberately created to clear the backlog created by previous failures of administration.[134] In addition, EU law now lays down minimum standards for support of asylum seekers including the right to access the labour market in the event of delay in considering their claims.[135] On the other hand, a recent Court of Appeal judgment has held that failed asylum seekers are not entitled to free medical care under the National Health Service because they cannot be said to be 'ordinarily resident' in England, as required by relevant legislation.[136]

(VI) CULTURE AND ETHNICITY

Cultural diversity is not, however, entirely characterized by negative features. Britain's society is instead enriched by its newly attained multicultural qualities. Differences in family structure, religion, language, and dress all contribute to a rich and diverse society. Dress is perhaps the most visible feature of cultural diversity, and is often intimately bound up with religion. The Fourth National Survey of ethnic minorities in Britain in 1997 found that the majority of women of South Asian origin, particularly women of Pakistani origin, wore Asian clothes (although few men of Asian origin do); and most women of Pakistani and Bangladeshi origin wore their heads covered, even

---

[131] House of Commons Home Affairs Committee, 'The Detention of Children in the Immigration System', First Report of Session 2009–10 (HC 73, November 2009).

[132] ECHR, Art 3; *R (on the application of Limbuela) v Secretary of State for the Home Department* [2005] UKHL 66, [2006] 1 AC 396 (HL).

[133] ECHR, Art 3.

[134] *Tekle* [2008] EWHC 3064 (Admin).

[135] Council Directive 2003/9/EC of 27 January 2003 laying down minimum standards for the reception of asylum seekers (the Reception Directive).

[136] *R (A) v Secretary of State for Health* [2009] EWCA Civ 225 (CA).

among the younger generations.[137] At the same time, a distinctive way of dressing was becoming less common among younger members of minority groups, particularly among Hindus. Notably, too, fewer young Sikh men wore turbans than older men. By contrast, Caribbean cultural dress is a growing, dynamic force with a charisma which has influenced the dominant cultural dress. It is the younger generation of Caribbeans who are infusing Caribbean culture with new energy and vitality, a vitality often attractive to members of other ethnic groups, particularly young whites. Religion was also a distinguishing feature. Whereas only a tiny minority of young whites saw religion as very important to how they lead their lives, the large majority of those of Pakistani and Bangladeshi origin considered religion a central defining characteristic of their identity. Significant minorities of those of Indian and Caribbean origins were religious; but it is notable that, according to the Fourth National Survey, their black identity was much more prominent in the self-description of people of Caribbean origin than religion. By contrast only a minority of people of South Asian origin thought of themselves as black. Language was a further measure of cultural identity. The Fourth National Survey found that, with the exception of those of Caribbean origin, nearly all ethnic minority persons spoke a language other than English, with Punjabi being the most commonly used South Asian language. Unfortunately, there has not yet been a Fifth National Survey, making it difficult to describe more recent trends.

Different ethnic groups also exhibit quite different social and cultural characteristics. Thus Bangladeshi households tend to be the largest, followed by Pakistani and Indian households. These families tend to have more children, as well as being multi-generational, often living with the father's parents. This family structure therefore plays a central role in the care of the elderly. The Fourth National Survey found that as many as two-thirds of Asian elders living in Britain residing in the same household as one or more of their adult children.[138] Arranged marriages were still customary in some families although there are fewer among British-born Asians. Families of Afro-Caribbean origin are at the other end of the spectrum, with a large number of unattached single adults (particularly men) and an unusually high proportion of single parent families. In 2002, 54 per cent of all Black Caribbean families with dependent children were lone-parent families, the highest proportion being among those of mixed ethnicity (61 per cent). White families

---

[137] Modood et al, above n 65.   [138] Ibid, p 58.

differ again: the number of children in white families is falling, and there is a striking increase in marital breakdown, single parent families, and cohabitation.

In addition, the combination of cultures can produce new and exciting syntheses. Nowhere is this better manifested than in marriage or partnership between men and women of different ethnic backgrounds. The 2001 census found significant proportions of inter-ethnic marriages among some ethnic minorities in England and Wales. This was particularly so for young black people born in Britain, and Black Caribbean people. Almost five in ten men who identified as 'Other Black' men (48 per cent) and three in ten Black Caribbean men (29 per cent) were married to women outside the black ethnic group, in most cases white women.[139] The census also found that those who identified mixed 'White and Black Caribbean' constituted over 42 per cent of the 'Black Caribbean' group, and there were more children of mixed white and Black Caribbean origin than those of Black Caribbean origin. Indeed, the prominence of children under 5 of mixed origin heralds a significant demographic change: almost 4 per cent of all under-5s and 25 per cent of the minority ethnic population in England and Wales were of mixed origin.[140] This is an important indicator of the relative openness of British society to a common sense of belonging. In other countries, such as South Africa and the USA, the prohibitions, both legal and cultural, of any form of racial inter-marriage were a core perpetuating feature of racism. It also has important implications for the definition and concept of ethnic identity itself.[141]

On the other hand, the 2001 census found that people from South Asian backgrounds were the least likely of the minority ethnic groups to be married to someone from a different ethnic group. Only 6 per cent of Indians, 4 per cent of Pakistanis, and 3 per cent of Bangladeshis had married someone outside the Asian group. This may well be explained by religious or cultural taboos on inter-marriage.[142]

---

[139] National Statistics, *Inter-Ethnic Marriage* (March 2005, available at: <http://www.statistics.gov.uk/cci/nugget_print.asp?ID=1090>).

[140] C Owen, 'The Mixed Category Census 2001' in J Mai Sims (ed), *Mixed Heritage* (Runnymede Trust, 2007).

[141] Ibid, p 31.

[142] *Inter-Ethnic Marriage*, above n 139.

III GYPSIES AND TRAVELLERS

Also subject to a long history of prejudice, hostility, and repression is the Gypsy and Traveller community.[143] Indeed, the failure of the dominant settled population to accommodate the nomadic existence of Gypsies and Travellers had meant that this is probably the poorest and most marginalized minority in the modern UK.[144] Since they were not included in the census before 2011, there are no reliable estimates of the Gypsy and Traveller population in Britain, with figures ranging from 82,000 to 300,000. Their desire for a nomadic existence, which in the past facilitated their participation in seasonal work, remains a central element in their culture and self-perception. Although many now prefer to remain in a particular location, with access to schools and other local amenities, nomadism continues to be a state of mind, if not a way of life. Even if they do not travel frequently, or at all, they want to live in a caravan or mobile home, with proximity to the outdoor world, in a community of family and friends.[145]

Yet it is this aspect of Gypsies' and Travellers' culture that the dominant community has resisted vehemently and often with hostility. Legislation passed in 1968 placed an obligation on local authorities to make provision for gypsy sites,[146] but this was repealed in 1994,[147] and had in any event been routinely ignored. Since 1994, many local authorities have regarded their role in relation to Gypsies and Travellers as purely a matter of enforcement against unauthorized sites, without making any new site provision. This is despite the fact that constant costs of eviction might well exceed costs of new provision. The result is a dire picture of overcrowded and unsanitary public sites, unauthorized encampment, harassment, and evictions from privately owned land.

---

[143] Comprising a range of groups with different histories, cultures, and beliefs, and including Irish Travellers, Scottish Gypsies/Travellers, English Gypsies, Romanies, and Welsh Gypsies.

[144] The information and statistics in this section are taken from Department for Communities and Local Government, 'Gypsies and Travellers: Facts and Figures' (2006, available at: <http://www.communities.gov.uk/documents/housing/pdf/158454.pdf>); Office of the Deputy Prime Minister: Housing, Planning, Local Government and the Regions, 'Thirteenth Report' (October 2004, available at: <http://www.parliament.the-stationery-office.co.uk/pa/cm200304/cmselect/cmodpm/633/63302.htm>); S Spencer, 'Gypsies and Travellers: Britain's Forgotten Minority' (2005) 4 European Human Rights Law Review 335–43.

[145] See 'Thirteenth Report', ibid, para 55.

[146] Caravan Sites Act 1968.

[147] Criminal Justice and Public Order Act 1994, s 77.

Gypsy and Traveller communities exhibit poor levels of health, high rates of infant mortality, poor school attendance, and high levels of illiteracy.[148] There is a serious shortage of authorized sites and those that exist are dismal. Over a quarter are adjacent to runways, rubbish tips, or sewage farms. A further 25 per cent are next to or under motorways. They are generally far from shops and schools and lack public transport.[149] Although Gypsies and Travellers were encouraged to buy their own land, most local authorities failed to identify appropriate sites. The result was that many Gypsies and Travellers, who bought land where they could, have found it almost impossible to get planning permission to site caravans on their land. In 2009, of at least 17,437 Gypsy and Traveller caravans in England, 13 per cent were on sites which they owned but for which planning permission had not been granted. A further 9 per cent were unauthorized encampments on others' land. In total, one in five of the travelling community has no legal place where they can stop their caravan. This has in turn fuelled antagonism against them, often fanned by a hostile press.

In principle, all those without anywhere to park their caravans are homeless and entitled to local authority assistance. Nevertheless, the vast majority of local authorities have not included Gypsies and Travellers in their homelessness strategies. Since 2006, government has made funds available to local authorities for the refurbishment of existing public sites and development of new facilities.[150] However, these sums remain small compared to identified need, and there is considerable variation across the country in local authorities' willingness to apply for funding. In any event, this stops well short of the recommendation of the Joint Committee of Human Rights for a statutory duty on local authorities to provide or facilitate the provision of accommodation.[151] On the other hand, there has been a plethora of guidance to local authorities as to how to manage perceived 'anti-social behaviour' of Gypsies and Travellers. While this guidance includes advising authorities to make proper provision for permanent and temporary sites, and urges them to treat Gypsies and Travellers in the same way as they would equivalent behaviour among the settled population, there remain

---

[148] Joint Committee on Human Rights, '14th Report on the Convention on the Elimnation of All Forms of Racial Discrimination, 2004–5', para 141.
[149] Spencer, above n 144.
[150] A total of £56 million was made available in the period 2006–8, with a further £97 million of grants available from 2008–11.
[151] '14th Report', above n 148, para 103.

strong stigmatic undertones to the advice, and a continuing inability to tackle structural causes of inequality.

In the meanwhile, Gypsies and Travellers have been increasingly resorting to courts to claim their rights. The results have been mixed. It took a trip to the Court of Appeal before Romany Gypsies were recognized as an ethnic group and therefore protected against discrimination under the RRA.[152] It took even longer for Irish Travellers and Scottish Gypsies to achieve similar recognition.[153] While some have successfully challenged outright discrimination under the RRA, the Act, with its emphasis on individual complaints, was not capable of achieving the structural change necessary.[154] More impact might have been expected of the positive duty to pay due regard to the need to promote equality of opportunity and good relations between racial groups. In a recent decision, the Court of Appeal recognized that Gypsies and Travellers suffer the worst health and education status of any disadvantaged group in England and that an effective way of alleviating this is to increase the number of Gypsy and Traveller sites in appropriate locations with planning permission. However, the duty to pay 'due regard' did not require action to be taken. To discharge the positive duty, a planning inspector was merely required to take the predicament of Gypsies and Travellers into account, alongside other planning factors. How much weight she should give to the various factors was a matter for her planning judgment.[155]

Others have relied on their human rights under the ECHR, particularly the right to respect for their home, private life, and family in Article 8. Here too the results have been mixed. On the one hand, the European Court of Human Rights (ECtHR) has acknowledged that a caravan is a 'home' for the purposes of Article 8.[156] In addition, the Court has affirmed that occupying a caravan is an integral part of the ethnic identity of Gypsies and Travellers even though many no longer live a wholly nomadic existence. Measures affecting the stationing of their caravans can therefore affect their ability to maintain their identity as Gypsies and Travellers and to lead their private and family life

---

[152] *Commission for Racial Equality v Dutton* [1989] 2 WLR 17, [1989] QB 783 (CA).

[153] *O'Leary v Punch Retail* (Westminster County Court, 29 August 2000, unreported) (Irish Travellers).

[154] See further Chapter Six.

[155] *R (on the application of Baker & Ors) v Secretary of State for Communities and Local Government, London Borough of Bromley* [2008] EWCA Civ 141 at para 40.

[156] *Buckley v UK* (1993) 23 EHRR 101.

accordingly.[157] Indeed, there is a positive obligation upon Contracting States to facilitate the Gypsy way of life: the vulnerable position of Gypsies as a minority means that special consideration should be given to their needs and their different lifestyle.[158] On the other hand, the ECtHR has been quick to accept that limitations on this right are justifiable, affording Contracting States a wide margin of appreciation.[159] Thus in *Chapman*, the applicant was refused planning permission to station her caravan on her own land. She argued that because the number of Gypsies is greater than the number of places available in authorized Gypsy sites, this constituted an unjustifiable limit on her right to respect for her home and family life. The Court rejected the argument. To accept it, it declared,

> would be tantamount to imposing on the United Kingdom, as on all the other Contracting States, an obligation by virtue of Article 8 to make available to the gypsy community an adequate number of suitably equipped sites. The Court is not convinced that Article 8 can be interpreted to involve such a far-reaching positive obligation of general social policy being imposed on States.[160]

The Court has been less deferent, however, when it comes to procedural protection. It has taken a particularly robust stand in relation to regulations under which Gypsies or Travellers can be evicted without the right to be given reasons. These have been held to be unjustifiable restrictions on Gypsies' and Travellers' Article 8 rights, all the more so in light of the fact that evictions from other mobile homes were required to be accompanied by reasons.[161] This has led to grudging recognition by domestic courts[162] and an amendment of the relevant legislation.[163]

Other developments at European level, aimed at European Roma people, might in due course assist Gypsies and Travellers in the UK. The Roma are the largest single minority in Europe, and, as in the UK, also the most marginalized. Both the Council of Europe and the EU have express policies in relation to the Roma, and Roma are in principle protected by the EU Race Directive, the ECHR, the European Social Charter, and the Framework Convention for the Protection of National

---

[157] *Chapman v United Kingdom* (2001) 33 EHRR 18 at paras 73–4.
[158] *Connors v United Kingdom* (2005) 40 EHRR 9 at para 84.
[159] *Buckley v UK*, above n 156; *Connors v United Kingdom*, above n 158, paras 82, 90–2.
[160] *Chapman v United Kingdom*, above n 157, para 98; followed in *R (on the application of McCarthy) v Basildon DC* [2009] EWCA Civ 13.
[161] *Connors v United Kingdom*, above n 158; *Chapman v United Kingdom*, above n 157, paras 93–4.
[162] *Doherty v Birmingham City Council* [2008] UKHL 57.
[163] Housing and Regeneration Act 2008, s 318; see Hansard, cols 142–3 (9 March 2010).

Minorities. However, as in the UK, while the Roma have scored some successes under these instruments, real change remains illusory.

IV RELIGION AND BELIEF

(I) CHALLENGES AND DILEMMAS

Protection against discrimination on grounds of religion has been a core value of international human rights law since its inception. As Boyle and Sheen put it,

from the Holocaust, the ultimate outworking of centuries of European intolerance against Jews, came a new idea, that of individual human rights, to be internationally defined and guaranteed to all persons everywhere in virtue of their humanity, without distinction as to race, sex, language or religion.[164]

At the same time, religious discrimination is arguably a good deal more complex than other related grounds. At one level, it bears strong similarities to, and is indeed closely allied with, other types of discrimination. Religious discrimination can be a form of racism at its most vicious, as witnessed by the atrocities committed by the Nazis against the Jews in the Second World War, in the name of pure racist ideology. In other contexts, religious discrimination constitutes a form of ethnic or cultural discrimination. Thus Modood regards anti-Muslim prejudice as 'cultural racism'. Religious discrimination can also be closely linked to discrimination on grounds of political affiliation, as in Northern Ireland, where the conflict between Catholics and Protestants is rooted as much in communal identification, separate nationalisms, and political disagreement as in religion.

On the other hand, the relationship between religion and other grounds of discrimination is shifting and often conflicting. Religions find their source of authority in faith rather than reason, and in some cases, their allegiance is to God and a transcendental morality, rather than to the democratic legal system. This might make it difficult to find common ground either between one religion and another or between individual religions and a secular human rights regime.[165] For example, should a teacher be permitted, for religious reasons, to cover her face while giving language instruction to young children, even if as a result

---

[164] K Boyle and J Sheen (eds), *Freedom of Religion and Belief: A World Report* (Routledge, 1997), p 4.
[165] F Raday, 'Culture, Religion and Gender' [2003] 1:4 International Journal of Constitutional Law 663 at 669.

the children's learning is impeded by their inability to see the expression on her face? Religions may also breed intolerance of other religions, and religious adherents might even discriminate against others of the same faith, because they are less observant or have a different interpretation of religious doctrine.

Perhaps most problematic is the reliance on religious belief to justify other forms of discrimination. Should individuals be permitted to discriminate against others on the grounds that this is required by their religion or belief? Particularly extreme was the use by the Afri-kaner Nationalist Party of religious precepts to justify institutionalized racism in the apartheid State in South Africa. More common are attempts to defend sexism or homophobia on the grounds of religion. As will be seen, both British and EU law have permitted priority to be given in specific circumstances to religious belief over the protection of others' rights, particularly those of women and homosexuals.

These conflicts have led some to argue that protection against religious discrimination has no place within the traditional lexicon of British discrimination law. McColgan argues that 'requiring the accommodation of practices or beliefs categorised as "religious" tends to perpetuate practices and beliefs which are problematic on equality and other grounds'.[166] Further complexities are added by the fact that it is not only religious belief, but also the right not to believe, that is usually protected by discrimination law. Other forms of belief are included too, usually encapsulated in the formula 'religion or belief'. This raises the troublesome question of whether all kinds of belief should be equally protected.[167]

Also complex is the relationship between religion, ethnicity, culture, and community. There is a tendency in the media and elsewhere to regard the Muslim population in Britain as synonymous with the Asian population. In fact, however, the Asian population is composed of several different religions, and there are many non-Asian Muslims living in Britain. Indeed, some Muslims would object to an approach which conflated Islamic norms with ethnicity, regarding the former as fundamentally religious in nature and transcending ethnic demarcations.[168] On the other hand, both Jews and Sikhs have long been regarded as

---

[166] A McColgan, 'Class Wars: Religion and (In)equality in the Workplace' (2009) 38 ILJ 1–29 at 1.

[167] L Vickers, *Religious Freedom, Religious Discrimination and the Workplace* (Hart Publishing, 2008) and see further Chapter Three.

[168] Boyle and Sheen, above n 164, p 316.

ethnic groups for the purposes of race discrimination law in Britain,[169] and many Jewish people regard themselves as primarily ethnic rather than religious. Moreover, there is a growing community dimension to religious adherence. The sense of identification of individual believers with other members of their faiths, particularly where they are in the minority, has deepened with the resurgence of general religious feeling in the twenty-first century, together with renewed Islamophobia and anti-Semitism following the terrorist attacks on the World Trade Center in New York in 2001. This has led to the concept of 'faith-based communities', an important acknowledgement that communities are increasingly identifying themselves by their bonds of faith. Recognition of faith-based communities can, however, raise its own dilemmas, particularly if this leads to self-segregation or isolation of some communities from the broader society. Earlier policies favouring multiculturalism led to fears that this merely encouraged isolated communities, without common bonds. On the other hand, more recent policies in favour of 'community cohesion' have been criticized as assimilationist. Both these approaches can be compared to the prescription of the Parekh Report on the Future of Multi-ethnic Britain, which argued that unity needs to be understood in terms 'both of a community of communities and a community of citizens'.[170]

(II) HISTORY AND CONTEXT

Religion was conspicuously lacking in British anti-discrimination law (outside Northern Ireland) until EU law made its inclusion mandatory in 2003. Absence of protection against religious discrimination did not, however, mean that there was no such discrimination. Formal discrimination on grounds of religion in the UK persisted until the closing decades of the nineteenth century. Institutionalized religious privilege in favour of the Church of England was matched by a mass of specific discriminatory laws against Jews, Catholics, and non-conformist Protestants. Thus Acts of Uniformity from as early as 1549 established the Church of England Prayer Book (the Book of Common Prayer) as the only legal form of worship. Even more problematic was the requirement, established by the Act of Supremacy 1559, that every person taking public office (including, subsequently, MPs and university students) should swear allegiance to the monarch as Supreme Governor of the Church of England. Failure to swear was treasonable. As well as

---

[169] See Chapter Three.   [170] Parekh, above n 68, para 4.36.

excluding Jews and Muslims, this had the effect of barring Catholics from public office and Parliament, because it entailed denial of the Pope's spiritual jurisdiction. For a period too, a series of penal laws known as the Test Acts made it a precondition for holding public office that the incumbent had received the communion of the Church of England. In 1677 it was enacted that all members of either House of Parliament should, before taking their seats, make a 'Declaration against Popery', and legislation also made this a pre-condition for owning or inheriting property. Requirements to disavow the authority of the Pope and other central tenets of the Catholic religion were particularly onerous to Roman Catholics. But all minority religions and non-conformist Protestants were effectively excluded from public office and Parliament.

It took many years of struggle before Catholic emancipation was achieved. It was not until the Catholic Relief Act of 1829 that public life, including the right to sit in Parliament, was opened up to Catholics and the last of these limitations was not removed until 1871. Even so, the British monarchy is still debarred to Catholics, and the monarch may not marry a Catholic. Substantive equality took longer to achieve. Irish Catholics, who formed a significant presence throughout the nineteenth century, were subject to 'a shared pool of insidious stereotypes... For the Protestant and liberal imagination they were the significant "other" in contrast to whom identity was defined.'[171] It was not until State funding was provided for Catholic schools in 1902 that Catholics began to feel that they were accepted members of society. By the mid-twentieth century, Hepple could argue that, while 'social inequality remains, Irish workers in Britain are rarely thought of with hostility as an alien group'.[172]

Jews, expelled from Britain in 1290, were only readmitted by Cromwell in 1656 because of the financial and political services which they could render to him. They were tolerated rather than welcomed, and although their community flourished, they continued to labour under severe legal disabilities. Like Catholics, they were barred from public life by the requirement to take the Christian oath in order to exercise central rights such as the right to vote, the right to stand for municipal election, and the right to be an MP. Emancipation was even slower in coming than

---

[171] P Lewis, 'Arenas of Ethnic Negotiation' in T Modood and P Werbner (eds), *The Politics of Multiculturalism in the New Europe: Racism, Identity and Community* (Zed Books, 1997), p 128.
[172] Hepple, above n 70, p 70.

that of the Catholics. Attempts in 1753 to permit Jewish immigrants to become naturalized failed after an upsurge of anti-Semitic protest. It was not until the mid-nineteenth century that these obstacles were gradually dismantled. Jews were permitted to become barristers in 1833 and to take the office of sheriff in 1835. The same year, a statute was passed revoking the power of returning electoral officers to insist on the Christian oath before allowing individuals to vote. This formally enfranchised those Jews who were otherwise eligible to vote.[173] They were permitted to take municipal office in 1845, while a statute of 1846 gave them undisputed rights to own land. But attempts to open up Parliament to Jews by lifting the requirement to take the oath were defeated on multiple occasions between 1834 and 1857.[174] Baron Lionel de Rothschild, who had been elected in 1847, consistently refused to take the oath and although elected in four further elections, was debarred from his seat. It was only in 1858 that a compromise was reached which permitted each House to determine its own oath and de Rothschild could finally take his seat as the first Jewish MP. In 1870, the University Test Act removed the obstacles in the way of Jews becoming university scholars or fellows, but it was not until 1890 that all restrictions for every position in the British Empire were removed, except for that of the monarch.

Despite the legal restrictions, the settled Jewish community in Britain was not subject to the rabid anti-Semitism of many parts of Europe. Although Jews were still stereotyped in pejorative forms, they had achieved a measure of integration by the end of the century, without the overt pressures of assimilation felt by Jewish communities elsewhere in Europe. This was, however, unsettled after 1881, when vicious pogroms against the Jewish population of Russia triggered an influx of Jewish refugees who, excluded from most of Europe, made their way to England. Between 1880 and 1914, between 150,000 and 200,000 Jews settled in Britain. Unlike their predecessors, who tended to be small traders, the vast majority of these immigrants entered the British workforce as workers in sweated industries.[175] In these unsanitary and crowded workshops, Jewish workers were paid starvation wages for working long hours producing cheap clothing, footwear, or furniture.

[173] In practice, some Jews had already been exercising the vote in boroughs where returning officers did not insist on the oath: Todd M Endelman, *The Jews of London 1656–2000* (University of California Press, 2002), p 103.
[174] D Cooper and D Herman, 'Jews and Other Uncertainties: Race, Faith and English Law' (1999) 19 Legal Studies 339 at 345.
[175] Endelman, above n 173, p 132.

For women, working conditions were particularly dire, with many of them working as homeworkers in dismal dwellings while at the same time looking after children and doing housework. Poverty-struck and often in ill health, these refugees inspired not sympathy but virulent anti-Semitism. Jews were blamed for their own plight and accused of undercutting local labour conditions. One consequence was the Aliens Act 1905, which gave immigration officers the power to refuse entry to 'undesirable' immigrants, and was clearly understood as an instrument to prevent further Jewish immigration.[176] It was only the enactment of effective factory legislation beginning in 1901, and the growth of Jewish trade unions, which led to the elimination of Jewish sweated labour.[177]

The Second World War signalled unparalleled horrors for the Jews of Europe. Although British Jews escaped the death and destruction that swept over their continental Jewish communities, they could not avoid their repercussions.[178] Despite the defeat of the Nazis, fascism and anti-Semitism continued to plague the Jewish communities in the immediate post-war period.[179] However, in the decades after the war, anti-Semitism gradually declined, economic mobility accelerated, and the inner-city, Jewish working class all but disappeared.[180] As with other minorities, a major factor which contributed to increasing prosperity in this period was the opening up of educational possibilities, assisted in particular by the abolition of secondary school fees in 1944 and the expansion of red-brick universities in the 1960s. Quotas limiting Jewish entry to private schools, which were the subject of much discussion in the 1970s, had receded from the scene in the 1980s and 1990s.[181] This coincided with the decline in social and economic discrimination against Jews. At the same time, there were more inner divisions. As with other communities, there has been an unexpected rise of religious Orthodoxy, while at the same time a trend towards secularization, cultural Judaism, and assimilation. Indeed, for most Jews at the end of the twentieth century, as for most non-Jews, religion was at the margins of their lives, replaced by cultural or national identification.

---

[176] Repealed 12 April 1920 by Aliens Order 1920 under Aliens Restriction (Amendment) Act 1919.
[177] Hepple, above n 70, pp 68–9. Note that by 1939 a further 50,000 Jews sought refuge here from the Nazis.
[178] Endelman, above n 173, p 183.   [179] Ibid, p 232.
[180] Ibid, p 229.   [181] Ibid, pp 242–3.

The Jewish community is now one of the smallest religious minorities, numbering about 285,000. Although well established and relatively prosperous, the Jewish community has again found itself the subject of increasing anti-Semitism in the past decade. Indeed, the All-Party Parliamentary Group against Anti-Semitism reported in 2006 that violence, desecration of property, and intimidation directed against Jews were on the rise.[182] Equally worrying was the fact that anti-Semitic discourse seemed to be gaining legitimacy in some contexts, including some university campuses. Swift responses by the government had some effect, but in 2008, the European Commission against Racism and Intolerance (ECRI) noted with concern that the total number of anti-Semitic incidents was still the third highest ever, and a total of 260 anti-Semitic incidents occurred in the first four weeks of 2009 alone. Anti-Semitic discourse in the press and radio websites also continues to rise.[183]

More recently, it has been the Muslim population which has borne the brunt of religious discrimination in the UK. By 2008, there were 2.42 million Muslims living in Britain,[184] the fastest growing and largest minority religion. Muslims have been in Britain for at least two centuries. From the very start, the Muslim population was characterized by wide ethnic and national diversity. Indeed, as Ansari argues, their Muslim identity was generally of less importance than their social, economic, and ethnic backgrounds.[185] The earliest settlers ranged from Turkish political refugees, to Moroccan and other Arab merchants, to maritime workers from India, Egypt, Malaya, Turkey, Yemen, and Somalia. After the Second World War, and particularly during the 1960s, Muslims began to migrate to Britain in much larger numbers, as part of the major migration already referred to. Most came from South Asia, but others came from parts of the Middle East, Africa, and Cyprus. After the institution of strict immigration controls, the nature of migration changed, from workers seeking jobs, to political and religious dissidents seeking asylum. These included Muslims from Africa and Arab countries: Iraqis, Algerians, Turkish Kurds, Libyans, Palestinians and Iranians. Similarly, asylum seekers from Somalia, Eritrea, Afghanistan, Algeria, and Bosnia tended to be largely Muslim.

---

[182] Report of the All-Party Parliamentary Inquiry into Anti-Semitism (The Stationery Office, 2006) <http://www.antisemitism.org.uk/publications/materials-publications>).

[183] European Commission on Racism and Intolerance (ECRI), Report on the United Kingdom (Fourth Monitoring Cycle Council of Europe, 2010), p 39.

[184] Labour Force Survey, September 2008.

[185] Ansari, above n 74.

As a result of this diversity in origin, culture, language, and even religious tradition, it is a mistake to regard British Muslims at the start of the twenty-first century as ethnically or ideologically homogeneous.[186] By far the largest group of British Muslims at the end of the twentieth century were Pakistani in origin, with significant numbers of Bangladeshi and Indian origin. However, there are also sizeable Turkish, Egyptian, and Iraqi Muslim populations, as well as relatively small groups of Muslims from Somalia, Yemen, and Morocco.[187] Evidence suggests that Muslim migrants have preferred to live in communities of their own ethnic group, seeking out similar communities even when moving out of poor areas into more affluent ones.[188] Similarly, the resulting socio-economic pattern is far from uniform. In a pattern remarkably similar to that of Jewish immigrants earlier in the century, first-generation immigrants tended to fill the most menial of jobs, gradually becoming small entrepreneurs once they had amassed sufficient capital. Punjabi Muslims worked in factories until they had saved up enough capital to set up as small traders, slowly expanding into wholesale and manufacturing, particularly in textiles.[189] Turkish Cypriots, by contrast, tended to be concentrated in the catering trade, setting up Turkish-run cafes which then acted as magnets for further Turkish Cypriot migration. Similarly, many Moroccans came specifically to work in Arab-owned casinos and nightclubs.[190]

Discrimination on religious grounds against Muslims takes various forms. The virulent wave of Islamophobia in the wake of the terrorist attacks on the World Trade Center in 2001 has been the source of chief concern. It is difficult to discern the extent of criminal action motivated by Islamophobia, since crime statistics do not monitor this as a separate category, but the ECRI expresses concern at the negative image of Muslims often portrayed in the British media.[191] Other research suggests that twice as many Muslim tenants (9 per cent) reported being the victim of harassment compared to 4 per cent of all tenants.[192] Nor is the extent of religious discrimination in access to the labour market clearly documented. However, cases before the courts have revealed

---

[186] Ibid, p 2.   [187] Ibid, p 168.
[188] Ibid, p 178.   [189] Ibid, p 150.
[190] Ibid, p 151.   [191] ECRI, above n 183, pp 41–2.
[192] J Flint, 'Faith and Housing in England: Promoting Community Cohesion or Contributing to Urban Segregation?' (2010) 36 Journal of Ethnic and Migration Studies 257 at 263.

discrimination on grounds of religious dress, time off for prayers on a Friday, and similar religious manifestation.

There is also a sizeable Hindu population in England, numbering about 546,982 at the last census. Hindu migration is relatively recent, dating from the post-war period: indeed the 2001 census found that 63 per cent of Hindus were born outside the UK. Hindus from India began arriving in 1947 at the time of Indian independence and partition, while others were actively recruited by the British government to fill skills shortages. A second group consists of East African Asians, expelled from Idi Amin's Uganda in the 1960s and 70s. Having lost all their wealth and property, these migrants were initially relatively poor, but quickly caught up and were, by the end of the twentieth century, well established. More recent immigrants have come as refugees from Sri Lanka's bitter civil war. Hindus are less ethnically diverse than British Muslims: of the Hindus identified by the 2001 census in England, 97 per cent classified themselves ethnically as Asian or Asian British. Nevertheless, in a survey conducted in 2006, 75 per cent of respondents to an online survey noted that they described themselves as Hindu, rather than by their ethnicity,[193] although the younger generation feel less strongly.

The Hindu population in the UK is predominantly urban, with by far the largest numbers living in London. Hindu communities are relatively successful compared to the general population. Hindus are over-represented in the professional and managerial categories. Hindu men are also more likely than average to be self-employed.[194] Hindus, both men and women, are more likely than the general population to have an educational qualification, although women are more likely to be unemployed than in other groups. It is notable that although 50 per cent of those questioned in the online survey felt that they had been discriminated against because they were Asian, less than a quarter (23 per cent) stated that they had been discriminated against because they were Hindus.[195] Some of the most important challenges for equality in relation to Hinduism come from internal inequalities, particularly the persistence of the caste system among British Hindus. Similarly 38 per cent of

---

[193] Department for Communities and Local Government, *Connecting British Hindus: An Enquiry into the Identity and Public Policy Engagement of British Hindus* (Runnymede Trust, commissioned by the Hindu Forum of Britain, 2006).

[194] Ibid, p 18.

[195] Ibid, pp 55–6.

female respondents to the online survey stated that they believed that women were not yet treated equally to men.[196]

Despite the removal of formal restrictions on specific religious minorities and the introduction of protection against religious discrimination, Britain remains culturally and politically primarily Christian. The Anglican Church of England retains its position as the established church in England, while the Presbyterian Church of Scotland performs the same role in Scotland. There are numerous formal links between State and Church. Thus the reigning monarch is head of the established Church, and appoints the bishops of the Church of England, on the advice of the prime minister (who, by convention, chooses from two nominees put forward by the Church itself). Conversely, the Church of England is represented in Parliament, with 25 seats in the House of Lords automatically allocated to Church of England archbishops and bishops.

The result is that religious minorities, while tolerated, have had in practice to find their place within the framework established by the culture and religion of Christianity. In 2009, Christianity remained by far the biggest single religion, with 42.66 million adherents.[197] Christians on the whole are less devout than other minorities: the Citizenship Survey of 2007–8 found that among people who said they were Christian, only 31 per cent said they were practising Christians, while among Muslims 76 per cent were practising, with similar proportions for Hindus, Sikhs, and Buddhists. Nevertheless, Britain is far from a secular society. Major Christian holy days are public holidays, and, because the English education system developed in partnership with the mainstream churches, a large proportion of State schools are maintained Church of England schools. Moreover, a daily act of collective worship is mandatory at all State schools,[198] and statute provides that 'the required collective worship shall be wholly or mainly of a broadly Christian character'.[199] In addition, religious education is compulsory at all State schools and although the syllabus can be decided locally, it must reflect the fact that 'the religious traditions in Britain are in the main Christian whilst taking account of the teaching and practices of the other principal religious represented in Great

---

[196] Ibid, p 65.
[197] Labour Force Survey (September 2008).
[198] School Standards and Framework Act 1998, s 70.
[199] Ibid, Sch 20.

Britain'.[200] Parents are, however, permitted to withdraw their children from religious education.[201]

One consequence of the Christian emphasis in schools has been the demand by minority religions for faith schools. Since 1944, communities of a particular faith have been able to apply to set up schools in the State sector in response to demand from parents.[202] Of the 20,000 State-maintained schools in England in 2010, almost 7,000 were faith schools.[203] Of these 98 per cent are associated with the major Christian denominations, with 30 per cent Catholic and 68 per cent Church of England. Of the remaining 58 maintained faith schools, 38 are Jewish, 11 Muslim, 4 Sikh, 1 Greek Orthodox, 1 Hindu, 1 Quaker, 1 Seventh Day Adventist, and 1 United Reform Church. In the private sector, there are a further 118 Muslim schools, 49 Jewish, 2 Hindu, 1 Buddhist, and 1 Sikh.[204] Faith schools in the maintained sector are permitted to give priority to applicants who are of the faith of the school. Some faith schools (voluntary aided faith schools) may fill all teaching places with staff of their faith and others (foundation and voluntary-controlled faith schools) may reserve up to one-fifth of their teaching posts for persons who are selected for their competence to teach religious education in accordance with the school's faith. However, maintained faith schools must follow the national curriculum.

Faith schools reflect some of the stark dilemmas raised by the principle of non-discrimination on grounds of religion. On the one hand, faith schools might constitute an appropriate accommodation of diverse religions and cultures. On the other hand, they may entrench boundaries between religious communities, fostering mutual suspicion and preventing interfaith dialogue. However, so long as there is no genuinely secular alternative within the State system, it will be difficult to resist demands for schools for adherents of other faiths.

(III) LEGAL DEVELOPMENTS

Protection from discrimination on grounds of religion was deliberately omitted from the protection afforded by the RRA. The statute did, however, include 'ethnic origins' as part of the definition of 'racial

---

[200] Education Act 1996, s 375(3).
[201] School Standards and Framework Act 1998, s 71.
[202] Ibid, s 69(3); Religious Character of Schools (Designation Procedure) Regulations 1998 (SI 1998/2535).
[203] Edubase, 2010.
[204] See: <http://www.teachernet.gov.uk/wholeschool/faithschools/>.

grounds'. The courts accepted that Jews and Sikhs could be regarded as ethnic groups.[205] But, as we have seen, Muslims cannot be so regarded. The only protection available was the possibility of indirect discrimination, for example on grounds of nationality.

It was only after intervention by the EU that discrimination on grounds of religion and belief became unlawful in the UK. The Employment Directive, passed under Article 13 of the Treaty of Amsterdam, required Member States to legislate to prohibit discrimination on grounds of religion or belief,[206] and this was implemented by regulations in 2003.[207] Religion or belief is now a protected characteristic for the purposes of the EA 2010, so that direct and indirect discrimination, as well as victimization on grounds of religion or belief are now unlawful. However, there is still no full equivalence with other grounds. In particular, although the EA 2010 protects individuals against harassment on grounds of religion or belief in employment, this protection does not extend to harassment on grounds of religion or belief in the provision of services, the exercise of public functions,[208] the disposal of premises,[209] and in recruitment or admission to schools. (As will be seen, harassment could, however, be a species of direct discrimination.) This reflects some concern at the possibility of conflict with the protection of freedom of expression under Article 10 ECHR.

More controversial is the question of how conflicting equalities can be managed. In particular, should it be permissible for religious people to argue that because of their religious convictions, they should be permitted to discriminate on grounds of gender, sexual orientation, or transsexuality? For example, should it be lawful to refuse to accept women priests or gay teachers? Should an individual marriage officer be permitted to refuse to perform a civil partnership ceremony for a same-sex couple on the grounds that this would be inconsistent with his or her religious beliefs? In balancing these conflicting demands, UK law has given priority to religion over other grounds of discrimination, but only in a narrow range of circumstances. Where employment is for the purposes of an organized religion, the employer may require a person to be of a particular sex or not be a transsexual, or may apply a requirement that is related to a person's sexual orientation or marriage

---

[205] *Mandla v Lee* [1983] 2 AC 548 (HL).   [206] Council Directive 2000/78/EC.
[207] Employment Equality (Religion or Belief) Regulations 2003 (SI 2003/1660).
[208] EA 2010, s 29(8).   [209] Ibid, s 33(6).

or civil partnership. In such a case, the employer must prove that the requirement is applied to comply with the doctrines of the religion, or to avoid conflict with the strongly held religious convictions of a significant number of the religion's followers.[210] Policy-makers claim that the scope of this exception is limited, for example to permit the Church to require priests to be male. The High Court, interpreting the slightly differently worded predecessor to the current exception, limited it to the appointment of religious leaders and teachers.[211] However, this limitation is not explicit. Earlier drafts of the EA 2010 did in fact include a provision expressly limiting the exception to purposes which mainly involved leading or assisting in the observation of religious liturgy or practice, or doctrinal explanation or promotion. However, this definition was removed from the legislation by the House of Lords at committee stage. The result is to open up the legislation to challenge under EU law. The European Commission, in a Reasoned Opinion in November 2009 has already warned that the UK exception to the principle of non-discrimination on grounds of sexual orientation is too broad, and therefore breaches EU law.[212]

Should it be lawful for a religion to discriminate against other religions? It makes sense to permit different religions to require religious leaders, such as priests, imams, or rabbis, to be a member of the relevant faith. Under both EU and UK law, employers may impose a requirement that a person be of a particular religion or belief. Again this is limited to specific circumstances: the employer must show that, having regard to the religious ethos and the nature or context of the work, being of a particular religion or belief is an occupational requirement, and that applying such a requirement is a proportionate means of achieving a legitimate aim.[213]

There are also other sources of protection against religious discrimination. The ECHR for its part includes religion as one of the prohibited grounds of discrimination under Article 14, as well as providing a freestanding right to freedom of religion under Article 9. In addition, it is now a criminal offence to stir up hatred against persons on religious grounds.[214] Also important has been the policy response from the UK government. From 2004, the government took a conscious decision to

---

[210] Ibid, Sch 9 para 2.
[211] *R (on the application of Amicus-MSF) v Secretary of State for Trade and Industry* [2004] IRLR 430 (High Court). See further L Vickers, above n 167, p 140.
[212] IP/09/1778.
[213] EA 2010, Sch 9 para 3.
[214] Public Order Act 1986, Pt 3A (inserted by Racial and Religious Hatred Act 2006).

work positively with faith-based communities rather than attempt to erect barriers between the supposedly public and private realms.[215]

V SEXUAL ORIENTATION

Discrimination on grounds of sexual orientation is a particularly vicious denial of dignity and equality, since it strikes out against the sexual intimacy at the very core of an individual's identity and well-being. It involves not just the equality right, but also the right to privacy and family life; and, even more fundamentally, the basic right to the free development of one's personality. Yet homosexuality was a criminal offence until 1967, and discrimination on grounds of sexual orientation remained lawful throughout the twentieth century. It is only in the past decade that real strides towards equality have been taken. Even with this progress, the basic right to equality before the law has still not been fully achieved. There are three dimensions to equality in this context: first, formal equality before the law in the form of decriminalization and removal of actual legal impediments; secondly, equal recognition of same-sex partnerships; and, thirdly, protection against discrimination of all kinds on the grounds of sexual orientation, including harassment and violence.

The first dimension, formal equality before the law, has been slow in coming. Same-sex sexual activity between men was decriminalized in 1967, although only for sexual activity between two consenting men in private. However, inequalities remained. The age of consent, which was set at 21 (compared to 16 for heterosexual or lesbian sexual activity[216]), was not fully equalized until 2000,[217] and then only after amendments to this effect had been twice rejected by the House of Lords. It took a further three years before the severe criminal prohibitions on homosexual behaviour in public were removed.[218] A particularly blatant manifestation of persecution of gay men and lesbian women was the policy of exclusion from the military. Attempts to put an end to this policy in

---

[215] Communities and Local Government, *Preventing Violent Extremism: Winning Hearts and Minds* (April 2007), p 10.

[216] Sexual Offences Act 1956, s 12(1).

[217] Sexual Offences (Amendment) Act 2000; see also *Sutherland v UK*, Application no 25186/94 (Commission Report, 1 July 1997). Note that it was reduced to 18 in 1994: Sexual Offences Act 1967, s 1 as amended by Criminal Justice and Public Order Act 1994.

[218] Sexual Offences Act 2003, Sch 7 para 1. See generally R Wintemute, 'Sexual Orientation Discrimination' in C McCrudden and G Chambers (eds), *Individual Rights and the Law in Britain* (Clarendon Press, 1994).

Parliament, in the EU, and in the domestic courts all failed, until a robust decision of the ECtHR in 1999 found this to be a breach of the right to respect for one's private life.[219] The policy of exclusion has now finally been lifted.

However, progress towards equality has been far from consistent. The Conservative government in power from 1979 to 1997 carried its hostility to homosexuality so far as to enact the notorious section 28 of the Local Government Act 1988, which prohibited local authorities from intentionally promoting homosexuality or promoting the teaching of the 'acceptability of homosexuality as a pretended family relationship'. Attempts by the Labour government elected in 1997 to repeal the legislation were repeatedly blocked by the House of Lords. The provision was not fully repealed until 2003.[220]

The second dimension, recognition of the depth and permanence of same-sex relationships, has been even slower in coming. However, the twenty-first century has seen remarkable progress. Shortly before the Human Rights Act 1998 (HRA) came into force, the House of Lords, in a surprisingly perceptive interpretation of the reference to 'family' in the relevant legislation, held that a man who had lived in a long-standing, loving, and monogamous homosexual relationship counted as a member of the family of his partner. He was therefore entitled under the Rent Act 1977 to succeed to his partner's tenancy rights.[221] This was reinforced after the HRA came into force. In the seminal case of *Ghaidan v Mendoza*, the House of Lords held that statutory provisions which treated same-sex partners less favourably than other co-habiting partners in relation to the right to inherit a statutory tenancy constituted a breach of Articles 8 and 14 ECHR (the rights to home and family life together with the right to equality).[222]

Particularly important has been the role of the ECtHR. The Court has always been unwilling to move ahead of what it regards as the consensus among contracting States. On the other hand, when a sufficient consensus appears to have been formed, it is capable of reaching a robust decision in favour of equality for same-sex couples. Thus in *Salgueiro da Silva Mouta v Portugal*,[223] a Portuguese court refused to give a father custody of his children on marital breakdown, on the

---

[219] *Smith and Grady v UK* (2000) 29 EHRR 493.
[220] Local Government Act 2003, Sch 8(1) para 1.
[221] *Fitzpatrick v Sterling Housing* [1999] 2 WLR 1113 (HL).
[222] *Ghaidan v Godin-Mendoza* [2004] UKHL 30, [2004] 2 AC 557.
[223] *Salgueiro da Silva Mouta v Portugal* [2001] 31 EHRR 1055.

grounds that he was a homosexual. The Court held that this was a breach of his right not to be discriminated against in respect of his right to family life.[224] Adoption by same-sex couples initially encountered more resistance. Thus in *Fretté v France* in 2004, the Court found that it was 'indisputable that there is no common ground on the question' of whether homosexual couples may adopt children.

Since the delicate issues raised in the case, therefore, touch on areas where there is little common ground amongst the Member States of the Council of Europe . . . a wide margin of appreciation must be left to the authorities of each State.[225]

Applying this analysis, the Court held that the differential treatment afforded to same-sex couples in relation to adoption was objective and reasonable and therefore not discriminatory. However, only four years later, in *EB v France*,[226] the Court reversed this decision and held that a person seeking to adopt cannot be prevented from doing so merely on the ground of his or her homosexuality. Notably, it observed that 'the Convention is a living instrument, to be interpreted in the light of present-day conditions'.[227]

A similar progression can be seen in relation to the granting of social security benefits to same-sex partners. As recently as 2001, the Court took the view that there was still little common ground between contracting States as to the extent to which they recognized same-sex relationships. Granting the State a wide margin of appreciation, it held that the applicant's relationships with his same-sex partner did not fall within the right to respect for family life.[228] However, by 2004, it was ready to acknowledge that contracting States should only have a narrow margin of appreciation in relation to difference in treatment based on sex or sexual orientation. In such cases,

the principle of proportionality does not merely require that the measure chosen is in principle suited for realising the aim sought. It must also be shown that it was *necessary* to exclude persons living in a homosexual relationship from the scope of [the relevant provision] . . . in order to achieve that aim.[229]

However, here too, progress has been uneven. In a case in 2006, the House of Lords still took the view that in the present state of Strasbourg

---

[224] Ibid.
[225] *Fretté v France* (2004) 38 EHRR 21 at para 41.
[226] *EB v France* (2008) 47 EHRR 21.
[227] Ibid, para 92.
[228] *Mata Estevez v Spain*, Reports of Judgments and Decisions 2001-VI, p 311.
[229] *Karner v Austria* (2004) 38 EHRR 24 at paras 40–1.

jurisprudence homosexual relationships did not fall within the scope of the right to respect for family life protected by Article 8. Therefore, although a statutory scheme drew a distinction based on sexual orientation, this was not sufficient in itself to bring the complaint within the ambit of discrimination under Article 14 or the right to respect for family and private life under Article 8.[230]

The biggest step forward in the recognition of the depth and permanence of same-sex relationships has been the Civil Partnership Act 2004. For the first time, couples who register themselves as civil partners are entitled to the same treatment as married couples with respect to wills, the administration of estates, and family provision.[231] Similarly, the relationship of civil partnership is recognized for the purposes of adoption,[232] and a civil partner can acquire parental responsibility for his or her civil partner's child in the same way as a married person.[233] Moreover, the civil partner of a woman who gives birth by means of artificial insemination is automatically recognized as the other parent of the child, unless she withdraws her consent.[234] The Act also provides for dissolution of civil partnerships.

The Act has had an immediate impact. A total of 33,956 partnerships were formed between December 2005 (when the Act came into force) and the end of 2008.[235] There were also a number of dissolutions. From April 2010, it is also possible for male couples who have a child through egg donation and surrogacy to apply for a Parental Order which, if granted, would enable them both to be named parents on the child's birth certificate.

However, the Act stops short of affording same-sex couples the fundamental right to marriage itself. Gay couples are still denied the right to marry under UK law;[236] and the ECtHR has confined the right in Article 12 ECHR to marry and found a family to the traditional marriage between persons of opposite sexes.[237] Reflecting its long-standing reluctance to enter into areas of political and social controversy, it has held that there is no sufficient consensus in Europe as a whole to

---

[230] *M v Secretary of State for Work and Pensions* [2006] UKHL 11.
[231] Civil Partnership Act 2004, s 71.
[232] Ibid, s 79.
[233] Ibid, s 75.
[234] Human Fertilisation and Embryology Act 2008, s 42.
[235] Office for National Statistics, 'Civil Partnerships' (2008, available at: <http://www.statistics.gov.uk/cci/nugget.asp?id=1685>).
[236] Matrimonial Causes Act 1973.
[237] *Rees v UK*, Series A No 106 (1986) 9 EHRR 56; *Cossey v UK*, Series A No 184 [1990] EHHR 622.

warrant recognition of the right of same-sex couples to marry. This stance was endorsed by the British High Court in a case brought by two women who wished their legal marriage in Wisconsin to be recognized in Britain. The court rejected their claim. According Porter J:

By withholding from same-sex partners the actual title and status of marriage, the Government declined to alter the deep-rooted and almost universal recognition of marriage as a relationship between a man and a woman, but without in any way interfering with or failing to recognise the right of same-sex couples to respect for their private or family life... Not only does English law recognise and not interfere with the right of such couples to live in a very close, loving, and monogamous relationship; it accords them also the benefits of marriage in all but name.[238]

Moreover, the judge held, that the discrimination between same-sex and opposite-sex couples was justifiable. Although the denial of the right to marry discriminated between same-sex and opposite-sex couples, it pursued the legitimate aim of 'preserving and supporting the concept and institution of marriage', while at the same time according, in the judge's view, all the rights, responsibilities, benefits, and advantages of civil marriages save the name.[239]

This contrasts strikingly with other jurisdictions, such as that in South Africa, which regard it as clearly discriminatory as well as deeply offensive and a breach of human dignity to preclude same-sex couples from the right to marry.[240] On this view, a 'separate but equal' regime, such as the Civil Partnership Act, ignores the fact that, regardless of legal rights and responsibilities, marriage and civil partnerships are not 'equal symbolically, when it is marriage that is the key social institution, celebrated and recognised around the world'.[241] Exclusion is inevitably demeaning and an assault on the dignity of same-sex couples.

The third element, anti-discrimination law, has been similarly slow to address sexual orientation. Until 2000, it was lawful both in domestic and EU law to discriminate against individuals on grounds of their sexual orientation. Attempts by litigants to argue that sexual orientation discrimination was a species of sex discrimination were rejected.[242] However, under new powers given by the Treaty of Amsterdam, the

---

[238] *Wilkinson v Kitzinger* [2006] EWHC 2022 (Fam) (High Court), para 88.
[239] Ibid, para 122.
[240] *Minister of Home Affairs v Fourie (CCT 60/04)* [2005] ZACC 19, 2006 (3) BCLR 355 (CC); 2006 (1) SA 524 (CC) (South African Constitutional Court).
[241] See affidavit of applicant in *Wilkinson v Kitzinger*, above n 238, para 19.
[242] Case C-249/96 *Grant v South-West Trains Ltd* [1998] ECR I-621.

EU Employment Directive was passed, requiring Member States to legislate to prohibit direct and indirect discrimination, as well as harassment, on grounds of sexual orientation.[243] Notably, the preamble states that the Directive is without prejudice to national laws on marital status and the benefits dependent thereon.[244] The Directive was implemented into UK law by regulations in 2003,[245] and this area is now governed by the EA 2010.

The new provisions make significant strides forward. Not only is sexual orientation now a protected characteristic for the purposes of most aspects of discrimination law; in addition, the list of protected characteristics now includes civil partnership, and marriage and civil partnership are almost invariably protected in the same ways. Discrimination on grounds of sexual orientation is now unlawful not only in relation to employment, but also to the provision of services, public functions, the disposal of premises, and education. Significantly, too, the prohibition on civil partnership ceremonies taking place on religious premises has now been lifted, although there is no obligation on religious organizations to host civil partnerships if they do not wish to do so.[246]

However, sexual orientation discrimination is still not treated as on a par with race and gender discrimination. Harassment on grounds of sexual orientation is specifically excluded from protection in the context of education, the provision of services, public functions, and disposal and management of premises,[247] although harassment on other grounds, such as gender, race, and disability is unlawful in these contexts. Instead, a victim of homophobic harassment or bullying in contexts outside employment would need to prove direct discrimination.[248] This reverses many of the gains made in turning harassment into a specific species of discrimination. Moreover, marriage and civil partnership are excluded from protection against discrimination in relation to the provision of services, public functions, education, and the disposal of premises. Finally, as we have seen, it is not unlawful to discriminate on grounds of sexual orientation where the employment is for the purposes of an organized religion and the employer applies a requirement related to sexual orientation so as to comply with the

---

[243] EC Directive 2000/78.   [244] Ibid, para 22.
[245] Employment Equality (Sexual Orientation) Regulations 2003 (SI 2003/1661).
[246] EA 2010, s 202.
[247] Ibid, ss 29(8), 33(6).   [248] Ibid, s 212(5).

doctrines of the religion or to avoid conflicting with the strongly held religious convictions of a significant number of the religion's followers.[249] The European Commission, in a Reasoned Opinion in November 2009, has already warned that the UK exception to the principle of non-discrimination on grounds of sexual orientation is too broad, breaching EU law.[250]

In many respects, the legal developments have reflected changing social attitudes towards lesbian, gay, and bisexual (LGB) people. While there have been rapid strides towards equality, there remain deep-seated currents of homophobia. The nature of inequality in this respect differs from that in relation to women and ethnic minorities in that it does not manifest primarily in socio-economic disadvantage. Indeed, the 2010 Triennial Review reports that the socio-economic position of LGB people is generally favourable, and poverty is not a major concern for the LGB community.[251] Instead, the dimension of equality which is most pronounced in relation to LGB people concerns failure to accord them equal dignity and respect. This is particularly true in relation to homophobic bullying at schools. Recent research has shown astonishingly high levels of such bullying. One survey of over 1,000 students in British schools in 2007 showed that almost two-thirds of LGB young people have experienced direct bullying, rising to three-quarters in faith schools. As many as 97 per cent reported regularly hearing homophobic language in school.[252] A survey of teachers found around half (46 per cent) of secondary school teachers in England acknowledged that bullying of pupils seen as LGB is common, but only 16 per cent of teachers said that their school was 'very active' in promoting equality and respect for LGB pupils.[253]

Indeed, fear of violence and suspicion remains pervasive. A recent survey found that as many as 70 per cent of LGB respondents believed that they are more likely to be insulted and harassed than heterosexual persons. Close to 50 per cent said that they were at greater risk of physical assault.[254] Moreover, many LGB people are concerned that they might encounter prejudice within the civil justice system, to the extent that about 75 per cent of victims of hate crime do not report the

---

[249] EA 2010, Sch 9 para 2.
[250] IP/09/1778.   [251] *How Fair is Britain?*, above n 77, Part II, p 486.
[252] Ibid, p 322; *Education for All: The Experiences of Young Gay People in Britain's Schools* (Stonewall, 2007), p 2.
[253] *How Fair is Britain?*, above n 77, p 322.   [254] Ibid, vol 2, p 243.

incident to the police.[255] A similar pattern can be seen in the workplace. Although there are not large-scale data on this topic, the Triennial Review in 2010 reports that LGB adults are twice as likely to report discrimination, bullying, or harassment at work than other employees. The cumulative effect is stark: LGB people are vulnerable to high levels of stress-related ill health. Indeed, they are identified as one of the most stressed groups of individuals in society.[256]

VI GENDER REASSIGNMENT

A similar host of legal disabilities has, until very recently, faced transsexual people but, here too, rapid strides have been made in the last two decades. This time, it was the ECJ which led the way. Thus in the seminal case of *P v S*,[257] the ECJ held that discrimination on the grounds of gender reassignment was a species of sex discrimination. Gender reassignment is now fully protected against direct discrimination, indirect discrimination, harassment, and victimization, whether in employment, public functions, services, disposal of premises, or education.[258] The protection does not depend on a person having gender reassignment surgery or being under medical supervision: it applies to anyone who is 'proposing to undergo, is undergoing or has undergone a process (or part of a process) for the purpose of reassigning the person's sex by changing physiological or other attributes of sex'.[259] The statute specifically provides that it is discriminatory to treat a person who is absent from work because he or she is undergoing the process of gender assignment less favourably than a person who is absent due to sickness or injury.[260] However, as in sexual orientation, harassment in schools on grounds of gender reassignment is not specifically protected, leaving the applicant to claim under the direct discrimination provisions.[261]

Important strides have also been made in relation to marriage. In the UK, the major impediment to marriage was found in the Matrimonial Causes Act 1973, which stated that a person's sex was that which appeared on their birth certificate. This confined transgendered persons to a double identity throughout their lives. Several

---

[255] Ibid, vol 2, p 161.   [256] Ibid, vol 2, p 452.

[257] Case C-13/94 *P v S and Cornwall County Council* [1996] ECR I-2143.

[258] Except in relation to harassment: see below.

[259] EA 2010, s 7.   [260] Ibid, s 16.   [261] Ibid, s 85(10).

attempts to argue that this was a breach of the right to marry under the ECHR received a hostile reception before the ECtHR, which refused to recognize that transsexual persons had a right to marry a person of the sex opposite to their reassigned gender.[262] In addition, the ECtHR has insisted that there was no sufficient consensus among contracting States on the moral, social, and legal issues raised in respect of transsexuality to permit the Court to interpret Article 8 as imposing an obligation on a State to recognize the transsexual partner of a woman as the father of the children she conceived by artificial insemination.[263]

However, in the seminal case of *Goodwin* in 2002,[264] the ECtHR reversed its previous jurisprudence. Although Article 12 refers in express terms to the right of a man and woman to marry, the Court held that the determination of gender should no longer be determined by purely biological criteria. 'The allocation of sex in national law to that registered at birth is a limitation impairing the very essence of the right to marry.'[265] Following the *Goodwin* decision, the UK House of Lords held that this aspect of the Matrimonial Causes Act 1973 was incompatible with the Convention.[266] The case provided added impetus for legislation already proceeding through Parliament in the form of the Gender Recognition Act 2004. Under this Act, transgendered persons can apply to a Gender Recognition Panel for a 'full gender recognition certificate' on the basis that they have or have had gender dysphoria, have lived in the acquired gender for at least two years, and intend to do so until death.[267] With a full gender recognition certificate, the person's gender becomes for all purposes the acquired gender. Most importantly, a person with such a certificate is able to marry someone of the opposite gender to his or her acquired gender.

However, legal equality for transgendered persons is still not complete. Clergymen, who are under a duty under the Marriage Act 1949 to marry anyone in their parish, are exempt from that duty where they reasonably believe that the gender of one of the parties' is acquired under the Gender Recognition Act.[268] Similarly, such a refusal does not

---

[262] *Rees v United Kingdom* (1987) 9 EHRR 56; *Cossey v United Kingdom* (1991) 13 EHRR 622; *Sheffield and Horsham v United Kingdom* (1999) 27 EHRR 163.
[263] *X, Y and Z v UK*, Case No 75/1995/582/667 (20 March 1997).
[264] *Goodwin v UK* (2002) 35 EHRR 18.
[265] Ibid, para 101.   [266] *Bellinger v Bellinger* [2003] UKHL 21.
[267] Gender Recognition Act 2004, s 2(1).   [268] Marriage Act 1949, s 5B.

amount to unlawful discrimination.[269] In this way, freedom of religion again takes priority over claims of discrimination on this ground.

VII DISABILITY

(I) CHALLENGES AND DILEMMAS

Disability differs from other types of discrimination in that it is a possibility which faces all members of society. The borderline between 'we' and 'they' is not only arbitrary but shifting. Nevertheless, able-bodied people tend to see disabled people as the 'Other', suppressing the knowledge, and the deep anxiety, that disability could come upon anyone at any time. Thus people with disabilities have always suffered from stigma, prejudice, and exclusion from society. The able-bodied norm is pervasive and exclusive: from public transport and pavements to working arrangements, to leisure and social facilities.

However, there remains considerable controversy as to how to formulate protection against discrimination in the context of disability. Central to the debate has been the conceptualization of disability itself. It has generally been assumed that the concept of disability points to functional limitations of an individual. This approach has come to be known as the 'medical model'. An alternative, 'social model', recognizes the role of society in creating disabling barriers. Social institutions, attitudes, and the built environment are constructed for able-bodied persons. Thus the problem consists not so much in functional limitations but in disabling barriers, whether attitudinal, physical, or political. This means that the social distinction which attaches to impairment, and not the impairment itself, should be the focus of legal intervention.

A second area of contention is the way in which discrimination against people with disabilities is characterized. One approach is to draw on the understanding of race discrimination, and regard people with disabilities as a 'discrete and insular' group which requires legal and human rights intervention because of its lack of voice in the democratic political process.[270] Thus in a striking parallel to the approach in early jurisprudence on race discrimination,[271] the Americans with Disabilities Act 1990[272] states that:

---

[269] EA 2010, Sch 3 para 24.
[270] *United States v Carolene Products Co* 304 US 144, 152 n4.
[271] See Chapter Three. [272] 104 STAT 327, 42 USC 1210.

Individuals with disabilities are a discrete and insular minority who have been faced with restrictions and limitations, subjected to a history of purposeful unequal treatment and relegated to a position of political powerlessness in our society, based on characteristics that are beyond the control of such individuals and resulting from stereotypic assumptions not truly indicative of the individual ability of such individuals to participate in and contribute to society.[273]

The advantage of this analysis is to emphasize the political and social aspect of disability. However, it also has some problematic implications. As a start, it depends on identifying people as 'disabled', which has proved notoriously difficult, both in the field of discrimination law and in that of social security.[274] This, argue opponents of the minority group analysis, is not just a technical legal difficulty. It reflects the social reality that disabled people do not form a discrete and insular group at all. Moreover, it is argued, a 'minority group' analysis sets people with disabilities apart as different and distinct. Disability is characterized as fixed and dichotomous: either one has a disability or one does not.[275] As Zola argues,

Seeing people with a disability as 'different' with 'special' needs, wants and rights in this currently perceived world of finite resources, they are pitted against the needs, wants and rights of the rest of the population.[276]

An alternative 'universalist view' suggests that, rather than demarcating a discrete and insular minority, disability should be regarded as fluid and continuous. 'Disability is a normal aspect of life; all kinds of disabilities can happen to all types of people at all stages in their normal lifecycles.'[277] As Bickenbach puts it: 'Disability is not a human attribute that demarks one portion of humanity from another; it is an infinitely various but universal feature of the human condition. No human has a complete repertoire of abilities.'[278] Advocates of universalism call for a

---

[273] Ibid, s 2(a)(7).

[274] D Mabbett, 'Why have Disability Categories in Social Security?' (2003) 11:3 *Benefits* 163–8.

[275] I K Zola, 'Towards the Necessary Universalizing of a Disability Policy' (1989) 67 *The Millbank Quarterly* 401; JE Bickenbach, S Chatterji, EM Badley, and TB Ustun, 'Models of Disablement, Universalism and the International Classification of Impairments, Disabilities and Handicaps' (1999) 48 Journal of Social Science and Medicine 1173 at 1182.

[276] Zola, ibid, at 406.

[277] UN Ad Hoc Committee on a Comprehensive and Integral International Convention on Protection and Promotion of the Rights and Dignity of Persons with Disabilities (New York, 2003), 'Issues and Emerging Trends Related to Advancement of Persons with Disabilities' Doc A/AC.265/2003/1, paras 9–10.

[278] Bickenbach et al, above n 275, p 1182.

policy that 'respects difference and widens the range of the normal'. Designing the environment only for people within a narrow range of ability is seen to accord special privilege to those who happen to fall within that range.[279] 'Disability policy is therefore not policy for some minority group; it is policy for all.'[280]

(II) LEGAL DEVELOPMENTS

Until the last decade of the twentieth century, disability was thought to be at most an issue for national assistance through social security or, in cases in which fault could be established, tort law. People with disabilities were depicted 'not as subjects with legal rights, but as objects of welfare, health and charity programs'.[281] The right to welfare came at a price: that of segregation, exclusion, and loss of self determination. In the employment field the only measure was one establishing 'special protection' for disabled people. The Disabled Persons (Employment) Act 1944 required employers of a substantial number of employees to employ a set quota of people registered as disabled, a quota which was enforced by criminal sanctions. However, compliance with the Act was negligible, partly because the conditions for registration as disabled were so severe as to exclude many genuinely disabled persons, and partly because of lack of proper enforcement. Major international human rights documents did not even mention disability as one of the grounds to be protected against discrimination. This is still true both of the ECHR and the International Covenant on Civil and Political Rights.

It was only in 1995, and after as many as 16 unsuccessful attempts, that the Disability Discrimination Act finally reached the statute books. Disability legislation at EU level was even more dilatory, with disability not included until the Employment Directive of 2000. Current anti-discrimination legislation in the UK and EU does not consistently follow any single model. On the one hand, the definition of disability has always followed a decidedly medical model. Thus the statutory definition of a disabled person refers to someone who has or had 'a physical or mental impairment and the impairment has a substantial and long-term adverse effect on [his or her] ability to carry out normal

---

[279] Ibid, p 1183.   [280] Ibid, p 1182.
[281] T Degener and G Quinn, 'A Survey of International Comparative and Regional Disability Law Reform' in *From Principles to Practice: An International Disability Law and Policy Symposium* (October 2000), p 3.

day to day activities'.[282] Much litigation has been expended on this definition, and many claims have fallen at this barrier.

On the other hand, in a strong affirmation of social model, the legislation includes a duty to make reasonable adjustments to avoid the disadvantage caused to disabled people by practices, criteria, or provisions or physical features of the environment. This includes a requirement to take reasonable steps to provide auxiliary aids.[283] In this way, it is expressly recognized that, instead of requiring conformity to the able-bodied norm, modification of the environment or of existing policies or practices is essential if people with disabilities are to have genuine equality of opportunity. Moreover, it is asymmetric: from the very start, the legislation has acknowledged that differential treatment of people with disabilities was necessary to achieve equality.

International law finally made express provision for people with disabilities in 2006, with the adoption of the UN Convention on the Rights of Persons with Disabilities. The Convention, in a powerful contrast to domestic legislation, manifests a culmination of the development of the 'social model' in relation to disability law. It rightly claims to signal a 'paradigm shift' in the approach to disability. Thus it comprehensively and emphatically views persons with disabilities as subjects with rights, rather than objects of charity, medical treatment, or social protection. Central to this is the principle, set out in the preamble, that 'disability results from the interaction between persons with impairments and attitudinal and environmental barriers that hinders their full and effective participation in society on an equal basis with others'. For example, a person using a wheelchair faces barriers to employment, not because of the wheelchair but because of the design of buses, buildings, and other parts of the built environment.

As well as a broad definition of disability, the Convention adopts an understanding of substantive equality which closely follows the multi-dimensional approach set out in Chapter One. This, it will be recalled, identified four dimensions of equality: the recognition dimension (respect for dignity and basic humanity), the redistributive dimension (redressing disadvantage), the transformative dimension (accommodation of difference), and the participative dimension. The first dimension, respect for dignity and basic humanity, is a basic principle of the Convention, which also emphasizes individual autonomy, including the freedom to make one's own choices; and independence. Notably, this

---

[282] EA 2010, s 6(1).   [283] Ibid, s 20.

includes respect for the evolving capacities of children with disabilities and respect for the right of children with disabilities to preserve their identities. So far as the redistributive dimension is concerned, the drafters of the Convention were well aware that equality could be no more than a gesture if it was not allied with the duty to ensure that basic minimum rights—such as education, housing, health, work, and social security—were genuinely equally accessible to people with disabilities. For example, States parties undertake to ensure not only that people with disabilities have the same range, quality, and standard of health care available to others, but also to provide those health services needed specifically by people with disabilities particularly because of their disability. The same is true for education. The transformative dimension is reflected in the reference to respect for difference and acceptance of persons with disabilities as part of human diversity and humanity. Central to this is the duty of reasonable accommodation, which requires

the necessary and appropriate modification and adjustments... where needed in a particular case, to ensure to persons with disabilities the enjoyment or exercise on an equal basis with others of all human rights and fundamental freedoms.

Fourthly, it stresses the central role of full and effective participation and inclusion in society. This is expressed as the duty to ensure both accessibility, and full and effective participation in political, public, and cultural life. The UK signed and ratified the Convention in 2009, As of April 2010, there were 144 signatories and 85 ratifications.

(III) CURRENT INEQUALITIES

People with disabilities constitute a significant section of the population. The Family Resources Survey estimates that the disabled constitute 21 per cent of the population of Britain.[284] There is, however, little data on specific impairments. As *How Fair is Britain* points out, we are therefore reliant on an aggregate definition which hides a wide diversity of experience.[285] There has been some positive progress. Thus a growing number of disabled students are going to universities.[286] However, the overall picture is one of continuing disadvantage. Even in times of growing employment, which saw significant improvements in the

---

[284] *How Fair is Britain?*, above n 77, Part II, p 63: this defines the disabled as those with a long-standing illness, disability, or impairment, and who have substantial difficulty with day-to-day activities.
[285] Ibid, Part II, p 67.   [286] Ibid, p 300.

percentage of women and of black people in employment, disabled groups remained on the margins of the labour market. This has been particularly true for disabled people without qualifications. In particular, the decades between the mid-1970s and the early 2000s witnessed a 50 per cent drop in the employment rate for disabled men without qualifications.[287] But this is not confined to those without qualifications. Overall, the employment rates of disabled people in Britain remain low. Whereas 70 per cent of non-disabled adults are employed, this figure drops to 50 per cent for their disabled counterparts.[288] Of these only 33 per cent are employed full time, compared with 60 per cent of non-disabled people.[289] At the same time, it is important not to see disabled people as a homogenous group. Those with impairments such as diabetes and skin conditions have employment rates which are close to the average. However, this plummets to 23 per cent for people with depression or 'bad nerves'.[290]

Barriers to employment are multiple and widespread. These include lack of access to appropriate transport, negative attitudes by employers, who regard employing disabled people as risking productivity, and lack of awareness among disabled people themselves of available opportunities.[291] For those disabled people in work, there is ongoing evidence of discrimination in the workplace. Bullying and harassment are particularly prevalent. Indeed, claims to employment tribunals of disability discrimination have risen every year for the three years up to 2010.[292]

Poor employment prospects affect the standard of living of disabled people and their families. These effects are not confined to disabled adults. There are greater than average levels of poverty among families with disabled children, in part due to the cost of providing care, and the limits care-giving can place on parents' workforce participation.[293] Bullying and harassment are problematic throughout a disabled person's life: indeed research shows that the majority of learning disabled young people have experienced bullying.[294]

Despite this picture of ongoing disadvantage, particularly in times of recession, the Coalition Government which came into power in 2010 is intent on cutting benefits for disabled people. In the budget delivered in June 2010, the Chancellor announced measures to reduce the number of disabled people who would be eligible for disability living allowance.

---

[287] Ibid, p 380.   [288] Ibid, p 385.   [289] Ibid, p 397.
[290] Ibid, p 399.   [291] Ibid, p 400.   [292] Ibid, p 446.
[293] Ibid, p 258.   [294] Ibid, p 317.

Stating that three times as many people now claim this benefit, at a cost of more than £11 billion per year, the Chancellor set out plans for a more stringent medical assessment, to be applied from 2013.[295] It is estimated that the move will save £1 billion by 2015, suggesting that a significant number of claimants will no longer be eligible. The Chancellor claimed that the objective is to 'benefit those with the greatest needs, while significantly improving incentives to work for others'.[296] However, no attempt was made to put in place complementary measures to provide work for those disabled people who will no longer qualify for the benefit. In any event, as the chief executive of one of the foremost disability charities put it, disability living allowance should not be regarded as a benefit but a recognition that it is more expensive to live as a disabled person.[297]

VIII AGE DISCRIMINATION

(1) CHALLENGES AND DILEMMAS

The issues raised by age discrimination differ in important respects from those discussed so far.[298] Since we have all been young and many of us will become old, the opposition between 'Self' and 'Other' prevalent in other kinds of discrimination is not as stark. Indeed, there is no clearly demarcated boundary between the group subject to discrimination and others. Unlike US legislation, which focuses on a 'protected group' of people aged 40 or over, UK and EU legislation refer to discrimination between any age groups. This means that there is no easily recognizable distinction between a dominant and subordinate group, a 'discrete and insular minority' defined by age. In fact, there may be patent conflicts of interest: the interests of younger workers may be compromised in order to cater for the interests of older workers and vice versa. Indeed, 'ageism' is often justified on the grounds that older people should in fairness be required to make space for younger people.

The notion that differentiation on the grounds of age might constitute unlawful discrimination is a very recent phenomenon. Classifications on the grounds of age abound in the law, and some, such as age limits for voting or driving, or legislation restricting children's ability to undertake paid work,[299] might be thought to be eminently justifiable. At

---

[295] Hansard (22 June 2010), col 173. [296] Ibid.

[297] Cited in *The Guardian*, 22 June 2010.

[298] See further S Fredman, 'The Age of Equality' in S Fredman and S Spencer (eds), *Age as an Equality Issue* (Hart Publishing, 2003).

[299] Council Directive 94/33/EC on the Protection of Young People at Work.

the same time, there remain significant areas of negative discrimination, both in State policy and in the labour market as a whole. Thus minimum wage legislation sets a lower hourly rate for workers under 22 than for workers above that age, and a still lower rate for those aged 16 or 17.[300] Similarly, it is true that older people are provided with a range of specific age-related benefits, such as concessionary travel, or free NHS prescriptions. But they are also vulnerable to detrimental treatment on grounds of age, particularly in the workforce, but also in relation to health care, education and training, or the provision of public services.[301]

The issue of age discrimination has been pushed to the foreground by several interlocking factors. The first is demographic: the UK is ageing rapidly. Average life expectancy is increasing, and fertility rates have fallen below replacement levels. In the 25 years up to 2008, the population aged 65 and over increased from 15 to 16 per cent; while the population aged 16 and under decreased from 21 to 19 per cent. By 2033, a greater proportion of the population will be old than young.[302] This pattern is repeated throughout the EU: the growth of the working-age population is slowing rapidly; whereas the population over 60 is growing steadily. Within the next 50 years, it is estimated that the EU will move from a ratio of four working-age people for every person aged over 65 to a ratio of only two to one.[303] On the other hand, the last three decades of the twentieth century witnessed a steep decline in employment rates of older workers. In 1971 in the UK, 83 per cent of men aged 60–64 were in employment. By 2000, this figure had slumped to less than half.[304] This was partly because in the periods of high unemployment and industrial restructuring in the 1980s and 1990s, older workers tended to be concentrated in contracting or 'sunset' industries, such as coal and manufacturing; but also because older people were deliberately made redundant before younger people. Indeed, State social policy actively encouraged early exit from the workforce, and trade unions frequently supported early retirement as a solution to redundancy.

[300] National Minimum Wage Act Regulations 1999 (SI 1999/584), reg 13.
[301] Fredman, above n 298.
[302] Office for National Statistics, 'UK Snapshot: Ageing' (2009, available at: <http://www.statistics.gov.uk/cci/nugget.asp?ID=949>).
[303] Communication from the Commission to the European Parliament, the Council, the European Economic and Social Committee and the Committee of the Regions, *Dealing with the Impact of an Ageing Population in the EU* (2009 Ageing Report) (COM(2009) 180 final) Brussels, 29 April 2009.
[304] D Smeaton and S Vegeris, 'Older People Inside and Outside the Labour Market: A Review', Research Report 22 (Equality and Human Rights Commission, 2009), p 14.

This pattern of early retirement, combined with increased longevity, has serious implications for public finances, as the need for public provision of age-related services and particularly pensions increases. Over the next 50 years, age-related public expenditure is likely to increase in the EU as a whole by 4.75 per cent on average, and between 4 and 7 per cent in the UK.[305] At the same time, the shrinking labour force raises the prospect of labour shortages. As a result, prolonging labour force participation has become a key labour market objective, both in the UK and the EU more widely.[306] Age discrimination legislation was one of the measures put in place to achieve this end, together with a range of other policy initiatives. For example, the State pension age is set to rise from 60 to 65 for women in 2010, and to 68 for all workers by 2046. Pension rules have been modified to permit access while still at work, thereby encouraging a phased withdrawal from paid work.

The decline of workers over 50 in the workforce does indeed appear to have reversed, although it is too soon to tell whether this has been a result of 'active ageing' policies or of economic upturn. Thus, while the employment rate of those aged between 50 and the State pension age was only 64.9 per cent in 1997, this figure had grown to 71.8 per cent in 2009, compared to just over 80 per cent of those aged 25 to 49.[307] Particularly marked is the increase in the proportion of women in the workforce in this age group, rising from 61.1 per cent in 1997 to reach 71.1 per cent in 2009, only 1.1 percentage point behind that of men.[308] Nevertheless, labour market participation among both men and women drops precipitously at age 50,[309] and in the EU as a whole, only about 50 per cent of people are still in employment by the age of 60.[310] Moreover, both older and younger people are particularly vulnerable in times of recession such as those precipitated by the banking crisis of 2008.

The new emphasis on combating age discrimination is not, therefore, a result of a sudden appreciation of the need for fairness, but gains its

---

[305] 2009 Ageing Report, above n 303, p 4.

[306] Smeaton and Vegeris, above n 304, p 15.

[307] Department for Work and Pensions, 'Older Workers Statistical Information Booklet' (available at: <http://webarchive.nationalarchives.gov.uk/+/http://www.dwp.gov.uk/asd/asd5/rports2007-2008/agepos27.pdf>).

[308] Ibid.

[309] Smeaton and Vegeris, above n 304, p iv.

[310] See 2009 Ageing Report, above n 303.

chief impetus from macroeconomic imperatives. Nevertheless, this should not obscure the fact that age discrimination is a source of injustice in its own right, regardless of instrumental justifications. The human and social costs of age discrimination, particularly when it leads to exclusion from the labour force, should not be under-estimated. Increased poverty, ill health, and depression, as well as low self-esteem and social isolation, are themselves strong justifications for legal intervention.

Older workers in particular suffer from some of the central hallmarks of discrimination. A substantial proportion of the population report having experienced age discrimination,[311] and this impression is borne out by surveys of employers, a significant proportion of whom consider age to be an important criterion in the recruitment of staff. Stigma and stereotyping of older workers make it more difficult for them to retain their jobs or re-enter the labour market than younger workers. Notably, stereotyping may be positive as well as negative: older staff may be regarded as more reliable or hard-working than younger employers; but both positive and negative perceptions contribute to employers 'age-typing' jobs.[312] Prejudice against older workers is most evident at the stage of recruitment, but it also manifests in relation to training, development opportunities, and promotion. Many companies overtly restrict training opportunities on the grounds that older people are perceived to be more inflexible and not worth the investment of training resources. Older people are also very likely to suffer from indirect discrimination, in the form of apparently neutral practices which in fact operate to exclude more older than younger people. This is particularly evident in respect of educational qualifications. The Triennial Survey in 2010 found a striking difference between older and younger people in this respect. Whereas 1 in 5 people between 25 and 34 have degrees, this drops to fewer than one in ten for those aged between 55 and 64.[313] Yet many employers include specific reference to job qualifications in advertisements. Undue emphasis on formal qualifications rather than relevant experience or transferable skills disproportionately excludes older workers. As a result, once unemployed, workers over 50 remain unemployed for longer than other age groups.

---

[311] D Abrams and D M Houston, 'Equality, Diversity and Prejudice in Britain: Results from the 2005 National Survey: Report for the Cabinet Office Equalities Review October 2006' (available at: <http://archive.cabinetoffice.gov.uk/equalitiesreview/upload/assets/www.theequalitiesreview.org.uk/kentequality.pdf>).
[312] Smeaton and Vegeris, above n 304, p 16.
[313] *How Fair is Britain?*, above n 77, Part II, p 347.

However, there are important differences within the over-50 age group, demonstrating the ways in which interlocking identities affect one another. At least 'two nations in early retirement' have been identified. One group has access to relatively good pensions and are able to retire to pursue other interests. A second group, frequently from lower social classes, have been compelled to leave work due to redundancy, poor skills, or bad health.[314] In addition, age and ethnicity frequently combine to intensify disadvantage. Thus, in the 50–65 age group, black, Indian, Pakistani, and Bangladeshi men are more likely to be unemployed than white men in the same age group. There are also significant levels of poverty among the pension age population. Although there has recently been a decline in pensioner poverty, it is still estimated that about 1.8 million pensioners live in poverty. This too is intensified by cumulative sources of disadvantage. Women and ethnic minorities are particularly vulnerable to poverty in old age. Thus as many as 42 per cent of retired people of Pakistani or Bangladeshi origins lived in poverty in 2007. Equally disturbing is the fact that two-thirds of pensioners living in poverty are women. For every £1 of benefits received by a retired man, a woman receives 32p.[315]

(II) LEGISLATIVE DEVELOPMENTS

The above discussion has demonstrated that age discrimination legislation may have divergent purposes. The demographic impetus suggests that the focus should be on keeping older workers in the workforce, which in turn points towards more instrumental aims and objectives of anti-discrimination legislation. Thus policy documents both at EU and UK level regularly highlight the efficiency benefits of including older workers in the workforce. In particular, it is argued that businesses benefit by avoiding the loss of expertise and experience resulting from prejudice and exclusion of older workers. This instrumental approach can be contrasted with an intrinsic view of the aims of anti-discrimination law. These emphasize the protection of individual dignity and the expansion of genuine choice for older or younger people.

At the same time, the impetus for the introduction of age discrimination legislation in the UK came directly from the EU. Age was included as a ground of discrimination together with sexual orientation, religion and belief, and disability in the 2000 Employment Directive.[316]

---

[314] Smeaton and Vegeris, above n 304, p 17. [315] Ibid, p 39.
[316] Council Directive 2000/78/EC establishing a General Framework for Equal Treatment in Employment and Occupation.

However, it took the UK six years to implement the Directive.[317] The legislation which finally emerged, like the Directive itself, reflected the ongoing tension between instrumental and intrinsic aims. In particular, age is set apart from other protected characteristics by permitting direct age discrimination to be justified provided it is an appropriate and necessary means to achieve a legitimate aim. The Directive pinpoints a series of aims which are considered legitimate, including employment policy, labour market and vocational training objectives. These span both instrumental and intrinsic objectives. Thus Article 6 permits differences of treatment to promote the vocational integration or ensure the protection of young people, older workers, and persons with caring responsibilities. These are intrinsic reasons. On the other hand, the right not to be discriminated against on grounds of age can be subordinated to instrumental ends. Thus Article 6 also potentially permits differences of treatment which fix a minimum condition of age for employment or other benefits; or which fix a maximum age of recruitment based on the training requirements of the post or the need for a reasonable period of employment before retirement.[318]

Possibly the clearest manifestation of the unresolved tension between instrumental and intrinsic justifications concerns mandatory retirement ages. Legislation introduced to implement the EU Directive permitted employers to retain a mandatory or default retirement age (DRA). It was not unfair to dismiss an employee aged 65 or over on grounds of retirement. The legislation also deprived employees who have reached or were about to reach 65[319] of any protection against age discrimination in recruitment. In addition, workers under 65 might be dismissed by reason of retirement if the employer could show that this was a proportionate means of achieving a legitimate aim.[320] An employee's only right was to request to remain on after retirement age, a request which the employer was under a duty to consider.[321]

However, the Coalition Government, in power since May 2010, immediately announced its intention to phase out the DRA.[322] Its

---

[317] Employment Equality (Age) Regulations 2006 (SI 2006/714).
[318] Council Directive 2000/78, Art 6.
[319] Or the normal retirement age set by that employer, if that is higher.
[320] EA 2010, Sch 9 Part 2 paras 8–9. (For original measures see Employment Equality (Age) Regulations, reg 30.)
[321] Employment Equality (Age) Regulations, Sch 6, paras 5–6. These remain in force after the EA 2010.
[322] Department for Business, Innovation and Skills, *Phasing out the Default Retirement Age: Consultation Document* (July 2010, available at: <http://www.bis.gov.uk/policies/employment-matters/strategies/default-retirement>).

aims are primarily instrumental: demographic changes mean that people are living longer and the ratio of older to younger people is dropping. It could also be good for the economy: government statistics suggest that extending average working lives by one year would lead to an increase of GDP of about 1 per cent. In addition, people do not save enough for retirement, and working longer could increase their income. Finally, there is a gesture towards an intrinsic aim: people's work often provides a sense of identity, contributes to their social network, or constitutes a source of enjoyment. The proposal is therefore to phase out the DRA by 1 September 2011, after a six-month transitional period. Employers will only be permitted to retain a DRA, whether for over-65s or under-65s, if they can show that it is a proportionate means of achieving a legitimate aim.[323] At the same time, the proposal aims to phase out existing protections for workers, including the right to six months' notice before retiring, and the right to request to stay on after retirement.

A similar tension between the instrumental and intrinsic aims of age discrimination law can be seen in respect of young workers. The original implementing regulations permitted the government to continue its practice of setting a lower minimum wage for younger people under the National Minimum Wage Act 1998,[324] and this has been maintained in the EA 2010.[325] This exception has not yet been challenged under the standard of proportionality required by the Directive.

Age discrimination legislation was initially confined to employment, vocational training, and membership of employers' and professional organizations. Not only did this mean that key areas of age discrimination were excluded, it also limited the effectiveness of the protection against employment-based discrimination. Older or younger people might fare less well in the labour market because of discrimination outside the labour market, such as in education, transport, health care, or other public services. The EA 2010 signals a more holistic approach to age discrimination, in that discrimination is generally prohibited in relation to services and public functions (except in relation to children under 18);[326] and higher education and vocational training (except in relation to schools).[327] Age is also now included in the positive duty on public bodies

---

[323] The DRA was upheld under the proportionality test in *R (Age UK) v Secretary of State for Business, Innovation and Skills* [2009] EWHC 2336 (Admin).
[324] Employment Equality (Age) Regulations, reg 31.
[325] EA 2010, Sch 9 Part 2 para 11.
[326] Ibid, s 28.
[327] Ibid, s 84 (schools).

to pay due regard to the need to promote equality of opportunity, eliminate unlawful discrimination, and foster good relations.[328]

IX CONCLUSION

This chapter has attempted to provide the social and legal context within which anti-discrimination law operates. As we have seen, each protected ground has its own history and particular sets of inequalities, all of which are crucial components in the understanding and evaluation of the legal concepts underpinning anti-discrimination law. The following chapters constitute an in-depth examination of this conceptual framework. In this examination, the focus is primarily on courts and legislative or constitutional measures. However, the ways in which anti-discrimination laws interact with the lived experience of the victims of anti-discrimination law should not be lost sight of.

---

[328] Ibid, s 149.

3

The Scope of Discrimination Law

Discrimination law poses a central dilemma. On the one hand, individuals should be judged according to their personal qualities. This basic tenet is contravened if the treatment accorded to individuals is based on their status, their group membership, or irrelevant physical characteristics. On the other hand, not every distinction is discriminatory. Governments classify people into groups for a wide variety of reasons and many of them are legitimate. In addition, there are many group characteristics which are a valued part of the identity of individuals. The challenge therefore is to frame laws which are sensitive enough to outlaw invidious distinctions; while permitting and even supporting positive difference.

Which characteristics, then, ought to be protected against discrimination and why? Although there is now general consensus that sex and race should be within the list of grounds of discrimination, even these were only achieved after struggle and controversy. It is only relatively recently that other grounds, such as disability and sexual orientation, have been accepted as attracting special protection, and the inclusion of age in more recent years came as a surprise to some. But is there a unifying principle drawing all these together into a coherent whole and, if so, what is it? To what extent can the choice of grounds be explained by the underlying aims of equality? Part I of this chapter addresses these questions.

A related concern is the reach of equality law. Should discrimination on these grounds be unlawful in all walks of life, or only in specific spheres, such as employment and education? Should both public and private actors be bound? Equality laws in many jurisdictions derive from a constitutional guarantee, which may well bind only the State and not private actors. Only if legislation is specifically passed pursuant to such guarantees will private actors be bound. In the UK, the trend has been in the opposite direction. Discrimination law originally bound private actors in specified fields, such as employment, education, and the provision of goods and services, and public bodies were only bound to the extent that they engaged in these activities. It is only since the turn of the century that public functions more generally have been engaged. Part II of the chapter examines the reach of anti-discrimination law in the UK, while Part III considers who is bound by such laws.

I GROUNDS OF DISCRIMINATION

What sort of distinctions should be outlawed as illegitimate and unacceptable? The answer to this question is heavily influenced by the political and social context in which discrimination law has developed. In the US, the development began with race. Expansion into other grounds has taken place primarily by way of extrapolation of principles developed for race. In the EU, by contrast, equality law began with nationality and gender. Race was not included until as recently as 2000, together with sexual orientation, disability, age, and religion and belief.[1] The list of grounds in the European Convention on Human Rights (ECHR) similarly reflects the immediate post-war context in which it was formulated. Hence it expressly includes such characteristics as birth, political opinion, and property,[2] but not disability or sexual orientation. More modern equality guarantees range over new grounds, unforeseeable in earlier decades. The EU Charter of Fundamental Rights includes genetic features as one of 14 listed grounds,[3] while the new UK Equality Act (EA) 2010 includes gender reassignment and civil partnership amongst its list of eight grounds. The South African Constitution has a non-exhaustive list of 17 grounds, including sex, gender, pregnancy, and marital status; as well as race, ethnic or social origin, colour, religion, conscience, belief, culture, language, and birth. Sexual orientation, age, and disability feature in all three.[4] Even then, there are other contenders for a position in the magic circle of protection. Should HIV status be an independent ground? Should socio-economic disadvantage or poverty?

Other complex questions quickly emerge. Is it enough for an individual to identify herself as having a particular identity, or is it necessary to formulate objective criteria? Should all grounds be considered equally

---

[1] Council Directive 2000/43/EC of 29 June 2000 [2000] OJ L180/22; and Council Directive 2000/78/EC of 27 November 2000 [2000] OJ L303/16.
[2] ECHR Art 14.
[3] Charter of Fundamental Rights of the European Union, Art 21.
[4] EU Charter, Art 21; EA 2010, s 4; Constitution of South Africa, s 9(3).

invidious, or are distinctions on the basis of some grounds more invidious than others? It will be seen that there is frequently an inverse relationship between the willingness of judges to extend categories of protection and the strictness with which such distinctions are scrutinized. And how should the law deal with those who belong to more than one specified group, such as black women?

We could search for a unifying principle which explains existing grounds of discrimination and generates the answer to new questions. Or we could argue that the decision is simply a political one, reflecting the balance of opinion in society at a particular time. If there is no 'right answer' to this question, the real debate concerns which institution is most appropriate to make the decision: the courts or the legislature? On the one hand, the main reason for providing protection for particular groups is their political powerlessness. This suggests that the decision as to which groups should be protected should not lie with the majoritarian political process, but the judiciary. On the other hand, judges may not have the legitimacy or competence to make value judgements of this sort. Alternatively, it could be argued that the decision should be taken at international or regional level. This transcends the particular balance of power in any participating State.

In reality, the determination of protected grounds operates as a result of a creative tension between several different sources: constitutional instruments, statutes, judicial interpretation, and international or regional instruments. Judicial decisions might trigger legislative action on behalf of minorities and a similar dynamic might operate between supranational and national mechanisms. In the UK, the EU and ECHR have exerted a key influence on the expansion of protected grounds of discrimination. As will be seen below, the European Court of Justice (ECJ), by extending sex discrimination protection to transgender persons, had an effect of this sort.[5] This dynamic interaction between different sources goes some way towards resolving the tension between the needs of minorities to be protected from majoritarianism, and the democratic deficiencies of the judiciary.

More radical still is Iris Marion Young's challenge to the very assumption that groups are identified on the basis of apparently fixed attributes. Instead, she argues, a group is better described in terms of a sense of affinity between individuals, and a social process of interaction. Moreover, groups intersect, so that different groups share some

---

[5] Case C-13/94 *P v S and Cornwall County Council* [1996] ECR I-2143.

common experiences and even have some common membership. This in turn entails a reconceptualization of the notion of difference itself. Instead of difference connoting 'absolute otherness', or deviance from a single norm, difference is about relationships between and within groups. This allows groups to define themselves, rather than being subject to a devalued essence imposed from outside.[6] Thus group membership is conceived of as having fluid boundaries, not dependent on a rigid definition of the group itself. This fluidity has proved difficult to capture in legal forms. At most, small steps have recently been taken in the direction of intersectional or cumulative discrimination affecting a person because she belongs to more than one group.

(i) DEFINING THE GROUNDS: THREE MODELS

There are three ways in which constitutional or legislative instruments formulate protected grounds of discrimination. The first is by means of an exhaustive list of grounds. Here the choice of ground is made wholly within the political, constitutional, or treaty-making process, with no discretion left to the judges. Grounds can be added or removed only legislatively or by amendment of the constitution or treaty. This 'fixed category' approach is found in both UK domestic and EU anti-discrimination legislation. A second model, at the other end of the spectrum, is to frame a broad, open-textured equality guarantee, stating simply that all persons are equal before the law, without specifying any particular grounds. This approach leaves it to judges to decide when a classification is prohibited under the constitution. It is epitomized by the US Constitution, which simply states, in the Fourteenth Amendment, that no State may 'deny to any person within its jurisdiction the equal protection of the laws'.

In between these two extremes is the third model, which specifies a list of grounds of discrimination, but indicates that the list is not exhaustive, using the terms 'grounds such as . . .', 'including . . .', 'in particular . . .', or 'other status'. This is the approach adopted in the ECHR, the EU Charter of Fundamental Rights, the Canadian Charter of Rights, and the South African Constitution. This approach gives judges some discretion to extend the list according to a set of judicially generated principles; but judicial discretion is shaped by the existence of enumerated grounds. In both the second and third models, courts tend

---

[6] I MYoung, *Justice and the Politics of Difference* (Princeton University Press, 1990), pp 168–72.

to regard their role as one of determining not just whether to extend protection to a new ground but also how intensely such grounds should be scrutinized. As will be seen, expansion into a new ground is often tempered by a reduction in the intensity of scrutiny. Thus in examining each of these models below, it is necessary to consider both the determination of grounds and the degree of scrutiny. Having examined each model, I ask whether there is an underlying theoretical coherence. Are there unifying principles which allow us to understand and predict the emergence of grounds, or is this simply a result of the confluence of political, historical, and social factors?

(a) An exhaustive list: specifying the grounds

The first model, which is found in UK and EU anti-discrimination law,[7] is to formulate an exhaustive set of grounds, which cannot be extended by the judiciary, but only through legislation or constitutional amendment. This does not, however, mean that courts have no role. Groups which are only marginally outside the delineated boundaries inevitably attempt to persuade courts to re-characterize recognized grounds in order to bring their members within the scope of protection. If sex is protected but not sexual orientation or transsexuality, then members of the latter groups will try to persuade courts that they are being discriminated against on grounds of sex. If ethnic origin is protected but not religion, then religious groups will claim on grounds of ethnicity. This results in complex and anomalous distinctions. Such pressures on the boundaries of existing grounds have been endemic in British and EU law. It is only when these pressures are powerful enough to generate change at the political level that such anomalies can be properly addressed. The result has been that incipient or marginalized groups seeking protection have been able to use both judicial and political means to achieve inclusion.

This pattern can be seen in British and EU law, where the protected grounds have gradually been expanded by the legislature to respond to a variety of legal and political pressures to incorporate excluded groups. The earliest British statutes were concerned with gender and race discrimination, with the Sex Discrimination Act 1975 (SDA) covering sex and being married, while the Race Relations Act 1976 (RRA) covered discrimination on grounds of colour, race, nationality, or ethnic or national origins. Discrimination on grounds of religion and political

---

[7] The EU Charter of Fundamental Rights is considered separately from EU discrimination law (see following section).

opinion, although prohibited in Northern Ireland, was deliberately excluded from protection in Great Britain.[8] It was not until 1995 that disability discrimination was prohibited by the introduction of the Disability Discrimination Act 1995.[9]

The coverage of EU law has until very recently been even more limited. EU anti-discrimination law has been shaped by the basic imperatives behind the formation of the European Community, namely the creation of a common market in Europe. From the inception of the Community, therefore, equality as a principle was only relevant insofar as it was needed in the creation of a European-wide labour market.[10] In particular, free movement of labour required a legal prohibition of discrimination by one Member State against nationals of other Member States. Outside of nationality, there was only one area within traditional discrimination law that was considered relevant to the creation of a common market: pay discrimination between men and women. Member States which permitted lower wages for women than men doing the same work would, it was argued, enjoy a competitive advantage over those with equal pay laws.[11] The original treaty therefore created a right to equal pay for equal work for men and women, a right which was to grow into a powerful equality tool.[12] However, the elimination of race discrimination was simply not considered necessary to the project of creating a common market, and indeed raised awkward questions in relation to discrimination against non-EU nationals. As a result, the right not to be discriminated against on grounds of race was conspicuously absent, apart from several soft law initiatives.[13]

Such uneven coverage made it inevitable that excluded groups would attempt to bring themselves within established grounds. This in turn necessitated bright-line distinctions between different grounds of discrimination. For example, as we have seen, the omission of sexual orientation and transsexuality led litigants to argue that discrimination on these grounds was a species of sex discrimination. The judicial

---

[8] RRA, s 3(1); SDA, ss 1–3; Fair Employment (Northern Ireland) Act 1989, s 49.

[9] See s 4.

[10] See eg W Streeck, 'From Market Making to State Building' in S Leibfried and P Pierson (eds), *European Social Policy: Between Fragmentation and Integration* (Brookings Institution, 1995), p 397.

[11] International Labour Organization, 'Social Aspects of European Economic Co-operation' (1956) 74 International Labour Review 107.

[12] Art 119 of the Treaty of Rome, which became Art 141 after the Treaty of Amsterdam, now Art 157 after the Treaty of Lisbon.

[13] See eg Joint Declaration on Fundamental Rights, 5 April 1977 (OJ C103/1); Action Plan on the Fight against Racism (COM(1998) 183 final of 25.03.1998).

response has been mixed and unpredictable. In the ground-breaking case of *P v S*,[14] the ECJ held that discrimination against transsexuals was a species of sex discrimination. To tolerate discrimination against a transsexual would be tantamount to a failure to respect the dignity and freedom to which he or she is entitled. As a result of *P v S*, the SDA was explicitly amended to include transsexuality as a prohibited ground of discrimination. More importantly still, the ECJ appeared to be developing a much wider equality principle, akin to the US constitutional guarantee. Thus in its judgment, the ECJ declared that the Equal Treatment Directive, which established the principle of equal treatment between men and women, was 'simply the expression, in the relevant field, of the principle of equality, which is one of the fundamental principles of Community law'.[15] However, the ECJ took a very different stance in relation to sexual orientation. In *Grant v South-West Trains Ltd*, it refused to hold that the prohibition of sex discrimination in the Equal Treatment Directive included a prohibition on sexual orientation discrimination.[16] One possible explanation is that it was aware that sexual orientation was already the subject of legislative proposals. In this context, the Court was unwilling to pre-empt the political process.

The boundary between ethnicity and religion has been similarly contested, again leading to mixed judicial responses. Under the RRA, the inclusion of 'ethnic origin' but the exclusion of religion meant that Sikhs, Muslims, Jews, and Rastafarians had to argue that they were groups defined by their ethnic origin and not by their religion. Domestic courts were willing to develop the understanding of 'ethnicity' to incorporate Sikhs[17] and Jews, but not Rastafarians[18] or Muslims.[19] Also disputed has been the borderline between sex discrimination and age discrimination. Before the introduction of age discrimination, attempts were made to challenge the removal of employment protection rights from employees over 65 by arguing that this constituted sex discrimination against men, who were more likely to remain in employment over 65 than women.[20] The House of Lords rejected the claim. According to Lord Scott:

---

[14] *P v S and Cornwall County Council*, above n 5.

[15] At para 18. See also Case C-555/07 *Kücükdeveci v Swedex Gmbh & Co KG* [2010] 2 CMLR 33 (ECJ); Case C-144/04 *Mangold* [2005] ECR I-9981.

[16] Case C-249/96 *Grant v South-West Trains Ltd* [1998] ECR I-621.

[17] *Mandla v Lee* [1983] 2 AC 548 (HL).

[18] *Dawkins v Department of the Environment* [1993] IRLR 284 (CA).

[19] *J H Walker v Hussain* [1996] IRLR 11 (EAT).

[20] *Secretary of State for Trade and Industry v Rutherford (No 2)* [2006] UKHL 19.

The disadvantage of which complaint is made in this case is certainly a result of discrimination on the ground of age. Age discrimination is not yet unlawful. . . . But the age discrimination cannot, in my opinion, be passed off as sex discrimination.[21]

The impetus to remedy this jagged coverage came from the EU. Article 13 of the Treaty of Amsterdam (now Article 19 of the Lisbon Treaty) gave legislative competence in relation to discrimination based on sex, racial or ethnic origin, religion or belief, disability, age, or sexual orientation. This power was swiftly used to pass two directives. The first, 'implementing the principle of equal treatment between persons irrespective of racial or ethnic origin' was adopted in June 2000.[22] The second extended the principle of equal treatment to prevent discrimination on grounds of age, disability, religion, and sexual orientation in relation to employment and vocational training, and was adopted five months later.[23] Provisions were enacted piecemeal in the UK to provide protection for the missing grounds of age, religion and belief, and sexual orientation. The resulting tangle of legislative provision was finally reorganized and pulled together by the EA 2010. The grounds of discrimination, now known as 'protected characteristics', consist of age; disability; gender reassignment; race; religion or belief; sex; sexual orientation; marriage and civil partnership; and pregnancy and maternity.[24]

The expanded range of protected characteristics, and their inclusion into a single statute, represent an important step forward. Nevertheless, the assumption that there are fixed boundaries between categories within an exhaustive list will continue to raise serious demarcation disputes. As a start, the EA 2010 treats protected characteristics differently for some purposes. For example, whereas harassment on the grounds of gender, race, and disability is unlawful in all contexts, there is no protection against harassment on grounds of sexual orientation or religion or belief in the provision of services, the exercise of public functions,[25] the disposal of premises,[26] and in recruitment or admission to schools. Moreover, marriage and civil partnership are excluded from protection against discrimination in relation to the provision of services, public functions, education, and the disposal of

---

[21] Ibid, para 22.
[22] Council Directive 2000/43/EC of 29 June 2000 [2000] OJ L180/22.
[23] Council Directive 2000/78/EC of 27 November 2000 [2000] OJ L303/16.
[24] EA 2010, ss 4–12.   [25] Ibid, s 29(8).   [26] Ibid, s 33(6).

premises. In addition, discrimination on grounds of religion is permitted in relation to designated State schools. In these contexts, there will inevitably be disputes as to whether harassment or discrimination is on the grounds of sexual orientation or sex, of religion or ethnicity, or of marriage or a different category.

The attempt to create a bright-line distinction between ethnicity and religion continues to create serious anomalies. This has already been starkly demonstrated in relation to the religious exception for designated 'faith' schools. Such schools can reserve entry, in case of oversubscription, to pupils of the designated faith without being guilty of a breach of discrimination law. However, in a recent decision, a designated Jewish faith school was found to have discriminated on grounds of race when it refused to admit a pupil who was not Jewish. This was because the UK Supreme Court held that the ancient Jewish rule that a person is Jewish if his or her mother is Jewish or has converted to Judaism is not a religious but an ethnic rule. By a 5:4 majority, the court held that because Jewish law as to who is Jewish is based on descent rather than practice of the faith, this was not a distinction on grounds of religion, but of ethnic origin. It therefore constituted unlawful race discrimination under the RRA.[27] As Lord Brown stated in his dissent: 'The difficulty in the case arises because of the obvious overlap here between the concepts respectively of religious and racial discrimination.'[28] Indeed, he continued,

the Court of Appeal's judgment insists on a non-Jewish definition of who is Jewish . . . The root question for the court is simply this: can a Jewish faith school ever give preference to those who are members of the Jewish religion under Jewish law. I would answer: yes, it can. To hold the contrary would be to stigmatise Judaism as a directly racially discriminating religion. I would respectfully disagree with that conclusion. Indeed I would greatly regret it.[29]

In fact, the real concern of the case was a dispute as between Orthodox and other sects of Judaism in relation to what kinds of conversion were acceptable. The complainant and his mother had been converted to Judaism under the non-Orthodox Mazorti tradition, which was not recognized under Orthodox Judaism. Therefore, as Lord Brown recognized, 'the differential treatment between Jews recognised by the [Chief

---

[27] *R (E) v Governing Body of JFS* [2009] UKSC 15.
[28] Ibid, para 243.   [29] Ibid, para 248.

Rabbi] of Orthodox Jewry and those not so recognised within the wider group of ethnic Jews . . . is plainly on the ground of religion rather than race.'[30] The result of the decision has been that the Jewish Free School and other schools designated as Orthodox Jewish faith schools, now require evidence of outward manifestations of the Jewish faith, which goes against the essence of the Jewish understanding of Jewish identity.

(b) An open-textured model: leaving it to the judiciary

The second model is at the opposite end of the spectrum. Instead of an exhaustive list of categories, this approach is based on an open-ended constitutional equality guarantee. This is epitomized by the US Constitution, which simply states, in the Fourteenth Amendment, that no State may 'deny to any person within its jurisdiction the equal protection of the laws'. In principle, then, any classification whatsoever may be challenged, be it a welfare law providing specific protection to vulnerable members of society or one that unduly burdens a group for reasons of pure prejudice. The only way in which the breadth of this provision can be handled is by adjusting the intensity of judicial scrutiny. In practice, then, the question of which classifications are illegitimate is determined by the judiciary through its power to decide how closely to scrutinize a legislative or other classification.

It is in this sense that the US Supreme Court has taken on itself the full responsibility of determining protected groups. To do this, it has developed the well-known double standard of scrutiny. In relation to most classifications, the Court will defer to the legislature, expecting the State to show only that the classification is 'rationally related' to a legitimate State interest. However, 'strict scrutiny' will be applied to legislative classifications which impermissibly interfere with the exercise of a fundamental right or operate to the particular disadvantage of a particular group, or 'suspect class'. Strict scrutiny differs from rational review in that the classification must further not just a legitimate but a compelling State interest. Moreover, rather than being rationally related to that interest, the classification must be 'narrowly tailored' to achieve it, in the sense that no other alternatives are available. Classifications attracting the deferent rationality standard of scrutiny almost invariably pass muster, whereas strict scrutiny almost invariably constitutes a fatal attack. It is in determining which groups count as suspect classes that

---

[30] Ibid, para 245.

the Court has been at the forefront of the development of protected grounds of discrimination law.

It was in relation to racism that the most dramatic developments occurred in the jurisprudence of the Court. Early cases applied a mere rationality standard to blatantly racist classifications. Thus in the notorious case of *Plessy v Ferguson*,[31] the US Supreme Court held that laws segregating blacks and whites did not breach the equality guarantee. The leading judgment held that the State had every right to use classifications, as long as the classification was not capricious, arbitrary, or unreasonable. Although the segregation (in this case of train carriages) was clearly part of a widespread set of laws aimed at reinforcing the power structure which elevated whites and stigmatized Afro-Americans, the Court held that the government had done its duty by securing equal rights to all of its citizens. 'If one race be inferior to the other socially, the Constitution of the United States cannot put them upon the same plane.'[32]

It was thus of enormous historical significance when the Court eventually recognized the perniciousness of racial classifications. Thus, in a seminal case concerning internship of Japanese citizens during the Second World War, the Court held: 'Legal restrictions which curtail the civil rights of a single racial group are immediately suspect... Courts must subject them to the most rigid scrutiny.'[33] Although this in principle leaves open the possibility of justification of a racial classification, in practice the strict scrutiny test has almost invariably led to the Court striking down racial classifications operating to the detriment of Afro-Americans.[34] Most recently, this has been reaffirmed and indeed arguably extended to include scrutiny of decisions within prisons, which had previously been thought to attract a more deferent standard. Thus in *Johnson v California*,[35] the US Supreme Court was faced with a Fourteenth Amendment challenge to racial segregation of prisoners. The Californian Department of Correction had followed an unwritten policy of placing new or transferred inmates with cellmates of the same race during an initial evaluation period. The respondent argued that this was necessary to prevent violence caused by racial gangs. The court below upheld the segregation policy on the basis that it was 'reasonably

---

[31] *Plessy v Ferguson* 163 US 537, 16 S Ct 1138 (1896).

[32] 163 US 537 at 552.

[33] *Korematsu v United States* 323 US 214, 65 S Ct 193 (1944) at 216.

[34] See eg *McLaughlin v Florida* 379 US 184, 85 S Ct 283 (1964); *Loving v Virginia* 388 US 1, 87 S Ct 1817 (1967).

[35] *Johnson v California* 125 S Ct 1141 (2005) (US Supreme Court).

related to a legitimate penological interest'. However, the Supreme Court reaffirmed that all racial classifications, whether in prison or not, should be subject to strict scrutiny. The rational basis standard was not sufficient: instead, the respondent was obliged to demonstrate that the policy was narrowly tailored to serve a compelling State interest.

In the result, however, only alienage, race, and ancestry have qualified for strict scrutiny. Indeed, the Court has been deeply resistant to attempts to expand strict scrutiny beyond these grounds. For most other grounds, rational basis has been deemed sufficient. Thus when a classification based on age was challenged before the Supreme Court, its decision to subject it merely to rational scrutiny meant that age discrimination would go largely untouched by Fourteenth Amendment protection. In a case in 1976,[36] the applicants challenged a Massachusetts law which required uniformed State police officers to retire at the age of 50. The Supreme Court held that rationality, rather than strict scrutiny, was the proper standard in determining whether the statute violated the equal protection clause. Protection of the public by assuring physical preparedness of its uniformed police was a legitimate State interest, and a maximum age of 50 was a rational means of doing so. If the Court had applied a stricter standard of scrutiny, it might have insisted that the State determine fitness more precisely through individualized testing after the age of 50. The plaintiff was in fact physically and mentally capable of performing the duties of a uniformed officer. The majority opinion observed:

This inquiry employs a relatively relaxed standard, reflecting the court's awareness that the drawing of lines which create distinctions is peculiarly a legislative task and an unavoidable one. Perfection in making the necessary classifications is neither possible nor necessary.[37]

The rigid classification of grounds into those attracting strict scrutiny and those subject only to a rationality analysis has been harshly criticized by Marshall J in a series of dissenting judgments in the US Supreme Court. He points out that, because strict scrutiny invariably results in the court striking down the classification, it has

lost interest in recognizing further 'fundamental' rights and 'suspect' classes . . . It should be no surprise . . . that the Court is hesitant to expand the number of categories of rights and classes subject to strict scrutiny, when each expansion

---

[36] *Massachusetts Board of Retirement v Murgia* 427 US 307.
[37] Ibid at 314.

involves the invalidation of virtually every classification bearing upon a newly covered category.[38]

This problem has been particularly evident in relation to gender discrimination. In earlier cases, such as the exclusion of women from compulsory jury service, it was held that there was no parallel between sex and race discrimination. This meant that strict scrutiny did not apply: as long as any 'basis in reason' could be conceived for the discrimination, there was no violation of equal protection.[39] The reasons given for this conclusion simply show up the continuing prejudices of the judiciary. Thus it was stated that sex discrimination differed from race discrimination because there was no history of prejudice against women. A good enough reason for differentiating, according to Harlan J, was that

Despite the enlightened emancipation of women from the restrictions and protections of bygone years, and their entry into many parts of community life formerly considered to be reserved to men, woman is still regarded as the centre of home and family life.[40]

In 1971, for the first time, the US Supreme Court ruled in favour of a woman who complained that her State had denied her the equal protection of its laws.[41] Nevertheless, the Court has consistently refused to regard gender classifications as suspect. Instead of requiring the most intense scrutiny, as applied to race, an 'intermediate' test is applied.[42] As reformulated in *US v Virginia* in 1996, this test requires the State to produce a justification which is 'exceedingly persuasive'.[43] This means that the State must show that the discriminatory classification is substantially related to the achievement of important governmental objectives. Ginsburg J in the *Virginia* case took care to draw a bright line between the rational review standard and the heightened scrutiny appropriate for gender. Thus, whereas under rational basis review, the defender of the classification is under no obligation to produce evidence to support its rationality, heightened review places a demanding burden

---

[38] Ibid at 318–19, there citing *San Antonio School District v Rodriguez* 411 US 1 at 98–110, 93 S Ct 1278 at 1330 (1973); and *Frontiero v Richardson* 411 US 677, 93 S Ct 1764 (1973).

[39] See eg *Goesart v Cleary* 335 US 464, 69 S Ct 198 (1948).

[40] *Hoyt v Florida* 368 US 57, 82 S Ct 159 (1961) at 61–2.

[41] *Reed v Reed* 404 US 71, 92 S Ct 251 (1971).

[42] *Craig v Boren* 429 US 190, 97 S Ct 451 (1976); *Orr v Orr* 440 US 268, 99 S Ct 1102 (1979); *Michael M v Superior Court, Sonoma Cty* 450 US 464, 101 S Ct 1200 (1981).

[43] *United States v Virginia* 116 S Ct 2264 (1996).

of justification on the defender. In addition, the justification must be genuine, not invented post hoc in response to litigation. Particularly importantly, it cannot rely on 'over-broad generalisations about the different talents, capacities or preferences of males and females'.[44] Finally, under heightened scrutiny, the discriminatory means must be 'substantially related' to an actual and important governmental interest. In other words, whereas the availability of other suitable means is irrelevant in relation to rational basis review, the availability of sex-neutral alternatives to a sex-based classification is of key importance in determining the validity of the classification.

On one level, the more flexible standard in relation to women is defensible. This is because it makes it possible to accommodate the more asymmetric understanding of equality law set out in Chapter One. This was articulated by Ginsburg J, who saw the lesser standard as providing an opportunity to frame legislation which positively promoted equal opportunities for women, while striking down legislation based on over-broad generalizations about different talents, capacities, or preferences of men and women. As we shall see in Chapter Five, the US Supreme Court has recently taken a strictly symmetrical approach to discrimination on grounds of race, holding that both invidious discrimination and discrimination designed to compensate for past disadvantage should be subject to strict scrutiny. Ginsburg J, however, made it clear that sex classifications can be used to compensate women for particular economic disabilities or to develop their talents and capacities fully. But they cannot be used to perpetuate the legal, social, and economic inferiority of women. Whereas supposed inherent differences are no longer accepted as a ground for race classifications, '"inherent differences" between men and women, we have come to appreciate, remain cause for celebration, but not for denigration of the members of either sex or for artificial constraints on an individual's opportunity'.[45]

However, it has been difficult to maintain an intermediate position which does not subtly slide into mere rational review. In the 2001 case of *Nguyen*, a majority of the US Supreme Court rejected a challenge of immigration rules which permitted unmarried mothers to give citizenship to their children without further proof, while requiring unmarried fathers to prove patrimony before the child was 18. Nguyen had lived with his American father for most his life, but the latter had not taken

---

[44] Ibid at 533.
[45] Ibid, text to footnotes 6 and 7.

the requisite steps before he turned 18. By a 5:4 majority, and over a blistering dissent by O'Connor J, the Court held that the additional requirements were substantially related to the important government objectives of ensuring reliable proof of the biological relationship between the father and child, and ensuring that the child and parent had the opportunity to develop real, everyday ties.[46] As O'Connor J argued, the majority recited the standard of heightened review, but applied a standard much closer to that of rational basis review. Thus, instead of taking seriously the possibility of a sex-neutral alternative, the majority simply declared that the requirement was a reasonable choice among several mechanisms and that there was no requirement that Congress choose one rather than the other. This relies on a stereotype, namely that mothers are significantly more likely than fathers to develop relationships with their children; and by doing so, perpetuates it. Application of the stereotype carries with it a particular pathos in this case, where the father had indeed been the primary carer of his son for almost all his life.

Leaving it to judges to develop grounds of discrimination has proved particularly controversial in relation to sexual orientation. Indeed, judges in the US Supreme Court have refused, until very recently, to insist even on formal equality before the law. Thus in the notorious case of *Bowers v Hardwick*[47] in 1986, by a narrow majority of 5:4, the US Supreme Court refused to strike down sodomy laws, which effectively made homosexuality a criminal offence. Arguing that strict scrutiny was only applicable in relation to a suspect class, or for breach of a fundamental right, the majority judgment held that strict scrutiny was not appropriate because the Federal Constitution did not confer a fundamental right upon homosexuals to engage in sodomy.

It was not until 2003 that this decision was reversed. In *Lawrence v Texas*,[48] a Texan statute prohibiting same-sex sexual activity was struck down. Giving judgment for the Court, Kennedy J stated:

To say that the issue in *Bowers* was simply the right to engage in certain sexual conduct demeans the claim the individual put forward ... Although the laws involved in *Bowers* and here purport to do no more than prohibit a particular sexual act, their penalties and purposes have more far-reaching consequences,

---

[46] Note that the case was decided under the Equal Protection Clause of the Fifth Amendment, which relies on substantially similar precedents to the Fourteenth Amendment.

[47] *Bowers v Hardwick* 478 US 186 (1986).

[48] *Lawrence v Texas* 539 US 558, 123 S Ct 247.

touching upon the most private human conduct, sexual behaviour, and in the most private of places, the home.[49]

Notably, however, the majority rejected the invitation to decide the case under the equal protection clause of the Fourteenth Amendment. This was because, taking a formal view of equality as requiring no more than consistent treatment, it did not regard equality as sufficiently robust to overturn the *Bowers* precedent.

Were we to hold the statute invalid under the Equal Protection Clause some might question whether a prohibition would be valid if drawn differently, say, to prohibit the conduct both between same-sex and different-sex participants.[50]

Instead, it relied on the guarantee of liberty from state intervention, found in the due process clause which is coupled with equal protection in the Fourteenth Amendment. Only O'Connor J held the sodomy laws to be unconstitutional because of a breach of the equality guarantee, on the grounds that the statute only prohibited homosexual and not opposite-sex sodomy. Nevertheless, Kennedy J regarded a decision on the liberty right as advancing both liberty and equality.

When homosexual conduct is made criminal by the law of the State, that declaration in and of itself is an invitation to subject homosexual persons to discrimination both in the public and the private spheres.[51]

The result is that judicial intervention in relation to sexual orientation has occurred outside the framework of strict scrutiny, rational review, or the intermediate standard. This is evident too in the 1996 case of *Romer v Evans*, where the Supreme Court struck down an amendment to the Constitution of Colorado which prohibited the enactment of any legislation outlawing discrimination on grounds of sexual orientation.[52] Kennedy J for the majority based his opinion on the fundamental principle that the Constitution 'neither knows nor tolerates classes among citizens'. It was held that the Equal Protection Clause was breached for two fundamental reasons: it imposed a broad and undifferentiated disability on a single named group, and, secondly, it raised the inevitable inference that the measure was born of animosity towards the

---

[49] Ibid, 539 US 558 at 567.
[50] Ibid at 575.   [51] Ibid at 575.
[52] *Romer v Evans* 517 US 620, 116 S Ct 1620 (1996).

class of persons affected. 'A State cannot so deem a class of persons a stranger to its laws.'[53]

(c) The non-exhaustive list

The third approach is a non-exhaustive list, which enumerates grounds but leaves it to judges to extend the list where appropriate. This is the approach adopted in the ECHR, the Canadian Charter of Rights, and the South African Constitution. Thus Article 14 of the ECHR states that the enjoyment of the rights and freedoms in the Convention shall be secured without discrimination 'on grounds *such as* sex, race, colour, language, religion, political or other opinion, national or social origin, association with a national minority, property, birth *or other status*...' The Canadian Charter of Rights and Freedoms states:

Every citizen is equal before and under the law and has the right to the equal protection and benefit of the law without discrimination *and in particular* without discrimination based on race, national or ethnic origin, colour, religion, sex, age or mental or physical disability.[54]

The South African Constitution prohibits unfair discrimination on grounds 'including' the listed grounds.[55]

The non-exhaustive list has made it possible for courts to 'update' the protected grounds in response to changing circumstances. This can clearly be seen by considering Article 14 ECHR. The list of grounds in Article 14 looks somewhat strange to modern eyes. While discrimination on grounds of property, birth, and association with a national minority are outlawed, there is no mention of disability, sexual orientation, or age, let alone pregnancy or civil partnership. However, the non-exhaustive nature of Article 14 has made it possible for the European Court of Human Rights (ECtHR) to fill these gaps. Indeed, it expressly regards the Convention as 'a living instrument, to be interpreted in the light of present-day conditions'.[56] The process of updating the list has been further facilitated by the Court's reluctance to use a fixed, categorical approach, preferring to regard the grounds as fluid and interchangeable. As a result, it is relatively rare for a case to be dismissed on the basis that it did not fall within a recognized ground.

---

[53] Ibid at 623, 1623 (per Kennedy J).
[54] Canadian Charter of Rights and Freedoms, s 15(1); emphasis added.
[55] See s 9.
[56] *EB v France* (2008) 47 EHRR 21, para 92.

This is particularly evident in relation to sexual orientation. In the earlier cases, the ECtHR had no difficulty regarding sexual orientation as an aspect of sex discrimination.[57] This contrasts with the more rigid approach of the ECJ, set out above. In more recent cases, the Court has been prepared to regard sexual orientation as a ground covered by Article 14 in its own right.[58] Indeed, the inclusion of sexual orientation is now considered so well established that when the Article 14 right was expanded in Protocol 12, it was deemed unnecessary to amend the list of enumerated grounds to include an explicit reference to sexual orientation.[59] Similarly, it is now taken as uncontentious that disability is protected under Article 14.[60]

With the incorporation of the Convention into UK domestic law, UK courts have had their first experience of dealing with a non-exhaustive list. The transition from a fixed categorical approach to the fluidity of the ECtHR has not been straightforward. Instead, UK courts have sought for a definition of the residual category 'other status', which would guide them in new and challenging situations. For this they have relied on a passing reference in ECHR jurisprudence to 'personal characteristics' as the defining feature.[61] Using this as a guideline, the House of Lords has, for example, found 'homelessness' to be a personal characteristic.[62] Similarly, being a single young adult was a category potentially protected by Article 14.[63]

The expansion of discrimination protection to include non-enumerated grounds, however, is counterbalanced by a sense that not all protected grounds should be regarded as equally invidious. This in turn triggers the impetus to create hierarchies, or differing levels, of scrutiny, similar to that found in the US Supreme Court. Thus the ECtHR has held that 'very convincing and weighty' reasons are required to justify a difference in treatment based on sex.[64] Similarly, where a 'difference of treatment is based on race, colour or ethnic origin, the notion of objective and reasonable justification must be interpreted as

---

[57] *Salgueiro da Silva Mouta v Portugal* (2001) 31 EHRR 47.

[58] *SL v Austria* (2003) 37 EHRR 39, para 37; *EB v France*, above n 56, paras 90–2.

[59] Protocol 12 Explanatory Report, available at: <http://www.humanrights.coe.int/Prot12/Protocol%2012%20and%20Exp%20Rep.htm>.

[60] *Glor v Switzerland*, Application no 13444/04, 30 April 2009. Available in French at: <http://cmiskp.echr.coe.int/tkp197/view.asp?item=4&portal=hbkm&action=html&highlight=13444/04&sessionid=65378998&skin=hudoc-pr-en>.

[61] *Kjeldsen, Busk Madsen and Pederson v Denmark* (1976) 1 EHRR 711, para 56.

[62] *R (RJM) v Secretary of State for Work and Pensions* [2008] UKHL 63.

[63] *AL (Serbia) v Secretary of State for the Home Department* [2008] UKHL 42.

[64] *Abdulaziz, Cabales and Balkandali v UK* [1985] 7 EHRR 471, para 78.

strictly as possible'.[65] Birth or adopted status,[66] nationality,[67] and religion[68] have also been held to fall into this category, and, more recently, sexual orientation.[69] As this demonstrates, the ECtHR has permitted a much wider range of grounds to come within the magic circle requiring particularly weighty justification than the US Court, which we have seen is limited to alienage, race, and ancestry. The UK courts have developed and consolidated this approach still further. Thus, as Lord Hoffmann explained in *Carson's* case,

Characteristics such as race, caste, noble birth, membership of a political party and ... gender, are seldom, if ever, acceptable grounds for differences in treatment. In some constitutions, the prohibition on discrimination is confined to grounds of this kind and I rather suspect that Article 14 was also intended to be so limited. But the Strasbourg court has given it a wide interpretation, approaching that of the Fourteenth Amendment, and it is therefore necessary, as in the United States, to distinguish between those grounds of discrimination which prima facie appear to offend our notions of the respect due to the individual and those which merely require some rational justification.[70]

The difficulty with imposing different levels of scrutiny, however, is that it introduces into the otherwise fluid approach of the ECHR, a requirement to determine which category is relevant in a particular case. This has not proved particularly problematic in the jurisprudence of the ECtHR, since it applies a proportionality test to all Article 14 claims, whether enumerated or not.[71] Intensive scrutiny is simply a stronger version of proportionality. In addition, as we have seen, the ECtHR has a dynamic and continually evolving notion of which grounds require particularly weighty reasons. In the UK courts, however, the standard of scrutiny has varied more widely as between grounds, making classification particularly important. Thus Lord Hoffmann himself acknowledged that there may be borderline cases in which it is not easy to allocate the ground of discrimination to one category or the other.[72] He cited age as an example of a borderline case.

---

[65] *DH v Czech Republic*, Application no 57325/00 (2008) 47 EHRR 3 at para 196.
[66] *Inze v Austria* (1987) 10 EHRR 394, para 41.
[67] *Gaygusuz v Austria* (1996) 23 EHRR 364, para 42.
[68] *Hoffmann v Austria* (1993) 17 EHRR 293 at 316, para 36.
[69] *EB v France*, above n 56, para 91; see also *SL v Austria*, above n 58, para 37; see also *Ghaidan v Godin-Mendoza* [2004] UKHL 30, para 19.
[70] *R (Carson) v Secretary of State for Work and Pensions* [2005] UKHL 37, para 15.
[71] *Belgian Linguistic Case (No 2)* (1968) 1 EHRR 252.
[72] *R (Carson) v Secretary of State for Work and Pensions*, above n 70, para 17.

In other cases, the UK Supreme Court has been prepared to include new grounds into the category of 'other status'. But it has generally declined to regard them as requiring particularly weighty reasons by way of justification. Thus although place of residence,[73] being a single young adult,[74] and homelessness[75] have all been found to be within the 'other status' category, a very deferential standard of scrutiny has been applied. For example, *RJM* concerned a policy which excluded homeless disabled people from entitlement to a disability benefit available to all other disabled people. Although the Supreme Court held that homelessness was a characteristic protected under Article 14, and therefore the policy prima facie discriminated against homeless people, there was no breach of that Article in this case. This was because the court should be slow to substitute its opinion for that of the State in a policy area such as this.[76] Lady Hale has stated that it is unlikely that the standard under the ECHR will be as relaxed as the rationality test in US law.[77] However, it is difficult to see how much more deferent the standard could be.

While UK courts interpreting the ECHR have focused on the meaning of 'other status', Canadian courts have concentrated on whether a ground is 'analogous' for the purposes of section 15 of the Charter. As was stated in *Corbiere*,

> What then are the criteria by which we identify a ground of distinction as analogous? The obvious answer is that we look for grounds of distinction that are analogous or like the grounds enumerated in s. 15—race, national or ethnic origin, colour, religion, sex, age, or mental or physical disability.[78]

The major missing ground, sexual orientation, was held to be an analogous ground in the 1995 case of *Egan v Canada*.[79] However, rather than dropping the standard of review to permit an increasingly wide range of grounds, the Supreme Court of Canada has held that certain grounds are simply not analogous. For example, in a recent case, school teachers were barred from seeking election as school trustees anywhere in their province. They claimed that they were discriminated against on the ground of their occupational status as teachers. The Court held that

---

[73] Ibid.

[74] *AL (Serbia) v Secretary of State for the Home Department*, above n 63, para 35.

[75] *R (RJM) v Secretary of State for Work and Pensions*, above n 62, para 56.

[76] Ibid, para 56.

[77] *R (Carson) v Secretary of State for Work and Pensions*, above n 70, para 55; *AL (Serbia)*, above n 63, para 31.

[78] *Corbiere v Canada (Minister of Indian and Northern Affairs)* [1999] 2 SCR 203.

[79] *Egan v Canada* [1995] 2 SCR 513.

there was no basis for identifying occupational status as an analogous ground.[80]

The South African Constitution has a different solution. The Constitution itself expressly distinguishes between enumerated and non-enumerated grounds in relation to the standard of scrutiny to be applied. All distinctions need to satisfy a basic rationality test.[81] But grounds which are enumerated raise a presumption of unfairness, whereas in the case of grounds which are not specified, unfairness must be proved by the applicant.[82] This approach has permitted the Constitutional Court to hold that a refusal to employ people living with HIV as cabin attendants amounted to unfair discrimination on grounds of HIV status. The alternative attempt to bring HIV status under the listed ground of disability was not deemed necessary.[83]

A further permutation is found in the Indian Constitution. In the seminal case of *Naz Foundation*,[84] the Delhi High Court held that the Indian Penal Code breached the constitutional equality guarantee insofar as it criminalized consensual sexual acts of adults in private. Section 15(1) of the Constitution provides that 'the State shall not discriminate against any citizen on grounds only of religion, race, caste, sex, place of birth or any of them.' Although this appears to be a closed list, the court used a purposive construction to hold that the prohibition on discrimination applied too to grounds which are analogous to those specified in section 15. Drawing on the Canadian and US case law referred to above, the court regarded personal autonomy as the principle behind the grounds in section 15(1).

personal autonomy is inherent in the grounds in Article 15. The grounds that are not specified in Article 15 but are analogous to those specified therein, will be those which have the potential to impair the personal autonomy of an individual.[85]

On this basis, it held that sexual orientation was analogous to sex as a ground of discrimination, and the criminalization of homosexual behaviour was discriminatory. This approach also opens up the possibility of

---

[80] *Baer v Alberta* [2007] 2 SCR 673 at para 64.

[81] South African Constitution, s 9(1).

[82] *Harksen v Lane NO and Others* [1997] ZACC 12, 1997 (11) BCLR 1489 (CC), 1998 (1) SA 300 (CC).

[83] *Hoffmann v South African Airways* (CCT17/00) [2000] ZACC 17, 2001 (1) SA 1, 2000 (11) BCLR 1235, [2000] 12 BLLR 1365 (CC).

[84] *Naz Foundation v Government of NCT of Delhi*, WP(C) No 7455/2001, 2 July 2009 (High Court of Delhi).

[85] Ibid, para 22.

holding that pregnancy and disability are analogous grounds.[86] The court also drew on jurisprudence from Canada, the US, and the ECHR to formulate a standard of strict scrutiny.

113. If a law discriminates on any of the prohibited grounds, it needs to be tested not merely against 'reasonableness' under Article 14 but be subject to 'strict scrutiny'.[87]

(II) A UNIFYING PRINCIPLE?

Underlying all these approaches is the question of whether the choice of grounds, whether political or judicial, is based on a unifying principle. Judges in the various jurisdictions covered here have used remarkably similar tests. The well-established US approach is summed up by the Supreme Court in *San Antonio v Rodriguez*:

A 'suspect class' requiring application of the strict scrutiny standard of equal protection analysis is one saddled with such disabilities, or subjected to such a history of purposeful unequal treatment, or relegated to such a position of political powerlessness as to command extraordinary protection from the majoritarian political process.[88]

A strikingly similar constellation of factors has been articulated by the Canadian Court to determine whether a group not specifically mentioned in the Canadian Charter should be protected by the equality guarantee. These include whether the targeted group has suffered historical disadvantage; whether it constitutes a 'discrete and insular minority'; and whether the distinction is based on an immutable characteristic.[89] Also a consideration for Canadian courts is whether the classification has the purpose or effect of demeaning or degrading the dignity of those affected. This section identifies the common factors used by these and other courts in demarcating the groups protected by equality guarantees. It also considers the ways in which the choice of factors reflects background assumptions about the meaning of equality itself. Each factor will be examined in turn, bearing in mind that these are analytic tools, which help to signal an analogous ground; but that no one indicator is required to be present.[90]

---

[86] T Khaitan, 'Reading Swaraj into Article 15: A New Deal for All Minorities' (2009) 2 NUJS L Rev 419.

[87] *Naz Foundation v Government of NCT of Delhi*, above n 84, p 113.

[88] *San Antonio Independent School District v Rodriguez* 411 US 959 (1973) at 40–1.

[89] See *Miron v Trudel* [1995] 2 SCR 418 at 496–7 (per McLachlan J).

[90] Ibid.

(a) Immutability, choice, and autonomy

To subject an individual to a detriment on the basis of a characteristic which she is powerless to change, appears to liberal thinkers to be particularly invidious. The first factor therefore focuses on whether the exclusion is a result of an immutable characteristic, or whether there are choices available to an individual which might make her eligible for the opportunity or benefit at stake. This places autonomy centre stage.

Immutability or absence of choice as a basis for delineating grounds of discrimination has appealed to judges across all the jurisdictions examined here. As Baroness Hale put it:

> It is not so very long ago in this country that people might be refused access to a so-called 'public' bar because of their sex or the colour of their skin; that a woman might automatically be paid three quarters of what a man was paid for doing exactly the same job; that a landlady offering rooms to let might lawfully put a 'no blacks' notice in her window. We now realise that this was wrong. It was wrong because the sex or colour of the person was simply irrelevant to the choice which was being made ... it was wrong because it was based on an irrelevant characteristic which the woman or the black did not choose and could do nothing about.[91]

Similarly, for the Supreme Court of Canada, the factor common to all the enumerated and analogous grounds is that 'they often serve as the basis for stereotypical decisions made not on the basis of merit but on the basis of a personal characteristic that is immutable ...'[92]

Although intuitively appealing, a reliance on immutability does, however, raise a host of further problems. The fact that some aspects of our identity are indeed a matter of personal choice, or can in principle be changed or suppressed, should not be a reason for denying such characteristics the protection of discrimination law. Thus, for many, religion is a matter of personal choice; but does that mean that a person's religion should be a reason for discriminating against her? Pregnancy may or may not be a personal choice. But either way, choice seems irrelevant to the question whether pregnancy should be a protected characteristic. Indeed, even the apparent immutability of sex itself is not unassailable. Many recent cases have concerned discrimination against transsexuals:

[91] *Ghaidan v Godin-Mendoza*, above n 69, para 130.
[92] *Corbiere v Canada (Minister of Indian and Northern Affairs)*, above n 78.

here it is the very mutability of their sex that has triggered the discrimination.

The Canadian Court has therefore refined the meaning of immutability to include characteristics that are 'changeable only at unacceptable cost to personal identity... or that the government has no legitimate interest in expecting us to change to receive equal treatment under the law.'[93] It is on this basis that the Court has held sexual orientation to be an analogous ground: it is 'unchangeable or changeable only at unacceptable personal costs'.[94] A similar approach led them to conclude that citizenship is an analogous ground. In *Andrews*, it was held that citizenship is typically not within the control of the individual and is, at least temporarily, a characteristic of personhood which is not alterable by conscious action and which in some cases is not alterable except on the basis of unacceptable costs.[95] A parallel approach has been followed by the South African Constitutional Court, where citizenship is also not an enumerated ground. Here too the Court has held that

citizenship is typically not within the control of the individual and is, at least temporarily, a characteristic of personhood not alterable by conscious action and in some cases not alterable except on the basis of unacceptable costs.[96]

On this basis, it has held that citizenship is unquestionably an analogous ground.

Drawing on this stream of jurisprudence, the Indian courts have grounded immutability and personal choice in the more fundamental principle of personal autonomy. Thus the Supreme Court held in the *Anuj Garg* case that the right to autonomy and self-determination were the key values underpinning the right not to be discriminated against in section 15 of the Constitution.

The bottom line in this behalf would be a functioning modern democratic society which ensures freedom to pursue varied opportunities and options without discriminating on the basis of sex, race, caste or any other like basis.[97]

---

[93] Ibid, para 13.

[94] *Egan v Canada*, above n 79, para 5.

[95] *Andrews v Law Society of British Columbia* [1989] 1 SCR 143, para 75 (per La Forest J).

[96] *Khosa and Mahlaule v Minister for Social Development* 2004 (6) BCLR 569 (South African Constitutional Court), para 71.

[97] *Anuj Garg & Ors v Hotel Association of India & Ors* [2007] INSC 1226, AIR 2008 SC 663 (Supreme Court of India), para 51.

This principle was used by the Delhi High Court in the *Naz Foundation* case to extend protection to discrimination on grounds of sexual orientation.[98]

However, even in this nuanced form, the concept of immutability or personal choice does not always yield straightforward or appropriate answers to the question of whether a ground should be protected under an equality guarantee. This can be seen by considering some of the very recent UK cases. In *Carson*, the question arose as to whether Article 14 ECHR was breached by a policy of granting pension increases to British citizens resident in Britain but excluding British citizens who were resident abroad. Place of residence is not in itself included in the list of protected grounds. It was therefore necessary to determine whether it was a personal characteristic which fell into the catch-all category of 'other status'. Lord Walker did not regard the role of choice as central to the question. Instead, he held that 'Where an individual lives is in principle a matter of choice. So although it can be regarded as a personal characteristic it is not immutable.'[99] Choice was, however, re-emphasized by Lady Hale in a later case where she stated:

In general, the list concentrates on personal characteristics which the complainant did not choose and either cannot or should not be expected to change. The *Carson* case is therefore unusual, because it concerned discrimination on the ground of habitual residence, which is a matter of personal choice and can be changed.[100]

These difficulties were even more acute in *AL (Serbia)*, where young adult asylum seekers without families were excluded from an amnesty extended to all asylum seekers in the UK with young families. Is 'being without a family' an immutable characteristic? To answer this, required a particularly complex understanding of immutability: 'being without a family may not be immutable, like sex and race, but it is something over which the young person has no control'.[101] But what about homelessness? The Court of Appeal in *RJM* held that being homeless did not fall into the 'other status' category in Article 14 ECHR. In coming to this conclusion, it placed great importance on the fact that being homeless was a voluntary choice. In the Supreme Court, however, Lord

---

[98]   *Naz Foundation v Government of NCT of Delhi*, above n 84.
[99]   *R (Carson) v Secretary of State for Work and Pensions*, above n 70, para 58.
[100] *AL (Serbia) v Secretary of State for the Home Department*, above n 63, para 26.
[101] Ibid, para 32.

Neuberger acknowledged the limitations of too great a reliance on the question of choice.

I do not accept that the fact that a condition has been adopted by choice is of much, if any, significance in determining whether that condition is a status for the purposes of Article 14. Of the specified grounds in the Article, 'language, religion, political or other opinion . . . association with a national minority [or] property' are all frequently a matter of choice, and even 'sex' can be.[102]

These difficulties have led Lord Walker to pose a more nuanced test, which regards the meaning of 'personal characteristics' as a set of concentric circles.

The most personal characteristics are those which are innate, largely immutable, and closely connected with an individual's personality: gender, sexual orientation, pigmentation of skin, hair and eyes, congenital disabilities. Nationality, language, religion and politics may be almost innate (depending on a person's family circumstances at birth) or may be acquired . . . Other acquired characteristics are further out in the concentric circles; they are more concerned with what people do, or with what happens to them, than with who they are; . . . I would include homelessness as falling within that range, whether or not it is regarded as a matter of choice . . . [103]

(b) Access to the political process: discrete and insular minorities

A second factor frequently used by courts to determine whether a group should be protected relates to the extent to which the group at issue is marginalized from the political process. Here the underlying assumption is that equality law should aim to redress imbalances in majoritarian democracy. This factor originated in one of the most famous footnotes in legal history, footnote 4 of the *Carolene Products* case.[104] According to Stone J, 'more searching judicial inquiry' may be required for statutes directed at particular religious or national or racial minorities, or where 'prejudice against discrete and insular minorities . . . tends seriously to curtail the operation of those political processes ordinarily to be relied upon to protect minorities'.[105] John Hart Ely builds on this approach to develop his 'representation-reinforcing' theory of judicial review. In his view, judicial review is particularly appropriate when

---

[102] *R (RJM) v Secretary of State for Work and Pensions*, above n 62, para 47.
[103] Ibid, para 5.
[104] *United States v Carolene Products Co* 304 US 144, 58 S Ct 778 (1938).
[105] Ibid at 152.

(1) the ins are choking off the channels of political change to ensure that they will stay in and the outs will stay out or (2) though no-one is actually denied a voice or a vote, representatives beholden to an effective majority are systematically disadvantaging some minority out of simple hostility or a prejudiced refusal to recognize commonalities of interest and thereby denying that minority the protection afforded other groups by a representative system.[106]

It was on this basis, as we have seen, that the US Supreme Court identified African-Americans as a suspect class, attracting strict scrutiny under the Fourteenth Amendment.

The 'representation-reinforcing' theory has had a seminal influence on courts in Canada and South Africa, as well as in the US. Thus, in the Canadian case of *Andrews*,[107] the complainant had been refused admission to the British Columbia Bar because he was not a Canadian citizen. A British subject permanently resident in Canada, he met all the other requirements of the Bar except for citizenship. Were 'non-citizens permanently resident in Canada' protected by the equality guarantee, although not expressly mentioned? The Court held that they were. The test to be applied, according to Wilson J, was whether this group was a 'discrete and insular minority' as specified in the *Carolene Products* case. Specifically citing John Hart Ely's representation-reinforcing theory, she held that non-citizens were one of 'those groups in society to whose needs and wishes elected officials have no apparent interest in attending'.[108] In that sense, they were held to be analogous to the groups specifically enumerated in the Charter.[109] The South African Constitutional Court has drawn expressly on *Andrews* and on the reference to Ely's theory embedded in it, to come to a similar conclusion about non-citizens permanently resident in South Africa. Thus regulations excluding non-citizens from being employed as educators was held to be discriminatory, in part because of the recognition that non-citizens had little political muscle.[110] This was reinforced in *Khosa*, where it was held that differentiation on the grounds of citizenship is clearly on a

---

[106] J H Ely, *Democracy and Distrust: A Theory of Judicial Review* (Harvard University Press, 1980), p 103.

[107] Above n 95.

[108] Ely, above n 106, p 151.

[109] *Andrews v Law Society of British Columbia* above n 95, at 51.

[110] *Larbi-Odam and Others v Member of the Executive Council for Education (North-West Province) and Another (CCT2/97)* [1997] ZACC 16, 1997 (12) BCLR 1655, 1998 (1) SA 745 (26 November 1997), para 19.

ground analogous to those listed in section 9(3) and therefore amounts to discrimination.[111]

By contrast, neither the ECtHR nor the UK courts have placed any emphasis on the extent to which the group at issue is marginalized from the political process in deciding whether it warrants protection under Article 14. This is unfortunate. It might well have been of value in deciding cases such as *AL (Serbia)*, which concerned asylum seekers, who, by definition, have no access to the political process. Similarly, in *RJM*, the fact that disabled homeless people are unlikely to have an effective voice in the political process might have led the domestic courts to scrutinize with greater intensity the decision to exclude them from benefits available to other disabled people. It is certainly a surer guide than choice or immutability.

At the same time, the representation-reinforcing theory suffers from its continuing alliance with the notion of 'discrete and insular minorities', which it inherited from the paradigm case of race discrimination in the US against Afro-Americans. In particular, it is difficult to see how women could be regarded as constituting a discrete and insular minority: yet they have certainly been under-represented in the political process. Moreover, as Ackermann shows, those who are in fact least likely to succeed in the political process are those who are neither discrete nor insular. It is precisely because they are diffuse that certain groups find it difficult or impossible to organize themselves sufficiently to compete. Those who have the least access to resources are possibly the most diffuse, and it is they who should have the greatest claim to judicial concern with the fairness of the political process.[112]

This is particularly evident in relation to poverty. In the *San Antonio* case, the US Supreme Court was asked to determine whether it was discriminatory against the poor to require communities to fund local schools through local taxes. The result was inevitably that poorer districts had fewer resources with which to fund their schools, leading to inferior education for poor children. Nevertheless, the Court held that this was not a breach of the Fourteenth Amendment. Poor people, in its view, did not constitute a discrete and insular minority; the boundaries of the group were shifting and definitions of poverty varied. Yet poor people are unlikely to have the resources to mobilize the political process in their favour and therefore could well be one of 'those groups in society to whose needs and wishes elected officials have no apparent

---

[111] Above n 96.
[112] B Ackerman, 'Beyond Carolene Products' [1985] 98 Harv L Rev 713 at 718.

interest in attending'.[113] A policy which locks poorer people into a cycle of disadvantage through the provision of inferior education appears particularly invidious. The representation-reinforcing theory, cut free from the requirement of a discrete and insular minority, should lead to the conclusion that classifications which burden the poor should be subject to particularly strict scrutiny.

(c) Dignity: treating individuals as less valuable members of society

Dignity constitutes a third factor frequently used by courts to delineate protected groups. Thus in *Egan v Canada*, a case concerning a legislative exclusion of same-sex couples, Cory J stated that 'the fundamental consideration underlying the analogous grounds analysis is whether the basis of distinction may serve to deny the essential human dignity of the Charter claimant'.[114] Similarly, the South African Constitutional Court has held that under the South African Constitution,

> there will be discrimination on an unspecified ground if it is based on attributes or characteristics which have the potential to impair the fundamental dignity of persons as human beings, or to affect them adversely in a comparably serious manner.[115]

The UK courts, in elaborating the ECHR understanding of personal characteristics, have similarly referred to the importance of dignity, particularly in relation to determining which characteristics should require more demanding justification. Thus Lord Walker in *Carson* stated that grounds of discrimination requiring particularly severe scrutiny are those personal characteristics which a person cannot change 'and which, if used as a ground for discrimination, are recognised as particularly demeaning for the victim'.[116]

However, as we have seen in Chapter One, dignity could just as easily act as a brake on expansion as operate in an inclusive manner. This is particularly true for characteristics such as age. The UK case of *Reynolds*[117] concerned regulations pursuant to which applicants under 25 were entitled to less by way of jobseeker's allowance and income support

---

[113] See *San Antonio v Rodriguez* above n 88; Ely, above n 106.

[114] *Egan v Canada*, above n 79, para 171. Although Cory J dissented in the outcome of the case, this part of his judgment is endorsed in later cases. See eg *Corbiere v Canada (Minister of Indian and Northern Affairs)*, above n 78, para 59.

[115] *Harksen v Lane NO and Others*, above n 82, para 46.

[116] *R (Carson) v Secretary of State for Work and Pensions*, above n 70, para 55.

[117] Ibid; *R (Reynolds) v Secretary of State for Work and Pensions* [2005] UKHL 37.

than those of 25 and over. It was argued that this breached Article 14 by discriminating against the applicant on grounds of her age. In the House of Lords, Lord Rodgers stated:

There is no doubt that the relevant regulations, endorsed by Parliament, deliberately gave less to those under 25. But this was not because the policy-makers were treating people under 25 years of age as less valuable members of society.[118]

This is remarkably similar to the Canadian case of *Gosselin*, where the claimant challenged a scheme according to which full benefit was only available to welfare recipients over 30.[119] The majority of the Supreme Court of Canada held that 'the provision of different initial amounts of monetary support to each of the two groups does not indicate that one group's dignity was prized above the other's.'[120] Notably, Indian juris-prudence has countered this somewhat by linking the conception of dignity to that of personal autonomy. Thus in the *Naz Foundation* case, the Chief Justice of the High Court in Delhi stated:

At the root of the dignity is the autonomy of the private will and a person's freedom of choice and of action. Human dignity rests on recognition of the physical and spiritual integrity of the human being, his or her humanity, and his value as a person, irrespective of the utility he can provide to others.[121]

(d) History of disadvantage

A fourth factor assisting courts to determine whether a group should be protected relates to whether the group has been subject to a history of disadvantage or prejudice. In the US Supreme Court, as we have seen, the list of factors in *San Antonio* includes 'a history of purposeful unequal treatment'.[122] In South Africa, this has also played a prominent role, although it goes to the issue of fairness, rather than the delineation of analogous grounds. Thus *Harksen* laid down the principle, oft-repeated in later cases, that in determining fairness under the equality guarantee, regardless of whether the discrimination is on a specified ground or not, a relevant factor is the position of the complainants in

---

[118] Ibid, para 45.
[119] *Gosselin v Quebec* 2002 SCC 84 (Canadian Supreme Court).
[120] Ibid, para 61 (per McLachlin J). See now *R v Kapp*, discussed in Chapter One.
[121] *Naz Foundation v Government of NCT of Delhi*, WP(C) No.7455/2001, 2 July 2009 (High Court of Delhi) at para 26.
[122] *San Antonio Independent School Dist v Rodriguez* 411 US 1, 93 S Ct 1278 (1973) (per Powell J).

society and whether they have suffered in the past from patterns of disadvantage.[123]

This is a powerful indicator of analogous grounds and fits well with the understanding of equality set out in Chapter One. Notably, however, there may be further contestation over the meaning of disadvantage. Thus in the Canadian case of *Egan*, which concerned same-sex couples, the State argued that sexual orientation should only be considered an analogous ground if the appellants could show that homosexuals suffered a specific form of economic disadvantage which was exacerbated by the legislation in question. In the case at hand, treating the applicants as single rather than cohabitees gave them access to better benefits than married couples. However, in the Supreme Court of Canada, it was recognized that disadvantage must be read in the context of the full social, political, and economical context, in all of which homosexuals have clearly suffered disadvantage.[124]

Thus, ultimately, there is no single element which can give a definitive answer to whether a characteristic should be within the inner circle of specially protected characteristics. Instead, courts have tended to use a constellation of factors. Although perhaps leaving too much discretion in the hands of judges, this approach has in practice proved to be an important vehicle for the law to develop dynamically in response to changing circumstances.

(III) CUMULATIVE DISCRIMINATION

One consequence of the focus on group identity of current equality law is the assumption that each individual belongs to a single, well-demarcated identity group. In reality, however, we all have multiple intersecting identities, constituted by our gender, sexual orientation, age, ethnicity, capabilities, and religion or lack of religion. While this can enrich our life experience and create community cohesion born from interlocking interests and concerns, it can also intensify disadvantage for those who belong to more than one disadvantaged group. For example, black women are subject to both sexism and racism, as well as bearing a 'third burden', namely, discrimination against black men. Ethnic minority women, older women, black women, and disabled women are among the most disadvantaged groups in many EU Member States. Similar cumulative or intersectional discrimination is experienced by gay or

---

[123] *Harksen v Lane NO and Others*, above n 82, para 50.
[124] *Egan v Canada*, above n 79, para 172.

lesbian members of ethnic minorities; disabled black people; younger ethnic minority members or older disabled people.

Such discrimination is not fully described by simply adding two kinds of discrimination together. Black women share some experiences in common with both white women and black men, but they also differ in important respects. Thus while white women may be the victims of sex discrimination, they may also be the beneficiaries and even the perpetrators of racism. The relationship of dominance between white 'madams' and black 'maids' is a well-known example. Conversely, black men may experience racism but be the beneficiaries and perpetrators of sexism. Nor is it accurate to generalize about 'black' women: this category fragments under the pressure of cultural diversity. As was seen in Chapter Two, the experience of women of Afro-Caribbean origin is quite different from that of women of Pakistani and Bangladeshi origin.

Recognition of intersectional discrimination has been pioneered in the US by African-American women, who have powerfully demonstrated the ways in which sex discrimination law focuses on white women, while race discrimination law is targeted at black men. As Kimberlé Crenshaw, the foremost thinker on this subject, has argued:

> The paradigm of sex discrimination tends to be based on the experiences of white women; the model of race discrimination tends to be based on the experiences of the most privileged blacks. Notions of what constitutes race and sex discrimination are, as a result, narrowly tailored to embrace only a small set of circumstances, none of which include discrimination against black women.[125]

However, Crenshaw argues, cumulative discrimination does not simply consist in the addition of two sources of discrimination; the result is qualitatively different, or synergistic. Thus the disadvantage experienced by black women is not the same as that experienced by white women or black men. For example, in *DeGraffenreid*, a US redundancy case,[126] black women, being the most recent entries to the company, were made redundant first. Since both white women and black men were among those who escaped redundancy, they could not claim that they had been less favourably treated on grounds of either gender alone or

---

[125] K Crenshaw, 'Demarginalising the Intersection of Race and Sex' (1989) University of Chicago Legal Forum 139.

[126] *DeGraffenreid v General Motors Assembly Division* 413 F Supp 142 (US Federal Court of Appeals).

race alone. It was only the cumulative situation, of being both female and black, which was the source of the discrimination.

In the UK and EU, this is best illustrated by considering the position of migrant women.[127] Migrants of both genders tend to be concentrated in particular segments of the market, but women with a migrant background are particularly restricted, largely in low paid and insecure jobs such as cleaning, catering, personal and domestic services, health, and care.[128] Women immigrants to the EU from Muslim countries have particularly low activity rates and are largely excluded from the labour market.[129] Women in such communities could be facing discrimination from their own communities on grounds of gender as well as discrimination from the broader society on grounds of ethnicity or religion. In particular, domestic violence should be seen in terms of the synergistic impact of gender combined with racial or religious discrimination. Women find it difficult to speak out against domestic violence, through fear of direct racism by the police, or because they are concerned in case reporting violence will reinforce negative stereotypes and expose their own communities to racist treatment, including deportation or injury. Migrant women whose status depends on marriage are particularly vulnerable, since they face deportation if they leave an abusive relationship, a vulnerability compounded by language difficulties, lack of knowledge of sources of protection, and difficulties in finding work or other sources of income to support themselves and their children.[130]

International human rights instruments are showing growing recognition of the issue. Most important was the contribution of the World Conference for Women held in Beijing in 1995, which drew attention to the fact that age, disability, socio-economic position, and membership of a particular ethnic or racial group could create particular barriers for women. A framework for recognition of multiple and coexisting forms of discrimination became a key part of the resulting Beijing Platform for Action. Similarly, the preamble to the United Nations Convention on the Elimination of Discrimination Against Women (CEDAW) emphasizes that the eradication of racism is essential to the full enjoyment of

---

[127] United Nations Division for the Advancement of Women, 'Gender and Racial Discrimination: Report of the Expert Meeting' (2000).

[128] EU Monitoring Centre on Racism and Xeonophobia, 'Migrants, Minorities and Employment: Exclusion, Discrimination and Anti-discrimination in 15 Member States of the European Union' (2003).

[129] Ibid.

[130] S Fredman, *The Future of Equality in Great Britain* (Equal Opportunities Commission, 2002), pp 25–6.

the rights of women. Correspondingly, in 2000, the Committee on the Elimination of Racial Discrimination adopted a general recommendation on gender-related dimensions of racial discrimination, which calls upon States parties to report on gendered aspects of race discrimination.

The synergistic nature of discrimination means that it has proved difficult to frame policy and law in ways which can address cumulative discrimination. As a start, judges and law-makers have been wary of opening a 'Pandora's box' to claims by multiple subgroups. For example, in *DeGraffenreid*, the US Federal Court of Appeals categorically refused to accept that black women formed a separate category, arguing that this gave them a 'super remedy' or 'greater standing' than black men or white women.[131] Subsequent US cases have been more promising. In *Jefferies*, the Fifth Circuit Federal Court of Appeal recognized that discrimination against black women can exist even in the absence of discrimination against black men or white women.[132] It is now accepted that black women constitute a distinct subgroup.[133] However, later courts took fright at the possibility that this would turn

employment discrimination into a many-headed Hydra, impossible to contain . . . . Following the *Jeffries* rationale to its extreme, protected subgroups would exist for every possible combination of race, color, sex, national origin and religion.[134]

To prevent the spectre that the benefits of the anti-discrimination legislation would be 'splintered beyond use and recognition',[135] it was held that cumulative discrimination should be restricted to a combination of only two of the grounds (the 'sex plus' approach).[136] The result is both artificial and paradoxical. The more a person differs from the norm, and the more likely she is to experience multiple discrimination, the less likely she is to gain protection.

UK law has evolved in a similar manner. In *Bahl v Law Society*,[137] the Court of Appeal held that a woman who complained of both race and sex discrimination was required to prove each type of discrimination separately. This was partly because each ground was protected by separate

---

[131] *DeGraffenreid v General Motors Assembly Division*, above n 126.

[132] *Jefferies v Harris County Community Action Assn* 615 F 2d 1025 (5th Cir 1980) (US Federal Court of Appeals).

[133] Ibid at 1034.

[134] *Judge v Marsh* 649 F Supp 770 (1986) at 779 (US District Court, District of Columbia).

[135] Ibid, p 779.

[136] See *Jeffries*, above n 132, at 1033–4.

[137] *Kamlesh Bahl v The Law Society* [2004] EWCA Civ 1070.

legislation. The advent of a single statute listing all grounds of discrimination therefore brought with it the possibility of directly addressing this issue. Section 14 of the EA 2010 does in fact make express provision for discrimination on more than one ground. However, the legislation has chosen to follow the US principle of confining the comparison to two protected characteristics. It also excludes marriage and civil partnership; and pregnancy and maternity. Thus although this is an important breakthrough, it remains the case that the more a person differs from the norm, the less likely she is to gain protection. This can be compared to the much more flexible approach of the South African Constitutional Court. In a recent case, Muslim women in polygynous marriages argued that they were being treated less favourably than non-Muslim women in polygynous marriages because whereas the latter were fully recognized, only one wife in Muslim polygynous marriage was recognized as an heir. The Court unanimously held that they were discriminated against on the triple grounds of religion, gender, and marital status.[138] Far from a Hydra-headed monster, this permitted the law to respond with appropriate sensitivity to a situation of multiple disadvantage.

II SCOPE OF DISCRIMINATION LAW

It is not always the case that discrimination is prohibited in all walks of life. The reach of equality law is delineated in different ways in different jurisdictions, but this depends on specific legal, historical, and cultural factors, rather than on overriding principles. This can be seen in the UK, where the scope of discrimination law has differed depending on the statutory source. While there have been pressures for harmonization, particularly as between domestic and EU law, the pattern of protection is still not uniform, and the ECHR continues to operate in parallel to anti-discrimination legislation.

The original race and sex discrimination laws in the UK applied only to education, employment, and the provision of goods, facilities, and services to the public. The Disability Discrimination Act 1995 was similarly limited, with the addition, in due course, of premises, and transport. Discrimination outside the specified areas was not outlawed by these statutes. EU law has also been restricted in its application, but in different ways and for different reasons. As we have seen, from the

[138] *Hassam v Jacobs NO and Others (CCT83/08)* [2009] ZACC 19, 2009 (11) BCLR 1148 (South African Constitutional Court).

inception of the Community, equality as a principle was only relevant insofar as it was needed in the creation of a European-wide labour market.[139] For this reason, discrimination law at EU level was narrower than UK domestic law, traditionally applying only to employment, vocational training, and membership of employers', workers', or professional organizations. Education and the provision of goods, facilities, and services to the public, which were covered by UK sex, race, and disability discrimination law, were not regulated by the EU.

Restriction to the labour market, however, inevitably curtails the effectiveness of anti-discrimination protection. This is because inequalities in the labour market are frequently a result of discrimination outside the labour market: in education, in housing, in the division of labour within the home, and in individuals' ability to access services such as health, banking, and transport. In a belated recognition of these issues, these boundaries were breached for the first time by the Race Directive in 2000, which ventured beyond the employment field to incorporate discrimination in relation to four new areas: social protection, including social security and health care; social advantages; education; and access to and supply of goods and services which are available to the public, including housing.[140] The preamble to the Race Directive highlights the link between protection against discrimination outside the market and labour market efficiency. Discrimination based on racial or ethnic origin, it is declared, may undermine the achievement of the objectives of the EC Treaty, in particular, the attainment of a high level of employment and of social protection. At the same time, the preamble stresses equity and justice as goals.

To ensure the development of democratic and tolerant societies which allow the participation of all persons irrespective of racial or ethnic origin, . . . [it is necessary to] go beyond access to employed and self-employed activities and cover areas such as education, social protection, social advantages and access to and supply of goods and services.[141]

Despite this recognition in relation to race, the other grounds of discrimination continued to be protected by EU law only in relation to the traditional labour market arena. The Employment Directive, also passed in 2000, which applies to sexual orientation, disability, religion or belief, and age restricted the reach of protection to employment, vocational

---

[139] See eg W. Streeck, above n 10, p 397.
[140] Directive 2000/43, Art 3(1).
[141] Ibid, recital 12.

training, and membership of professional associations. This restricted coverage was replicated in the measures brought into effect in the UK to comply with the Employment Directive. This was problematic in that it created a hierarchy of grounds: race and ethnicity, so long in the wilderness, were suddenly the best protected. This in turn created pressure on the definition of the grounds, as seen above. Since ethnicity fell within the wider zone of protection, and religion fell within the narrower, it became necessary to draw bright-line distinctions between ethnicity and religion.

This awkward patchwork of protection, with some grounds better protected than others, is gradually being remedied at EU level. Equal treatment for men and women outside the labour market was addressed for the first time in 2004, with a directive implementing the principle of equal treatment between women and men in the access to and supply of goods and services.[142] In July 2008, the Commission adopted a draft directive extending the protection provided against discrimination on grounds of disability, religion or belief, age, and sexual orientation, to areas outside the labour market (social protection, including social security and health care; social advantages; education; and access to goods and services, including housing).[143] Although this received the approval of the European Parliament in April 2009, its final adoption requires unanimity among members of the Council of Ministers. By June 2010, this had not yet been forthcoming.[144]

At UK level, a more comprehensive approach to harmonizing the coverage of anti-discrimination law has finally been undertaken in the form of the EA 2010, which brings all protected characteristics within the boundaries of a single statute. The familiar contours of existing statutory coverage remain: discrimination is prohibited in relation to work; education; the provision of goods, facilities, and services to the public; and the disposal or management of premises. Discrimination in relation to membership of associations is also covered, as is transport in relation to disabled persons. The Act still applies only within the demarcated areas, so that discrimination remains lawful outside these boundaries. Nevertheless, within those boundaries, the Act has generally aimed to provide uniform protection for all the protected characteristics. In several contexts this has entailed extending protection. For example, discrimination by associations against existing or potential

---

[142] Council Directive 2004/113/EC.
[143] COM(2008) 426.
[144] See: <http://www.equineteurope.org/773517_3.html>.

members was previously only unlawful in relation to race, disability, and sexual orientation. The new legislation extends protection to gender, age, religion or belief, pregnancy and maternity, and gender reassignment.[145] The same is true for employers' liability to take reasonable steps to prevent third parties from harassing employees or applicants for employment. Previously only applicable to gender, this now applies also to age, disability, race, and gender reassignment.[146] Particularly importantly, protection against discrimination in schools is now explicitly extended to include pregnancy and gender reassignment.[147] Finally, discrimination in relation to occupational pension schemes was previously only applicable to age, disability, religion or belief, and sexual orientation. It is now also required in respect of race, gender reassignment, marriage and civil partnership, and sex.[148] However, the coverage is still far from even. Marriage and civil partnership are excluded from protection in relation to most areas, except for aspects of discrimination at work. Discrimination on grounds of age is not prohibited in relation to schools, premises, and, for under-18s, provision of goods and services and public functions. Harassment on grounds of religion or sexual orientation is not prohibited in relation to provision of goods and services.

The ECHR has a very different approach to demarcating the scope of protection. As will be recalled, Article 14 ECHR states that 'the enjoyment of the rights and freedoms set forth in this Convention shall be secured without discrimination on grounds such as...' This means that, rather than being a free-standing equality guarantee, it only prohibits discrimination in the enjoyment of rights in the Convention itself. Hence Article 14 is often criticized for its parasitic nature. However, the ECtHR has considerably expanded the reach of Article 14 by holding that a claim can lie under Article 14 even if there has been no breach of a Convention right, as long as the issue in question falls within the 'ambit' of the right, or is linked to the exercise of a right. This has allowed Article 14 to operate in practice in a wide range of circumstances. Thus, as was stated in *Sejdić and Finci* in 2009:

The prohibition of discrimination in Article 14 thus extends beyond the enjoyment of the rights and freedoms which the Convention and the Protocols require each State to guarantee. It applies also to those additional rights falling

---

[145] EA 2010, s 101.   [146] Ibid, s 40.
[147] Ibid, s 84.   [148] Ibid, s 61.

within the general scope of any Convention article, for which the State has voluntarily decided to provide.[149]

The result is far-reaching. Although there is no right to housing, education, or social security under the ECHR, there is a duty not to discriminate if a State does in fact make provision in relation to these areas, since each of these is linked to the exercise of a right actually guaranteed.[150] For example, Article 8 protects the right to respect for home and family life. A State is not obliged to provide parental leave allowance. But if it does, its actions fall within the ambit of Article 8 and the duty not to discriminate in Article 14 is engaged.[151] The UK courts have followed a similar line of reasoning. For example, in *Ghaidan*,[152] legislation on social housing permitted married and unmarried heterosexual partners to inherit a statutory tenancy. Same-sex partners were, however, excluded. The House of Lords reaffirmed that there was no duty to provide a home under Article 8 on its own. However, in fact, the UK government had chosen to intervene in a factual area characteristic of those protected by Article 8, here the applicant's home. This meant that Article 14 was engaged. Thus the House of Lords found that the measure breached Article 14, together with Article 8.

Article 14, however, has no purchase where the State has not chosen to take any steps falling within the ambit of a right, or if there is no right which covers the situation at all. Some of these limitations have now been more directly addressed in Protocol 12, which was opened for signature in November 2000. Article 1(1) of Protocol 12 to the ECHR provides that 'the enjoyment of *any right set forth by law* shall be secured without discrimination' on any of the specified grounds.[153] This means that protection against discrimination is provided in relation to the enjoyment of any right specifically granted to an individual under national law, not just in the enjoyment of Convention rights. The importance of this extension was seen in *Sejdić and Finci v Bosnia and Herzegovina*.[154] In this case, the applicants, of Roma and Jewish origin respectively, challenged the constitutional settlement barring them from

---

[149] *Sejdić and Finci v Bosnia and Herzegovina*, Application nos 27996/06 and 34836/06, 22 December 2009, unreported (ECtHR), para 39.

[150] See *Belgian Linguistic Case (No 2) Stec v United Kingdom* (2006) 43 EHRR 47; *EB v France*, above n 56.

[151] *Petrovic v Austria* (2001) 33 EHRR 14, paras 27–9. The State can still argue that the differential treatment is justified.

[152] *Ghaidan v Godin-Mendoza*, above n 69.

[153] Emphasis added.

[154] *Sejdić and Finci v Bosnia and Herzegovina*, above n 149.

standing for election to the House of Peoples (the second chamber of the State Parliament) and the presidency (the collective Head of State). Only Bosniacs, Croats, and Serbs were eligible for these positions. The ECHR includes a guarantee of free periodic elections, but this does not in terms give the right to stand for election to the presidency.[155] Nevertheless, the Court held, the complaint concerned a 'right set forth by law', for the purposes of Protocol 12 and that the provision was indeed discriminatory under the Protocol.

Article 1(1) only covers rights which have been specifically granted by the State. Article 1(2) of the Protocol is even wider, stating that 'no-one shall be discriminated against by any public authority' on one of the specified grounds. Thus the non-discrimination guarantee applies in the exercise of public functions, regardless of whether a right has been specifically granted. The duty also arises in the exercise by a public authority of discretionary powers, for example the granting of certain subsidies, as well as in respect of any other act or omission of a public authority. Protocol 12 would cover, for example, the behaviour of law enforcement officers when controlling a riot.[156] The UK has not, however, ratified Protocol 12 and there do not appear to be any moves in train to do so. The scope of influence of the ECHR on UK domestic law is therefore confined to the reach of Article 14.

III WHO IS BOUND?

Closely linked to the question of the scope of discrimination law is that of who should be bound. In jurisdictions with a constitutional guarantee, it is generally assumed that the State, and not private actors, should be bound. In other words, like other human rights, the equality guarantee should have vertical but not horizontal effect. Both the ECHR and EU law in principle bind only the State, although several techniques have been developed to circumvent this limitation. By contrast, anti-discrimination legislation in the UK began by focusing on private functions, and has only recently included all the functions of the State.

Most closely tied to the vertical model is the ECHR, which, as a treaty, binds only the State. Its major effect on private individuals comes through the obligation on the State to protect individuals against other

---

[155] Article 3 of Protocol No 1.
[156] See para 22 of the explanatory report appended to Draft Protocol No 12 as transmitted by the Steering Committee for Human Rights CCDH 99(10), 25 June 1999.

individuals who breach their Convention rights.[157] The strictness of this model is softened in important ways by the Human Rights Act 1998 (HRA), which widens the range of actors bound by the Convention to include private bodies when performing public functions. Recognizing that many State functions are now delegated to private bodies, the HRA provides that human rights duties should apply to private or voluntary sector bodies when performing functions 'of a public nature'.[158] Domestic courts have, however, been reluctant to give this concept the breadth of interpretation originally intended,[159] resting the definition on the relationship of the body to the government, rather than the function itself.[160] The result has been to exclude important providers of public functions, such as housing providers or care homes. Instead, as the Joint Committee on Human Rights has proposed, the key test for 'public function' should be whether the relevant 'function' is one for which the government has assumed responsibility in the public interest.[161]

EU law has developed more sophisticated attempts to extend its reach from a purely vertical model to one which binds private individuals in some situations. It was initially envisaged that only the State would be bound, on the assumption that domestic legislation would be enacted to bind private individuals. However, a reluctance on the part of Member States fully to comply with EU law led the ECJ to develop a doctrine of horizontal direct effect. This has been particularly true in the equality field. Article 119 of the Treaty of Rome, which provided for equal pay for equal work for men and women, lay dormant for decades until, in the seminal case of *Defrenne v Sabena*,[162] the ECJ held that Article 119 was both vertically and horizontally directly effective. This meant that an individual could claim equal pay directly under Article 119, in domestic courts, against both her employer and the State, even in the absence of domestic legislation. Article 119 became Article 141 under the Treaty of

---

[157] *Costello-Roberts v United Kingdom*, Application no 13134/87 (1993) 19 EHRR 112, [1993] ECHR 16.

[158] HRA s. 6(3).

[159] See eg HC Deb, 16 February 1998, col 773 (Home Secretary); HC Deb, 17 June 1998, cols 409–10, 433 (Home Secretary), HL Deb, 24 November 1997, cols 800, 811 (Lord Chancellor).

[160] *YL (by her litigation friend the Official Solicitor) v Birmingham CC* [2007] UKHL 27, [2007] 3 WLR 112.

[161] Joint Committee on Human Rights, *The Meaning of Public Authority under the Human Rights Act*, Ninth Report of Session 2006–07 (HL Paper 77; HC 410) (The Stationery Office, 28 March 2007), para 7.

[162] Case 43/75 *Defrenne v Sabena* [1976] ECR 455 (ECJ).

Amsterdam, and has now been transferred to Article 157 of the Lisbon Treaty.

The ECJ has stopped short of holding that directives can have horizontal direct effect. Thus it held that the Equal Treatment Directive,[163] which provides for equal treatment of men and women in access to employment, promotion, vocational training, and working conditions, is directly binding on the State, but not private employers.[164] This principle continues to hold true for the newer version of the Equal Treatment Directive, the Recast Directive,[165] as well as the Race Directive and the Employment Directive. Thus, most recently, in *Kücükdeveci*, the Court stated as follows:

> In this respect, where proceedings between individuals are concerned, the Court has consistently held that a directive cannot of itself impose obligations on an individual and cannot therefore be relied on as such against an individual.[166]

This has led to some problematic anomalies, with State employees better protected against discrimination than their counterparts in the private sector.

The impact of this limitation has, however, been softened in two important respects. First, the ECJ has interpreted the notion of the State widely[167] including, for example, a nationalized industry which provides a public service under the control of the State.[168] Secondly, it has developed a principle of 'indirect effect', which means that,

> in applying national law, the national court called on to interpret it is required to do so, as far as possible, in the light of the wording and the purpose of the directive in question, in order to achieve the result pursued by the directive.[169]

This is true even when the case concerns a private body, with the effect that the latter is in practice bound.[170] Most recently, the ECJ has taken this still further, to have a similar effect even if national law is clear and

---

[163] Council Directive 76/207/EEC.

[164] Case C-152/84 *Marshall v Southampton Area Health Authority* [1986] ECR 723 (ECJ).

[165] 2006/54/EC.

[166] *Kücükdeveci v Swedex Gmbh & Co KG*, above n 15, para 46.

[167] Case C-409/95 *Marshall v Southampton and South West Hampshire Area Health Authority (Teaching) No 1* [1986] ECR 723 (ECJ).

[168] Case C-188/89 *Foster v British Gas plc* [1990] ECR I-3313.

[169] *Kücükdeveci v Swedex Gmbh & Co KG*, above n 15, para 48.

[170] Case 14/83 *Von Colson and Kamann v Land Nordrhein-Westfalen* [1984] ECR 1891 (ECJ); Case C-106/89 *Marleasing* [1990] ECR I-4135.

cannot be interpreted consistently with the Directive. Thus in *Kücük-deveci*, the Court held that the Employment Directive (2000/78)

> merely gives expression to, but does not lay down, the principle of equal treatment in employment and occupation, and that the principle of non-discrimination on grounds of age is a general principle of European Union law in that it constitutes a specific application of the general principle of equal treatment.[171]

This meant that the national court

> hearing a dispute involving the principle of non-discrimination on grounds of age as given expression in Directive 2000/78, to provide, within the limits of its jurisdiction, the legal protection which individuals derive from European Union law and to ensure the full effectiveness of that law, disapplying if need be any provision of national legislation contrary to that principle.[172]

The development of domestic law has been in the opposite direction. Anti-discrimination law in the UK has always applied to private bodies, albeit only in their capacities as employers, service providers, and education providers. Public bodies were not bound in respect of all their functions, but only insofar as they were employers, or service or education providers. Even then, there were specific exceptions for bodies acting within their statutory authority. The RRA did not apply to immigration control[173] nor to police when pursuing and arresting or charging alleged criminals.[174] Yet these are areas in which the individual is most vulnerable to racial discrimination, as was brutally demonstrated by the reaction of the police and other authorities to the racist murder of a young black man, Stephen Lawrence. The MacPherson inquiry, established to examine the response to the murder, found unequivocally that institutional racism was rife in the Metropolitan Police Service, in other police services, and in other institutions countrywide.[175] It was not until 2000 that the race legislation was amended to make it unlawful for a public authority to discriminate against or victimize a person on racial grounds in carrying out any of its functions. Similar amendments were later made to sex and disability discrimination legislation.

---

[171] *Kücükdeveci v Swedex Gmbh & Co* KG, above n 15, paras 20, 50; *Mangold*, above n 15, paras 74–7.

[172] *Kücükdeveci v Swedex Gmbh & Co KG*, above n 15, para 50.

[173] *R v Entry Clearance Officer (Bombay), ex p Amin* [1983] 2 AC 818 (HL).

[174] *Farah v Commissioner for Police for the Metropolis* [1998] QB 65 (CA).

[175] Home Office 'Report of the MacPherson Inquiry' (Cmd 4262, 24 February 1999), p 6.39.

The EA 2010 now consolidates this development by making it unlawful to discriminate in the exercise of all public functions. This means that so far as public bodies are concerned, the limitations of scope above do not apply: all public functions are covered, unless specifically excepted. This is true for all the protected grounds except for civil partnership, marital status, or age where this relates to a person under 18.[176] Moreover, the EA 2010 carries forward the trend already established by the HRA, by referring to all 'public functions' even if they are exercised by private bodies. At the same time, as we have seen, it has not been easy to define 'public functions' for the purposes of the HRA, a difficulty which the EA 2010 makes no attempt to resolve. Instead, it simply defines a public function as having the same meaning as that in the HRA.[177] This may, however, be less of a problem than under the HRA, given that a significant number of private functions, such as employment, the provision of services, and education, are also covered by the EA 2010.

---

[176] EA 2010, s 29(6).   [177] Ibid, s 31(4).

4

Legal Concepts: Direct, Indirect Discrimination, and Beyond

Anti-discrimination law has grown rapidly, in both scope and complexity. Yet true equality remains elusive. This prompts a closer examination of the different concepts of equality used in anti-discrimination law. Is the limited effect explained by flaws in the ways in which the equality principle is transposed into legal forms? Or are we expecting equality to achieve something of which it is incapable? It is to these difficult questions which we now turn.

The most basic principle is that of equality before the law, requiring the removal of specific legal impediments. Significant progress has been made to achieve equality for some groups, although there remain groups for whom even juridical equality has not yet been achieved. At the same time, it quickly became evident that equality before the law is insufficient on its own. For women, equal voting and property rights did not eliminate pay structures in which women were explicitly paid less than men doing the same work; women were still dismissed from paid employment on marriage or pregnancy; and women remained segregated into low paid, low status jobs. Similarly, the basic right to citizenship for ethnic minorities did not prevent racism, nor exclusion on grounds of colour from jobs or housing, nor institutionalized hostility from police forces and other service providers.

To tackle these phenomena, a more developed notion of equality was needed. Instead of simply removing juridical impediments, it was necessary to prohibit prejudiced behaviour and discrimination by public and private actors. The building block has been the basic conception that likes should be treated alike. In legal terms, this received its first major expression through women's right to equal pay for equal work. It is encapsulated more generally in the principle of direct discrimination, which prohibits less favourable treatment of two similarly situated individuals on grounds of a protected characteristic. However, as was seen in Chapter One, the concept that likes should be treated alike is limited in important ways. Most importantly, equal treatment in the context of pre-existing disadvantage will simply perpetuate or even exacerbate inequality of outcome. It was in recognition of this limitation that the US Supreme Court developed the concept of 'disparate impact'. Where equal treatment disproportionately disadvantages a group which already suffers from a history of discrimination, then it too can be unlawful, unless there is a good reason.[1] This concept was imported into UK law and gradually made its way into EU law. Known as indirect discrimination, it is formulated in different ways, but broadly speaking has three elements: equal treatment; a disproportionately exclusionary impact on those sharing a protected characteristic; and the absence of an acceptable justification. A similar concept, known as adverse effects discrimination, has been developed by the Supreme Court of Canada in relation to the equality guarantee in section 15 of the Canadian Charter.[2]

More recently, and primarily in the context of disability discrimination, a further concept has been introduced, in the form of a duty of reasonable accommodation or adjustment. Whereas the equal treatment principle requires conformity to the dominant norm, the duty of reasonable accommodation or adjustment expressly requires a modification of the able-bodied norm to facilitate equal participation of people with disabilities. In other jurisdictions, such as Canada, this concept has been used in the context of religious discrimination, requiring employers to provide exemptions or modifications of specific practices to accommodate individuals from minority religions.

Each of these differing legal formulations of equality invites a further question: how much weight should be given to equality in the face of competing priorities? If a finding of prima facie discrimination has been made, can it nevertheless be justified on the basis that the distinction serves other ends, such as the business interests of the employer, the social policies of the State, or the rights and interests of others? In UK domestic law, there has traditionally been a strong resistance to permitting a general justification defence for direct discrimination, except in specific contexts.[3] Indirect discrimination can, however, be justified. This fundamental difference in approach to justification has meant

---

[1] *Griggs v Duke Power Co* 401 US 424 (1971).
[2] *Ontario Human Rights Commission v Simpsons-Sears Ltd* [1985] 2 SCR 53 at 551.
[3] eg, genuine occupational qualification; equal pay; age; and disability.

that bright-line distinctions must be drawn between direct and indirect discrimination.

The relatively rigid framework of statutory anti-discrimination law, resting on a strict division between direct and indirect discrimination, contrasts with the more flexible notion of equality found in many constitutional documents, including Article 14 of the European Convention on Human Rights (ECHR). The primary guiding principle behind Article 14 is that not all distinctions are discriminatory: only those for which there is no objective and proportionate justification. This chapter considers the way in which the proportionality doctrine operates in this context and contrasts it with the approach in anti-discrimination legislation. Dignity is also the express basis of the legal formulation in some contexts, such as harassment and discrimination by association. These are dealt with briefly in Section VIII. Finally, a more wide-ranging set of positive duties to promote equality of opportunity have been introduced since 2000. However, unlike the duty of reasonable adjustment in UK law, these do not give rise to individual rights. Positive duties are discussed in detail in Chapter Six.

The Equality Act (EA) 2010 now incorporates and harmonizes what was previously a bewildering array of definitions of each of these concepts. This is complemented by Article 14 ECHR. In principle, these should provide powerful instruments to address the inequalities identified in Chapter Two. In many respects they do so. However, each concept has its own limitations, weaknesses which are only partially buttressed by strengths in alternative approaches within the statutory framework. In addition, the interface between different concepts, such as direct and indirect discrimination, can be uncomfortably jagged.

The aim of this chapter is to develop an understanding of these foundational concepts, and their relationship with each other. In particular, the extent to which they can achieve the four-dimensional understanding of equality posed in Chapter One will be analysed. It will be recalled that it was argued there that substantive equality resists capture by a single principle, whether it be dignity, equality of results, or equality of opportunity. I argued instead that it should be seen as a multi-dimensional concept, consisting of four overlapping aims: to break the cycle of disadvantage associated with status or out-groups (the redistributive dimension); to promote respect for the equal dignity and worth of all, thereby redressing stigma, stereotyping, humiliation, and violence (the recognition dimension); to restructure, accommodate and positively affirm different identities while maintaining a community of values (the transformational dimension); and to facilitate full participation in society (the participative dimension).

I EQUAL PAY LEGISLATION: THE SHACKLED GIANT

The right to equal pay for equal work was, as we have seen, originally enacted in the Equal Pay Act 1970 (EqPA). When the UK entered the EU in 1972, it also became subject to Article 119 of the Treaty of Rome, which, together with the Equal Pay Directive, provided for equal pay for work of equal value. Equal pay provisions are now incorporated into Chapter 3 of the EA 2010, under the heading 'Equality of Terms'. The provisions retain the basic structure inherited from the original EqPA: a woman has the right to equal pay for like work, work rated as equivalent, or work of equal value with a man employed by the same employer at the same or equivalent establishment. If equal work has been established, the burden shifts to the employer to justify the inequality of pay on grounds which do not directly or indirectly involve sex. The provisions apply equally to men seeking equal pay with women.[4] The legislation has radical potential, in the form of the concept of equal value. However, this potential is severely constrained by shackling equal value to the limited conception of equality as treating likes alike. This section begins with the radical potential of equal value before turning to the constraining factors.

(I) EQUAL VALUE: A RADICAL POSSIBILITY

Equal pay legislation was one of the earliest legal interventions, both in the EU and the UK, where separate pay scales for men and women doing the same work persisted well into the middle of the twentieth century. The removal of such flagrant pay discrimination was not, however, sufficient to resolve the pay gap between men and women. Job segregation, together with the widespread undervaluation of women's work, meant that the gender pay gap proved impervious to straightforward legal solutions. It was the concept of equal pay for work of equal value which had the potential to revolutionize women's role in the workforce. By penetrating job labels to examine the characteristics of women's work, the notion of equal value opens up dramatic possibilities for transcending evaluations of women's work which

---

[4] EA 2010, ss 64–80; Art 157, TFEU.

depend on deeply held stereotypes and entrenched inequalities in women's bargaining power. Properly handled, the concept of equal value reveals the extent to which women's work shares characteristics usually attributed only to men's work, such as heavy work and responsibility. It also requires recognition of chronically undervalued elements of women's work, such as manual dexterity and caring. As a result, a cook has been compared to a carpenter; a home help to a refuse collector; and learning support assistants to painters, drivers, and street cleaners.

The right to equal pay for work of equal value has the potential to achieve a rare synthesis of the redistributive, recognition, and participative dimensions of equality identified in Chapter One. The redistributive dimension is central to the mission of equal pay legislation: by correcting inequalities in pay, it clearly has the potential to redress disadvantage experienced by women because of their gender. Moreover, the concept of equal value acknowledges that many of these distributive consequences are a direct result of the underlying recognition harms: namely the undervaluation of certain types of work because it has traditionally been done by women.[5] Indeed, a central cause of unequal pay is absence of full recognition of the value of women's work. The redistributive and recognition dimensions of equal value together enhance women's ability to participate as equal citizens in the labour market, thus furthering the participative dimension. The concept of equal value is less adept at changing underlying structures, and therefore addressing the transformative dimension. For example, a major achievement of equal pay legislation has been to give part-time workers the right to receive equal pay pro rata for their work. Since women predominate among part-time workers, this has been an important step forward. However, it has not changed the underlying structure, whereby women are primarily responsible for childcare. Therefore, part-time work, while somewhat better paid, has remained predominantly female.

Much of the revolutionary potential of equal value has, however, been blighted by the limited concept of equality to which it has been shackled. The primary conception of equality behind equal pay laws is that likes should be treated alike. In addition, a far-reaching justification defence has always been available, potentially allowing arguments based on costs to trump equality. Equal pay legislation has also been particularly affected by the constraints of an individualized, complaint-based legal

---

[5] S Fredman, 'Redistribution and Recognition: Reconciling Inequalities' (2007) 23 South African Journal on Human Rights 214–34.

framework. This has meant that each complainant is required to prove her own case, based on a comparison with a specific male employed by the same employer who can be proved to be responsible for the difference in pay. The result has been a slow and cumbersome legal process in a field which is essentially collective. This final point is explored further in Chapter Six. The effects of the reliance on the equal treatment principle are dealt with below.

(II) TREAT LIKES ALIKE: THE SAME EMPLOYMENT REQUIREMENT

Under equal pay legislation in the UK, the notion that likes should be treated alike receives its most concrete formulation. A woman can only claim equal pay if she is paid less than a man doing equal work and employed contemporaneously for the same employer at the same or 'equivalent' establishment.[6] Not only must the comparator be employed by the same employer: he must also be at the same establishment. This severely curtails the reach of equal pay legislation. As we have seen, one of the chief causes of low pay among women is the fact that so many women work in segregated workplaces or in the lower grades of mixed professions. A woman working in a segregated workplace is unlikely to find a male comparator doing equal work for higher pay at the same establishment.

This is somewhat mitigated by permitting A to compare herself with B if B is employed by the same employer at a different establishment in situations in which 'common terms apply at the establishments (either generally or as between A and B)'.[7] This somewhat opaque formulation has not been easy to interpret. The clearest situation in which a woman can compare herself with a man at a different establishment of the same or associated employer is where both are covered by the same collective agreement.[8] This is helpful in parts of the public sector where there are still collective agreements which span more than one workplace. Thus a nursery nurse, working at a nursery school with no available male comparators, could compare herself with a male clerical worker working for the same authority at the town hall, because both job classes were covered by the same collective agreement.[9] Alternatively, it has been held that a cross-establishment comparison can be drawn where like

---

[6] EA 2010, s 79.   [7] Ibid.
[8] *Leverton v Clwyd County Council* [1984] IRLR 28 (HL).   [9] Ibid.

terms and conditions would apply if men were employed at her establishment in the particular jobs concerned.[10]

However, these conditions are increasingly difficult to meet, due to the steep decline in collective bargaining, particularly in the private sector, and the technical approach of courts to the interpretation of the statutory provisions. Moreover, where several collective agreements cover different parts of the workforce, a woman's right to equal pay might depend on historical patterns of collective bargaining.[11] The result can be seen in a case in 2009, where women classroom assistants and nursery nurses, employed at schools operated by Dumfries Council, sought equality of pay with male manual workers, including road workers and refuse collectors, employed by the same council and doing work of equal value. But the comparators were neither based at their schools, nor employed under the same collective agreement. Nor was there a real likelihood that the male workers might have been employed at the schools. Thus there was no appropriate comparator. Although the women and men were employed by the same employer in jobs with equal value, the women continued to be seriously underpaid relative to the men.[12]

Such a narrow understanding of the reach of the comparison required by the maxim 'likes should be treated alike' arguably confuses the role of comparison with that of justification. If it is believed that there might be good reasons why a woman is paid less than a man doing work of equal value at a different establishment of the same employer, this should be raised as part of a justification defence.[13] A regional differentiation, such as a London weighting, might well be justified in this way. A model for reform can be found in the comprehensive report of the Canadian Taskforce on Pay Equity, which recommended that comparisons should normally be based on all the operations of the employer. The normal rule could be modified where different operations of the same employer are carried out in different regions of the country with differing economic environments or in separate and distinct industrial sectors.[14]

Even more problematic is the requirement that the comparator be employed by the same employer. Since the 1980s, there has been an

[10] *British Coal Corpn v Smith* [1996] ICR 515 (HL) at 526.
[11] *South Tyneside Metropolitan Borough Council v Anderson* [2007] ICR 1581 (CA).
[12] *Dumfries and Galloway Council v North* [2009] ICR 1363 (EAT).
[13] EA 2010, s 69.
[14] Pay Equity Taskforce and Departments of Justice and Human Resources Development Canada, *Pay Equity: A New Approach to a Fundamental Right* (2004), Recommendation 6.10, pp 505–6 (hereinafter 'Canadian Taskforce').

increasing tendency to cut costs in the public sector by 'contracting out' services previously carried out in-house. This has led to the replacement of many public sector jobs with services provided by private contractors, particularly in low paid, predominantly female-dominated areas such as cleaning and catering. Indeed, it is their ability to cut pay rates that gives private contractors the advantage in the tendering process. The result is that low paid female cleaning or catering staff who are employed by a private contractor may work in the same establishment and do work of equal value as workers employed directly by a public employer. Yet because they are employed by a different employer, they would not be entitled to an equal pay claim.

EU law briefly signalled the promise of a wider scope of comparison. In the early case of *Defrenne*,[15] the European Court of Justice (ECJ) held that inter-industry comparisons were too complex to give rise to directly enforceable rights without domestic legislation. Nevertheless, it left open the possibility of a comparison between employees in the 'same service'. Later case law reaffirmed that the comparator need not be employed by the same employer. However, it very quickly withdrew the hope of a genuine broadening of the scope of comparison by sub-stituting the need for the 'same employer' by a requirement that the respondent be responsible for the pay differential.[16] Thus in *Laurence*, the ECJ held that:

> where the differences identified in the pay and conditions of workers performing equal work or work of equal value cannot be attributed to a single source, there is no body which is responsible for the inequality and which could restore equal treatment . . . The work and the pay of those workers cannot therefore be compared on the basis of [Article 141(1) EC].[17]

The focus on responsibility makes it impossible to address institutional or structural discrimination, which cannot be traced to the fault of any one individual. At the same time, it has the paradoxical effect of permitting deliberate avoidance by employers, who can minimize the scope for equal pay comparisons by contracting out and decentralizing pay structures. This was clearly demonstrated in *Allonby*,[18] where the employer transferred its part-time lecturers, who were predominantly female, to an agency, thereby avoiding the possibility of comparison

---

[15] Case 43/75 *Defrenne* [1976] ECR 455; see further *Scullard v Knowles* [1996] IRLR 344 (EAT).

[16] Case C-256/01 *Allonby v Accrington & Rossendale College* [2004] IRLR 224 (ECJ).

[17] Case C-320/00 *Lawrence v Regent Office Care* [2002] ECR I-7325, paras 17–18.

[18] *Allonby v Accrington & Rossendale College*, above n 16.

between full-time and part-time workers. The agency workers continued to do the same work at the same establishment, but on considerably worse terms and conditions.

One way forward would be to permit the use of a 'hypothetical' male comparator, as is found in the direct discrimination provisions (see below). Instead of pointing to a male colleague, a claimant could argue that she has been less favourably treated than a man would be. This would facilitate equal pay claims in cases of severe job segregation. An example of its use is the Canadian proxy method, which provides for comparison with job classes of a different employer. This is applied both in Ontario (albeit to the public sector only) and in Quebec (to both public and private sectors) and is one of the Taskforce recommendations for Federal pay equity legislation.[19] Indeed, when the Government of Ontario attempted to repeal the proxy method, the Ontario court held that this discriminated against women in segregated public sector jobs,

by denying them the opportunity of quantifying and correcting the systemic gender-based wage inequity from which they suffer, a benefit the [pay equity legislation] grants to other women working in the broader public sector.[20]

Equal pay in UK law has been traditionally separated from anti-discrimination law outside of pay and conditions. This has meant that the direct discrimination provisions, which do include a hypothetical comparator, have not applied in the equal pay field. However, EU law now requires Member States to provide protection against direct discrimination in relation to pay, which would include a hypothetical comparator provision.[21] A tentative first step in this direction has also been taken by the EA 2010, which provides that, although as a rule direct discrimination does not apply in relation to pay, it may do so if a sex equality clause (implying equal pay into the contract) 'has no effect'.[22] Arguably, then, direct discrimination, with its hypothetical comparator, would apply in a situation in which a sex equality clause has no effect due to the absence of an actual male comparator.

---

[19] Canadian Taskforce, above n 14, p 328.
[20] *SEIU, Local 204 v Ontario (Attorney General)* 151 DLR (4th) 273 (Ontario Court of Justice).
[21] Recast Directive 2006/54/EC.
[22] EA 2010, ss 70–1.

(III) CONSISTENCY BUT NOT SUBSTANCE

Treating likes alike requires consistent treatment, but does not dictate any substantive content. As we have seen, the principle will be satisfied even if both the man and the woman are equally badly paid. Thus if the only appropriate male comparator is equally badly paid, equal pay laws are of no assistance to a low paid woman. Yet this fails to address the structural causes of the gender pay gap. Men who work at a 'woman's' rate are most likely to be doing so in a transitory fashion, either as students, or as a route to promotion.[23] Women, by contrast, tend to remain in such jobs throughout their working lives.

The adherence to consistency rather than substance also means that the requirement that likes be treated alike could be fulfilled by lowering men's pay to that of women's, rather than raising women's pay to that of men's. This issue has become a major source of contention in local government in the UK.[24] A far-reaching job evaluation scheme has been agreed, promising to bring about a radical change in relation to under-valued women's work. However, several local authorities, in the absence of appropriate government funding, threatened to reduce men's pay instead of increasing that of women. In other words, relatively low paid men would be footing the bill to achieve equality of pay with very low paid women. This solution, not surprisingly, proved deeply unpalatable. However, instead of raising women's pay to that of men's, a number of local authority employers agreed to 'protect' the pay of the adversely affected (predominantly male) grades for periods of up to three years. The effect is simply to preserve the pay gap between men and women. This in turn led to further litigation by women, claiming equal pay with the men who were within the pay protection packages. In *Redcar v Bainbridge*,[25] the Court of Appeal agreed that the women would have been within the protected category had they not been the subject of past sex discrimination. However, the court did not require women's pay simply to be raised to that of men doing work of equal value. Instead, it left it open to employers to justify pay protection for male workers on the facts of the case.

---

[23] J Rubery, *The Economics of Equal Value*, Research Discussion Series, No 3 (Equal Opportunities Commission, 1992), p 50.

[24] See further S Fredman, 'Reforming Equal Pay Laws' [2008] 37 ILJ 193–218.

[25] *Redcar and Cleveland Borough Council v Bainbridge; Middlesbrough Borough Council v Surtees* [2008] EWCA Civ 885.

(IV) EQUAL TREATMENT VS PROPORTIONALITY

Equal pay legislation only requires that 'likes' should be treated 'alike'. There is no requirement that men and women be treated appropriately according to their difference. This leaves the law powerless to address the common situation in which a woman is doing work which is admittedly of less value than that of a man, but the difference in pay is disproportionately large relative to the difference in value. A claim lies only in extreme cases, where the woman is doing work of greater value but is paid less. In such a case, the ECJ has recognized that to exclude the claim would be to go against the spirit of the legislation.[26] Thus in *Redcar v Bainbridge*,[27] in a highly segregated workforce, female catering employees and care workers were unable to find an appropriate male comparator doing equal work. Instead, they sought to compare themselves with refuse collectors, who were on lower grades, but better paid than they were. The Court of Appeal was prepared to read words into the EqPA to make it clear that a woman could compare her pay to that of a man doing work of less value. However, the remedy was to award the woman the same pay as the man on the lower grade, instead of the higher pay which was appropriate to her grade. Moreover, this is limited to extreme cases where women are doing work of greater value. It does not deal with disproportionate pay differentials in cases in which a woman is doing work of lower value.

This can be contrasted with the approach in Canada, where the rigid equal treatment model has been relaxed in important ways. In particular, when directly equivalent male comparator jobs are not available within the same employment, provision may be made for proportionate pay. Under this system, the relationship between the points assigned to male job classes in a job evaluation process is determined. The same relationship is then applied to female job classes.[28]

(V) COMPETING PRIORITIES: JUSTIFYING UNEQUAL PAY FOR EQUAL WORK

Even if a woman can show that she is being paid less than a relevant male comparator doing work of equal value, the employer is still entitled to

---

[26] *Murphy v Bord Telecom Eireann* [1988] ICR 445 (ECJ).
[27] *Redcar and Cleveland Borough Council v Bainbridge; Middlesbrough Borough Council v Surtees*, above n 25.
[28] Canadian Taskforce, above n 14, p 328.

justify the difference.[29] The presence of a justification defence for equal pay reflects a long-standing sense among policy-makers, that equality should not impose 'burdens on business'. Such an argument has been particularly salient recently in relation to equal pay, where decades of indolence in redressing the pay gap have run up a large and costly backlog. Indeed, women's right to equal pay for equal work is often represented as an unreasonable demand on resources, carrying with it an unsustainable cost. In this context, therefore, special vigilance must be exercised to ensure that the equality value is not simply subordinated to the competing self-interest of the employer.

Under the EqPA, the defence was formulated as simply requiring objective justification by a material factor which was not the difference of sex.[30] This did not in terms rule out a justification which, while not explicitly based on sex, in effect reinforced existing patterns of discrimination. For example, there has been a widespread practice of paying part-timers less than full-timers for the same work. As we have seen, the fact that women remain primarily responsible for childcare has meant that the vast majority of part-time workers, in both the UK and elsewhere in the EU, are women. Can an employer justify paying a woman less than a man doing the same work on the grounds that she is part time, while the male comparator works full time? This is a material factor which is not expressly based on gender, but which in practice reinforces discriminatory structures.

The ECJ from early in its case law has been sensitive to this difficulty. In the seminal case of *Jenkins v Kingsgate*,[31] it was held that where a difference in pay is not directly based on sex, but in fact disproportionally affects women, it must be justified.[32] The standard of justification is searching: a difference can only be justified 'if the means chosen meet a genuine need of the enterprise, are suitable for attaining the objective pursued by the enterprise and are necessary for that purpose'.[33] Somewhat more latitude has been subsequently granted where the measure in question is a question of social policy, rather than one put in place by an individual employer. Here, rather than showing that the rule is necessary to attain a genuine need of the enterprise, the Member State must show it could 'reasonably consider that the means chosen were suitable' for

[29] EA 2010, s 69; Case 96/80 *Jenkins v Kingsgate* [1981] ECR 911 (ECJ).

[30] EqPA 1970, s 1(3) (see now EA 2010, s 69(1)(a)).

[31] *Jenkins v Kingsgate*, above n 29.

[32] Ibid.

[33] Case 1007/84 *Bilka-Kaufhaus* [1986] IRLR 317 (ECJ) at para 36.

attaining 'a legitimate aim of its social policy' which is unrelated to any discrimination based on sex.[34] This descent from necessity to reasonableness has been somewhat mitigated by the ECJ's insistence that mere generalizations are not sufficient to show that the aim is unrelated to sex discrimination, and that evidence must be provided on the basis of which 'it could reasonably be considered that the means chosen were suitable for achieving that aim'.[35] Moreover, the ECJ has held that a State cannot rely on the aim of restricting public expenditure to justify a difference in treatment on grounds of sex. To hold otherwise might mean that 'the application and scope of a rule of Community law as fundamental as that of equal treatment between men and women might vary in time and place according to the state of the public finances of Member States'.[36] Properly applied, this standard can, therefore, be exacting. In *Schönheit* in 2006, it was held that while it is acceptable to pay part-timers a pro rata pension, a measure which reduces the pension by a proportion greater than warranted by her part-time work is disproportionate and cannot be objectively justified.[37]

Domestic courts had some difficulty dealing with the problem of a justification defence which, while not expressly based on sex, had the effect of entrenching disadvantage. By trying to read indirect discrimination into the justification defence, courts in effect increased the burdens faced by women in proving an equal pay claim.[38] The EA 2010 has, however, moved towards resolving the problem. The statute distinguishes between a defence based on a material factor which is expressly based on sex and one which, while not expressly treating a woman less favourably on grounds of her sex, nevertheless puts her at a particular disadvantage compared to a man doing equal work. In the second case, the burden of justification is not discharged unless the material factor cited in defence is a proportionate means of achieving a legitimate aim.[39] For example, if an employer seeks to justify paying part-time workers less on the grounds that they work part time, it would be relying on a material factor which puts women at a particular

[34] Case C-167/97 *R v Secretary of State for Employment, ex p Seymour-Smith* [1999] ECR I-623, [1999] 2 AC 554, at para 77.
[35] Ibid, para 76.
[36] Joined Cases C-4 and 5/02 *Schönheit v Stadt Frankfurt am Main; Becker v Land Hessen* [2006] 1 CMLR 5, paras 84–5.
[37] Ibid.
[38] Fredman, above n 24.
[39] EA 2010, s 69(1)(b), (2); this mirrors the proposals in ibid at p 206. (This applies equally to men.)

disadvantage when compared with men. In such circumstances, the defence cannot succeed unless the employer can show that paying part-time workers less is a proportionate means of achieving a legitimate aim.

In a new provision, which holds out both promise and peril, the EA 2010 also provides that the long-term objective of reducing inequality between men's and women's terms of work is always to be regarded as a legitimate aim.[40] The means to achieve this aim must still be shown to be proportional to this long-term objective. This is an important means by which a programme of phasing in equal pay for a group as a whole can be defended against individual claims for immediate entitlements. However, it is important that the proportionality requirement is carefully observed. It would be unfortunate and regressive if this provision were used to justify long-term pay protection for men. This point is pursued further in Chapter Six.

II DIRECT DISCRIMINATION

The concept of direct discrimination, like that of equal pay, is based on the bedrock principle that likes should be treated alike. Its definition has changed little since its inception. In its harmonized form in the EA 2010, it is defined as follows: 'A person (A) discriminates against another (B) if, because of a protected characteristic, A treats B less favourably than A treats or would treat others.'[41] Similar definitions are found in modern EU directives. The Race Directive defines direct discrimination as occurring when 'one person is treated less favourably than another is, or would be treated in a comparable situation on grounds of racial or ethnic origin'[42] and equivalent definitions are found in relation to gender, disability, age, sexual orientation, and religion or belief.[43]

Direct discrimination continues to be fundamentally limited by its adherence to the principle that likes should be treated alike. This means that it suffers from all the weaknesses of the conception identified in Chapter One. In particular, it is a relative concept, and relies heavily on the possibility of finding an appropriate comparator. It is also a

---

[40] EA 2010, s 69(3).

[41] Ibid, s 13.

[42] Council Directive 2000/43 on equal treatment between persons irrespective of racial or ethnic origin, Art 2(1)(a).

[43] Recast Directive 2006/54, Art 2(1)(a); Framework Directive 2000/78, Art 2(2)(a).

symmetric conception, applying both to discrimination against the disadvantaged class and to that aimed at furthering equality for the disadvantaged class. These limitations have become particularly apparent in relation to aspects of direct discrimination, such as pregnancy and disability. So much so that there have been important attempts to reformulate the notion so as to free it of its shackles of the comparator. This has made it possible for direct discrimination to develop beyond the limitations seen above in relation to equal pay. Nevertheless, the concept of direct discrimination is highly restricted in its ability to achieve the four-dimensional understanding of equality set out in Chapter One. These points are elaborated below. The issue of justification of direct discrimination is also controversial, but discussion of this aspect is deferred until after the section on indirect discrimination, so that the intricate inter-relationship between these two approaches to justification can be made clear.

(i) CONSISTENCY RATHER THAN SUBSTANCE

Direct discrimination, with its emphasis on 'less favourable treatment', is primarily a relative concept. As in the case of equal pay, equality is achieved if both parties have been equally well treated; but it is also achieved if they have been equally badly treated. There is nothing to suggest that the first is more desirable than the second. For example, it has been stated that if a bisexual employer harasses both men and women, then there is no discrimination on grounds of sex because they are both treated equally badly.[44] In a UK case,[45] an employer permitted its predominantly male workforce to display calendars and other pictures of naked or semi-naked women all around the factory. A female employee complained of sex discrimination. The tribunal held that a man might well find this sort of display as offensive as the woman did, and therefore men and women were treated equally. It also held that the employer 'would have treated a man just as badly whether he was complaining about the display of nude women or nude men'. There was therefore no discrimination. The Employment Appeal Tribunal (EAT) upheld this finding.

Similarly, equality is fulfilled whether a benefit is removed from the advantaged group or extended to the disadvantaged group. This is clearly illustrated in the fraught area of protective legislation, which

---

[44] *Barnes v Castle* 561 F 2d 983 (US Court of Appeals (DC Cir, 1997)) at 990, n 55.
[45] *Stewart v Cleveland Guest (Engineering) Ltd* [1994] IRLR 440 (EAT).

provided for 'special' protection for women by, for example, prohibiting night work or underground work in mines. In recent decades, there has been a general consensus that such legislation breaches the equality principle. However, this led to two quite contradictory responses. The UK government, with few exceptions, simply repealed the protective legislation; thereby withdrawing protection from women without achieving any corresponding benefits to either men or women.[46] By contrast, the European Commission declared specifically that 'equality should not be made the occasion for a disimprovement of working conditions for one sex'.[47]

Even more problematic were the results of a series of cases in which men who were pensionable at 65 claimed that they were being treated less favourably than women, who were pensionable at 60. The ECJ held that equality had indeed been breached. But it went on to find that it was not necessary to drop men's pensionable age to achieve equality. The breach could just as well be remedied by raising women's pensionable age to 65, thus removing the extra benefit to women.[48] The result was stark. Equal treatment was achieved. But the position of women was worsened, while men were no better off.

(II) EQUALITY AS CONFORMITY:
THE ROLE OF THE COMPARATOR

Direct discrimination is somewhat more sophisticated than the equal pay concept. It does not require an actual comparator. Instead, it permits a 'hypothetical comparison', or a showing that A treats B less favourably than A *would treat* others. Even in this form, however, it is fundamentally a comparative concept. Indeed, the need for a comparator has been one of the most problematic aspects of direct discrimination. As a start, as was seen in Chapter One, the need for a norm of comparison, be it male, white, or able-bodied, has created powerful conformist pressures. In addition, the choice of comparator itself requires a value judgement as to which aspects of the comparator are relevant and which irrelevant. This has been particularly problematic in

---

[46] S Fredman, *Women and the Law* (Oxford University Press, 1997), p 306, and see S Kenney, *For Whose Protection?* (University of Michigan Press, 1992).

[47] Commission Communication, *Protective Legislation for Women in the Member States of the EC*, COM(87) 105 final.

[48] See Fredman, above n 46, p 350; see eg Case C-408/92 *Smith v Advel* [1994] IRLR 602 (ECJ).

relation to disability. Finally, there are important situations in which there is simply no appropriate comparator. These limitations can in principle be surmounted simply by discarding the comparative element. Rather than 'less favourable' treatment, the focus could be on 'unfavourable' or 'detrimental' treatment. This approach has now been followed in contexts in which the search for a comparator has led to absurd or unpalatable consequences. Thus in relation to pregnancy, disability, harassment, and victimization, it is possible to prove discrimination on the basis of 'unfavourable' rather than 'less favourable' treatment. In other contexts, such as harassment, the principle that likes should be treated alike has expressly been replaced by a reliance on breach of dignity as the basis of the harm. In addition, sensitivity to the underlying value of dignity has led to protection against discrimination by association and discrimination by perception. These points are discussed in more detail below.

(a) Pregnancy

The problem of equality as conformity is at its most glaring in relation to pregnancy discrimination.[49] Who is the relevant male comparator for a pregnant woman? In the early pregnancy cases, it was held that since there could be no pregnant men, pregnancy was simply excluded from the protection of the sex discrimination legislation.

In order to see if she has been treated less favourably than a man . . . you must compare like with like and you cannot. When she is pregnant a woman is no longer just a woman. She is a woman . . . with child and there is no masculine equivalent.[50]

The result was to dismiss claims of sex discrimination by women who were subjected to detrimental treatment on grounds of their pregnancy.[51] A similar approach can be found in the jurisprudence of the US Supreme Court, where pregnancy was routinely excluded from occupational insurance schemes which provided benefits in respect of sickness or injury. This, however, was held not to constitute a breach of constitutional or statutory equality guarantees. In the words of Stewart J: 'There is no risk from which men are protected and women are not.

---

[49] For a more detailed discussion, see Fredman, above n 46, pp 184–92; S Fredman, 'A Difference with Distinction: Pregnancy and Parenthood Reassessed' (1994) 110 LQR 106.

[50] *Turley v Allders Stores Ltd* [1980] ICR 66 (EAT) at 70D (per Bristow J).

[51] A similar route was followed in the US: see *Geduldig v Aiello* 417 US 484, 94 S Ct 2485 (1974) and *General Electric Co v Gilbert* 429 US 125, 97 S Ct 401 (1976).

Likewise, there is no risk from which women are protected and men are not.'[52]

Some progress was made when courts in various jurisdictions were prepared to hold that pregnancy was equivalent to illness in its effect on the capacity to work. If a pregnant woman was treated less favourably than an ill man, discrimination might be made out.[53] Similarly, the Pregnancy Discrimination Act in the US established that women affected by pregnancy, childbirth, or related medical conditions would be entitled to the same treatment as other persons who were similar in their ability or inability to work.[54] The 'ill male comparator' at least gave pregnant women the opportunity to claim protection from sex discrimination laws. But it did so at a cost. Pregnancy is not an illness and should not be stigmatized as 'unhealthy'. In addition, it assumes that the only dimension of pregnancy with which discrimination law should be concerned is its effect on an employee's ability to work. It thereby ignores the positive medical and social reasons for leave, such as the need to breastfeed and develop a relationship with the child.

It was only when courts and legislatures were able to move away from the need for a comparator at all that real protection for pregnancy and maternity could be achieved. In a series of important cases, both the ECJ[55] and the Canadian Supreme Court[56] have held that there is no need for a comparator of any sort. Since only women have the capacity to become pregnant, discrimination on grounds of pregnancy is necessarily discrimination on grounds of sex. Legislation has taken a similar route. Under the EA 2010, pregnancy and maternity are now protected characteristics in their own right.[57] Particularly important is the express removal of the need for a comparator. Thus the EA 2010 provides that a person discriminates against a woman simply if he treats her 'unfavourably' because of her pregnancy.[58] This also extends to unfavourable treatment because she is breastfeeding or has given birth in the past 26 weeks. In an entirely separate, albeit complementary, model, specific rights have been accorded to pregnant women and mothers, including maternity leave and pay, through employment protection legislation and

---

[52] *Geduldig v Aiello*, above n 51, at 497 and see *General Electric Co v Gilbert*, above n 51.
[53] *Webb v EMO* [1992] 2 All ER 43 (CA) at 52G (per Glidewell LJ). This point was not upheld by the ECJ. See below.
[54] Pregnancy Discrimination Act, 42 USC § 2000e(k).
[55] Case C-177/88 *Dekker* [1990] ECR I-394; Case C-32/93 *Webb* [1994] ECR I-3567.
[56] *Brookes v Canada Safeway Ltd* (1989) 1 SCR 1219.
[57] EA 2010, s 4.
[58] Ibid, ss 17,18.

social security. At EU level, the Pregnant Workers Directive gives women specific rights to protection in the event of pregnancy, thus moving away from the need for a comparator at all.[59]

Nevertheless, the ill male comparator has proved remarkably tenacious. Thus the ECJ has held that where pregnancy-related illness continues after the expiry of maternity leave, however short, a woman will only be able to prove a breach of the equality principle if she can show that she was treated less favourably than an ill man would have been treated.[60] The ill male comparator even haunts the operation of statutory rights to maternity leave and pay. The Pregnant Workers Directive, despite appearing to move away from the need for a comparator, provides that pay during maternity leave is adequate if it is equivalent to sickness pay.[61] This in turn has led to the use of the equality principle, not to enhance pregnant workers' rights, but to defeat claims by women for full pay while on maternity leave. Instead, such a claim is construed as a demand for preferential treatment. Thus in *Gillespie*[62] a claim by women that they should receive full pay while on maternity leave was dismissed on the grounds that benefits received by ill employees were far less. Yet there are many countries in Europe which have recognized that maternity is not comparable to illness and have therefore been prepared to see maternity pay as a full substitute for earnings.[63]

(b) Disability

The disability cases reveal a further difficulty with the principle that likes should be treated alike. This is that the choice of comparator requires a value judgement as to which of the myriad similarities and differences among people should be treated as relevant and which irrelevant. This choice must be made in a way which is sensitive to social meaning and context. Otherwise, the choice of comparator can empty anti-discrimination law of any real impact. This can be seen by considering the effects on the choice of comparator of a 'medical' as against a 'social' model of disability. The 'medical model' focuses on

[59] Council Directive (EEC) 92/85 on the protection of the safety and health at work of pregnant and breastfeeding workers [1992] OJ L348/1, Art 11(3).

[60] Case C-179/88 *Hertz* [1990] ECR I-3979. Illness during pregnancy or maternity leave still attracts protection without the need for a comparator; Case C-394/96 *Brown v Rentokill* [1998] ECR I-4185, [1998] IRLR 445.

[61] Council Directive (EEC) 92/85 on the protection of the safety and health at work of pregnant and breastfeeding workers [1992] OJ L348/1, Art 11(3).

[62] Case C-342/93 *Gillespie* [1996] ECR I-475.

[63] Women on maternity leave are paid in full in Austria, Belgium (for the first four weeks), Finland, Greece, Luxembourg, the Netherlands, Norway, Portugal, and Spain.

functional limitations of an individual. The social model, by contrast, maintains that an individual is not disabled by her personal character- istics but by the disabling effects of the built environment, individual attitudes, and institutional barriers. It is because society is structured around an able-bodied norm that disabled people are excluded.

These differing models are reflected in the choice of comparator. To take a commonly used example, assume that a restaurant which does not permit dogs, refuses entry to a blind person with a guide dog. On a medical model, the relevant difference is between a blind and a sighted person, both of whom have a dog. Since both would be excluded, there is no breach of the equal treatment principle and no direct discrimina- tion. But by abstracting the comparison from the real social context, this choice of comparator empties discrimination law of any value. The reality is that the role of the dog for the blind person is wholly different from that of a dog belonging to a non-blind person. The social model of disability suggests instead that in this situation it is the exclusion of the guide dog which disables the blind person, not the blindness itself. Thus the comparison should be between a blind person with a dog and a sighted person.

The crucial difference between these two approaches is starkly de- monstrated by the contrasting decisions of the Court of Appeal in 1999 in the case of *Clark v Novacold*,[64] and that of the House of Lords nine years later in *Malcolm*.[65] In *Clark*, the court came close to endorsing the social model. The case concerned the dismissal of a disabled employee after a long period of absence. In such a situation, who is the relevant comparator? On a medical model, the equivalence is between an ill person and a disabled person. If both would have been dismissed after the same period of absence, then there has been equal treatment. However, on a social model, the comparison should be between those whose access to the workforce is impeded by their disability and those whose access is not: that is, between a disabled and an able-bodied employee. It was this approach which was followed in *Clark v Nova- cold*.[66] Mummery LJ noted the 'futile attempts of the . . . courts to find and identify the characteristics of a hypothetical non-pregnant male comparator for a pregnant woman in sex discrimination cases'.[67] Noting the difference in wording between the disability provisions and those of

---

[64] *Clark v Novacold* [1999] 2 All ER 977 (CA).
[65] *Lewisham London Borough Council v Malcolm* [2008] UKHL 43.
[66] *Clark v Novacold*, above n 64.
[67] Ibid, para 63.

sex and race discrimination legislation, he held that, for disability, the main issue was whether the reason for the detrimental treatment was the individual's disability. The appropriate comparison was, therefore, with an able-bodied person at work; just as, in the restaurant example, the appropriate comparison was between a blind person with a guide dog, and a sighted person who did not need a dog. Given that in most cases, it is not simple prejudice against a disabled person, but the social or practical consequences of her disability which are the reasons for the detrimental treatment, this was a critical step forward for disability protection.

However, the House of Lords in *Malcolm*[68] reverted resoundingly to a medical model. Lord Bingham stated in his judgment that it was much more 'natural' to regard the comparator as an able-bodied person who was in all other respects similarly situated: that is, 'a person who had a dog but no disability'.[69] Thus where, as in this case, a disabled person was evicted for sub-letting premises in breach of the lease, the question was whether a non-disabled person who had sub-let the premises would be similarly evicted. Of course, such a person would have been evicted. Thus the disabled tenant had not been treated less favourably than the comparator. The result was to narrow the scope of disability discrimination law to those isolated cases in which a person was evicted simply because of express prejudice against her on the grounds that she was disabled.

The EA 2010 goes some way towards reconciling the tension between the two models. It does so by distinguishing between discrimination 'because of' disability[70] and discrimination 'arising from' disability.[71] The former retains the narrow basis of comparison established in *Malcolm*, thus reflecting a medical model. There must be no material differences between the circumstances of the disabled person and her comparator, where these circumstances 'include a person's abilities'.[72] Thus in *Clark*, the relevant comparator should have been the ill employee who was similarly unable to do the work. A very different approach is taken in relation to discrimination 'arising from' disability. Here the focus is on the social consequences of the disability rather than the disability itself. Moreover, for discrimination arising out of disability, the Act moves away from the need for a comparator at all: as in the

---

[68] *Lewisham London Borough Council v Malcolm*, above n 65.
[69] Ibid, para 15.   [70] EA 2010, s 13.
[71] Ibid, s 15.   [72] Ibid, s 23.

case of pregnancy, instead of 'less favourable' treatment, the statute simply requires a showing that A has treated B *unfavourably* because of something arising in consequence of B's disability.[73] At the same time, the 'arising out' claim is deliberately weaker than the 'because of' claim. Whereas the latter operates even if A did not know that B had the disability, the former is not made out if A did not know or could not be expected to know that B had the disability. In addition, there is no possibility of a justification or excuse for the 'because of' claim. However, in the 'arising from' claim, A can defend her actions if the treatment is a proportionate means of achieving a legitimate aim. Nevertheless, this is an important step towards a social model, and with it, a further acceptance of the inherent weakness of a model of equality which depends so heavily on the choice of comparator.

(c) Victimization

On the face of it, it is difficult to see why protection against victimization should require a comparator. As Lord Nicholls stated: 'The primary object of the victimisation provisions . . . is to ensure that persons are not penalised or prejudiced because they have taken steps to exercise their statutory rights or are intending to do so.'[74] Yet sex and race discrimination have always squeezed such protection into the formula 'likes should be treated alike'. Thus the Sex Discrimination Act 1975 (SDA) made it unlawful for A to treat B less favourably than A treats or would treat other persons who have brought proceedings under the SDA or EqPA.[75] This contrasts with EU law which has never used a comparator. Instead, EU law simply requires employees to be protected against adverse treatment as a reaction to complaints or legal proceedings.[76] The question of who should be the appropriate comparator in domestic law was subject to some vexed litigation,[77] although Lady Hale rightly took the view that, since there is no equivalent comparison question in EU law, 'we must beware of introducing too many niceties into this aspect of our domestic legislation'.[78] The need for a comparator and less favourable treatment has finally been extinguished by the EA 2010. The

---

[73] Ibid, s 15.
[74] *Chief Constable of the West Yorkshire Police v Khan* [2001] ICR 1065 (HL), para 16.
[75] SDA, s 4(1)(a); see also RRA, s 2.
[76] Equal Treatment Directive, Art 7 (as amended by Directive 2002/73, Art 6); Race Directive (2000/43/EC), Art 9; Employment Directive (2000/78/EC), Art 11.
[77] *Chief Constable of the West Yorkshire Police v Khan*, above n 74.
[78] *Derbyshire v St Helens Metropolitan Borough Council* [2007] UKHL 16, para 40.

Act now simply provides that victimization takes place where A subjects B to a detriment because B in good faith does a 'protected act'.[79]

(III) DIRECT DISCRIMINATION AND SYMMETRY

The third limitation of direct discrimination is that it is a symmetric concept. In other words, it prohibits less favourable treatment regardless of whether such treatment redresses or entrenches disadvantage. According to the definition of direct discrimination, measures which give preference to a disadvantaged group constitute 'less favourable treatment' of the advantaged group and therefore breach the principle of direct discrimination even if they aim to achieve substantive equality. This aspect of the conception of equality as embodied in the principle that likes should be treated alike is dealt with in detail in Chapter Five. For present purposes, it is worth focusing briefly on the potential impact of symmetry on maternity rights. In parallel to protection for pregnancy and maternity against discrimination, most jurisdictions considered here have developed specific rights, such as the rights to maternity leave and pay, which apply only to women. This raises the question of whether the equal treatment principle can be used to obstruct pregnancy and maternity rights, on the grounds that they permit women to be *more favourably* treated than men.

This argument was raised in the US Supreme Court in the case of *Guerra*.[80] Here a Californian statute required employers to provide women with unpaid maternity leave of four months. An employer contended that this breached the Pregnancy Discrimination Act, which, as we have seen, gave pregnant women the right to the same treatment as other persons who were similar in their ability or inability to work.[81] By requiring employers to treat pregnant women better than other disabled employees, the employer argued, the equal treatment provision was breached. Fortunately, the US Supreme Court rejected the challenge. Marshall J for the majority held that the legislation 'does not compel California employers to treat pregnant workers better than other disabled employees; it merely establishes benefits that employers must, at a minimum, provide to pregnant workers.' Even more important was his explicit preference for a 'levelling up' option.

---

[79] EA 2010, s 27(1)(a).
[80] *California Federal Savings and Loan Assn v Guerra* 479 US 272, 107 S Ct 683 (1987).
[81] Pregnancy Discrimination Act, 42 USC § 2000e(k).

Employers are free to give comparable benefits to other disabled employees, thereby treating 'women affected by pregnancy' no better than 'other persons not so affected but similar in their ability or inability to work'.

UK legislation has taken a different approach, creating a specific exception to the principle of equal treatment in relation to pregnancy. Thus the EA 2010 provides specifically that 'no account is to be taken of special treatment afforded to a woman in connection with pregnancy or childbirth'.[82] However, this is less desirable than the levelling-up option proposed by Marshall J above. By treating parenting rights as a case of 'special treatment' of women, there is a risk that women's primary responsibility for childcare will simply be reinforced. If parenting rights are reserved for women, only women will interrupt their working lives to look after children, with long-term detrimental consequences for pay and pensions. It is only when the responsibility of both parents is fully recognized that structural change will be achieved. Thus a radically different way forward would take a substantive approach to equality, by constructing a female rather than a male norm. This would entail extending women's entitlements to all parents. While there are some signs of developments in this direction, fathers' entitlements are invariably inferior to those of mothers.[83]

(iv) aims

How then does direct discrimination advance the four-dimensional conception of equality established in Chapter One? Its primary contribution is in relation to the recognition dimension: namely to address stigma, stereotyping, and humiliation because of a protected characteristic. Enhanced judicial sensitivity to the dangers of stereotyping have indeed made direct discrimination an effective instrument in this respect. As Baroness Hale put it, 'the object of the legislation is to ensure that each person is treated as an individual and not assumed to be like other members of the group'.[84] Thus when UK immigration officers at Prague airport treated Roma more sceptically than others, with the result that Roma were 400 times more likely than non-Roma to be refused permission to enter the UK, the House of Lords held that

---

[82] EA 2010, s 13(6)(b).

[83] S Fredman, *Making Equality Effective: The Role of Proactive Measures* (European Commission, 2010).

[84] *R (European Roma Rights Centre) v Immigration Officer at Prague Airport* [2004] UKHL 55, [2005] 2 AC 1, para 82.

this was discriminatory.[85] This was because, rather than judging each individual on her merits, the immigration officers assumed that all Roma applicants would be making false claims and therefore warranted particularly intensive questioning. Lord Carswell stated: 'What the officers must do is treat all applicants, whatever their racial background, alike in the method of investigation.'[86] Racial profiling in the use of police stop and search powers might similarly breach the principle of discrimination.[87] However, even this dimension is undermined by the possibility that equality might be achieved by 'levelling down' rather than up. If everyone is treated in the same humiliating or stigmatic way, there would be no recourse under the direct discrimination provisions.

The remaining dimensions of equality are out of the range of direct discrimination. Its symmetry makes it difficult to advance the redistributive dimension. Nor can direct discrimination further the participative or transformational dimension. Instead, the insistence on a comparator, hypothetical or otherwise, means that direct discrimination requires conformity to the dominant mode as a condition of equal treatment. Only with the kind of modifications seen above, is its potential in this respect released.

III INDIRECT DISCRIMINATION

(1) THE DEVELOPMENT OF THE CONCEPT

We have seen that equal treatment is not in itself sufficient to address inequality in society. Equal treatment may well lead to unequal results. Selection criteria based on educational qualifications, although equally applicable to all, will exclude those who have been deprived of proper schooling; jobs which require full-time working and mobility will exclude those with primary responsibility for childcare. It is in recognition of this that the concept of indirect discrimination was shaped, initially by the US Supreme Court in the pioneering US case of *Griggs v Duke Power*.[88] The case was a clear demonstration of the way in which apparently neutral criteria sustain and reinforce the disadvantaged position of blacks in the US. The employer, Duke Power, had followed a long-standing practice of excluding blacks from the jobs in question. Following the passage of the Civil Rights Act 1964, which prohibited

---

[85] Ibid.   [86] Ibid, para 113.
[87] *R (Gillan) v Commr of Police of Metropolis* [2006] UKHL 12, [2006] 2 AC 307, para 45.
[88] 401 US 424, 91 S Ct 849 (1971).

exclusion of black workers, the employer removed the express exclusion, but instead instituted requirements of a high school education and satisfactory scores in an aptitude test as a condition of employment or transfer. The same test was applied to all candidates, but because black applicants had long received inferior education in segregated schools, both requirements operated to disqualify black applicants at a substantially higher rate than whites. Neither standard was shown to be significantly related to successful job performance. The Court responded by expanding the principle of equality. As Burger CJ, delivering the judgment of the Court put it:

The Act proscribes not only overt discrimination but also practices that are fair in form, but discriminatory in operation. The touchstone is business necessity. If an employment practice which operates to exclude Negroes cannot be shown to be related to job performance, the practice is prohibited.[89]

Thus equal treatment was held to be discriminatory if the result was that fewer blacks could comply, unless the requirement was necessary for the proper execution of the job in hand.

This conception was codified 20 years later in the Civil Rights Act 1991.[90] Under this statute, a plaintiff establishes a prima facie violation by showing that an employer uses 'a particular employment practice that causes a disparate impact on the basis of race, color, religion, sex, or national origin'.[91] An employer may defend against liability by demonstrating that the practice is 'job related for the position in question and consistent with business necessity'.[92] However, even if the employer establishes this defence, a plaintiff may still succeed by showing that the employer refuses to adopt an available alternative employment practice that has less disparate impact and serves the employer's legitimate needs.[93]

This concept rapidly made its way across the Atlantic, first to Britain, then to Europe, where it mingled with a similar concept already developing under EU law of freedom of movement. The result has been a variety of statutory formulations, each built around three basic elements. First, there must be equal treatment. Secondly, despite being equal, the treatment must have disparate results. Thirdly, however, the disparate impact can be justified if there are good reasons for the treatment in question. Each of these elements has been formulated differently over

---

[89] *Griggs v. Duke Power Co*, above n 1, at 431.   [90] 105 Stat 1071.
[91] 42 USC § 2000e-2(k)(1)(A)(i).   [92] Ibid.
[93] §§ 2000e-2(k)(1)(A)(ii) and (C).

time and in different jurisdictions. Earlier UK statutes defined the first element (equal treatment) as a 'requirement or condition' which was equally applied to all.[94] This was interpreted rigidly by the courts to exclude informal practices, or flexible policies.[95] In later definitions, originating in the EU, the equal treatment element was reformulated in the much more flexible form of a 'provision, criterion or practice',[96] thereby capturing a wider range of situations in which equal treatment has a disparate impact.

The second element (unequal impact) has been more contentious, since it applies the comparative dimension of equality in a collective sense. This raises difficult questions about the role of statistics, as well as the interaction between the group and the individual. The original legislation in the UK attempted to formulate the *Griggs* criterion in a relatively tight statutory definition. Thus the SDA definition defined indirect discrimination as a requirement or condition which was applied equally to men and women but which was 'such that the proportion of women who can comply with it is considerably smaller than the proportion of men who can comply with it, and . . . which is to her detriment because she cannot comply with it.'[97] A substantially similar provision was found in the Race Relations Act 1976 (RRA).[98] EU-inspired definitions, however, have downplayed the group dimension. Thus the Race Directive refers to an 'apparently neutral provision, criterion or practice [which] would put persons of a racial or ethnic origin *at a particular disadvantage* compared with other persons.'[99] This definition has now been incorporated into the EA 2010 to apply to all protected characteristics bar pregnancy and maternity.

The third element is concerned with when a disparate impact can be excused or justified. The original statutory definition permitted disparate impact to be justified without specifying the level of scrutiny to which potential justifications should be subjected. It was left to courts to determine the level of scrutiny, and judicial responses varied widely, especially as between domestic and EU courts. The newer definitions,

---

[94] SDA, s 1(1)(b).
[95] *Perera v Civil Service Commission (No 2)* [1983] IRLR 166 (CA).
[96] Directive 97/80/EC on the burden of proof in cases of discrimination based on sex ('Burden of Proof Directive'), Art 2(2); Race Directive, Employment Directive, EA 2010 s 19(1).
[97] SDA, s 1(1)(b).
[98] RRA, s 1(1)(b).
[99] Council Directive 2000/43/EC of 29 June 2000 implementing the principle of equal treatment between persons irrespective of racial or ethnic origin, Art 2(2)(b) (emphasis added).

again originating in the EU, explicitly import a proportionality analysis, stating that any disparate impact must be justified by a legitimate aim, that the means of achieving that aim should be appropriate or necessary, and that the justification should be objective.

The EA 2010 represents a synthesis of these developments. Indirect discrimination is now defined as follows:

A person (A) discriminates against another (B) if A applies to B a provision, criterion or practice which . . .

(a) A applies, or would apply, . . . to persons with whom B does not share the characteristic,

(b) [the provision, criterion or practice] puts, or would put, persons with whom B shares the characteristic at a particular disadvantage when compared with persons with whom B does not share it,

(c) it puts, or would put, B at that disadvantage, and

(d) A cannot show it to be a proportionate means of achieving a legitimate aim.[100]

This definition now applies widely across all the protected characteristics, except pregnancy and maternity. After much equivocation by the UK government, it also applies to disability. Outside the legislative framework, the European Court of Human Rights (ECtHR), after initially resisting a concept of indirect discrimination, has now embraced the EU definition in the case of *DH*.[101] This is discussed further under the heading of proportionality.

(II) AIMS AND OBJECTIVES

Indirect discrimination is often thought of as aiming to achieve equality of results. However, on closer examination, it can be seen that this is only partially true. Unequal results will not breach the principle of indirect discrimination if the inequality can be justified by reference to business needs or State social policy; or if no exclusionary provision, criterion, or practice can be identified. Even if the aim were equality of results, the expansion of protected characteristics makes it increasingly difficult to identify what equality of results should entail. Should a workforce reflect precisely the demography of the population, in relation to age and religion as much as in relation to gender, disability, sexual orientation, and race?

---

[100] EA 2010, s 19.
[101] *DH v Czech Republic*, Application no 57325/00 (2008) 47 EHRR 3 (ECtHR, Grand Chamber).

This demonstrates that, instead of constituting the aim of indirect discrimination, results are part of the diagnosis of discrimination, exposing the existence of obstacles to entry rather than the pattern of outcome. The assumption is that, in a non-discriminatory environment, there will be a fair distribution of men and women, ethnic and religious groups, heterosexuals and homosexuals, able-bodied and disabled people. Under-representation of one of these groups is a sign that there might be a hidden obstacle to entry, which, unless justifiable, should be removed. This is particularly useful where the practice is opaque and informal, such as a pay policy which is characterized by a total lack of transparency,[102] or a recruitment policy based on unwritten and subjective criteria. It is also useful in situations in which the measure itself is not suspect and there is clearly no intention on the part of the perpetrator.[103] However, if there is no exclusionary practice, or the requirement is necessary for the job, the presumption of discrimination is displaced. For example, a glance at the statistics shows that there are very few women airline pilots, an inequality of results which potentially diagnoses a discriminatory practice. If the unequal outcome is due to the fact that airline pilots are hired on the basis of personal recommendations from existing pilots, or because of specific height or weight requirements which are unnecessary for the job, then discrimination may be made out. However, if it is shown that there are not enough women with the training necessary to be an airline pilot then, despite the inequality of results, the presumption of indirect discrimination is displaced.

To what extent then does indirect discrimination match the four goals set out in Chapter One? It is certainly capable of furthering the redistributive dimension. It has been particularly effective in dealing with criteria which specifically disadvantage women with childcare responsibilities. Thus a maximum age limit of 28 for new entrants to the civil service has been held to be a condition with which fewer women than men can comply because many women spend their twenties having babies and caring for them.[104] Similarly, a range of measures disadvantaging part-time workers have been held to be indirectly discriminatory against women on the grounds of their sex. Policies or practices

---

[102] Case C-109/88 *Handels- og Kontorfunktionærernes Forbund I Danmark (Union of Clerical and Commercial Employees) v Dansk Arbejdsgiverforening (Danish Employers' Association)* [1991] 1 CMLR 8 (ECJ).

[103] O DeSchutter, 'Three Models of Equality and European Anti-Discrimination Law' (2006) 57 Northern Ireland Legal Quarterly 1–56.

[104] *Price v Civil Service Commission* [1977] IRLR 291 (EAT).

precluding part-time workers from access to pensions, protection against unfair dismissal, and equal hourly pay have thus been held to be indirectly discriminatory.[105]

Indirect discrimination has also made some progress towards the transformational goal and, in particular, accommodating diversity. By examining the impact of apparently neutral practices and criteria, indirect discrimination reveals the extent to which the dominant culture or religion is favoured. Thus in the landmark case of *Mandla v Lee*[106] the court held that a school had unlawfully discriminated against a Sikh boy by excluding him from the school when he refused to take off his turban in order to comply with a school rule requiring boys to come bareheaded to school. An apparently neutral rule, applying equally to all pupils, was recognized as in practice requiring conformity to a Christian way of dressing and therefore creating unacceptable barriers to those of different cultures or religions.

However, its effectiveness in relation to real structural change is limited. This is primarily because of the role of the justification defence. Indirectly discriminatory barriers need not be dismantled if they can be justified. Criteria which are job-related remain legitimate even though disadvantaged groups, by virtue of their disadvantage, might find it impossible to comply. Thus certain qualifications may be necessary for a job, yet an individual may lack those qualifications precisely because of past or ongoing discrimination. In one British case, training places for management jobs were only available to applicants with previous work experience in Britain. This made it impossible for those who, due to prejudice in the labour market, or due to the fact that they were recent arrivals, were unable to gain a place.[107] Nor does indirect discrimination on its own give rise to any obligation to ensure that applicants are equipped for a job or other benefit; for example, by training or provision of childcare. Furthermore, the remedy for indirect discrimination does not necessarily entail a requirement that the discriminatory barrier must be removed, although many employers may in fact do so to avoid further proceedings.

This means that, in order to advance the transformational goal of equality, justification defences should be subject to a high level of scrutiny before being accepted. Most importantly, the respondent should be

---

[105] *Bilka-Kaufhaus*, above n 33; *R v Secretary of State for Employment, ex p Equal Opportunities Commission* [1994] IRLR 176 (HL).
[106] [1983] 2 AC 548 (HL).
[107] *Ojutiku v Manpower Services Commission* [1982] IRLR 418 (CA).

required to consider ways of modifying the discriminatory practice better to accommodate the excluded class. Thus the respondent should need to show that the practice is necessary to achieve a legitimate aim and that there are no other less discriminatory alternatives, which should themselves include possible ways of accommodating the complainant. The benefits and limitations of indirect discrimination are clearly evident in respect of part-time work. As we have seen, the indirect discrimination provisions have made significant progress in the removal of specific detriments attached to part-time work. But they do nothing to change the underlying division of power within the family which leaves women with the primary responsibility for childcare. The result is that women part-time workers might find their position at work improved as a result of the prohibition of indirect discrimination. But the fact that the vast majority of women are part-time workers remains unchanged.

(III) THE ROLE OF THE COMPARATOR: INDIVIDUAL OR GROUP

Indirect discrimination, like its direct counterpart, is based on a comparison. However, because it is concerned with impact, rather than treatment, the role of the comparator is complex. Both in US and UK law, the comparison is group-based: equal treatment can be unlawful because of its disproportionate exclusionary impact on a group sharing a protected characteristic. But how should the group dimension be established? What proportion of the group should be excluded and relative to whom?

The use of statistics is clearly a potent tool to determine such questions. As noted by a recent study,

the indirect discrimination concept . . . [is] intrinsically linked to statistics by their logic and objectives. The definition of indirect discrimination is based on quantitative concepts: significant effects and comparisons between groups. The cognitive tools used to capture indirect discrimination, which is the reasoning on which legal and political developments are based, are statistical. The group concept is the focus: treatment is no longer personalised, it is collective and only relates to individuals in terms of their real or assumed affiliation to a protected group. This shift from the individual to a group is strictly analogous to the operations carried out by statistics: impersonal aggregates that highlight a collective situation.[108]

---

[108] P Simon (coord), *Comparative Study on the Collection of Data to Measure the Extent and Impact of Discrimination Within the US, Canada, Australia, Great Britain and the Netherlands* (Medis Project (Measurement of Discriminations), INED—Economie and Humanisme), August 2004, p 82.

The importance of statistics is vividly demonstrated in the ECtHR case of *DH*,[109] where psychological tests were used to determine whether children should go to 'special' schools, which were in practice educationally undemanding and inferior. Statistics showed the disproportionate impact on Roma children, who were over-represented in special schools. The Chamber of the ECtHR, which initially heard the case, refused to examine the statistics and insisted on considering only the individual case. This made it impossible for it to recognize that tests which it regarded as professionally administered with no intention to discriminate were in practice operating to consign dramatically more Roma children to special schools than the representation in the population.[110] By contrast, when the case was re-heard by the Grand Chamber, statistical evidence was accepted, enabling the Court to uphold the claim of indirect discrimination.[111] This follows the pattern set by the early conceptions of indirect discrimination, which reflected the centrality of statistics to a group-based view of discrimination.

However, a statistical focus brings with it several complex problems. As a start, many States, particularly in the EU, do not collect data. This is in part because of an aversion to requiring individuals to reveal their identities, for the very reason that this might trigger discrimination against them. This should not, however, be a long-term bar, in the light of sophisticated means of data gathering, particularly on a population-wide level, which do not require individuals to expose themselves to individual prejudice. But even when statistics are available, they have proved difficult to apply. As a start, it has not been easy to reach a consensus as to which groups are relevant in determining the scope of comparison. As many cases have shown, the figures might differ substantially depending on which statistics are chosen and how the comparable groups are identified.[112] The difficulties with a statistical approach were aggravated by the much tighter statutory definition in UK sex and race discrimination law. Under the SDA, the complainant had to establish that 'considerably fewer women than men' could comply with a particular requirement. An equivalent provision applied to race. This required an assessment, first, of the relevant pool of comparison. Should a comparison be drawn between all women and all men, or only between qualified women and qualified men, or between women and men who

---

[109] *DH v Czech Republic*, above n 101.
[110] Ibid at 41.
[111] See further below.
[112] See eg *Wards Cove v Atonio* 490 US 642, 109 S Ct 2115 (1989).

had actually applied for the job or promotion? Even if agreement can be reached as to which statistics are relevant, it may be difficult to decide whether the difference is 'considerably smaller'.

This was well illustrated by *R v Secretary of State, ex p Seymour Smith and Perez*,[113] which challenged legislation excluding employees who had been employed for less than two years from the benefit of protection against unfair dismissal. The applicants argued that the proportion of women who could comply with the two-year eligibility requirement was considerably smaller than the proportion of men, thus raising a prima facie case of indirect discrimination. The figures showed that over the period from 1985 to 1991, the ratio of qualified men to qualified women was roughly 10:9 over the relevant period. It was accepted that the difference in the impact of the requirement was statistically significant, in that it could be said with confidence that they were due to social facts rather than to chance. But was the proportion of women who could comply 'considerably smaller' as required by the legislation? The case was aired before four different courts, including the ECJ, and all came to different conclusions. When the House of Lords finally decided the issue, six years after the first hearing, it fortunately took a perceptive view, holding that the latitude afforded by the word 'considerably' should not be exaggerated.[114] Although the impact was relatively small, the fact that it was persistent meant that it should not 'be brushed aside and dismissed as insignificant or inconsiderable'. Notably, however, the court went on to find the measure justifiable.

The difficulties in defining the appropriate pool of comparison and in determining the appropriate margin of difference have continued to perplex courts and lawyers, leading Mummery LJ to comment on the 'increasingly voluminous and incredibly intractable' legal materials on indirect discrimination.[115] In *Rutherford*,[116] Lord Walker pointed out that

the comparison of proportions (inherent in any assessment of indirect discrimination) produces startlingly different results depending on whether the comparison focuses on (i) proportions of advantaged men and women respectively ('advantage-led') or (ii) proportions of disadvantaged men and women respectively ('disadvantage-led').

---

[113] (No 1) [1994] IRLR 448 (DC), [1995] IRLR 464 (CA), [1997] IRLR 315 (HL), [1999] IRLR 253 (ECJ), (No 2) [2000] IRLR 263 (HL).
[114] [2000] IRLR 263 at 270, para 57 (per Lord Nicholls).
[115] *Secretary of State for Trade and Industry v Rutherford* [2005] ICR 119 (CA), para 3.
[116] *Secretary of State for Trade and Industry v Rutherford (No 2)* [2006] UKHL 19.

The case concerned the removal of rights to protection against unfair dismissal and redundancy from employees over the age of 65. Because more men than women stay on at work over the age of 65, it was argued that this constituted indirect discrimination against men. Although the claim was unanimously rejected, their Lordships took somewhat different approaches to the statistical data. Lord Walker held that the pool for purposes of comparison comprised the 'advantaged group', namely those under 65 who were entitled to employment protection rights. Lord Scott, Lord Rodger, and Baroness Hale held that the appropriate group for comparison comprised all those still in the workforce at age 65. Lord Nicholls considered both those under 65 and those over 65 and found that the disparities over 65 were not significant enough to amount to discrimination.[117]

The result of these complexities has been that many indirect discrimination cases have become mired in the preliminary stages. In *Rutherford* itself, the first applicant began proceedings in December 1998, well before age discrimination legislation was even contemplated. The House of Lords decision on this preliminary point was handed down in May 2006. Even if the claim had been successful, it would have had to return to the employment tribunal to make a finding on the merits.

None of these conundrums are insurmountable. Statistical techniques exist to determine appropriate comparator groups. Statisticians weed out differences which are random or fortuitous by use of the concept of statistical significance.[118] It should be sufficient to show that the difference in impact between the groups is statistically significant, for the burden of proof of justification to pass on to the respondent. A different approach has been used in the US. Here, the Equal Employment Opportunity Commission has developed a rule of thumb, known as the 'four-fifths' rule. On this approach,

a selection rate for any race, sex, or ethnic group which is less than four-fifths (4/5) (or eighty percent) of the rate for the group with the highest rate will generally be regarded by the Federal enforcement agencies as evidence of adverse impact.[119]

For example, if the hiring rate for whites is 60 per cent and that for American Indians is 45 per cent, then the ratio for American Indians is

---

[117] Ibid.

[118] This was suggested by the European Commission in *R v Secretary of State for Employment, ex p Seymour-Smith*, above n 34, para 57.

[119] 29 CFR § 1607.4(D) <http://www.eeoc.gov/policy/docs/qanda_clarify_procedures. html>.

45:60, or 75 per cent, which is less than four-fifths. In the same example, if the hiring rate for Hispanics is 48 per cent, then the ratio for Hispanics is 48:60 or 80 per cent. The result is that there is a prima facie case of disparate impact in relation to American Indians but not Hispanics. The Agency stresses however, that

This '4/5ths' or '80%' rule of thumb is not intended as a legal definition, but is a practical means of keeping the attention of the enforcement agencies on serious discrepancies in rates of hiring, promotion and other selection decisions.[120]

EU law has, however, veered away from the statistical approach, using instead the terminology of 'particular disadvantage'. The 'particular disadvantage' test derives from EU law on free movement of workers, which outlaws discrimination on the grounds of nationality against EU workers migrating to other EU Member States.[121] The seminal case on this point was *O'Flynn*,[122] in which it was held that, although a set of criteria for eligibility for a particular benefit applied equally to all workers, it was indirectly discriminatory against non-UK workers. The court did not require statistical proof. Instead it held that

unless objectively justified and proportionate to its aim, a provision of national law must be regarded as indirectly discriminatory if it is intrinsically liable to affect migrant workers more than national workers and if there is a consequent risk that it will place the former at a particular disadvantage.[123]

It was not necessary to prove that the provision *in practice* affects a substantially higher proportion of migrant workers, as long as it was *liable* to have such an effect.[124] In other words, this approach is based on the risk or liability of disparate impact, rather than requiring proof that such impact has in fact occurred. This approach was transplanted into the Race and Employment Directives and has now been comprehensively introduced into UK domestic law through the EA 2010. Thus, as we have seen, indirect discrimination is established where, subject to a justification defence, the provision or practice 'puts, or would put,

---

[120] Ibid.
[121] Directive 2004/38/EC of the European Parliament and of the Council on the right of citizens of the Union and their family members to move and reside freely within the territory of the Member States, amending Regulation (EEC) No 1612/68 on freedom of movement for workers within the Community, Art 39.
[122] Case C-237/94 *O'Flynn v Adjudication Officer* [1996] 3 CMLR 103 (ECJ).
[123] Ibid, para 20.
[124] Ibid, para 21.

persons with whom B shares the characteristic at a particular disadvantage when compared with persons with whom B does not share it'.[125]

On one level, this can be a more flexible test. While statistics may be used, courts might in principle take a commonsense view, based on judicial notice, or on obvious facts.[126] This is helpful, particularly where statistics are not available or are contentious, or numbers are small. For example, in *Ladele*,[127] the applicant, a marriage registrar employed by Islington Borough Council, refused to perform civil partnership proceedings because she believed they were contrary to the will of God. When she was subjected to disciplinary proceedings, she claimed that she had been indirectly discriminated against on the ground of her religion. Here there was no need to find statistics to establish a prima facie case. Instead of the tortuous process described above, Neuberger LJ was able to devote just one sentence to the decision that

There is no doubt but that Islington's policy decisions to designate all their registrars civil partnership registrars, and then to require all registrars to perform civil partnerships, put a person such as Ms Ladele, who believed that civil partnerships were contrary to the will of God, 'at a particular disadvantage when compared with other persons', namely those who did not have that belief.[128]

This meant that the court could immediately turn its attention to whether the discriminatory impact was justified, which it was. The aim of the requirement, namely promotion of equality and diversity, was legitimate, and the means chosen were proportionate, in that the requirement did not impinge on the claimant's freedom to hold her beliefs. The great advantage of this approach, then, is that the real weight of the decision falls on the question of justification, rather than on the threshold question of whether disparate impact has been established.

However, the role of statistics in establishing the group dimension should not be discarded simply because of technical difficulties. The

---

[125] Council Directive 2000/43/EC of 29 June 2000 implementing the principle of equal treatment between persons irrespective of racial or ethnic origin; Council Directive 2000/78/EC of 27 November 2000 establishing a general framework for equal treatment in employment and occupation; EA 2010, s 19(2)(b).

[126] C Tobler, *Limits and Potential of the Concept of Indirect Discrimination* (European Commission, 2008), p 40.

[127] *Islington London Borough Council v Ladele* [2009] EWCA Civ 1357.

[128] Ibid, para 43.

notion of 'particular disadvantage', while useful in situations of obvious disparate impact, would not be sufficient to flush out measures which appear wholly neutral and are not in any way suspect.[129] If not confronted with actual evidence of a disproportionate impact, courts are tempted to view such measures as non-discriminatory unless they can find an express link with the protected characteristic. This simply reverts to a direct discrimination approach. Thus in *Homer*,[130] the claimant, aged 61, was employed as a legal adviser to a police authority. Under a new grading structure, a law degree was determined to be essential for admission to the highest pay grade. This had not been required on his appointment. The employment tribunal held that the law degree requirement put persons in the 60 to 65 age group at a particular disadvantage when compared with other persons, because the former were not able to obtain a degree before retirement. The Court of Appeal, however, held that the particular disadvantage did not result from the claimant's age but the proximity of his retirement. It is submitted that this misunderstands the operation of indirect discrimination. Indirect discrimination by definition does not require proof that the detriment was because of the claimant's age. Instead, it must be shown that a disproportionate number of people in his age group were excluded because of an apparently neutral criterion: the requirement of a law degree.

Of particular concern was the Court of Appeal's finding that this was a claim for more favourable treatment on account of age. The whole point of indirect discrimination is to recognize that equal treatment may itself be discriminatory. Rather than demanding more favourable treatment, a finding of indirect discrimination requires a practice to be changed in order to achieve substantive equality. Of course, a finding of particular disadvantage might still be justifiable: for example, a law degree might be necessary for the effective discharge of the job. The rejection at the earlier stage meant, however, that the justifiability of the measure could not even be canvassed in the court. It is therefore crucial that statistics remain an alternative and complementary method of proving disparate impact. Aptitude tests, interview and selection processes, and other apparently scientific and neutral measures might never invite scrutiny unless data is available to dislodge these assumptions.

[129] DeSchutter, above n 103, pp 18–20.
[130] *Chief Constable of West Yorkshire Police v Homer* [2010] EWCA Civ 419.

IV COMPETING PRIORITIES:
JUSTIFYING DISCRIMINATION

For each of the conceptions discussed above, a crucial question arises. When will discrimination be capable of being excused or justified? What competing priorities can displace a finding of discrimination? This question has received very different answers in relation to direct as against indirect discrimination. While there is no general justification for direct discrimination, indirect discrimination has always been justifiable. It is largely for this reason that direct and indirect discrimination have been held to be separate and mutually exclusive. As Lady Hale has put it:

> Direct and indirect discrimination are mutually exclusive. You cannot have both at once.... The main difference between them is that direct discrimination cannot be justified. Indirect discrimination can be justified if it is a proportionate means of achieving a legitimate aim.[131]

It will be seen below, however, that this distinction is coming under increasing strain, particularly with the extension of the reach of anti-discrimination law well beyond its original arena of race and sex discrimination.

This throws the spotlight on the degree of scrutiny to be applied to a justification defence. There has been a welcome development from an open-textured statutory formula to one expressly based on proportionality. Proportionality requires close scrutiny of the stated aims, and the means to achieve those aims. It thus structures judicial decision-making in important ways. Proportionality is, however, open to varying interpretations, both as to which aims should be legitimate and how close the 'fit' should be between the means and the ends. This section considers the extent to which such a defence has been calibrated to give the appropriate weight to the right of equality as against competing claims. Particularly neglected is the question of how much evidence must be produced to substantiate a claim that the means fit the ends. It is argued here that the key is to find a formulation of the justification defence which does not permit costs arguments to trump equality, nor facilitate legitimation of prejudice and stereotypes, but at the same time

---

[131] *R (on the application of E) v Governing Body of JFS and the Admissions Appeal Panel of JFS* [2009] UKSC 15, para 57.

recognizes when unequal treatment is acceptable or appropriate. The section begins with indirect discrimination, where justification is a familiar issue, before turning to the far more contentious issues that arise in relation to direct discrimination.

(I) JUSTIFYING INDIRECT DISCRIMINATION

Indirect discrimination has always been structured in such a way as to permit a prima facie case of discrimination to be justified if the exclusionary practice is required for the job or other legitimate aim. The impact of indirect discrimination is therefore dependent on formulating a test for justification which gives due weight to the right to equality, while insisting on a high level of scrutiny of competing values.

The original definition of indirect discrimination in the SDA (and its equivalent in the RRA) gave no direct guidance on this issue, simply requiring that the measure 'be justifiable irrespective of the sex of the person to whom it is applied'.[132] However, ECJ jurisprudence has developed a more structured approach. It is a defence to indirect discrimination to show that the provision, criterion, or practice in question is 'objectively justified by a legitimate aim and the means of achieving that aim are appropriate and necessary'.[133] The EA 2010 now imports this standard, albeit in truncated form: indirect discrimination can be justified if the respondent can show that the measure is 'a proportionate means of achieving a legitimate aim'.[134]

Proportionality is not, however, self-executing. It depends on the judicial approach to each of its main dimensions: the stated aims of the respondent; and the means–end relationship. Unpacking these two dimensions of a proportionality analysis requires us to pay closer attention to a further set of questions. The first is the closeness of the fit between the discriminatory measure and the purported justification. Should the means be *necessary* to achieve the end, or is it sufficient if there is a reasonable link? In answering this question a second question arises, namely how much attention must be paid to the possibility of alternative less discriminatory means capable of achieving the stated aims? A strict 'necessity' criterion requires a showing that the measure chosen is the only alternative. Allied to this are the questions of whether

---

[132] SDA, s 1(1)(b).
[133] Council Directive 2000/43/EC, Art 2(2)(b); Council Directive 2000/78/EC, Art 2(2)(b); European Parliament and Council Directive 2006/54/EC, Art 2(1)(b).
[134] EA 2010, s 19(2)(d).

the respondent should have actually considered the alternative, or whether *ex post facto* justification is permitted; and who has the burden of proving that alternative measures are possible. Thirdly, is the decision as to whether the means fit the ends judged by objective criteria, or is it sufficient if the respondent could 'reasonably consider' that the means fit the ends? In answering this question, is there a difference between private and public respondents, in that a wider margin of discretion might be granted to the latter? The fourth question concerns the role of evidence. Is it sufficient for a respondent simply to assert that the indirectly discriminatory requirement was considered appropriate to achieve the stated aim, or should an evidential basis be required?

The seminal US case of *Griggs* set the value of equality high, requiring proof that the exclusionary practice was necessary for the business of the employer or that it was essential to effective job performance. Even if the employer could prove business necessity and job-relatedness, it remained open for the plaintiff to argue that there was a less discriminatory alternative which would also serve the employers' business interest.[135] A similar set of priorities was evidenced in the earliest UK cases, requiring the employer to show both that the requirement was necessary and that no non-discriminatory alternative was available.[136] However, the extent to which the tribunals and courts were prepared to prioritize equality issues soon waned, and the standard of justification progressively slipped. A particular low point was reached in the race discrimination case of *Ojutiku v Manpower Services Commission*,[137] in which the Court of Appeal held that an act was justified merely if the reasons for doing it were such that they would be acceptable to right-thinking persons as sound and tolerable reasons for so doing. A similar decline in the standard of justification in the US[138] was only partially arrested by legislation.[139] Current US law requires the respondent to demonstrate that 'the challenged practice is job related for the position in question and consistent with business necessity'.[140] Nevertheless, commentators note that there remains room for manoeuvre, in particular because 'consistent with business necessity' can be read as 'nothing

---

[135] *Griggs v Duke Power Co* 401 US 424, 91 S Ct 849 (1971); *Albermarle v Moody* 422 US 405, 95 S Ct 2362 (1975).

[136] *Steel v UPW* [1978] ICR 181 (EAT).

[137] Above n 107.

[138] *Wards Cove v Atonio*, above n 112.

[139] Civil Rights Act 1991, s 105; and see (1992) 105 Harv L Rev 913; (1993) 106 Harv L Rev 1621.

[140] 42 USC § 2000e-2.

more than an important business reason for engaging in a facially neutral policy'.[141]

The governing principles are now set by EU law. In the seminal case of *Bilka*,[142] the ECJ set a high standard of justification. The respondent must show that the means chosen serve a real business need, that they are appropriate to achieve that objective, and are necessary to that end.[143] In one of the clearest examples of the application of this test, the House of Lords in *EOC*[144] struck down a legislative measure which excluded part-time employees from the right to claim unfair dismissal for the first five years of their employment. Given that women predominate amongst part-time workers, this exclusion was prima facie indirectly discriminatory. The government argued that the exclusion was necessary to reduce unemployment among flexible workers. In a highly significant decision, the House of Lords rejected this justification, holding that the empirical evidence for the government's claim was not available.

However, some equivocation on the standard is evident in the later case of *Nolte*,[145] which seems to grant a wider margin of discretion when the respondent is the State. Instead of demonstrating that the means are *necessary* to achieve the State's legitimate ends, it was held that it is sufficient for the State to demonstrate that *it could reasonably consider* that the means were suitable for attaining a legitimate aim.[146] This contrasts with the earlier case of *Rinner-Kuhn*, where the same court had held that where legislation or social policy has a discriminatory impact, the State can only justify its continuation if the means correspond to an objective which is necessary for social policy, and which are appropriate and necessary to achieve that end.[147] The more lenient test in *Nolte* led Lord Nicholls in the House of Lords in *Seymour Smith* to declare that the burden placed on the government in this type of case was not as heavy as previously thought. 'Governments must be able to govern. . . . National courts, acting with hindsight, are not to impose an impracticable burden on governments which are proceeding in good

---

[141] W Gordon, 'The Evolution of the Disparate Impact Theory of Title VII: A Hypothetical Case Study' (2007) 44 Harv J on Legis 529.
[142] *Bilka-Kaufhaus*, above n 33.
[143] Ibid.
[144] *EOC*, above n 105.
[145] Case 371/93 *Nolte* [1995] ECR I4625.
[146] Contrast Case 171/88 *Rinner-Kuhn* [1989] ECR 2743 (ECJ).
[147] *Rinner Kuhn*, ibid.

faith.'[148] This case concerned legislation depriving employees of rights to unfair dismissal and redundancy unless they had worked for two years. The government argued that the two-year qualification period was adopted in order to reduce the reluctance of employers to take on more employees. Lord Nicholls acknowledged that government evidence amounted to no more than the citation of reports indicating that various small percentages of employers considered that the unfair dismissal legislation might inhibit the recruitment of employees. But the test was merely whether the Secretary of State was reasonably entitled to consider that the longer qualifying period might help to reduce the reluctance of employers to take on more employees. Thus, the court held, the evidence submitted was sufficient to discharge the burden of justification.[149]

More recent case law has, however, arrested the drift away from a high standard of scrutiny of justification tests. Generally speaking, courts are likely to be relatively deferent in relation to the aim articulated by the respondent. However, the relationship between the means and the ends attracts more careful judicial scrutiny. Thus the ECJ in *Seymour Smith*, while acknowledging that the State should have a wider margin of appreciation, nevertheless insisted that mere generalizations should not suffice. An evidential basis was necessary to establish a defence of justification.

Mere generalisations concerning the capacity of a specific measure to encourage recruitment are not enough to show that the aim of the disputed rule is unrelated to any discrimination based on sex nor to provide evidence on the basis of which it could reasonably be considered that the means chosen were suitable for achieving that aim.[150]

Nor is it for the complainant to prove that there is a less discriminatory alternative. As Mummery LJ emphasized in *Elias*, the burden remains with the respondent throughout. Moreover, he continued: 'I would also add that the onus is not on the court, as part of the exercise of margin of appreciation or area of discretionary judgment allowed by the court to the state, to search around for a justification.'[151] Should these alternatives have been considered at the time of making the decision? The ECJ has held that in some circumstances an *ex post facto* justification might

---

[148] *R v Secretary of State for Employment (No 2)* [2000] ICR 244 (HL) at 260.
[149] Ibid.
[150] *R v Secretary of State for Employment, ex p Seymour-Smith*, above n 34, para 71.
[151] *R (Elias) v Secretary of State for Defence* [2006] 1 WLR 3213 (CA), para 131.

be acceptable. However, this is likely to be unusual: generally speaking, there must be evidence that the respondent, at the time of making the decision, considered whether there were other, less discriminatory ways of achieving the objective.[152] An important reason for this is that, if the respondent failed to address the effects of a measure, there is generally no evidential basis for assessing the comparative discriminatory effects of other possible criteria.[153] For example, in *Hockenjos*[154] and *Elias*, the absence of any consideration to possible less discriminatory alternatives was a key factor in the rejection of the justification defence. As Mummery LJ put it

As there was no proper consideration of whether there were other less discrim-inatory means of restricting payments to those with a close link to the UK, there is no evidential basis for finding that the [chosen] criteria were the only criteria that were reasonably necessary and proportionate to achieving the legitimate aim.[155]

The opposite was the case in *Azmi v Kirklees*,[156] where the applicant, a devout Muslim employed as a bilingual support worker at a school, complained that she had been subject to indirect discrimination on grounds of her religion because she was required to remove her veil while teaching. The court accepted the respondent's justification, which was that it was necessary for children to see their teacher's face when learning language. The court set a great deal of store on the fact that the respondent had considered all possible alternatives. At the same time, courts should not be tempted to defer to the respondent simply because it did consider alternatives: the court should still ask whether the alternatives were less discriminatory.[157]

The measure chosen need not be the only possible means of achieving the stated aim. However, as Scott Baker LJ put it in the Court of Appeal in *Hockenjos*,

There is a point at which it becomes no longer possible or appropriate to defer to the Member State's broad margin of appreciation on social policy. That point is reached when the effect of doing so would be to frustrate the implementation of

---

[152] Ibid.   [153] Ibid.
[154] *Hockenjos v Secretary of State for Social Security* [2004] EWCA Civ 1749.
[155] *R (Elias) v Secretary of State for Defence*, above n 151.
[156] *Azmi v Kirklees Metropolitan Borough Council* [2007] ICR 1154 (EAT).
[157] See eg *Humphreys v The Commissioners for Her Majesty's Revenue and Customs* [2010] EWCA Civ 56 (decided under Art 14 rather than EU law).

a fundamental principle of community law. It is therefore necessary to feed into the question of proportionality the importance of the principle of equality.[158]

The most succinct and best-calibrated approach to the justification of indirect discrimination is that of Mummery LJ in the Court of Appeal in *Elias* where he posed a three-stage test:

First, is the objective sufficiently important to justify limiting a fundamental right? Secondly, is the measure rationally connected to the objective? Thirdly, are the means chosen no more than is necessary to accomplish the objective?[159]

In answering the questions posed, it is hoped that courts will continue to be vigilant in resisting the temptation to accept generalizations by respondents under the guise of deference and in lieu of close scrutiny of actual evidence. It is also particularly important to maintain the emphasis on possible alternatives which are less discriminatory. Otherwise, the possibility of justification allows the status quo to be maintained without giving proper attention to whether the discriminatory practice can be adjusted better to accommodate the excluded group.

(II) JUSTIFYING DIRECT DISCRIMINATION?

The question of whether direct discrimination can be justified is hotly contested. Whereas a justification defence has always been available for indirect discrimination, there has been strong resistance to allowing direct discrimination to be justified. One reason for this is that direct discrimination is concerned with unequal treatment because of a personal characteristic. It is arguably a central affront to individual dignity to permit such treatment to be excused.[160] This argument certainly holds true in relation to justifications based on costs, which constitute a hidden but powerful agenda behind much of equality policy and legislation. As has been seen in the context of equal pay, there is a danger that allowing costs to trump equality claims will mean that 'unlawfulness of any treatment will be determined by its "market value" or cost'.[161] There is also a danger that stereotypes will be reinforced by permitting less favourable treatment on a protected ground to be justified.[162]

---

[158] *Hockenjos v Secretary of State for Social Security*, above n 154, para 44.

[159] *R (Elias) v Secretary of State for Defence*, above n 151.

[160] T Gill and K Monaghan, 'Justification in Direct Sex Discrimination Law: Taboo Upheld' (2003) 32 ILJ 115.

[161] Ibid, p 116.

[162] *R (European Roma Rights Centre) v Immigration Officer at Prague Airport* [2004] QB 811 (CA), para 86. This approach was rejected in the House of Lords: see *R (European*

The strength of the argument against permitting justification based on costs or stereotypes, however, should not obscure the possibility that there may be other legitimate justifications, not least when called for by other conceptions of equality. Thus there is a strong argument that inequality of treatment might in principle be justifiable if it aims to redress previous disadvantage. For example, under the European Convention on Human Rights, it is recognized that

the fact that there are certain groups or categories of persons who are disadvantaged, or the existence of de facto inequalities, may constitute justifications for adopting measures providing for specific advantages in order to promote equality, provided that the proportionality principle is respected.... [163]

More broadly, the possibility of justification can make direct discrimination more context-sensitive. This is particularly so in the light of the extension of protected characteristics beyond race and gender, and beyond the employment context. Whether a classification amounts to invidious discrimination requires a court to look beyond the actual classification to the way in which it operates within the social contexts. Thus the key is to provide for a justification defence which can differentiate between furthering a substantive understanding of equality, on the one hand, and subordinating equality to costs or perpetuating stereotypes, on the other. Moreover, the possibility of justification should not be a pretext for maintaining the status quo. Instead of permitting justification, a finding of discrimination should trigger a duty to make reasonable adjustments. The role of justification therefore needs to be seen in conjunction with the possibility of accommodating the individual.

UK and EU law have generally resisted the possibility of a general justification for direct discrimination. Indeed, the absence of the possibility of justification is one of the key differences between direct and indirect discrimination. Nevertheless, in practice there are a growing number of ways in which direct discrimination can indeed be justified. As we have seen, equal pay legislation has always permitted employers to justify differences of pay for equal work by reference to a material factor which is not itself the difference in sex. In addition, it has always been

Roma Rights Centre and Others) v Immigration Officer at Prague Airport [2004] UKHL 55, [2005] 2 AC 1, para 37.

[163] Protocol No 12 to the Convention for the Protection of Human Rights and Fundamental Freedoms and Explanatory Report: <http://www.humanrights.coe.int/Prot12/Protocol%2012%20and%20Exp%20Rep.htm#EXPLANATORY%20REPORT>.

possible to justify direct race and sex discrimination where sex or race is a genuine occupational qualification. This has now been extended to most of the protected characteristics, subject to a proportionality requirement.[164] Similarly, direct discrimination in relation to age is expressly capable of justification, and there has been a long-standing equivocation in relation to disability. This makes it particularly important to be in a position to shape a justification defence which is context-sensitive without permitting costs arguments to trump equality or reintroducing the very stereotypes that direct discrimination aims to eliminate.

This raises the further question as to whether it is more appropriate to do so by regarding justification as a defence or excuse to a finding of discrimination, or to follow the pattern of most constitutional understandings of equality, where mere differentiation does not amount to discrimination in the first place if it can be legitimated by reference to its purpose and the 'fit' between the means and the legitimate aim. This is the approach of Article 14 ECHR. Alternatively, the South African Constitution distinguishes between discrimination and 'unfair' discrimination. Neither of these latter approaches necessarily weakens the equality principle[165] provided a high standard of proof is required to show that the differentiation is indeed legitimate. They do, however, escape the appearance of 'excusing' discrimination.

In order to assess ways in which a justification defence could operate, it is useful to consider one context in which a justification defence has been available for direct discrimination, and that is age discrimination. Age is singled out among the grounds protected in EU law in that it permits direct discrimination to be justified. It has been argued that this should not be 'interpreted as putting age discrimination at the bottom of a perceived "hierarchy" of discrimination grounds', but instead, a recognition of the fact that age discrimination is different and its scope needs more careful demarcation.[166] This suggests, as was seen in Chapter Two, that there are contexts in which age differentiation is appropriate and even necessary. The challenge is to find a sufficiently incisive tool to distinguish between legitimate and illegitimate differentiation.

---

[164] EA 2010, Sch 9 Part 1.

[165] As is argued by Gill and Monaghan, above n 160, p 116.

[166] Case C-388/07 *R (Incorporated Trustees of the National Council on Ageing (Age Concern England) v Secretary of State* ('Heyday' case) [2009] ICR 1080 per Advocate-General Mazák at para 76.

As we have seen, there are two quite different types of possible justification.[167] One is instrumental or cost-based. In the case of age discrimination, these would aim to address the demographic problems of an ageing population and its implications for the labour market and social security. A second is intrinsic, focusing on the recognition, redistributive, or transformative dimensions of equality (protection of individual dignity, redressing disadvantage, or accommodating difference). Intrinsic justifications would make it lawful to use age-based classifications if the aim was to ameliorate the effects of old age or youth. Examples might include concessions for older people, such as free bus passes or medical prescriptions.

The instrumental aim is clearly dominant in the EU Employment Directive, which was the first to include age within the sphere of protection of anti-discrimination law. Direct age discrimination may be 'objectively and reasonably justified by a legitimate aim, including legitimate employment policy, labour market and vocational training objectives'.[168] More specifically, it may be justifiable to require workers to be over a given age, experience, or seniority before they are given access to employment or advantages linked to employment. In addition, a maximum age for recruitment may be set if it is based on the training requirements of the employer, or the need for a reasonable period of employment before retirement.[169] There are, however, gestures towards the intrinsic aim: differential treatment may be justified in relation to positive action (such as the setting of special conditions on access to employment or training, or in relation to such issues as dismissal and conditions of remuneration) if it is aimed at promoting the vocational integration of young people, older workers, or persons with caring responsibilities.

Given the predominantly instrumental nature of potentially legitimate aims of age differentiation, the weight of responsibility for achieving an appropriate role for a justification defence must be borne by the relationship between the age classification and these legitimate aims. The Directive stipulates that the means for achieving the aim must be 'appropriate and necessary'.[170] Much therefore depends on the extent to which courts are prepared to demand a high standard of proof that age

---

[167] See further S Fredman, 'The Age of Equality' in S Fredman and S Spencer (eds), *Age as an Equality Issue* (Hart Publishing, 2003).
[168] Council Directive 2000/78, Art 6(1).
[169] Ibid, Art 6.   [170] Ibid, Art 6.

discrimination is indeed necessary to achieve these ends. The ECJ will generally accept governments' stated aims, while requiring a reasonably strict standard of proof to demonstrate that age-related policies are in fact proportionate to those aims. Particularly important is its demand for actual evidence.

Mere generalisations concerning the capacity of a specific measure to contribute to employment policy, labour market or vocational training objectives are not enough to show that the aim of that measure is capable of justifying derogation from that principle and do not constitute evidence on the basis of which it could reasonably be considered that the means chosen are suitable for achieving that aim.[171]

This can be demonstrated by *Kükücdeveci*,[172] which concerned a provision in the German Civil Code providing that periods of employment completed before the age of 25 were not to be taken into account in calculating a notice period. The German government claimed that a shorter notice period for younger workers facilitated their recruitment by increasing the flexibility of personnel management. Moreover, it claimed, young workers generally reacted more easily and more rapidly to the loss of their jobs and greater flexibility could be demanded of them. Despite the fact that such generalizations clearly stereotype workers on grounds of their age, the ECJ held that these were acceptable employment and labour market objectives. However, the means were not acceptable, because the exclusion of periods of employment completed before age 25 was not an appropriate and necessary means of achieving this aim. It was over-inclusive in that its effects were felt throughout a worker's life, not just when she was under 25. This was because periods of employment under 25 were discounted for the rest of a workers' working life, and therefore did not apply only to young workers. Moreover, the impact was felt disproportionately severely by the most disadvantaged, namely those who entered the labour market at a young age without further vocational qualifications. Germany was therefore held to be in breach of the Directive.

In the UK, it is in relation to mandatory retirement ages that the role of justification has been most hotly contested. Until 2010, the UK government was intent on retaining the possibility of lawful mandatory retirement ages. The question therefore arose whether it was justifiable to enact a general statutory exclusion from anti-discrimination and

---

[171] *Heyday* case, above n 166, para 51.
[172] Case C-555/07 *Küçükdeveci v Swedex Gmbh & Co KG* [2010] 2 CMLR 33 (ECJ).

employment protection laws, such as the right to unfair dismissal, for all workers over 65.[173] In defending this exclusion, the government of the time made a gesture towards an intrinsic view, to the effect that

the default retirement age was needed to protect the dignity of workers by avoiding a situation in which employers were obliged to dismiss elderly employees on grounds of declining competence at the end of an otherwise unblemished career.[174]

However, subjecting everyone to automatic dismissal at a fixed age, regardless of individual capacities or desires seems an odd way to protect individual dignity. Instead, the real focus is on the instrumental aim of

improving the participation of the 50 to 64 age group in the labour market. . . . Those employers who would otherwise be concerned about recruiting older workers because of the possible need to deal with their declining competence at a later stage, can recruit such workers in the knowledge that they can retire them without the uncertainty of when and how their working lives will end.[175]

The question of whether this was proportionate under EU law was aired before the ECJ in the *Heyday* case.[176] The ECJ held that in principle it was permissible for a Member State to include such an exception, but only if the exception reached the high standard of justification required. It also stressed that the derogation was available for public policy reasons, and not necessarily for purely individual reasons such as cost reduction or improving competitiveness.[177] The ultimate decision on the proportionality issue, however, was left to the UK courts. The decision of the UK High Court is instructive. It held that the government's stated labour market aims were legitimate and the adoption of a designated retirement age was a proportionate way of giving effect to those aims. Despite this overall deference, the High Court was prepared to subject the specific choice of age 65 to more searching scrutiny. Although proportionate at the time of implementation, it would not have been proportionate had it been adopted in 2009.

---

[173] EA 2010, Sch 9 Part 2 paras 8–9 (for original measures see Employment Equality (Age) Regulations 2006 (SI 2006/714), reg 30); Employment Equality (Age) Regulations 2006, Sch 6 paras 5–6. These remain in force after the EA 2010.
[174] Cited in *R (Age UK) v Secretary of State* [2009] EWHC 2336 (Admin) at para 74.
[175] Ibid, para 75.
[176] *Heyday* case, above n 166.
[177] Ibid, para 46.

It creates greater discriminatory effect than is necessary on a class of people who are both able to and want to continue their employment. A higher age would not have any general detrimental labour market consequences or block access to high level jobs by future generations.[178]

It is unfortunate that the court did not demand a stronger evidential basis for the justification. However, the willingness to insist that the specific categorization be necessary to achieve the specified aim and to reject simple assertions by government is a valuable pointer to the way in which a justification defence could be judicially managed.

It should be noted that the EA 2010 has retained the contested provisions,[179] but the newly elected government announced in 2010 that the default retirement age of 65 was to be removed. It remains to be seen how courts might react if a similar challenge is brought against regulations setting a lower minimum wage for younger people under the National Minimum Wage Act 1998,[180] a distinction which has been maintained in the EA 2010.[181] This exception has not yet been challenged under the standard of proportionality required by the Directive.

It has also been difficult to find the appropriate role for justification in relation to disability. UK law permitted a defence of justification for disability discrimination from the start. In this respect, the UK has been at odds with the EU which has always required Member States to introduce a provision outlawing direct discrimination without permitting a justification defence. The UK's response has been to split the definition of direct discrimination in relation to disability into two: discrimination *because of* disability, which cannot be justified,[182] and discrimination *arising from* disability, which can.[183] In the latter case, A discriminates against B if A treats B unfavourably because of something arising in consequence of B's disability and A cannot show that the treatment is a proportionate means of achieving a legitimate aim. This, together with the duty to make reasonable adjustments, constitutes a valuable alternative model to the rigid divide between direct and indirect discrimination in relation to justification. It will be explored further below.

---

[178] *R (Age UK) v Secretary of State* above n 174, para 128.
[179] EA 2010, Sch 9 Part 2 paras 8–9 (for original measures see Employment Equality (Age) Regulations 2006, reg 30).
[180] Employment Equality (Age) Regulations 2006, reg 31.
[181] EA 2010, Sch 9 Part 2 para 11.
[182] Ibid, s 13.
[183] Ibid, s 15.

V THE DIFFICULT DIVIDE: THE ROLE OF MOTIVE AND INTENTION IN DIRECT AND INDIRECT DISCRIMINATION

Direct discrimination is distinctive in its focus on a perpetrator's actions and the reason for those actions. A discriminates against B if A treats B less favourably because of a protected characteristic. There is a necessary link between the treatment and the reason for it: if the 'less favourable' treatment is not 'because of' the protected characteristic, there is no discrimination. This underlies the demarcation between direct and indirect discrimination. Whereas direct discrimination is based on the ground of or reason for A's actions, indirect discrimination focuses on its impact. The distinction is important because, as we have seen, less favourable treatment cannot be justified, whereas disparate impact can. Advocate General Maduro has formulated this relationship particularly clearly:

The distinguishing feature of direct discrimination ... is that [it] bear[s] a necessary relationship to a particular suspect classification. The discriminator relies on a suspect classification in order to act in a certain way. The classification is not a mere contingency but serves as an essential premise of his reasoning. An employer's reliance on those suspect grounds is seen by the Community legal order as an evil which must be eradicated. Therefore, the Directive prohibits the use of those classifications as grounds upon which an employer's reasoning may be based. By contrast, in indirect discrimination cases, the intentions of the employer and the reasons he has to act or not to act are irrelevant. In fact, this is the whole point of the prohibition of indirect discrimination: even neutral, innocent or good faith measures and policies adopted with no discriminatory intent whatsoever will be caught if their impact on persons who have a particular characteristic is greater than their impact on other persons.[184]

The relationship between A's conduct and the protected characteristic has been more contentious in domestic UK law. In particular, there has been some difficulty in distinguishing between the 'ground' or reason for the differential treatment, which must be established in the case, and a 'justification' for that treatment, which is not relevant. Courts have attempted to achieve this by drawing a bright line between A's motive or intention, and the 'ground' for or 'cause' of A's action. Motive or

---

[184] Case C-303/06 *Coleman v Attridge Law* [2008] ECR I-5603, [2008] IRLR 722.

intention are equated with 'justification' and therefore regarded as irrelevant. Thus, according to Lord Goff:

> The intention or motive of the defendant to discriminate . . . is not a necessary condition of liability. . . [Otherwise] it would be a good defence for an employer to show that he discriminated against women not because he intended to do so but (for example) because of customer preference, or to save money, or even to avoid controversy.[185]

For example, in the *Roma* case, immigration officers explained their targeting of Roma on the grounds that Roma were disadvantaged in their country of origin and thus were more likely to claim asylum. To allow such explanations, it has been argued, would amount to a justification of direct discrimination. For this reason, it is now settled law that the motive of the perpetrator is irrelevant.

However, it has not always been easy to distinguish 'motive' from the 'ground' or cause of the treatment. In the attempt to exclude motive, courts have at times slipped over the boundary between differential *treatment on the ground of* a protected characteristic and differential *impact*. It is true that the fact that A is not hostile to B should not excuse A's actions. On the other hand, A's action must be *because of* the protected characteristic. If the treatment was for an entirely different reason, but has the effect of discriminating, then it should fall under the indirect discrimination provisions and be capable of justification. Instead of ignoring the perpetrator's real reason, this would allow courts to determine on proportionality grounds whether the real reason should be allowed to outweigh the differential impact. In the examples given by Lord Goff above, the fact that an employer was following customer preference, or saving money, or avoiding controversy, should not be sufficient to outweigh the fact that women have been excluded. Similarly, stereotypical assumptions, as in the *Roma* case, would not displace the detrimental effect. On the other hand, if the reason for the treatment was to compensate for past disadvantage, this may well outweigh the exclusionary effect.

The jurisprudence of the UK courts on this issue has been problematic because the principle that the perpetrator's *motive* is irrelevant has subtly transformed into an assertion of the irrelevance of the perpetrator's *reason* for the less favourable treatment. Courts have held that even if the reason is not on its face based on a protected characteristic, it

---

[185] *R v Birmingham City Council, ex p Equal Opportunities Commission* [1989] AC 1155 (HL), para 175.

might nevertheless be 'inherently' sex- or race-based. This severs the notion of direct discrimination from its moral anchor in fault and responsibility of the perpetrator, and instead makes A responsible for putting in motion a series of steps which have a detrimental *effect* on B, thus crossing the border between direct and indirect discrimination. This can be seen by considering the string of Supreme Court cases on this topic over the past decade and a half, from the earliest case, *Birmingham CC v EOC*,[186] which was able to sustain the appropriate demarcation, to the later cases of *James v Eastleigh*[187] and *JFS*,[188] which slipped over the boundary.

The *Birmingham* case was concerned with the fact that in the area in question, fewer places were available in girls' selective grammar schools than in boys'. As a result, the council required girls to obtain higher marks in the entry examination than boys.[189] The council argued that its motive was not to discriminate against girls, but to ensure that the most meritorious pupils were given places. The House of Lords held that to establish direct discrimination, it was not necessary to prove that the council's motive was to put girl pupils at a disadvantage compared with boy pupils in the area. Instead, the causative factor was crucial.

The question is whether, *but for her sex*, a qualified girl would have been given treatment and education opportunities equal to those given to a comparable boy. In the present case, there is no dispute that it is because of her sex that a qualified girl is given less favourable treatment than a qualified boy. Were she male, she would have access to almost twice as many selective places.[190]

The court in this case did not traverse the boundary between treatment on the grounds of sex and effect. This was because the council was itself responsible for maintaining selective schools. As Dillon LJ in the Court of Appeal put it (upheld by Lord Goff in the House of Lords),

in truth the council's position really is that they are knowingly continuing their acts of maintaining the various boys' and girls' selective schools, which inevitably results in discrimination against girls in the light of the great disparity in the numbers of places available.[191]

---

[186] Ibid.   [187] *James v Eastleigh BC* [1990] 2 AC 751 (HL).
[188] *R (on the application of E) v Governing Body of JFS and the Admissions Appeal Panel of JFS*, above n 131.
[189] *R v Birmingham City Council, ex p Equal Opportunities Commission*, above n 185.
[190] Ibid at 1184.   [191] Ibid at 1196.

The 'but for' test was taken a step further in *James v Eastleigh BC*,[192] which introduced the concept of an 'inherently' discriminatory criterion, which breaches the law regardless of A's reason for the classification. *James* concerned a challenge to Eastleigh Borough Council's policy of free access to swimming pools and other council facilities to anyone over pensionable age. The aim of the concessions was to compensate for the drop in income generally accompanying the end of one's working life. The problem arose because State pension ages are set at 60 for women and 65 for men. This meant that although both Mr James and his wife were 61, she was entitled to free swimming, but he was not. He argued that he had been discriminated against on grounds of his sex. The authority defended the policy by arguing that people living on pensions are almost always less well off than when in employment. The criterion of pensionable age, while somewhat broad brush, was the most practical way of identifying people living on pensions. The reason for the differentiation was not the sex of the complainant, but the fact that he had not reached pensionable age.

However, the majority of the House of Lords found that the reason why the policy was adopted could not alter the fact that the man would have received the benefits 'but for' his sex. The reason for the difference, namely to give concessions to pensioners to compensate for their loss of income, was irrelevant. Instead, it was held that the criterion of pensionable age '*itself*. . . treats women more favourably than men "on the ground of their sex"',[193] and was 'inherently' discriminatory.[194] The result was paradoxical. As Lord Griffiths put it in his dissenting opinion:

> The result of your Lordships' decision will be that either free facilities must be withdrawn from those who can ill afford to pay for them or, alternatively, given free to those who can well afford to pay for them. I consider both alternatives regrettable. I cannot believe that Parliament intended such a result and I do not believe that the words 'on the grounds of sex' compel such a result.[195]

This difficulty arises because the court has focused, not on the reason for A's actions, but on its effect. In this case, the court assumed that pensionable age was simply a proxy for sex; whereas in reality the council regarded pensionable age as a proxy for relative disadvantage. It is true that this had a differential impact on men and women; but this was because, for reasons beyond the council's control, the pensionable

---

[192] *James v Eastleigh BC*, above n 187.   [193] Ibid at 763.
[194] Ibid at p 769.   [195] Ibid at p 768.

age was different for men and women. Although the council could foresee this effect, this was not the reason for its actions.[196] If pensionable age were the same for men and women, it would still have used this criterion. Thus it treated Mr James less favourably than his wife because he was not yet of pensionable age, not because he was a man. Of course, it might be argued that pensionable age is too crude a mechanism for determining low income and therefore, given its exclusionary effect on men, the choice of pensionable age was not appropriate or necessary to achieve the aim of ameliorating the loss of income post pensionable age. This, however, should be considered separately, in the form of a justification defence. This strongly suggests that, if intention and motive are excluded from the original decision, a defence of justification should be permitted.

The paradoxical effect of ignoring the perpetrator's real reason for his or her action (as against the motive for so acting) is further underscored in the *JFS* case,[197] where the notion that a ground can be 'inherently' discriminatory was entrenched within the structure of direct discrimination. Here both Lord Mance and Lord Clarke expressly held that direct discrimination could arise in one of two ways: 'because a decision or action was taken on a ground which was, however worthy or benign the motive, inherently racial, or because it was taken or undertaken for a reason which was subjectively racial'.[198] In this case, as we saw in Chapter Three, a boy was refused admission to JFS, a Jewish faith school, because he was not recognized as Jewish according to the Orthodox religious rule. This rule, as set out by the Orthodox Chief Rabbi, requires Orthodox conversion or descent from a mother who is herself Jewish or has been converted according to the Orthodox faith. Although the boy's mother was a practising Jewess, she had been converted to Judaism according to Masorti rather than Orthodox tenets. Designated faith schools are permitted to discriminate on grounds of religion, but not on grounds of race or ethnicity. Was the school's decision, therefore, on grounds of his religion or his ethnicity?[199] There was no doubt, according to Lord Mance, that the reason for the exclusion was the school's reliance on its admissions policy. But did that

---

[196] Ibid at p 781.
[197] *R (on the application of E) v Governing Body of JFS and the Admissions Appeal Panel of JFS*, above n 131.
[198] Ibid, para 78; and see Lord Clarke at para 132.
[199] It has already been argued that this exception is problematic because it relies on a distinction between religion and ethnicity which only truly works from a Christian perspective. See Chapter Three.

admissions policy 'religiously motivated as it was, involve grounds for admission or refusal of admission which were in their nature inherently ethnic?'[200]

The majority of the court found that although the Chief Rabbi and the governors of the school were entirely free from moral blame, and acted on what must have seemed to them an entirely legitimate religious objective, the religious element was a mere motive, and therefore irrelevant to the outcome. Instead, the ground was his ethnicity: any rule which relies on descent is an ethnic rule, and, 'but for' the fact that his mother was not Jewish by Orthodox standards, he would have been admitted to the school.

The result was that the policy was held to be discriminatory on grounds of race. Yet the majority was at pains to stress that a breach of the prohibition of direct race discrimination did not connote that the school or the Chief Rabbi was racist. It was simply a technical application of the law. This disjuncture between a moral condemnation of racism and a breach of race discrimination legislation should itself give pause for thought. As Lord Rodger points out in his dissent:

> The majority's decision leads to such extraordinary results, and produces such manifest discrimination against Jewish schools in comparison with other faith schools, that one can't help feeling that something has gone wrong.[201]

What then might have gone wrong? First, the notion that a criterion is 'inherently' discriminatory ignores the structure of direct discrimination, which is to focus on why a person acted in the way she did. A decision or action is only 'inherently' discriminatory because of its effect; it is this which distinguishes it from an action which is, in the words of Lords Mance and Clark, 'subjectively racial'.[202] Focusing on the effect is the province of indirect discrimination. As we saw above, it is in indirect discrimination cases that the intentions of the respondent and the reasons she acts as she does are irrelevant. Direct discrimination, by contrast, requires a finding that the reason for the perpetrator's action was based on a protected characteristic.

Secondly, the 'but for' test gives the misleading impression that it is a value-free standard, which can find a single and unequivocal cause for the less favourable treatment. In this case, however, it yields several

---

[200] *R (on the application of E) v Governing Body of JFS and the Admissions Appeal Panel of JFS*, above n 131, para 78.

[201] Ibid, para 226.

[202] Ibid, para 78; and see Lord Clarke at para 132.

different answers. 'But for' the fact that he was a Masorti rather than an Orthodox Jew, the boy would have been admitted to the school. This would be a religious reason. Alternatively, 'but for' the fact that his mother was a Masorti rather than an Orthodox Jew, he would have been admitted. This combines a religious and a descent-based reason. Or, 'but for' the fact that Judaism recognizes only the matrilineal and not the patrilineal line, the boy would have been admitted. This is a gender-based, religious, and descent-based reason. The majority of the court took the view that as long as one of the reasons was descent-based, it did not matter that there were other non-descent-based reasons. But the freedom of the court to choose amongst different reasons undercuts the thrust of the 'but for' test. Only by referring back to the actual reason or set of reasons used by the perpetrator can a 'but for' test make sense.

Thirdly, the relegation of the real reason to a mere motive undercuts any moral rationale which might underpin direct discrimination. It will be recalled that Advocate General Maduro identified the 'evil' of direct discrimination as the fact that a suspect classification is an 'essential premise' of the discriminator's reasoning; or constitutes grounds on which the person's reasoning is based. It is the perpetrator's reasoning which is in issue. By contrast, in the context of indirect discrimination, the intentions of the perpetrator and the reasons she or he acts are irrelevant.[203] As both Lord Hope and Lord Rodger pointed out in their dissenting opinions in *JFS*, to reduce the religious element to the status of a mere motive entirely misrepresents the position,[204] removing the link between A's actions and the reason for A's actions. The real reason for the Chief Rabbi's action was religious: he recognized some conversions to Judaism but not others. Indeed, the real dispute in the case was between the Orthodox and non-Orthodox understandings of who should be Jewish, a profoundly religious dispute. Yet the impact of the majority decision is not to require recognition of non-Orthodox conversions. It is to prevent the school from basing its selection policy on the Jewish definition of Judaism at all. Instead, it requires a practice-based definition, familiar to Anglicanism but alien to Judaism. Jewish faith schools have now changed their admissions policy to require evidence of practice of the Jewish faith, through attendance at synagogue twice a month on the Sabbath as well as on all holy days. This is a result which profoundly undermines the stated mission of the school, which is to give

---

[203] *Coleman v Attridge Law*, above n 184.
[204] *R (on the application of E) v Governing Body of JFS and the Admissions Appeal Panel of JFS*, above n 131, para 201.

a Jewish education to children with no knowledge of Judaism as much as to those who already have such a knowledge. As Lord Brown put it, the result is

a test for admission to an Orthodox Jewish school which is not Judaism's own test and which requires a focus (as Christianity does) on outward acts of religious practice and declarations of faith, ignoring whether the child is or is not Jewish as defined by Orthodox Jewish law.[205]

The extent to which this result empties the concept of direct discrimination of moral weight can be seen by the fact that the majority of the court regarded the Jewish rule as equivalent to that of the Dutch Reformed Church in apartheid South Africa, which refused to admit blacks because of a belief that God made them inferior. However, the analogy is fundamentally unsound. First, the Dutch Reformed Church rejected blacks because it regarded them as inferior. In *JFS*, there was no aspersion that non-Jewish children were inferior to Jewish children, nor that they should not go to school nor that exclusion from the school was stigmatic. The only assumption was that a child needed to be Jewish to go to a Jewish faith school. Secondly, a black person could not become white and therefore become a member of the Church. On the other hand, while it may be difficult to convert to Judaism, it is not impossible. It is in fact quite easy for children under 13 to convert. The court paid surprisingly little attention to the question of conversion.

Earlier formulations of direct discrimination, on which these cases are based, referred to less favourable treatment *on the grounds* of race or sex. The EA 2010 states that direct discrimination occurs when A treats B less favourably *because of* a protected characteristic. The explanatory notes state that this is not intended to change the law, but to make the law more easily understood. Nevertheless, since 'because of' denotes the reason for the less favourable treatment, it is possible that courts might use this as an opportunity to reinstate the focus on the reason for A's conduct rather than its effect. This would elaborate on previous House of Lords jurisprudence which appeared to be reinstating the centrality of the perpetrator's actual reason, although the *JFS* majority held that these cases only applied where on the facts it is not clear which of two possible grounds is the 'real' ground.[206]

There are several possible ways forward. One way might be to permit direct discrimination to be justifiable. As we have seen, there has been a

---

[205] Ibid, para 258.
[206] *Shamoon v Chief Constable of the Royal Ulster Constabulary* [2003] IRLR 285 (HL).

deep resistance in both UK and EU law to allow a general justification defence for direct discrimination, although this is no longer true in relation to equal pay, age, and disability. There is something to be said for such a resistance where the discrimination is intentional, or the protected characteristic is an explicit reason for A's actions. However, it makes less sense now that direct discrimination is regarded as including situations in which the protected characteristic is not the reason for A's actions, but instead the criterion used is somehow intrinsically discriminatory. In such situations, permitting justification would make it possible to situate a policy, criterion, or practice within its context and test its purpose and function against the seriousness of its discriminatory consequences. For example, in *James* the council would have been required to show that there was no other less discriminatory means of achieving its aim of assisting pensioners. Similarly, in *JFS* the school would have had to prove that there was no less discriminatory manner of achieving its legitimate objective of providing a Jewish education for Jewish children. Permitting non-Orthodox conversions may have been such a means.

An alternative way forward is to regard intrinsically discriminatory rules as a species of indirect discrimination and therefore justifiable. This permits the real reason to be scrutinized to determine whether it is proportionate and necessary in the light of its exclusionary effect. For example, Lord Hope held that the admissions policy in the *JFS* case was not directly but indirectly discriminatory, in that it was not proportionate or necessary to insist on Orthodox conversion in the admission criteria. By classifying the requirement that a child be Jewish as direct discrimination, the majority of the court prevented any real consideration being given to the real, genuinely religious reason.

There has been a reluctance to rely on indirect discrimination in such cases, because the act or decision excludes everyone with the relevant protected characteristic. It will be recalled that indirect discrimination is understood as a practice, provision, or requirement which, although ostensibly neutral, in practice excludes significantly more of those with a particular protected characteristic than others. When all members of the group are excluded, it might be thought that there is too much of a coincidence between the criterion applied and the exclusionary effect to regard the criterion as neutral.[207] Indeed, it is this that prompts the conclusion that the criterion is 'intrinsically' discriminatory. However,

---

[207] See eg *R (on the application of E) v Governing Body of JFS and the Admissions Appeal Panel of JFS*, above n 131, para 71.

the criterion is neutral for the purposes of indirect discrimination as long as the same criterion is applied to everyone. This is not changed if the criterion excludes significantly more of one group than another, or all of the group. For example, in *Mandla v Lee*[208] the House of Lords held that a school uniform rule which required pupils to go bare-headed was indirectly discriminatory because, although applied to all students, it excluded Sikhs. The fact that all Sikhs were excluded by the rule did not prevent this result.

This argument is strengthened by the new definition of indirect discrimination which, as we have seen, requires that the measure subjects B to a particular disadvantage. It will be recalled that this formulation originated in the case of *O'Flynn*,[209] in which the ECJ explicitly stated that a provision would be regarded as indirectly discriminatory if it was 'intrinsically liable' to affect migrant workers more than national workers, with the consequent risk that they would be placed at a particular disadvantage.[210] It has made no difference to the ECJ that the apparently neutral criterion in effect excludes all members of a particular group. In *Schnorbus*,[211] a legal training course was mandatory in order to qualify for the higher civil service or the judicial service. Priority for places on this course was given to individuals who had completed national service. Yet only men were eligible for national service. The ECJ held that regardless of statistics, the provisions at issue were themselves evidence of indirect discrimination since, under the relevant national legislation, women were not required to do military or civilian service and therefore could not benefit from the priority. This analysis closely resembles the 'intrinsically discriminatory' class identified by UK courts as directly discriminatory. By classifying it as indirectly discriminatory, however, the ECJ was able to consider the justification for the rule. Since its aim was to compensate for the delay necessitated by military service, and the detriment to others lasted for only 12 months, it was held to be proportionate and justified.

A third way forward is to relax the boundary between direct and indirect discrimination. This route has been followed by the Supreme Court of Canada. Although the definitions of direct and indirect discrimination differ in important respects from those used in UK law, the critique of the distinction mounted by the Supreme Court of Canada in

---

[208] *Mandla v Lee* [1983] 2 AC 548 (HL).
[209] *O'Flynn v Adjudication Officer*, above n 122.
[210] Ibid, para 20.
[211] Case C-79/99 *Schnorbus v Land Hessen* [2001] 1 CMLR 40 (ECJ).

a case in 1997 (the *'Firefighters'* case) is instructive.[212] The case was brought by a woman firefighter, who complained that a new rule requiring a certain standard of aerobic fitness was indirectly discriminatory against women, because the test was designed for a male physique, and women were unable to achieve the level required. The Court upheld her claim. The aerobic standard was prima facie discriminatory and there was no credible evidence showing that the prescribed aerobic capacity was necessary for either men or women to perform the work of a forest firefighter satisfactorily.

McLachlan J took the opportunity of revisiting the conventional bifurcated approach which categorized discrimination as either 'direct', meaning discriminatory on its face, or 'adverse effect', meaning discriminatory in effect. She recognized that 'the conventional analysis was helpful in the interpretation of the early human rights statutes, and indeed represented a significant step forward in that it recognized for the first time the harm of adverse effect discrimination'.[213] However, it no longer served the purpose of human rights legislation. There were a number of reasons for this. Most important for our purposes was the fact that few cases could be neatly categorized as direct or adverse effect discrimination. The example given by McLachlan J is particularly instructive. She referred to a rule requiring all workers to appear at work on Fridays or face dismissal. This could be directly discriminatory, in that no workers whose religious beliefs preclude working on Fridays may be employed there. Or it could be characterized as a neutral rule that merely has an adverse effect on a few individuals (those same workers whose religious beliefs prevent them from working on Fridays).[214] The same analysis would work in British law: the rule would be 'intrinsically' directly discriminatory under the *JFS* test; or indirectly discriminatory because workers whose religious beliefs prevent them from working on Fridays would be subject to a particular disadvantage. She also recognized that the size of the 'affected group' is easily manipulable, mirroring the concerns raised above. The difficulty in classification led McLachlan J to conclude that it was not appropriate for the distinction to constitute the basis for diverging remedial or other outcomes. Instead, she established a unified approach. Where a standard is prima facie discriminatory, it can only be justified if the employer can

---

[212] *British Columbia (Public Service Employee Relations Commission) v BCGEU* (1999) Carswell BC 1907 (Supreme Court of Canada).

[213] Ibid, para 25.

[214] Ibid, para 27.

show that the purpose of the standard is rationally connected to the performance of the job, the standard was adopted in a bona fide belief that it was necessary to fulfil a legitimate work-related purpose, and the standard is reasonably necessary to the accomplishment of that purpose.

A different possible way of bridging the divide between direct and indirect discrimination is found in the context of disability. As we have seen, the EA 2010 splits the definition of direct discrimination in relation to disability into two: discrimination *because of* disability, which cannot be justified,[215] and discrimination *arising from* disability, which can.[216] In the latter case, A discriminates against B if A treats B unfavourably because of something arising in consequence of B's disability and A cannot show that the treatment is a proportionate means of achieving a legitimate aim. This formulation is conceptually very close to the notion of a criterion which is 'inherently' discriminatory and, notably, it can be justified on the standard proportionality analysis. It differs in that it is a defence to a claim of discrimination arising from disability for an employer to show that she did not know that the person was disabled. Nevertheless, shorn of the requirement of knowledge, it represents the seeds of a possible alternative way forward to the existing rigid divide.

VI DUTY OF ACCOMMODATION OR ADJUSTMENT

The advent of disability discrimination legislation in the UK brought with it a recognition that it is not sufficient to require individuals to conform to the dominant norm. The norm should be adapted to facilitate equal participation of people with disabilities. Thus when the Disability Discrimination Act 1995 was introduced, it included a duty of reasonable adjustment.[217] The duty applies to situations in which a disabled person is put at a substantial disadvantage in comparison with non-disabled persons by a provision, criterion, or practice, a physical feature, or the absence of an auxiliary aid. In such circumstances, the employer, service provider, or other relevant body must take such steps as is reasonable to avoid the disadvantage, or to provide an auxiliary aid.[218] A failure to comply constitutes discrimination. A similar duty applies in the US, where the Americans with Disabilities Act of 1990

---

[215] EA 2010, s 13.   [216] Ibid, s 15.
[217] DDA, s 3A(6).   [218] EA 2010, s 20.

provides that it is discriminatory for an employer to fail to make 'reasonable accommodations to the known physical or mental limitations of an [employee] with a disability' unless the employer 'can demonstrate that the accommodation would impose an undue hardship on the operation of [its] business'.[219] Although in the UK this concept is confined to disability, in other jurisdictions it extends further. In the US, the duty of reasonable accommodation also applies for religious purposes. An employer is required to make 'reasonable accommodations' to the religious needs of its employees, short of 'undue hardship'.[220] Similarly, in Canada the duty has its origins in religious discrimination. Thus in *Simpson-Sears*[221] the applicant argued that a rule requiring employees to be available for work on Saturdays discriminated against those observing a Saturday Sabbath, thus contravening the Ontario Human Rights Code.[222] The Supreme Court of Canada held that the respondent had an obligation to take reasonable steps to accommodate the religious observance of the complainant, short of undue hardship in the operation of its business. This approach has been expressly adopted in relation to the constitutional guarantee of equality in the Canadian Charter.[223] Moreover, it is not confined to religion and disability in Canadian law. It has become an integral part of the broader understanding of adverse effects discrimination. This raises the more general question of whether the duty should sensibly be extended to other grounds in UK law, and what its relationship with indirect and direct discrimination should be.

There are several important ways in which the duty of reasonable adjustment represents an advance towards substantive equality. The first is that equality is explicitly asymmetric, aiming to redress disadvantage even if this entails different or more favourable treatment. Indeed, the EA 2010 specifically protects such action against a challenge under the equal treatment principle.[224] This asymmetry in the specific context of disability has been endorsed by the courts.

---

[219] 42 USC § 12112(b)(5)(A).

[220] 42 USC § 2000e(j) (1970 ed, Supp V). See also § 703(a)(1) of the Civil Rights Act of 1964, Title VII, 78 Stat 255, 42 USC § 2000e-2(a)(1) (prohibits religious discrimination in employment).

[221] *Ontario Human Rights Commission v Simpsons-Sears Ltd*, above n 2.

[222] Section 4(1)(g) of the Ontario Human Rights Code prohibiting discrimination on grounds of 'creed'; since superceded by the differently worded Section 10 of the Human Rights Code, 1981.

[223] *Eldridge v British Columbia* [1997] 3 SCR 624, para 63.

[224] EA 2010, s 13(3).

In the [Sex Discrimination Act 1975 and Race Relations Act 1976], men and women or black and white, as the case may be, are opposite sides of the same coin. Each is to be treated in the same way. Treating men more favourably than women discriminates against women. Treating women more favourably than men discriminates against men. Pregnancy apart, the differences between the genders are generally regarded as irrelevant. The 1995 Act, however, does not regard the differences between disabled people and others as irrelevant. It does not expect each to be treated in the same way. It expects reasonable adjustments to be made to cater for the special needs of disabled people. It necessarily entails an element of more favourable treatment.[225]

In this spirit, too, the role of the comparator has been broadly construed so that, in effect, it is sufficient to show that, because of her disability, a person is at a substantial disadvantage.[226]

The express endorsement of an asymmetric approach has been shown to be essential to protect the duty of reasonable accommodation or adjustment against challenges for breach of the basic equal treatment principle. In a case before the US Supreme Court, an employer argued that the duty of reasonable accommodation in effect constituted preferential treatment for disabled employees. By requiring an exception to rules which apply equally to all, it was argued, the duty was a breach of the principle of equal treatment specified in the US Disability Discrimination Act. The response of the US Supreme Court was emphatic:

While linguistically logical, this argument fails to recognize what the Act specifies, namely, that preferences will sometimes prove necessary to achieve the Act's basic equal opportunity goal. The Act requires preferences in the form of 'reasonable accommodations' that are needed for those with disabilities to obtain the *same* workplace opportunities that those without disabilities automatically enjoy.... The simple fact that an accommodation would provide a 'preference'—in the sense that it would permit the worker with a disability to violate a rule that others must obey—cannot, *in and of itself,* automatically show that the accommodation is not 'reasonable'.[227]

Similarly, the Supreme Court of Canada has stressed that avoidance of discrimination on grounds of disability will frequently require distinctions to be made to take into account the actual personal characteristics of disabled persons.[228]

[225] *Archibald v Fife Council* [2004] UKHL 32, paras 47, 57.
[226] Ibid, para 64.
[227] *US Airways v Barnett* 535 US 391 (2002) at 397–8.
[228] *Eldridge v British Columbia*, above n 223, para 65.

The second important way in which the duty of reasonable adjustment advances substantive equality is its focus on modifying the environment to facilitate the participation of those affected. In the context of disability, this endorses a social model of disability, highlighting the disabling effect of an environment adapted to able-bodied people. As Sopinka J put it in the Supreme Court of Canada:

Exclusion from the mainstream of society results from the construction of a society based solely on 'mainstream' attributes to which disabled persons will never be able to gain access. . . . . [I]t is the failure to make reasonable accommodation, to fine-tune society so that its structures and assumptions do not result in the relegation and banishment of disabled persons from participation, which results in discrimination against them.[229]

Thirdly, the duty of reasonable adjustment goes beyond other conceptions of equality in that it expressly imposes a positive duty to make changes. This applies not just to neutral rules or practices but also to a failure to provide specific aids. Thus in the Canadian case of *Eldridge*,[230] the court emphasized that the adverse effects suffered by disabled people need not stem only from the imposition of a burden not faced by the mainstream population, but also from a failure to ensure that they benefit equally from a service offered to everyone. In this case, the failure to provide sign language interpreters for deaf people in the health service was discriminatory and constituted a failure to accommodate their needs. In the EA 2010, as we have seen, express provision is made for a duty of accommodation arising from the absence of an auxiliary aid.

It will be seen in Chapter Six that there has been a more general development in UK anti-discrimination law towards the imposition of positive duties on public bodies in the context of equality ('the public sector duty'). The duty of reasonable adjustment is, however, more focused and specific. Whereas the public sector duty requires only that consideration be given to the need to take action, the duty of reasonable adjustment requires specific and focused action. It also differs from the public sector duty in that breach constitutes discrimination and therefore gives rise to an individually enforceable right. In addition, it is not confined to the public sector.

The duty therefore fulfils at least three of the dimensions of equality identified in Chapter One: the distributive dimension of redressing disadvantage, the transformative dimension of accommodating difference,

---

[229] *Eaton v Brant County Board of Education* [1997] 1 SCR 241, paras 66–7.
[230] *Eldridge v British Columbia*, above n 223, para 66.

and the participative dimension of facilitating participation. At the same time, the duty confronts an ambiguity in the understanding of the need to accommodate difference. Does accommodating difference require general structural change, or is it sufficient to create exceptions for individuals, while maintaining the general rule? An 'exceptionalist' approach has attracted criticism on the basis that, as Brodsky and Day have argued,

> The difficulty with this paradigm is that it does not challenge the imbalances of power, or the discourses of dominance, such as racism, able-bodyism and sexism, which result in a society being designed well for some and not for others. It allows those who consider themselves 'normal' to continue to construct institutions and relations in their image, as long as others, when they challenge this construction are 'accommodated' . . . In short, accommodation is assimilationist. Its goal is to try to make 'different' people fit into existing systems.[231]

However, the dichotomy between exceptionalism and structural change might be overstated. There are clearly situations, particularly in the context of gender discrimination, in which the norm should be changed. However, in other situations it might be appropriate to retain the norm as a whole, but with specific exceptions to cater for religious differences. For example, if Sikhs are unable to wear a hard hat on a construction site because of their religious duty to wear a turban, the creation of an exception is preferable to the wholesale rejection of the rule.

An attempt to achieve an appropriate balance between creating an exception and structural change can be seen in the EA 2010, where the duty of reasonable adjustment can be either anticipatory or reactive.[232] In some contexts it is reactive, only arising if the practice substantially disadvantages a particular disabled person or on request by a particular disabled person. For example, in relation to common parts of let residential premises, the duty is not owed to disabled persons generally, but only to those where a request for an adjustment is made.[233] Similarly, employers need not take any action in relation to job applicants unless they have been notified by a person that she is applying for work, and they know or could be expected to know that she is disabled.[234] In such

---

[231] S Day and G Brodsky, 'The Duty to Accommodate: Who Will Benefit?' (1996) 75 Can Bar Rev 433 at 447–57.
[232] Bob Hepple, *Equality: The New Framework* (Hart Publishing, 2011), ch 3.
[233] EA 2010, Pt 4 Premises, s 36 and Sch 4.
[234] Ibid, s 39; Sch 8 Part 2.

situations, the duty functions as a specific exception. In other contexts, however, it is 'anticipatory'. Thus service providers and those exercising public functions must anticipate the needs of disabled people and make appropriate reasonable adjustments. For example, the duty might require the installation of ramps, automatic doors, and hearing induction loops in national chain stores. A rail service provider might need to provide an alternative catering service for disabled people who cannot get to the buffet car.[235] In this way, the service is modified proactively, so that it is as close as possible to that offered to the rest of the public.[236] In this sense, it signals structural change and can be transformative.

As with direct and indirect discrimination, the question arises as to how to balance competing priorities against the duty of accommodation. Generally, the balance between priorities is not formulated as a separate defence, but is built into the notion that any accommodation or adjustment need only be reasonable. This in turn requires greater attention to the meaning of reasonableness. In Canadian and US jurisprudence, this standard is made more specific than in the UK, in that the accommodation should not cause undue hardship.

Also problematic is the question of who should bear the cost. Generally, this cost falls on the employer or service provider, although a substantial contribution is often provided by the State through the welfare system. But what if the cost falls on other employees, who need to make way to accommodate the needs of a disabled or religious colleague? This question was starkly put to the US Supreme Court in a case in 2002, in which the employer asked the court whether the Americans with Disabilities Act required an employer to assign a disabled employee to a particular position even though another employee was entitled to that position under the employer's 'established seniority system'.[237] It was held that, generally speaking, it would not be reasonable to expect an employer to override another employee's rights to a particular job, earned through her seniority, unless special circumstances could be shown.[238] The Court came to the same conclusion in relation to accommodation in the context of a Title VII religious discrimination case, holding that an employer need not adapt to an employee's special worship schedule as a 'reasonable

---

235 EA 2010 explanatory notes para 686.
236 Hepple, above n 232, ch 3.
237 *US Airways v Barnett*, above n 227.
238 Ibid.

accommodation' where doing so would conflict with the seniority rights of other employees.[239]

More difficult is the attempt to find the balance between specific religious requirements and general laws promulgated purportedly for the good of the population as a whole. This question has generally arisen in relation to general public safety laws which impinge on particular religious practices. For example, should a prohibition on cannabis or peyote be subject to an exception to accommodate the religious practices of Rastafarians or First Americans? Should a requirement to wear a hard hat or a motorcycle helmet be lifted to accommodate turban-wearing Sikhs? Even more problematic, should a ban on corporal punishment be modified to accommodate Christians who maintain that their religion requires that children be disciplined in this manner? Should a teacher be permitted to wear a veil covering her face if this interferes with her ability to teach effectively? There has been a general reluctance by courts in different jurisdictions to create such exceptions, particularly where others are affected. Thus in both the US and South Africa, courts have rejected a claim that criminal prohibitions on drug-taking should be relaxed to accommodate Rastafarians and First Americans.[240] In both the UK and South Africa, the same has been true for the challenge to prohibitions on corporal punishment in schools.[241] In the UK, as we have seen, it was held that it was not discriminatory to refuse to accommodate a Muslim teacher who believed she should cover her face when this interfered with children's education,[242] or a Muslim pupil who believed that her religion required her to wear a jilbab, rather than the shalwar kameez which was permitted by the uniform rules.[243] This has even been true in the case of less conspicuous religious symbols, such as the wearing of a cross, if it conflicted with an employer's uniform requirements. However, there have been decisions in the opposite direction. Thus the South African Constitutional Court upheld a claim by a Hindu student that an exception should be made to

---

[239] *Trans World Airlines, Inc v Hardison* 432 US 63, 79–80 (1977).

[240] *Prince v President of the Law Society of the Cape of Good Hope* (CCT36/00) [2002] ZACC 1, 2002 (2) SA 794 (South African Constitutional Court); *Employment Division, Department of Human Resources of Oregon v Smith* 494 US 872 (1990).

[241] *Christian Education South Africa v Minister of Education* 2000 (4) SA 757 (CC), 2000 (10) BCLR 1051 (CC) (South African Constituitonal Court).

[242] *Azmi v Kirklees MBC* above n 156.

[243] *R (SB) v Governors of Denbigh High School* [2006] UKHL 15 (HL). The 'shalwar kameez' is described in the judgment as a combination of a sleeveless smock-like dress and loose trousers tapering at the ankles. The 'jilbab' is described as a long coat-like garment which effectively concealed the shape of the female body.

school uniform rules to permit her to wear a bracelet which was part of her cultural identity. [244] There has always been a statutory exception for Sikhs from the requirement to wear hard hats on construction sites and motorcycle helmets.

One way of reconciling these decisions might be to distinguish between claims for accommodation which affect only the religious adherent and those which affect others. However, this distinction soon breaks down. It was argued in *Denbigh* that if one girl was permitted to wear the burka, this would put pressure on others to do the same. [245] A Sikh who is injured in a motorcycle accident will still have the right to publicly funded health care. A more useful approach would be to ask whether the general rule genuinely serves all, or is simply a normalization of the dominant culture. Apparently secular rules, such as dress codes or days of rest, are frequently modelled on Christian customs. Where this is the case, there should be a duty to accommodate, unless there is a clear conflict with another's rights, as in the corporal punishment cases or the wearing of a veil in school. However, religious accommodation might well continue to create conflicts which have no easy solution.

VII EQUALITY AS PROPORTIONALITY

Instead of the precise set of definitions found in statutory anti-discrimination law, constitutional equality guarantees tend to be open-textured, simply stipulating that all persons are equal before the law. However, since the State inevitably differentiates between people in a variety of legitimate contexts, such as taxation, it is necessary to distinguish between legitimate classifications and invidious discrimination. To do so, courts in various jurisdictions have used a proportionality test. The State must show that the classification has been instituted for a legitimate purpose, and that it is appropriate to achieve that aim. This approach is particularly visible in the jurisprudence of the ECtHR. The ECtHR has consistently held that not all differences of treatment are discriminatory, even if based on one of the specified grounds. A difference is only discriminatory, according to the Court, if it has 'no objective and reasonable justification', that is, if does not pursue a legitimate aim or if there is not a 'reasonable relationship of proportionality between the means

---

[244] *MEC for Education: Kwazulu-Natal and Others v Pillay* (CCT 51/06) [2007] ZACC 21, 2008 (1) SA 474 (CC), 2008 (2) BCLR 99 (CC).

[245] Above n 243.

employed and the aim sought to be realised'.[246] The US court as we saw in Chapter Three, has approached this question by establishing differing standards of review. Distinctions used as part of the normal administration of the State need only be 'rationally related' to a legitimate State interest. However, invidious distinctions, such as race, will be subject to strict scrutiny, passing muster only if they are necessary for a pressing State interest.

Despite the difference between the open-textured nature of constitutional equality guarantees and the structured statutory approaches found in anti-discrimination legislation at domestic and EU level, there are growing convergences in approach. This is particularly evident in relation to indirect or adverse effects discrimination. As we have seen, the Supreme Court of Canada has found little difficulty in developing the constitutional equality guarantee in the direction of adverse impact discrimination. Interpreting the equality guarantee in the Ontario Human Rights Code, McIntyre J stated that the main aim was

not to punish the discriminator, but rather to provide relief for the victims of discrimination. It is the result or the effect of the action complained of which is significant.... if its effect is to impose on one person or group of persons obligations, penalties, or restrictive conditions not imposed on other members of the community, it is discriminatory.[247]

This definition of adverse effects discrimination has been expressly adopted in the context of the equality guarantee in s 15(1) of the Canadian Charter.[248]

In its earlier case law, the ECtHR was unwilling to move beyond a focus on equal treatment to one of adverse impact. Thus in the early case of *Abdulaziz*,[249] the Court refused to hold that the UK's 1980 Immigration Rules were discriminatory on the grounds of race. Because the rules did not contain regulations expressly differentiating between persons or groups on the grounds of their race or ethnic origin, there could be no breach of Article 14 even though their primary effect was to exclude a disproportionate number of would-be immigrants from the New Commonwealth and Pakistan.

---

[246] *Belgian Linguistic Case (No 2)* Series A No 6 (1968) 1 EHRR 252 at para 10; *Marckx v Belgium* Series A No 31 (1979) 2 EHRR 330 at para 33; *Abdulaziz, Cabales and Balkandali v UK* Series A No 42 (1985) 7 EHRR 471 (ECtHR), para 72.

[247] *Ontario Human Rights Commission v Simpsons-Sears Ltd*, above n 2, para 12.

[248] *Egan v Canada* [1995] 2 SCR 513, para 138.

[249] *Abdulaziz, Cabales and Balkandali v UK*, above n 246.

That the mass immigration against which the rules were directed consisted mainly of would-be immigrants from the New Commonwealth and Pakistan, and that as a result they affected at the material time fewer white people than others, is not a sufficient reason to consider them as racist in character: it is an effect which derives not from the content of the 1980 Rules but from the fact that, among those wishing to immigrate, some ethnic groups outnumbered others.[250]

This, approach, however, has altered significantly. The first stage was to hold that equal treatment could itself be discriminatory if applied to persons in significantly different circumstances. Thus in *Thlimmenos*[251] the applicant refused to serve in the army because of his religious convictions, a criminal offence in Greece. He was later barred from becoming an accountant because of a rule excluding anyone with a criminal conviction. The Court stated: 'The right not to be discriminated against . . . is also violated when States without an objective and reasonable justification fail to treat differently persons whose situations are significantly different'.[252] His situation was significantly different because the criminal conviction was due to his religious beliefs, and he should have been treated differently.

The Court was still unwilling to develop a full-blown indirect discrimination analysis until the *DH* case came to the Grand Chamber.[253] This case concerned the situation in Ostrava, in which educational psychology tests applied to children had the effect that Roma children were 27 times more likely than non-Roma children to be placed in a school for children with special needs. This apparently neutral treatment in practice had significantly adverse effects. Special schools or classes generally meant an inferior curriculum, as well as being accompanied by the stigmatic labelling of Roma children as less intelligent or capable. Moreover, as the Commissioner for Human Rights pointed out in the case,

Segregated education denies both the Roma and non-Roma children the chance to know each other and to learn to live as equal citizens. It excludes Roma children from mainstream society at the very beginning of their lives, increasing the risk of their being caught in the vicious circle of marginalisation.[254]

The Court accepted expressly that a difference in treatment may take the form of disproportionately prejudicial effects of a general policy or

---

[250] Ibid, para 85.   [251] *Thlimmenos v Greece* (2001) 31 EHRR 4 (ECtHR).
[252] Ibid, para 44.   [253] *DH v Czech Republic*, above n 101.
[254] Ibid, para 50.

measure which, although couched in neutral terms, discriminates against a group. Taking its cue from the indirect discrimination provisions in EU law, the Court held that such discrimination did not necessarily require discriminatory intent.

Significantly out of line with this approach has been the US Supreme Court. Despite the fact that adverse effects discrimination was pioneered in that court in the context of the statutory equality guarantee in Title VII of the Civil Rights Act, the Court was unwilling to carry over this analysis to the constitutional guarantee. In *Washington v Davis*, the Court held: 'Our cases have not embraced the proposition that a law or other official act, without regard to whether it reflects a racially discriminatory purpose, is unconstitutional *solely* because it has a racially disproportionate impact.'[255]

The incorporation of an indirect discrimination analysis into the proportionality doctrine at the centre of the ECHR guarantee has not, however, led to rigid distinctions between direct and indirect discrimination as found in recent UK case law, particularly in relation to the availability of justification. This is because, under a proportionality approach, the tension between competing interests is at its core, rather than functioning as a defence after a prima facie finding of discrimination has been made. As was made explicit when Protocol 12 was agreed, it is unnecessary to include a separate defence or restriction: distinctions for which an objective and reasonable justification exists simply do not constitute discrimination.[256] This means that differentiation can be justified whether it is direct or indirect.

Much therefore depends on the sensitivity to equality goals with which the Court applies the proportionality formula. On the one hand, unequal treatment should be justifiable where appropriate. On the other hand, the Court should be in a position to exercise sufficient control to ensure that the equality right is not displaced without careful scrutiny by the court of its underlying justification, including evidence.

The judicial response to this issue has also been closely bound up with questions of separation of powers, and judicial deference to stated governmental aims. Thus the ECtHR has consistently stressed that

the contracting state enjoys a margin of appreciation in assessing whether and to what extent differences in otherwise similar situations justify a different

---

[255] *Washington v Davis* 426 US 229, 96 S Ct 2040 (1976) at 239.
[256] Draft Protocol 12, Explanatory Report, paras 18 and 19.

treatment. The scope of this margin will vary according to the circumstances, the subject matter and the background. A wide margin is usually allowed to the state under the Convention when it comes to general measures of economic or social strategy.[257]

The result has been that, like the ECJ, the ECtHR has generally been deferent in relation to the stated aims of a classification, but demanding as to the means. This is particularly true in relation to grounds such as race, sex, or sexual orientation, where the Court demands 'very weighty reasons' to justify differentiation. A good example of the reasoning process is found in the ECtHR decision in *Karner v Austria*,[258] in which the applicant argued that he should have the same rights to succeed to the tenancy of his same-sex partner as an opposite sex partner would have. So far as the aim was concerned, the Court was prepared to accept that 'protection of the family in the traditional sense is, in principle, a weighty and legitimate reason which might justify a difference in treatment'. However,

the aim of protecting the family in the traditional sense is rather abstract and a broad variety of concrete measures may be used to implement it. In cases in which the margin of appreciation afforded to Member States is narrow, as the position where there is a difference in treatment based on sex or sexual orientation, the principle of proportionality does not merely require that the measure chosen is in principle suited for realising the aim sought. It must also be shown that it was necessary to exclude persons living in a homosexual relationship from the scope of application of s.14 of the Rent Act in order to achieve that aim. The Court cannot see that the Government has advanced any arguments that would allow of such a conclusion.[259]

Nevertheless, there remains the risk that equality will be regarded as no more than a factor to be weighed in the balance. One way forward is to give express weight to the equality value in the constitutional text itself. This is the approach of the South African Constitution, which distinguishes between fair and unfair discrimination, with a presumption that all discrimination is unfair unless proved fair. Even unfair discrimination can be justified if the limitation is reasonable and justifiable in an open and democratic society based on human dignity, equality, and freedom, taking into account all relevant factors including the

---

[257] *Carson v United Kingdom* (2010) 51 EHRR 13, para 61.
[258] *Karner v Austria* (2004) 38 EHRR 24 (ECtHR).
[259] Ibid, paras 40–1.

nature of the right; the importance of the purpose of the limitation; the relation between the limitation and its purpose; and less restrictive means to achieve the purpose.[260] However, even the most sophisticated tests depend on judicial application, and it is not always the case that a sufficiently nuanced test has been developed.

To what extent then has the proportionality doctrine been capable of achieving some of the central aims of equality? The ECtHR has been sensitive to the need to further the recognition dimension through its insistence that particular grounds, such as sexual orientation, require very weighty justification. The redistributive dimension is furthered by the Court's acceptance of the principle of indirect discrimination, and even more so by its asymmetric approach. Thus the Court has consistently stated that Article 14 does not prohibit a Member State from treating groups differently in order to correct 'factual inequalities' between them. Indeed, it has held that in certain circumstances a failure to attempt to correct inequality through different treatment may in itself give rise to a breach of the Article.[261] This contrasts with more recent jurisprudence of the US, where the Supreme Court by a majority held that steps taken to reduce disparate impact could breach the prohibition against disparate treatment.[262] Scalia J in his dissenting opinion in that case cast doubt on whether the disparate impact principle in Title VII is capable of reconciliation with the constitutional guarantee of equal treatment.[263]

The transformative dimension recently surfaced in ECtHR jurisprudence in relation to accommodating diversity. Thus in *DH* the Court referred to the emerging consensus that the special needs of minorities should be recognized. It held that there is an obligation to protect their security, identity, and lifestyle, both for minorities themselves and to preserve a cultural diversity of value to the whole community.[264] In *Connors* this was reinforced, with the Court holding that the vulnerable position of gypsies as a minority means that some special consideration should be given to their needs and their different lifestyle.[265]

---

[260] Constitution of South Africa, s 36(1).

[261] *Case relating to certain aspects of the laws on the use of languages in education in Belgium* (Merits), Judgment of 23 July 1968, Series A No 6, para 10 and *Thlimmenos v Greece* above n 251, para 44.

[262] *Ricci v DeStefano* 129 S Ct 2658 (2009).

[263] Ibid, per Scalia J at 2681–2.

[264] *DH v Czech Republic*, above n 101.

[265] *Connors v United Kingdom* (2005) 40 EHRR 9 (ECtHR).

VIII EQUALITY AS DIGNITY

It was argued in Chapter One that a commitment to the underlying value of human dignity can provide a valuable underpinning to the concept of equality. To what extent has this permeated the legal definitions of discrimination? At its most general level, dignity can operate as a guiding principle. This has been its role in the text and judicial development of the South African Constitution. In one of the first equality cases to be decided, the South African Constitutional Court declared:

At the heart of the prohibition of unfair discrimination lies a recognition that the purpose of our new constitutional and democratic order is the establishment of a society in which all human beings will be accorded equal dignity and respect regardless of their membership of particular groups. The achievement of such a society in the context of our deeply inegalitarian past will not be easy, but that that is the goal of the Constitution should not be forgotten or overlooked.[266]

Similarly, the Canadian Supreme Court has used dignity as a fundamental principle in deciding to whom the equality guarantee should apply. Thus, the Court stated:

Equality means that our society cannot tolerate legislative distinctions that treat certain people as second-class citizens, that demean them, that treat them as less capable for no good reason, or that otherwise offend fundamental human dignity.[267]

A similar sentiment has been articulated at EU level. According to Advocate General Maduro, the aim of the equal treatment principle in the EU Treaty is

to protect the dignity and autonomy of persons belonging to those suspect classifications.... Treating someone less well on the basis of reasons such as religious belief, age, disability and sexual orientation undermines this special and unique value that people have by virtue of being human.[268]

Reliance on dignity has some important advantages over direct discrimination, with its basis in equality as consistent treatment. As a start, it is incompatible with a 'levelling down' option. It also avoids the need

---

[266] *President of the Republic of South Africa v Hugo* CCT 11/96 (18 April 1997), 1997 (4) SA 1 (CC), para 41.
[267] *Egan v Canada* (1995) 29 CRR (2d) 79 at 104–5.
[268] *Coleman v Attridge Law*, above n 184, AG9.

for a comparator. This has been particularly important in relation to sexual harassment. In the UK, dignity has been the crucial additional ingredient in transforming the principle of direct discrimination to encompass a prohibition on sexual harassment. Indeed, in the field of harassment, the stress on dignity has facilitated a transformation of direct discrimination from a principle based entirely on consistency, to one embedded in substantive values. Thus, in the first UK case to recognize harassment as a species of sex discrimination, Lord Elmslie had no difficulty in finding it to be 'a particularly unacceptable form of treatment which it must be taken to have been the intention of Parliament to restrain'.[269] Canadian jurisprudence has been most explicit in recognizing sexual harassment as a demeaning practice, constituting a profound affront to the dignity and self-respect of the victim both as an employee and a human being.[270]

Dignity is now the basis of the statutory definition of harassment, both in the EU and in the UK. The EU Race Directive defines harassment as unwanted conduct related to racial or ethnic origin which 'takes place with the purpose or effect of violating the dignity of a person and of creating an intimidating, hostile, degrading, humiliating or offensive environment'.[271] Such conduct is deemed to be discriminatory. EU law also contains a specific application to sexual harassment, outlawing

unwanted conduct related to sex... with the purposes or effect of affecting the dignity of a person and/or creating an intimidating, hostile, offensive or disturbing environment, in particular if... rejection of or submission to such conduct is used as a basis for a decision which affects that person.

These definitions have now been imported and harmonized in the EA 2010, which prohibits

unwanted conduct related to a relevant protected characteristic, which has the purpose or effect of violating another's dignity, or creating an intimidating, hostile, degrading, humiliating or offensive environment for another person.[272]

There is a similar definition of sexual harassment to that in the EU.[273]

---

[269] *Strathclyde Regional Council v Porcelli* [1986] IRLR 135 (Court of Session).
[270] *Janzen v Platy Enterprises Ltd* [1989] 1 SCR 1252, 59 DLR (4th) 352.
[271] Directive 2000/43, Art 2(3).
[272] EA 2010, s 26.
[273] Ibid, s 27.

Dignity has also been the basis for the very recent recognition by the ECJ that discrimination can affect more than just the person with the particular characteristic.

One way of undermining the dignity and autonomy of people who belong to a certain group is to target not them, but third persons who are closely associated with them and do not themselves belong to the group. A robust conception of equality entails that these subtler forms of discrimination should also be caught by anti-discrimination legislation, as they, too, affect the persons belonging to suspect classifications.[274]

Known as discrimination by association, this has been used to uphold a claim by a mother and carer of a disabled child that she should be protected against discrimination on the grounds of her child's disability.[275] Similarly positive in this context is the acceptance that direct discrimination includes situations in which a person mistakenly believes another has a protected characteristic, for example that she is HIV positive. Both discrimination by association and discrimination by perception are now expressly included in the EA 2010.[276]

A similar stress on dignity led the European Commission on Human Rights to accept that racism can constitute a breach of the right not to be subjected to cruel and unusual treatment. The boldest decision in this area was that in the *East African Asians* case,[277] which concerned the explicit exclusion from Britain of East African Asians who were being forced out of Uganda and Tanzania. The Commission held that discrimination based on race could, in certain circumstances, amount to degrading treatment contrary to Article 3 ECHR, which states that 'no-one shall be subjected to torture or to inhuman or degrading treatment or punishment'. In the case in hand, the Commission found that the UK legislation in question was racially motivated and destined to harm a specific racial group. However, the Commission was careful to stress that it was not faced with a general question of whether racial discrimination in immigration constituted degrading treatment as such. Instead it was specifically concerned with the Commonwealth Immigrants Act 1968 which explicitly subjected Asians in Tanzania and Uganda to particularly restrictive immigration control.[278] The classification of

---

[274] *Coleman v Attridge Law*, above n 184, AG12.
[275] Ibid.
[276] EA 2010, ss 13(1), 24(1) except in relation to marriage and civil partnership.
[277] *East African Asians v United Kingdom* (1981) 3 EHRR 76.
[278] Ibid at para 196; the Committee of Ministers held, however, that there had been no violation, largely because of measures taken by the UK to meet the Commission's objections.

immigration controls as explicitly racist and therefore constituting inhuman and degrading treatment is therefore unlikely to function as the primary source of challenge to immigration rules.

Put together, all these developments can be seen as deepening the notion of equality beyond consistency into a substantive concept, based on the fundamental values of dignity and respect for the individual. However, as was seen in Chapter One, dignity has also been used by courts in various jurisdictions as a means of blocking or obstructing equality claims. In particular, in the Canadian case of *Gosselin*, a measure giving lower benefits to welfare recipients under the age of 30 was held not to be discriminatory on grounds of age because 'the provision of different initial amounts of monetary support to each of the two groups does not indicate that one group's dignity was prized above the other's'.[279] The Supreme Court of Canada has now recognized that dignity thus construed has 'proven to be an additional burden on equality claimants, rather than the philosophical enhancement it was intended to be'.[280] Thus, as was argued in Chapter One, rather than subsuming the concept of equality in that of dignity, dignity should be regarded as one element of a multi-dimensional conception of equality.

IX POSITIVE DUTIES TO PROMOTE EQUALITY

The recognition of the limits of existing models of discrimination has led law-makers to strike out in a new direction, namely the imposition of positive duties to promote equality. These duties are analysed in detail in Chapter Six. For present purposes, it is worth highlighting the radical ways in which they can reconfigure discrimination law. Most importantly, positive duties recognize that societal discrimination extends well beyond individual acts. This has implications for both the nature of the duty and that of the duty-bearer. Instead of a tort-based model, whereby proof of fault by a perpetrator gives rise to an individual right of compensation, the proactive model aims to restructure institutions. Rather than requiring proof of individual wrongoing, it is triggered by evidence of structural discrimination. Correspondingly, the duty-bearer is identified as the body in the best position to perform this duty, regardless of whether he or she is responsible for creating the problem in the first place.

---

[279] *Gosselin v Quebec* 2002 SCC 84, para 61 (per McLachlin J).
[280] *R v Kapp* 2008 SCC 41 (Supreme Court of Canada), paras 21, 22.

The proactive nature of positive duties does more than change the structure of equality law. It also changes the way of thinking about the aims of discrimination law. If discrimination law is not only about compensating an individual victim, what are its aims? It is in this context that the four-dimensional understanding of the aims of equality in Chapter One are particularly helpful. To be targeted and effective, proactive programmes should be aimed at specified outcomes, such as redressing disadvantage, accommodating difference, increasing participation, or protecting dignity, or a combination of the above. These questions are explored in Chapter Six.

X CONCLUSION

This chapter has mapped the architecture of anti-discrimination law in the UK and EU, drawing on comparative insights where appropriate to highlight different possible models and ways of addressing weaknesses. It can be seen that while important advances have been made, both in the depth and reach of anti-discrimination laws, these have brought with them new challenges and raised new questions about established understandings and demarcations. In the following chapter, a particularly challenging issue, that of reverse discrimination, is explored in more detail.

5

Symmetry or Substance:
Reverse Discrimination

Possibly the most controversial issue in anti-discrimination law is the question of whether reverse discrimination is legitimate. Reverse discrimination, or affirmative action,[1] entails the deliberate use of gender, race, or other protected characteristic to benefit a disadvantaged group. Yet this appears to offend against basic principles of equality. Much of the century has been spent convincing judges and legislators that race and gender are irrelevant and their use in the allocation of benefits or rights is invidious. How then can it be legitimate to permit their use for purportedly remedial purposes?

The answer to this question depends on whether a formal or substantive conception of equality is used. Reverse discrimination is clearly a breach of formal equality. However, on a substantive view, deliberate preferences for a disadvantaged group could well be regarded as a means to achieve equality, rather than a breach or exception. At the same time, reverse discrimination does not automatically achieve substantive equality. Reverse discrimination may change the colour or gender composition of those in power. But the structure might remain intact. Inequalities between middle class whites and blacks might diminish. But the gap between poor blacks and wealthy blacks might increase. Colour consciousness might be necessary to redress racism. But it might also entrench racial difference. Some check is necessary in order to ensure that affirmative action genuinely furthers substantive equality before unequal treatment on otherwise protected grounds is regarded as legitimate.

This function is now widely performed by a proportionality test. As we have seen, proportionality requires scrutiny of whether the aims are

---

[1] Reverse discrimination, preference policies, and affirmative action will be used interchangeably in this chapter.

legitimate and whether the means fit the ends. Several potentially legitimate aims have been identified. These include remedying past discrimination, increasing participation, and enhancing diversity. Even more difficult is to determine the relationship between the selected aims and the means. This requires answers to a further set of inter-related questions. First, how close should the 'fit' be between the affirmative action measure and the identified aim? Is it enough that the measure is a reasonable means to achieve the end, or must it be necessary in the sense that there is no alternative means to achieve the end? Secondly, how should the class of beneficiaries be delineated? Can it include individuals who have not themselves suffered disadvantage (over-inclusiveness); or exclude others who have (under-inclusiveness); or must the class of beneficiaries precisely match the aim? Thirdly, what evidence is necessary to demonstrate that the measure is actually capable of achieving the identified aim? Fourthly, should there be a 'sunset' clause when it is believed the measure has been successful? All this needs to be balanced against the cost to those who are deliberately excluded. Finally and particularly important for our purposes is the question of who should make these decisions. What degree of deference should a court show to legislative or executive decision-making?

Part I of this chapter briefly rehearses the main contours of the debate between formal and substantive equality and how this affects the legitimacy of reverse discrimination. Part II considers how reverse discrimination is viewed in various jurisdictions. Three types of approach can be discerned. The first views reverse discrimination as a breach of equality. The second considers it as an exception to equality, to be narrowly construed. The third approaches reverse discrimination as a means to achieving substantive equality. It is in this context that the further challenges arise. These are dealt with in Part III.

I CONCEPTS OF EQUALITY AND REVERSE DISCRIMINATION

Given its deliberate use of protected characteristics to allocate benefits, it is not surprising that the legitimacy of reverse discrimination is highly problematic. Indeed, the arguments presented by opponents of reverse discrimination appear at first sight to be unassailable. If equality is the goal, how can it be possible to justify policies requiring unequal treatment on the grounds of sex or race?

This argument, however, only appears irrefutable because it is based on a particular formal conception of equality. There are three salient characteristics of formal equality which make it inevitable that reverse discrimination will constitute an illegitimate breach. First, formal equality presupposes that justice is an abstract, universal notion, and cannot vary to reflect different patterns of benefit and disadvantage in a particular society. If discrimination on grounds of gender or race is unjust, it must be unjust whether it creates extra burdens on a group already disadvantaged, or whether it redistributes those burdens to a previously privileged group. Equality must therefore always be symmetrical, applying with equal strength regardless of whether it is directed against or in favour of a disadvantaged group. As the US Supreme Court Justice Powell declared in the famous case of *Bakke*: 'The guarantee of equal protection cannot mean one thing when applied to one individual and something else when applied to an individual of another colour.'[2] There is a moral and constitutional equivalence between laws designed to subjugate a race and those that distribute benefits. As another Supreme Court Justice, Thomas J, put it in a later case, government-sponsored racial discrimination based on benign prejudice should be considered to be just as noxious as discrimination motivated by malicious prejudice.[3] Other judicial statements have made it clear that the aim is not the alleviation of disadvantage: discrimination on grounds of race is considered to be odious even if directed against a group that has never been the subject of governmental discrimination.[4]

The second premise of formal equality which makes reverse discrimination internally contradictory is its individualism. Status such as sex or race should always be disregarded in distributing benefits or allocating jobs or promotion; instead, individuals must be rewarded only on the basis of individual merit. Moreover, reverse discrimination is not only unfair but also inefficient: it simply permits the appointment of people less well qualified and therefore less able to do the job properly.[5] Correspondingly, burdens should only be allocated on the basis of individual responsibility. Individuals may only be treated as responsible for their own actions; they should not be held accountable for more general societal wrongs. This means in particular that an individual man or

---

[2] *Regents of the University of California v Bakke* 438 US 265 (1978) at 288–90.
[3] *Adarand v Pena* 515 US 200, 115 S Ct 2097 (1995) at 241, 2119 (per Thomas J).
[4] *Wygant v Jackson Board of Education* 476 US 267, 106 S Ct 1842 (1986).
[5] M Abram, 'Affirmative Action: Fair Shakers and Social Engineers' (1986) 99 Harv L Rev 1312 at 1322.

white person should not be required to compensate for historical or institutional sex or race discrimination by being excluded from a job or promotion for which he is well qualified. There can, on this view, be no 'creditor or debtor race'.[6]

Thirdly, formal equality entails equality before the law. The State should be neutral as between its citizens, favouring no one above any other.

Without doing violence to the principles of equality before the law and neutral decision-making, we simply cannot interpret our laws to support both colour-blindness for some citizens and colour-consciousness for others.[7]

The proposition that a group should be favoured on account of gender or race, even in a remedial sense, is therefore anathema. Moreover, argues Abram, any attempt to move from the individual to the group is bound to degenerate into a 'crude political struggle between groups seeking favoured status'.[8] State neutrality also entails a State which intervenes as little as possible in the 'free market'. In particular, the State should not use its contractual powers within the market to pursue public policies such as the elimination of discrimination. This necessarily outlaws the use of contract compliance or 'set-asides' of State funds for the purpose of aiding minorities or women.

Reliance on substantive rather than formal equality gives rise to a very different analysis of reverse discrimination. The substantive approach to reverse discrimination rejects an abstract view of justice and instead insists that justice is only meaningful in its interaction with society. The unfortunate reality is that it is women rather than men who have suffered cumulative disadvantage due to sex discrimination; blacks rather than whites who have suffered from racism. Once this is accepted, it becomes clear that to adopt a symmetrical approach, whereby unequal treatment of men is regarded as morally identical to discrimination against women, is to empty the equality principle of real social meaning. As Dworkin puts it: 'The difference between a general racial classification that causes further disadvantage to those who have suffered from prejudice, and a classification framed to help them, is morally significant.'[9]

---

[6] *Adarand v Pena*, above n 3, at 239, 2118 (per Scalia J).
[7] Abram, above n 5, at 1319.
[8] Ibid at 1321.
[9] R Dworkin, *A Matter of Principle* (Harvard University Press, 1985), p 314.

Similarly, the substantive approach rejects as misleading the aspirations of individualism. It is true that the merit principle has played a valuable role in advancing equality of opportunity by displacing nepotism and class bias in the allocation of jobs or benefits. However, in the context of sex or race, the uncritical use of merit as a criterion for employment or promotion could perpetuate disadvantage. This is because, despite the appearance of scientific objectivity, the choice of criteria for deciding merit may well reinforce existing societal discrimination or incorporate implicit discriminatory assumptions. Equally misleading is the reliance on a notion of individual fault, which generates an image of an 'innocent' third party who is deprived of a job or other opportunity because he is white or male. A substantive view of equality suggests that the responsibility for correcting disadvantage should not be seen to rest merely with those to whom 'fault' can be attributed. Instead, all who benefit from the existing structure of disadvantage should be expected to bear part of the cost of remedy. A community structured on racial or gender discrimination has conferred benefits on the dominant group as a whole. Each member of the community should, therefore, be required to bear part of the costs of correction, provided these costs are not disproportionate for the individual.

Finally, the substantive approach rejects the possibility of a neutral State which is separate from society with its current set of power relations. The State is no more than an emanation of the democratic process, the aim of which is to function as a conduit for or resolution of the cross-currents of social power. The modern State plays a central role in distributing benefits in society. It cannot therefore be truly neutral: if it refuses to take an active role in reducing disadvantage, it is in fact supporting the existing dominant groups in maintaining their position of superiority over groups which have suffered from discrimination and prejudice. A substantive view of equality would view the State as having a duty to act positively to correct the results of such discrimination. On all these counts, then, reverse discrimination could be entirely legitimate if a substantive view of equality is accepted.

Even then, important questions remain. The first concerns the definition of disadvantage. Does it cover both recognition and redistributive ills? Is it sufficient to be black, or a woman, or should it be necessary in addition to prove socio-economic disadvantage? A second question concerns how the demands of different disadvantaged groups should be balanced against each other. With the widening of the scope of anti-discrimination laws to include grounds such as religion or age, these issues loom larger. Thirdly, how should the burden be spread between those who benefit and those who bear the costs? These issues are examined further in Part III.

II REVERSE DISCRIMINATION AND THE LAW: CONTRASTING JURISDICTIONS

The arguments rehearsed above have been part of a lively debate in various jurisdictions about the legality of reverse discrimination. But the dominant model has differed widely between countries. Three broad approaches can be discerned. The first is to regard affirmative action as a breach of the right to equality (the 'formal' approach). The legislative framework in Britain broadly accepts this view. The second is to regard affirmative action as an exception to the prohibition against discrimination (the 'derogation' approach). As an exception, it is construed strictly but remains legitimate in defined circumstances. This has been the approach of the EU. The final approach views affirmative action not as a derogation from the right to equality, but as an aspect of equality. On this view, affirmative action is a legitimate means to fulfil the non-discrimination principle, provided it is proportional (the 'substantive' approach). This approach can be seen in Canada, South Africa, and India, as well as in an increasing number of human rights instruments, both at domestic and international level, where express permission is given for affirmative action. The dispute has been at its fiercest in the US, where the battle between formal and substantive equality has yielded different victors at different stages of its development.

(I) SYMMETRY: THE BRITISH APPROACH

Traditionally, anti-discrimination legislation in Britain has left little room for reverse discrimination. The dominant characteristic is one of symmetry. The legislation explicitly provides that the provisions are applicable equally to the treatment of men and women;[10] and to all races or ethnic groups. Similarly, the legislation protects not just homosexual and bisexual but also heterosexual individuals.[11]

This symmetry is reinforced by judicial interpretation. As we saw in the previous chapter, in the case of *James v Eastleigh Borough Council*,[12] the House of Lords held that the simple question to be considered was whether the complainant would have received the same treatment from the defendant 'but for' his or her sex. This line of reasoning is explicitly

---

[10] EA 2010, s 11.   [11] Ibid, s 12.   [12] [1990] 2 AC 751 (HL).

symmetrical, relying on a formal notion of justice which is abstracted from the social power relations within which it operates. Thus, Lord Ackner declared, 'the reason why the policy was adopted can in no way affect or alter the fact that . . . men were to be treated less favourably than women, and were to be so treated on the ground of, because of their sex'.[13] This can be contrasted with the substantive notion of justice expressed in the dissenting judgment of Lord Griffiths. On his view, it could not be discriminatory to attempt to redress the result of an unfair act of discrimination by offering free facilities to those disadvantaged by the earlier act of discrimination.[14]

Important inroads have now been made into the overall symmetry of the legislative framework. However, this is primarily by way of statutory exceptions, thus preserving the foundational commitment to formal equality. As we have seen, disability is regarded as asymmetric, so that it is not discriminatory to treat a disabled person more favourably than a non-disabled person.[15] Similarly, no account is to be taken of special treatment of a woman in connection with pregnancy and childbirth.[16]

More specific instances of permitted preferential treatment were found in the Sex Discrimination Act 1975 (SDA), which always permitted trade unions and employers or professional organizations to reserve seats on an elected executive for persons of one sex where this was necessary to secure a 'reasonable lower limit to the number of members of that sex serving on the body'.[17] In addition, both the SDA and the Race Relations Act 1976 (RRA) permitted sex or race conscious remedial action in training. If there were comparatively few or no members of one sex or racial group doing a particular type of work, it was not unlawful to reserve access to training facilities to members of that group to help equip them for that work.[18]

The Equality Act (EA) 2010 has deepened and extended these sporadic exceptions, applying them to all the protected characteristics, and extending them beyond the employment relationship. Thus section 158 of the Act applies to situations in which a person reasonably thinks that persons with a protected characteristic are at a disadvantage, or have different needs from others, or their participation in any activity is

---

[13] Ibid at 769.
[14] Ibid at 768.
[15] EA 2010, s 13(3).
[16] Ibid, s 13(6)(b).
[17] SDA, s 49.
[18] See also SDA, ss 47–8; RRA, ss 37–8; and SDA, s 47(3) (training for those who have been fully engaged in family responsibilities).

disproportionately low. In such circumstances, proportionate action may be taken to address these issues. This will, for example, allow measures to be targeted to particular groups, including training to enable them to gain employment, or health services to address their needs. Charities are also permitted to provide benefits to persons with the same protected characteristic (apart from colour) to prevent or compensate for disadvantage.[19]

The Act also expressly permits more favourable treatment in recruitment and promotion of those with a protected characteristic if their participation is disproportionately low, or they suffer disadvantage connected to that characteristic.[20] However, this provision is hedged about with limitations. It only applies to those who are equally well qualified. It cannot be part of a general preference policy. Instead, individual assessments are required. It is permissive rather than mandatory. In addition, it must be proportionate to the aim of enabling or encouraging persons who share the protected characteristic to overcome or minimize that disadvantage, or participate in that activity. Even in this limited form, however, it went sufficiently against the grain of the underlying adherence to symmetry for the newly elected Coalition Government in 2010 to have delayed its implementation indefinitely.

This ambivalence can also be seen in relation to the positive duties to promote equality discussed further in Chapter Six. The duty requires public bodies to pay due regard to the need to eliminate unlawful discrimination, promote equality of opportunity, and advance good relations. The statute provides that

Compliance with the duties in this section may involve treating some persons more favourably than others; but that is not to be taken as permitting conduct that would otherwise be prohibited by or under this Act.[21]

It is in the area of political participation that the struggle between symmetry and substance has been most evident. The Labour Party introduced all-women shortlists in a limited number of constituencies[22] in 1993, a major factor in almost trebling the number of women Labour Party MPs returned to Parliament after the 1997 election.[23] However, an employment tribunal struck down the policy as unlawful

---

[19] Provided that this is permitted by their charitable instrument: EA 2010, s 193.
[20] EA 201, s 159.
[21] Ibid, s 149(6).
[22] 50 per cent of the constituencies were either (i) marginal, (ii) new, or (iii) the sitting Labour MP was not standing at the next election.
[23] See M Eagle and J Lovenduski, *High Time or High Tide for Labour Women*, Fabian Pamphlet 585 (Fabian Society, 1998).

sex discrimination,[24] regarding the matter as conclusively decided by the 'simple' answer to the 'simple' test of whether the complainant would have received the same treatment but for his sex. 'It is obvious direct discrimination on grounds of sex.'[25] In response, a provision was introduced in 2002 permitting political parties to use women-only shortlists in order to reduce the inequality in the numbers of men and women elected as candidates of the party.[26] The 2002 provision was originally introduced with a 'sunset clause', so that it would expire at the end of 2015. The EA 2010 extends the permission for single-sex shortlists until 2030. The EA 2010 also broadens this provision to cover all protected characteristics. Under this measure, political parties may make arrangements in relation to the selection of candidates to address the under-representation of any of those with protected characteristics in relevant elected bodies. However, arrangements in relation to protected characteristics other than gender cannot include shortlists restricted to that group. In addition, with the exception of gender, such arrangements must be proportionate to the aim of redressing inequality in representation.[27]

The growth of such exceptions to the principle of formal equality may signal a change in the underlying conception of equality itself. In an important recognition of substantive equality, Moses J refused to interpret the provision permitting the provision of training to meet the special needs of a particular racial group as an exception to the anti-discrimination principle.[28]

[This provision] is not an exception to the 1976 Act. It does not derogate from it in any way. It is a manifestation of the important principle of anti-discrimination and equality measures that not only must like cases be treated alike but that unlike cases must be treated differently... [S]ervices for a racial minority from a specialist source are anti-discriminatory and further the objectives of equality and cohesion.[29]

However, at present, this remains an isolated view.

---

[24] *Jepson v The Labour Party* [1996] IRLR 116 (IT).
[25] Ibid at 117.
[26] SDA, s 42A.
[27] EA 2010, s 104.
[28] RRA, s 35.
[29] *R (on the application of Kaur, Shah) v London Borough of Ealing* [2008] EWHC 2062 (Admin) (High Court of Justice (QBD)), paras 52, 58.

(II) EQUALITY OF OPPORTUNITY: THE EU APPROACH

From early on in the development of gender discrimination law at EU level, it was accepted that it might be necessary to go beyond equality of treatment and take measures in favour of women to achieve equality in practice. However, this has been formulated as a derogation from the principle of equality, rather than as a means to achieve substantive equality. Derogations from fundamental principles are always strictly construed. The governing provision was originally found in Article 2(4) of the Equal Treatment Directive 1976.[30] This states that the principle of equal treatment 'shall be without prejudice to measures to promote equal opportunity for men and women, in particular by removing existing inequalities which affect women's opportunities'. Current provisions continue to take the form of a derogation from equality. Thus in the Treaty itself, Article 157(4) provides as follows:

With a view to ensuring full equality in practice between men and women in working life, the principle of equal treatment shall not prevent any Member States from maintaining or adopting measures providing for specific advantages in order to make it easier for the under-represented sex to pursue a vocational activity or to prevent or compensate for disadvantages in professional careers.[31]

This approach is mirrored in the Recast Equal Treatment Directive. Article 3 now states: 'Member states may maintain or adopt measures within the meaning of Article 141(4) with a view to ensuring full equality in practice between men and women in working life.'[32] Similarly, the Race Directive states as follows:

With a view to ensuring full equality in practice, the principle of equal treatment shall not prevent any Member State from maintaining or adopting specific measures to prevent or compensate for disadvantages linked to racial or ethnic origin.[33]

The Employment Directive contains an identically worded provision in relation to religion or belief, disability, age, or sexual orientation.[34]

---

[30] Directive 76/207 EEC.
[31] Treaty on European Union (2010). This was identically worded in Art 141(4) of the previous Treaty.
[32] Directive of the European Parliament and of the Council 2006/54/EC on the implementation of the principle of equal opportunities and equal treatment of men and women in matters of employment and occupation (Recast Directive), Art 3.
[33] Race Directive, Art 5.
[34] Framework Directive, Art 7(1).

The 'derogation' approach reflects an underlying tension between a recognition of the limits of formal equality, on the one hand, and a firm adherence to individual merit, on the other. Thus the European Court of Justice (ECJ) has reiterated on numerous occasions that measures may be authorized which 'although discriminatory in appearance, are in fact intended to eliminate or reduce actual instances of inequality which may exist in the reality of social life'.[35] At the same time, as Advocate General Maduro put it in his perceptive opinion in *Briheche*,

The Court attempts to reconcile positive discrimination with the general principle of equality by allowing the former only to the extent that it does not lead to discrimination that favours a certain group at the expense of particular individuals: achieving a more equal representation of men and women in the workforce does not justify derogating from the right of each individual not to be discriminated against.[36]

These apparently opposing imperatives have been reconciled by the ECJ through a conception of equality of opportunity.[37] Equality of opportunity goes beyond equal treatment in its recognition that because of previous discrimination and disadvantage, affected groups are not in a position to compete on equal terms with others. Using the graphic metaphor of a running race, it is acknowledged that individuals who suffer from discrimination begin the race from different starting points. It is part of the function of equality to equalize the starting point, even if this might necessitate special measures for the disadvantaged group. However, equality of opportunity stops short of demanding equality of results. Once the starting point has been equalized, individuals enjoy equality of opportunity, and fairness demands that they be treated on the basis of their individual merit. As Advocate General Maduro explains:

Equality of opportunities prevails over equality of results. The Court assumes that positive discriminatory measures can be accepted only if they are designed, in effect, to prevent discrimination in each individual case by forcing the employer to place women in a similar position to men.[38]

---

[35] Case C-265/95 *Commission v France* [1997] ECR I-6959; Case C-450/93 *Kalanke v Freie Hansestadt Bremen* [1995] IRLR 660 (ECJ); Case C-409/95 *Marschall v Land Nordrhein-Westfalen* [1998] IRLR 39 (ECJ), para 26; P Alston, 'Strengths and Weaknesses of the ESC's Supervisory System' in G de Búrca and B de Witte (eds), *Social Rights in Europe* (Oxford University Press, 2005), para 22.

[36] Case C-319/03 *Briheche v Ministre de L'Interieur* [2005] 1 CMLR 4, AG49.

[37] *Kalanke v Freie Hansestadt Bremen*, above n 35, para 23.

[38] *Briheche v Ministre de L'Interieur*, above n 36, AG42.

By embracing the principle of equality of opportunity, the Court has been able to recognize important limitations on women's ability to compete equally in the labour market. Thus in *Marschall*,[39] the Court recognized that an apparently objective merit-based system could incorporate prejudicial assumptions:

Even where male and female candidates are equally qualified, male candidates tend to be promoted in preference to female candidates particularly because of prejudices and stereotypes concerning the role and capacities of women in working life and the fear, for example, that women will interrupt their careers more frequently, that owing to household and family duties they will be less flexible in their working hours, or that they will be absent from work more frequently because of pregnancy, childbirth and breast-feeding.[40]

Thus a measure giving preference to women candidates 'may counteract the prejudicial effects on female candidates of the attitudes and behaviour described above and thus reduce actual instances of inequality which may exist in the real world'.[41]

At the same time, the Court's endorsement of equality of opportunity is tempered by its adherence to a principle of individual merit. This manifests in two ways. First, preference policies should not be automatic and unconditional. Meritorious individuals from outside the beneficiary class should have the possibility of individual assessment.

National rules which guarantee women absolute and unconditional priority for appointment or promotion go beyond promoting equal opportunities and overstep the limits of the exception in Article 2(4) of the Directive.[42]

Thus a measure giving priority to women in under-represented sectors of the public service would only be compatible with Community law if (i) it does not automatically and unconditionally give priority to women when women and men are equally qualified; and (ii) the candidatures are the subject of an objective assessment which takes into account the specific personal situations of all candidates.[43]

For example, in *Kalanke*[44] a measure giving preference to equally qualified women was struck down. In *Marschall*,[45] by contrast, a similar

---

[39] *Marschall v Land Nordrhein-Westfalen*, above n 35.
[40] Ibid at para 29.
[41] Ibid at para 31.
[42] *Kalanke v Freie Hansestadt Bremen Kalanke*, above n 35, para 22.
[43] Case C-158/97 *Badeck* [2000] IRLR 432 (ECJ) at para 23.
[44] *Kalanke v Freie Hansestadt Bremen*, above n 35.
[45] *Marschall v Land Nordrhein-Westfalen*, above n 35.

measure was softened by a proviso allowing exceptions if 'reasons specific to another candidate predominate'. For this reason, the Court upheld the plan. The result was a highly circumscribed endorsement of such measures. A rule which gave priority to the promotion of female candidates was permitted where there were fewer women than men in the relevant post and both female and male candidates for the post were equally qualified, as long as the priority accorded to female candidates could in principle be overridden where an objectively assessed individual criterion tilted the balance in favour of the male candidate.[46]

It was this principle which the Norwegian government was found to have breached when, in an effort to remedy the under-representation of women in high-level academic positions, it provided funding for a small number of post-doctoral research grants and academic posts on the basis that they should be specifically earmarked for women. The EFTA Court, which follows the jurisprudence of the ECJ, held that this measure was contrary to the principle of equal treatment and could not be regarded as falling within the exception defined in Article 2(4).[47] This was because it automatically excluded male applicants from the earmarked posts. Because the Directive was based on the 'recognition of the right to equal treatment as a fundamental right of the individual', the EFTA Court explained, 'there must, as a matter of principle, be a possibility that the best qualified candidate obtains the post'.[48]

Secondly, the emphasis on individual merit has meant that preference measures can only be legitimate in the narrowly circumscribed situation in which all the candidates are equally qualified. That is, the preference policy can only operate as a 'tie-break'. It was for this reason that the ECJ struck down the measure in *Abrahamsson*.[49] In this case, the Swedish government was faced with a severe under-representation of women in professorial posts. It therefore promulgated a regulation requiring preference to be granted to a candidate of the under-represented sex provided she possessed sufficient qualifications, even if she were less qualified than a candidate from the opposite sex, unless the difference between the candidates' qualifications was so great as to give rise to a breach of the requirement of objectivity in the making of appointments. In the case in question, a woman had been appointed who, although sufficiently

---

[46] Ibid at para 35.
[47] Case E-1/02 *EFTA Surveillance Authority v Norway* [2003] 1 CMLR 23 (EFTA Court).
[48] Ibid, para 45.
[49] Case C-407/98 *Abrahamsson v Fogelqvist* [2000] IRLR 732 (ECJ).

qualified, had been ranked below a male candidate for the job. Again, the ECJ held that individual merit should trump the demands of substantive equality. The measure was in breach of Article 2(4) because selection was 'ultimately based on the mere fact of belonging to the under-represented sex, and this is so even if the merits of the candidates so selected are inferior to those of a candidate of the opposite sex'. Nor were candidates subjected to an objective assessment which took account of their specific personal situations. Similarly, when dealing with Article 141(4) (now 157(4)), the ECJ held that the measure was 'on any view... dispropor-tionate to the aim pursued'.[50]

More recent case law has stressed that it is through the principle of proportionality that the legitimacy of positive measures and their excep-tionality should be determined. This was initially most clearly articu-lated by Advocate General Saggio in *Badeck*,[51] whose opinion reiterates the dual emphasis on substantive equality and the primacy of the individual. The reconciliation of the two, he argues, lies in the develop-ment of a proportionality criterion. Equal treatment, or formal equality, comes into conflict with substantive equality only if the remedial meas-ure, in this case positive action in favour of women, is disproportionate, either in that it demands excessive sacrifices from those who do not belong to the group, or when the social reality does not justify it. Positive action could therefore be lawful if it is proportionate in this sense. Nevertheless, individual merit, provided it is purified of discriminatory assumptions, remains the governing principle. It is only permissible to institute automatic preferences for women to redress under-representation if there is an objective examination of the professional and personal profile of each candidate and there is no bar on the selection of a man if he is more suitable for the job.

Although the more recent formulations in Article 157(4) and the new Directives might give Member States somewhat wider discretion in formulating positive measures than Article 2(4),[52] these foundational values remain. This was summed up well by Advocate General Maduro in *Briheche*.[53] He rejected an interpretation of Article 157(4) which subordinated individuals' rights not to be discriminated against to the aim of achieving equality between groups. 'Such a reading is hardly compatible with the priority which the Court has given to equality of

---

[50] Ibid, para 55.
[51] *Badeck*, above n 43.
[52] Alston, above n 35, para AG48.
[53] *Briheche v Ministre de L'Interieur*, above n 36.

opportunities and to its traditional understanding of the general principle of equal treatment.' Instead, he favoured an interpretation according to which

the purpose of compensatory measures of this type becomes that of re-establishing
equality of opportunities by removing the effects of discrimination and promoting
long-term maximisation of equality of opportunities... To base the acceptance of
compensatory forms of positive discrimination on equality of opportunities and
not on equality of results would still make equality among individuals prevail over
equality among groups.[54]

Similarly, as we have seen, in *Abrahamsson*,[55] when dealing with Article
157(4), the ECJ held that the measure in question, which gave preference to women even if they were less well qualified than male competitors, was 'on any view... disproportionate to the aim pursued'.[56] The
Court in *Briheche* was similarly of the view that Article 157(4) did not
permit a measure which was disproportionate because it gave automatic
and unconditional preference to women.[57]

Thus in its more recent case law, the Court has repeated the following
formula:

In determining the scope of any derogation from an individual right such as the
equal treatment of men and women laid down by the Directive, due regard must
be had to the principle of proportionality, which requires that derogations must
remain within the limits of what is appropriate and necessary in order to achieve
the aim in view and that the principle of equal treatment be reconciled as far as
possible with the requirements of the aim thus pursued.[58]

However, even proportionality needs to be applied with care so as to
ensure that positive measures genuinely further substantive equality,
rather than reinforcing stereotypes. Protective legislation for women is
an example of a measure which could be misinterpreted as a measure
remedying disadvantage for women when in fact it reinforces stereotypes. This danger is particularly evident in relation to pregnancy and
parenting. While specific rights for women in relation to pregnancy and
childbirth should not be regarded as a breach of the principle of equality,
this is not the case for parenting rights. If the distribution of labour in

---

[54] Ibid, AG49–51.
[55] *Abrahamsson and Anderson v Fogelqvist*, above n 49.
[56] Ibid at para 55.
[57] *Briheche v Ministre de L'Interieur*, above n 36, para 30.
[58] Ibid, para 24; Case C-476/99 *Lommers v Minister Van Landbouw, Natuurbeheer En Visserij* [2004] 2 CMLR 49 (ECJ) at para 39.

the home is to be altered, parenting rights available to women should also be available to men.

The ECJ, however, has rejected a claim that it was discriminatory on grounds of sex to provide childcare facilities for working mothers and not for working fathers. Such a measure, it held, 'although discriminatory in appearance, [is] in fact intended to eliminate or reduce actual instances of inequality which may exist in the reality of social life'.[59] The case concerned provision by the Dutch Ministry of Agriculture for a workplace nursery catering for children of female but not male employees. According to Dutch law, the programme was legitimate because it was a 'distinction intended to place women in a privileged position in order to eliminate or reduce *de facto* inequalities' and was reasonable in relation to that aim.[60] The ECJ endorsed this approach. The Court pointed out that there was a significant under-representation of women in the Ministry of Agriculture and particularly in the higher grades, and that there was similarly a proven insufficiency of suitable and affordable nursery facilities, which it regarded as likely to induce women employees to give up their jobs. The Court was not oblivious to the danger that 'a measure such as that at issue . . . , whose purported aim is to abolish a *de facto* inequality, might nevertheless also help to perpetuate a traditional division of roles between men and women'.[61] However, it was not prepared to hold that the measure was disproportionate for failing to include working fathers. In line with *Marschall*, the Court took into account the fact that the employer could grant requests from male officials in cases of emergency, to be determined by the employer and the Ministry assured the Court that male officials who bring up their children by themselves should, on that basis, have access to the nursery scheme.

Nevertheless, it is submitted that the Court did not exercise sufficient scrutiny in this case. It is not sufficient to permit measures which exclude men from rights related to parenting on the ground that exceptions can be created for fathers who are the primary carers. The scheme should be available to all fathers on the same terms as mothers. Genuinely transformative change can only occur when both parents are equally responsible for childcare.[62] Special measures for women, however well intentioned,

---

[59] *Lommers v Minister Van Landbouw, Natuurbeheer En Visserij*, above n 58, para 32; see Equal Treatment Directive, Art 2(4).

[60] Netherlands Law on Equal Treatment of Men and Women, art 5.

[61] *Lommers v Minister Van Landbouw, Natuurbeheer En Visserij*, above n 58, para 41.

[62] See further S Fredman, *Women and the Law* (Oxford University Press, 1997).

run the risk of reinforcing their primary role as childcarers, and therefore perpetuating their disadvantage.

(III) SYMMETRY V SUBSTANCE: THE US SUPREME COURT

Nowhere has the dichotomy between the formal and substantive approaches been more vividly demonstrated than in the US Supreme Court. Indeed the Court has been the arena of fierce struggle between judicial proponents of a formal, symmetrical view of equality and those who advocate a more substantive position. Earlier case law witnessed the triumph of a vigorous substantive approach. This entailed an emphatic movement away from the core elements of formal equality: namely adherence to a view of justice abstracted from its social context, individualism, and the principle of a neutral State. Thus, far from an abstract view of justice, a strong stream of Supreme Court jurisprudence recognized that although 'the enduring hope is that race should not matter; the reality is that too often it does'. Mandated by Title VII of the Civil Rights Act 1964, courts began to order affirmative action as a remedy in cases of proven past discrimination.[63] Having signalled a clear departure from an abstract, formal view of justice, the Court soon began to move beyond individualism, with its emphasis on individual merit and individual fault. As a start, it accepted that court-ordered reverse discrimination need not be restricted to the victim. Non-victims may also be beneficiaries provided they are members of a group previously suffering from invidious discrimination.[64] In addition, the emphasis on individual fault was replaced by a consideration of who would be in the best position to bring about change. This facilitated the development beyond affirmative action as a remedy for proven discrimination, to the acceptance of voluntarily instituted affirmative action programmes. Instead of proof of fault, the court only required sufficient evidence of imbalances and segregation for which the employer appeared responsible.[65]

With the departure from formal justice and individualism, came a rejection of the principle that the State should remain neutral. Instead, the Court upheld both the right and the responsibility of the State to use its public and market powers in remedying discrimination. Thus *Fullilove v Klutznick*[66] concerned a policy according to which 10 per

---

[63] *Franks v Bowman Transportation Co* 424 US 747, 96 S Ct 1251 (1975).

[64] *United States v Paradise* 480 US 149, 107 S Ct 1053 (1988).

[65] *United Steelworkers v Weber* 443 US 193, 99 S Ct 2721 (1979); *Johnson v Santa Clara* 480 US 616, 107 S Ct 1442 (1987).

[66] 448 US 448, 100 S Ct 2758 (1980).

cent of federal funds granted for the provision of public works were set aside to procure services from minority-owned businesses, even if the latter were not the lowest bidder. It was argued that this was in breach of the Fourteenth Amendment right to equality. The Court rejected the challenge. Chief Justice Burger stated specifically that in a remedial context, it was not necessary for Congress to act in a wholly colour-blind way. Indeed, substantive reverse discrimination was a necessary means to achieve equal economic opportunities.

However, recent cases have been marked by the ascendancy of a far more formal approach. This is reflected in the controversies within the case law on two main issues: the 'innocent' third party who is discriminated against on grounds of race in the process of preferring minorities; and the standard of scrutiny. So far as the 'innocent third party' is concerned, the Court has attempted to reach a balance whereby individuals who are not members of the target group are not expected to bear too great a burden in redressing the disadvantage of the preferred group. Since no one has an absolute right to a job, promotion, or training place, the person refused a position on grounds of sex or race is not unduly burdened. However, loss of an existing job (for example in a redundancy situation) has been held to be too serious a prospect to permit individual interests to be subordinated. The result has been that, except in the case of identified victims of discrimination, the vested interests of 'dispreferred' workers to retain seniority rights and therefore remain in work have generally trumped the goals of achieving and maintaining a balanced workforce. The effects of this compromise are evident in *Wygant v Jackson Board of Education*,[67] in which a collective agreement was struck down as contrary to the Fourteenth Amendment because it gave preferential protection against layoffs to minority employees. The result was, however, largely to undermine the effects of positive action programmes incorporating under-represented workers: such workers were the 'last in' and therefore inevitably the 'first out'.

The second controversial issue in US case law concerns the standard of scrutiny which should be applied in affirmative action cases. As we have seen, the Supreme Court has a well-developed jurisprudence requiring 'strict scrutiny' of any classifications which burden blacks: such a classification must serve a compelling governmental interest and be narrowly tailored to achieve that aim.[68] In practice, the insistence on strict scrutiny has outlawed most racist policies or practices discriminating against

---

[67] 476 US 267, 106 S Ct 1842 (1986).
[68] *Korematsu v United States* 323 US 214, 65 S Ct 193 (1944).

blacks. This raises the question: does an equally strict standard of review apply to racial classifications which benefit blacks at the expense of whites? US case law is criss-crossed with deeply conflicting judicial statements on this point. In *Bakke* Powell J, consistent with his symmetrical stance, was unequivocal in his rejection of the argument that strict scrutiny applies only to classifications that disadvantage discrete and insular minorities. Instead, he argued, all kinds of race-conscious criteria should be subject to the 'most exacting of judicial examination'.[69] By contrast four judges (Brennan, White, Marshall, and Blackmunn JJ), taking a substantive asymmetric view, held that a less stringent standard of review should apply to racial classifications designed to further remedial purposes than to pernicious classifications. On this view, it was sufficient for the policy to be 'substantially related' to the achievement of an important government objective, a standard known as intermediate review.[70]

The issue remained unresolved until in two crucial cases in the last decades of the twentieth century, *City of Richmond v JA Croson*[71] and *Adarand v Pena*,[72] the exacting standard of strict scrutiny won the day. Thus in *Adarand v Pena*, the Court decided by a majority of 5:4 that even in cases of 'benign' racial classification, or affirmative action, the standard of strict scrutiny should apply. Nevertheless, a closer examination of the judgments in *Adarand* reveals that the dispute between the asymmetric and the symmetric approaches continues despite the triumph of strict scrutiny. While O'Connor J agreed with Thomas and Scalia JJ on the standard of strict scrutiny, in fact their interpretation of that standard differed markedly. Thomas and Scalia JJ upheld the strict standard from a strongly symmetrical and individualistic camp. O'Connor J, giving judgment for the court, articulated a sensitive synthesis of the difficult opposing views. She was at pains to dispute the notion that strict scrutiny is strict in theory but fatal in fact.[73] Indeed, she held, the federal government might well have a compelling interest to act on the basis of race to overcome the 'persistence of both the practice and lingering effects of racial discrimination against minority groups'.[74] In this respect, her approach incorporates important elements of the clearly substantive

---

[69] *Bakke*, above n 2.
[70] *Fullilove v Klutznick*, above n 66 (per Marshall J).
[71] 488 US 469, 109 S Ct 706 (1989).
[72] *Adarand*, above n 3.
[73] Ibid at 2117.
[74] Rehnquist, Kennedy, and Thomas JJ all agreed.

view expressed in dissent by Stevens J,[75] who rejected the strict scrutiny standard by reasserting the fundamental difference between a policy designed to perpetuate a caste system and one seeking to eliminate racial discrimination.

Post-*Adarand* cases have concerned two main issues: voting rights and education. An important part of the strategy of redressing electoral disadvantage among Afro-Americans has included the redrawing of electoral districts to give black voters a better opportunity to influence the outcome of elections.[76] The deliberate creation of districts with black majorities has caused deep controversy within the US, particularly in recent years.[77] Not surprisingly, it has led to a spate of litigation[78] in which the Supreme Court has been required to decide whether such gerrymandering is necessary to ensure that blacks have equal opportunity to elect representatives of their choice; or whether it reinforces harmful racial stereotypes and impedes progress towards a multi-racial society. The divergence between those members of the Supreme Court who take a substantive approach and those who take a symmetrical approach emerges more clearly than ever. Thus in the 1996 case of *Shaw v Hunt*,[79] the majority struck down a congressionally mandated redistricting plan on the ground that it was not narrowly tailored to serve a compelling State interest. Rehnquist J for the Court declared emphatically that all laws classifying on racial grounds are constitutionally suspect. This is true even if the reason is benign or the purpose remedial. This fiercely symmetrical approach was countered for the minority by Stevens J, who declared that the sorry state of race relations in North Carolina was sufficient reason to attempt to facilitate greater participation of blacks in the electoral process. The crucial casting vote remained that of O'Connor J, who attempted, as she did in *Adarand*, to use the strict scrutiny test in a way which was sensitive to the range of conflicting interests. Most importantly she has reaffirmed her position that strict scrutiny should not be equated with total prohibition of affirmative action. Thus she declared in *Bush v Vera* that the State

---

[75] Joined by Souter, Ginsburg, and Breyer JJ.

[76] Voting Rights Act 1965, amended in 1982 to include a 'results-based' test to ascertain whether the right had been violated.

[77] See eg A Thernstrom, 'Voting Rights: Another Affirmative Action Mess' (1996) 43 UCLA L Rev 2031.

[78] *Shaw v Reno* 509 US 630, 113 S Ct 2816 (1993); *Miller v Johnson* 515 US 900, 115 S Ct 2475 (1995); *United States v Hays* 5 US 737, 115 S Ct 2431 (1995); *Bush v Vera* 517 US 952, 116 S Ct 1941 (1996).

[79] *Shaw v Hunt* 517 US 899, 116 S Ct 1894 (1996).

could indeed have a compelling interest in pursuing equality of opportunity of voters to elect representatives of their choice; and that it was
possible to find means which were 'narrowly tailored to those ends' by
producing electoral districts which aim to produce black majorities, but
which do not deviate too much from established districting principles.[80]
By contrast, the strictly symmetrical judges (although concurring with
O'Connor J) make it extremely difficult if not impossible to justify
deliberate use of race in drawing districts.[81] At the same time, a vocal
minority[82] continues to advocate a more substantive approach.

The current position is that strict scrutiny applies whenever race is
the predominant factor motivating a districting decision, in that other
race-neutral districting principles are subordinated to racial considerations. This means that the State must justify its districting decision by
establishing that it was narrowly tailored to serve a compelling State
interest. Importantly, however, compliance with the Voting Rights Act is
itself a legitimate reason. Under § 1973(b) of the Voting Rights Act, a
State is in breach

if, based on the totality of circumstances, it is shown that the political processes
leading to nomination or election in the State or political subdivision are not
equally open to participation by members of [a racial group] in that its members
have less opportunity than other members of the electorate to participate in the
political process and to elect representatives of their choice.[83]

The ongoing tension between substantive and symmetrical approaches
to equality has been even more pronounced in the education cases. In
Grutter, the legitimacy of affirmative action measures in favour of Afro-
Americans in higher education was again before the Court. In this case,
the University of Michigan's affirmative action strategy was challenged
on the grounds that its preference for Afro-Americans breached the
Fourteenth Amendment equality guarantee. The Court upheld the plan.
Signalling the narrow triumph of O'Connor J's approach, the Court
stated:

Although all governmental uses of race are subject to strict scrutiny, not all are
invalidated by it . . . . Not every decision influenced by race is equally objection-
able, and strict scrutiny is designed to provide a framework for carefully

---

[80] *Bush v Vera*, above n 78, at 1969–70.
[81] Ibid at 1971 (per Kennedy J), at 1972–3 (per Thomas and Scalia JJ).
[82] Stevens, Ginsburg, and Breyer JJ.
[83] 42 USC § 1973(b); see *League of United Latin American Citizens v Perry* 548 US 399
(2006).

examining the importance and the sincerity of the reasons advanced by the governmental decision-maker for the use of race in that particular context.[84]

In applying strict scrutiny, the legitimacy of such programmes therefore depends on two crucial questions. First, what interests are recognized as compelling under the strict scrutiny test? Secondly, how does the court determine whether the programme is narrowly tailored? In answering the first question, two acceptable interests have been identified in Supreme Court case law. The first is well established: the interest in remedying the effects of past intentional discrimination. The second is more complex: the interest in diversity. The idea that diversity could be a compelling interest first surfaced in the judgment of Powell J in the *Bakke* case. It was this interest that the Court emphasized in *Grutter*, which upheld the University of Michigan's race-conscious policy on the grounds that it furthered the legitimate aim of diversity in higher education. These aims are evaluated later in this chapter. So far as the second question is concerned, *Grutter* held that for a race-conscious programme to be 'narrowly tailored' it must be flexible and allow individual evaluation.[85] This approach has striking similarities to that of the ECJ.

However, recent case law indicates that the dispute between formal and substantive approaches is far from over. The most recent dispute concerns school districting measures aimed at avoiding re-segregation and countering the effects of residential segregation. In *Parents Involved in Community Schools v Seattle*,[86] a challenge was mounted against a school district student assignment plan that relied on racial classification to allocate slots in oversubscribed high schools with these aims in mind. The Court struck down the plan by a majority of 5:4. The swing judgment, by Kennedy J, concurred in the result but did not agree with everything in the plurality decision. Thus the case is authority only for the principles in respect of which a majority was achieved, through the agreement by Kennedy J with either the plurality approach or that of the dissent.

The first question which attracted differing approaches concerned what constituted a 'compelling interest' for the purposes of strict scrutiny. Most importantly, Kennedy J disagreed with the plurality finding that diversity could not constitute a compelling State interest outside

---

[84] *Grutter v Bollinger* 539 US 306 (2003) (US Supreme Court) at 327.
[85] This point is elaborated below in Part III(II) pp 269 ff.
[86] *Parents Involved in Community Schools v Seattle School Dist No 1* 551 US 701, 127 S Ct 2738 (2007).

higher education. Instead, he agreed with the dissent that 'diversity, depending on its meaning and definition, is a compelling educational goal a school district may pursue'.[87] Thus the interest in diversity, begun in *Bakke* and continued in *Grutter*, remains a compelling State interest even outside higher education, extending at least to school districts.

In addition, all the judges in *Community Schools* agreed that the need to remedy intentional past discrimination constituted a second compelling reason. However, Kennedy J agreed with the plurality that this did not extend to de facto discrimination.

Our cases recognized a fundamental difference between those school districts that had engaged in de jure segregation and those whose segregation was the result of other factors. School districts that had engaged in de jure segregation had an affirmative constitutional duty to desegregate; those that were de facto segregated did not.[88]

In this respect he echoed the view in the earlier case of *Wygant*:

This Court never has held that societal discrimination alone is sufficient to justify a racial classification. Rather, the Court has insisted upon some showing of prior discrimination by the governmental unit involved before allowing limited use of racial classifications in order to remedy such discrimination.[89]

Nor was the State permitted to voluntarily institute such measures. When de facto discrimination is at issue, the State must 'seek alternatives to the classification and differential treatment of individuals by race'.[90]

The second question which attracted differing approaches concerned whether the means used (the affirmative action programme in question) were 'narrowly tailored'. Kennedy J took the view that in the case at bar, the schools could have achieved their stated ends through different means, and therefore the programme was not narrowly tailored for the purposes of strict scrutiny. At the same time, he rejected the plurality view that race should never feature in a government decision and was particularly opposed to the statement by Thomas J to the effect that the US Constitution is colour-blind. In the view of Kennedy J, parts of the plurality opinion

---

[87] Ibid, 551 US 701 at 784.
[88] Ibid at 794.
[89] *Wygant v Jackson Bd of Ed* 476 US 267 at 274.
[90] *Community Schools*, above n 86, 551 US 701 at 796.

imply an all-too-unyielding insistence that race cannot be a factor in instances when, in my view, it may be taken into account. The plurality opinion is too dismissive of the legitimate interest government has in ensuring all people have equal opportunity regardless of their race. The plurality's postulate that '[t]he way to stop discrimination on the basis of race is to stop discriminating on the basis of race,' is not sufficient to decide these cases.[91]

He therefore held that it is permissible for school administrators to consider the racial make-up of schools and to adopt general policies to encourage a diverse student body. In particular, he held, if school authorities were concerned that the student-body compositions of certain schools interfere with the objective of offering an equal educational opportunity to all their students, they were free to devise race-conscious measures to address the problem in a general way, provided they did not treat each student on the basis of a systematic individual typing by race. Acceptable race-conscious mechanisms could include strategic site selection of new schools; drawing attendance zones with general recognition of the demographics of neighbourhoods; allocating resources for special programmes; recruiting students and faculty in a targeted fashion; and tracking enrolments, performance, and other statistics by race. In fact, he concluded, because these mechanisms are 'race conscious but do not lead to different treatment based on a classification that tells each student he or she is to be defined by race, it is unlikely any of them would demand strict scrutiny to be found permissible'.[92] In his view, strict scrutiny would, however, be appropriate where each student was assigned a personal designation 'according to a crude system of individual racial classifications'. Individual racial classifications employed in this manner may be considered legitimate only if they were a last resort to achieve a compelling interest.[93]

Thus it is clear that even in the US there remains a clear role for race-conscious programmes. Kennedy J's judgment strongly suggests that where such programmes do not involve individual racial classifications, there may be no need for a strict scrutiny analysis. But even if they do, it is possible for an affirmative action programme to be upheld if it is narrowly tailored to achieve a legitimate State interest. Remedial programmes to correct previous *de jure* discrimination will fulfil this standard if narrowly tailored (in the sense described above), as will programmes to promote diversity, whether in higher education, in schools, or potentially elsewhere. For a programme to be

---

[91] Ibid at 788.   [92] Ibid at 789.   [93] Ibid at 789.

narrowly tailored, it is not necessary for a body to have exhausted every conceivable race-neutral possibility.

As we saw in Chapter Three, gender is not considered a suspect class that is subject to strict scrutiny. Thus affirmative action programmes in favour of women need not reach the standard of strict scrutiny required in race cases. In *US v Virginia*,[94] the Court reiterated that

> sex classifications may be used to compensate women for particular economic disabilities they have suffered, to promote equal employment opportunity, to advance the full development of talent and capacities of nation's people; but such classifications may not be used to create or perpetuate legal, social, and economic inferiority of women.

(IV) SUBSTANTIVE EQUALITY: NEW INSIGHTS AND NEW CHALLENGES

In contrast with the UK, EU, and US, a substantive approach to affirmative action is found in a variety of jurisdictions, including South Africa, Canada, and India. According to section 9(2) of the South African Constitution: 'To promote the achievement of equality, legislative and other measures designed to protect or advance persons, or categories of persons, disadvantaged by unfair discrimination may be taken.' The meaning of this provision was elaborated in *Van Heerden*.[95] The case was concerned with a measure which enhanced the pension contributions of post-apartheid members of Parliament but not apartheid members. Since black South Africans were prohibited from participating in Parliament during apartheid, the class of individuals excluded from the measure was almost entirely white. White members, however, had had the opportunity of accruing their pensions over many years, and therefore were significantly better off in relation to pension entitlement than black MPs. The aim of the measure was, therefore, to redress this disadvantage by enhancing the pension benefits of all post-apartheid MPs. A white Afrikaner member brought a claim of race discrimination.

The High Court took an emphatically formal view of equality, regarding the relatively advantaged position of the affected white members as irrelevant. It therefore struck down the programme as unfair discrimination. The Constitutional Court reversed the decision. As Moseneke J

---

[94] *US v Virginia* 518 US 515 (1996).
[95] *Minister of Finance v Van Heerden* 2004 (6) SA 121 (CC), 2004 (11) BCLR 1125 (South African Constitutional Court).

stressed, instead of being an exception to equality, restitutionary measures are an essential part of it.

What is clear is that our Constitution and in particular section 9 thereof, read as a whole, embraces for good reason a substantive conception of equality inclusive of measures to redress existing inequality... Such measures are not in themselves a deviation from, or invasive of, the right to equality guaranteed by the Constitution. They are not 'reverse discrimination' or 'positive discrimination' as argued by the claimant in this case. They are integral to the reach of our equality protection. In other words, the provisions of section 9(1) and section 9(2) are complementary; both contribute to the constitutional goal of achieving equality to ensure 'full and equal enjoyment of all rights.'[96]

Similarly, the Canadian Charter makes it clear that measures the object of which is to ameliorate the conditions of disadvantaged individuals or groups will not be a breach of the equality guarantee in the Charter. Thus section 15(2) states:

Subsection (1) does not preclude any law, program or activity that has as its object the amelioration of conditions of disadvantaged individuals or groups including those that are disadvantaged because of race, national or ethnic origin, colour, religion, sex, age or mental or physical disability.[97]

While there was some suggestion in earlier cases that section 15(2) should be read as an exception to the equality guarantee, the Supreme Court of Canada in its 2008 decision in *Kapp*,[98] emphatically held that

Sections 15(1) and 15(2) work together to promote the vision of substantive equality that underlies s. 15 as a whole. Section 15(1) is aimed at preventing discriminatory distinctions that impact adversely on members of groups identified by the grounds enumerated in s. 15 and analogous grounds. This is one way of combating discrimination. However, governments may also wish to combat discrimination by developing programs aimed at helping disadvantaged groups improve their situation. Through s. 15(2), the Charter preserves the right of governments to implement such programs, without fear of challenge under s. 15(1). This is made apparent by the existence of s. 15(2). Thus s. 15(1) and s. 15(2) work together to confirm s. 15's purpose of furthering substantive equality.[99]

Moreover, 'Section 15(2) supports a full expression of equality, rather than derogating from it.'[100]

---

[96] Ibid, para 30.
[97] Canadian Charter of Rights, s 15(2).
[98] *R v Kapp* 2008 SCC 41.
[99] Ibid, para 16.
[100] Ibid, para 37.

At international level, affirmative action is again endorsed. Thus the Convention on the Elimination of Discrimination Against Women (CEDAW) states that adoption by States parties of temporary special measures aimed at accelerating de facto equality between men and women 'shall not be considered discrimination'. Article 2(2) of the International Convention on the Elimination of Race Discrimination (CERD) similarly declares:

States Parties shall, when the circumstances so warrant, take, in the social, economic, cultural and other fields, special and concrete measures to ensure the adequate development and protection of certain racial groups or individuals belonging to them, for the purpose of guaranteeing them the full and equal enjoyment of human rights and fundamental freedoms.[101]

The equality guarantee in the European Convention on Human Rights (ECHR), found in Article 14, does not contain a specific reference to affirmative action. It simply requires that Convention rights 'shall be secured without discrimination' on any of the prohibited grounds. However, the European Court of Human Rights (ECtHR) has interpreted 'discrimination' in a way which has made it clear that the concept of discrimination is not necessarily a symmetric one that simply outlaws all distinctions made on the prohibited ground. Instead, in the seminal case of *Belgian Linguistics*, it held that not all distinctions constitute discrimination.

The competent national authorities are frequently confronted with situations and problems which, on account of differences inherent therein, call for different legal solutions; moreover, certain legal inequalities tend only to correct factual inequalities.[102]

In its more recent case law, the ECtHR has consolidated its view that Article 14 is not breached when a State treats groups differently in order to correct factual inequalities. Indeed, in some circumstances, failure to do so might be a breach of Article 14.[103] The controlling factor remains the proportionality test.

---

[101] CERD, Art 2(2).
[102] *Belgian Linguistic Case (No 2)* (1968) 1 EHRR 252 (ECtHR), para 10.
[103] *Stec v United Kingdom* (2006) 43 EHRR 47 (ECtHR), para 51; *DH v Czech Republic*, Application no 57325/00 (2008) 47 EHRR 3 (ECtHR, Grand Chamber), para 175.

III AIMS AND EFFECTIVENESS

The discussion above has demonstrated that the principled objections to affirmative action can be plausibly repudiated. Indeed, there is a growing acceptance that affirmative action is not a breach of or even an exception to equality. Instead, it is a means to achieve equality. But there remain important challenges for affirmative action measures. The line between invidious discrimination and appropriate steps to achieve equality may not always be clear. This part considers the two main questions which need to be answered in determining which side of the line a measure falls. First, what aims are legitimate? And, secondly, how close should the fit be between the measure and the identified aims? The aims articulated by courts in various jurisdictions closely resemble the dimensions of equality set out in Chapter One. These can be grouped under three main headings, namely: (i) the removal of discriminatory barriers or redressing past disadvantage; (ii) participation, or the representation of the interests of the previously excluded group; and (iii) the fostering of diversity and the creation of role models. The second question, the means–end fit, on closer inspection, requires answers to a further set of issues. One such question is how we delineate the beneficiary class. Should the criterion be solely based on membership of a group which has suffered prejudice, or should the criterion include socio-economic disadvantage? Should those who have succeeded in socio-economic terms, despite their colour, gender, or other status, be excluded? This in turn requires a deeper understanding of the relationship between status and socio-economic disadvantage. A different question is whether a programme singling out one group for special protection may perpetuate stereotypes and freeze individuals into the very status identity which substantive equality aims to eliminate. At what point should it be accepted that the time has come to move beyond classifying individuals according to their status? Behind these issues is a further challenge, namely the extent to which affirmative action can be genuinely transformative. Can it bring about structural change, rather than simply changing the colour or gender composition of classes within the existing structure? These questions are considered in more detail below.

(I) AIMS OF AFFIRMATIVE ACTION

(a) Removal of barriers and redressing past disadvantage

The most familiar function of affirmative action is to remedy past discrimination. The major question before the courts has been whether affirmative action can only be used as a remedy for intentional discrimination on the part of the respondent, or whether it can extend to de facto, unintentional discrimination. This question is answered in different ways in different jurisdictions. As we have seen, the use of reverse discrimination as a remedy for past intentional discrimination is well established in the US. The US Supreme Court has, however, refused to go beyond intentional discrimination. In *Bakke*, Powell J rejected an interest in 'reducing the historic deficit of traditionally disfavored minorities in medical schools and in the medical profession'.[104] He also refused to accept that race-conscious policies could be legitimated on the grounds that they remedy societal discrimination. This was because, he argued, such measures risk placing unnecessary burdens on innocent third parties 'who bear no responsibility for whatever harm the beneficiaries of the special admissions program are thought to have suffered'.[105] This was confirmed in the *Community Schools* case, as we have seen above, in which the majority of the justices held that de facto discrimination did not constitute a compelling interest potentially justifying race conscious desegregation measures in schools.

This contrasts with the Canadian Charter, which explicitly permits programmes that aim to 'ameliorate' the condition of disadvantaged groups identified by the enumerated or analogous grounds.[106] Indeed, affirmative action measures may be particularly effective where intentional discrimination cannot be proved, but there remain hidden and structural barriers to advancement which can be more easily overcome by affirmative action than by individual claims for indirect discrimination. Despite apparently objective eligibility standards and ostensible equal opportunity policies, there remain many hidden obstacles to the advancement of disadvantaged groups. On the assumption that, in the absence of barriers, there would be a random spread of men and women, blacks and whites, and members of different ethnic groups across the labour force and government, the very fact that a group is seriously

---

[104] *Regents of the University of California v Bakke*, above n 2, at 306–7.
[105] Ibid at 310.   [106] Section 15(2).

under-represented in a sphere or activity is evidence of the subtle operation of often invisible barriers.

A good demonstration of this phenomenon is found in the facts of *Kalanke* and *Marschall*, two major ECJ cases.[107] Because the formal assessment process in the public services produced too many equally qualified candidates, informal selection criteria had come into being, including duration of service, age, and number of dependants. It is well established that all these criteria, despite being equally applicable to both men and women, in practice exclude substantially more women than men. Indeed, the ECJ is aware of this process, acknowledging in *Marschall* that the 'mere fact that a male candidate and a female candidate are equally qualified does not mean that they have the same chances'.[108] It was to overcome these hidden barriers to women's advancement that the City of Bremen took the decision to institute a policy giving preference to women if they had equal formal qualifications.

Yet could this not be dealt with by the familiar principle of indirect discrimination? Indirect discrimination expressly aims to remove apparently neutral barriers which in fact function to exclude more women than men or more blacks than whites unless they can be justified.[109] However, as we have seen, indirect discrimination has proved to be too clumsy a tool to achieve its aims. A complainant seeking to prove indirect discrimination must initiate court proceedings and show disparate impact, often on the basis of complex statistics. Even if she can surmount all these barriers, she may find that an employer successfully shows that the criteria, despite being exclusionary, are justifiable by reference to the needs of the business. Affirmative action resolves many of these difficulties. Instead of relying on litigation by individual victims, the employer takes the initiative. Nor is it necessary to prove that an exclusionary rule has had a disproportionate impact. Instead, it is sufficient to demonstrate a clear pattern of under-representation of women in particular grades or occupations. The complex questions above are unnecessary. Moreover, discriminatory selection criteria are unequivocally removed by drouting a prosumption in farion of women in

---

[107] *Kalanke*, above n 35, *Marschall*, above n 35; D Schiek, 'More Positive Action in Community Law' [1998] ILJ 155; D Schiek, 'Positive Action in Community Law' [1996] ILJ 239.

[108] *Marschall*, above n 35, para 30.

[109] SDA, s 1(1)(b)(i).

in conditions of equal merit, it makes it impossible for such criteria to be reintroduced surreptitiously through subjective decision-making.

This approach has, until very recently, been well established in the US, where there has been a long tradition of encouraging voluntary action on the part of employers to avoid disparate impact suits. Indeed, as Ginsburg J put it: 'This Court has repeatedly emphasized that the statute "should not be read to thwart" efforts at voluntary compliance.'[110] There have also been a significant number of disparate impact settlements.[111] However, in the 2010 case of *Ricci v DeStefano*,[112] the US Supreme Court, by a majority of 5:4, struck down an attempt by the city of Haven to take proactive action to prevent disparate impact. The case arose in relation to a selection test for promotion of firefighters. The results, if used, would have led to significant racial disparities in promotion. The pass rate for both African-American and Hispanic candidates was about half the rate for white candidates, with the result that none of the candidates from these groups would have been eligible for promotion to the eight lieutenant positions then vacant. Similarly only two Hispanic candidates and no African-Americans would have been eligible for the seven vacant captain positions. In response to these figures, the city decided not to certify the results of the tests.

The applicants, who were white firefighters and one Hispanic firefighter, argued that they had been discriminated on grounds of their race, in breach of the principle of equal treatment in Title VII. Kennedy J, giving judgment for the Court, stated:

Without some other justification, this express, race-based decision-making violates Title VII's command that employers cannot take adverse employment actions because of an individual's race.[113]

Only if the respondent had a strong basis in evidence that it would lose a disparate impact case would it be entitled to take race-based actions to prevent such disparate impact. This was not the situation on the facts of this case, since the examinations were job-related and consistent with business necessity. Even more worryingly, this could function as an immunity to a disparate impact case.

---

[110] *Ricci v DeStefano* 129 S Ct 2658 (2009) at 2701.

[111] R Belton, 'Title VII at Forty: A Brief Look at the Birth, Death and Resurrection of the Disparate Impact Theory of Discrimination' (2005) 22 Hofstra Lab & Emp LJ 431 at 470.

[112] *Ricci v DeStefano*, above n 110.

[113] Ibid at 2673.

If, after it certifies the test results, the City faces a disparate-impact suit, then in light of our holding today it should be clear that the City would avoid disparate-impact liability based on the strong basis in evidence that, had it not certified the results, it would have been subject to disparate treatment liability.[114]

This approach can be contrasted with the dissenting opinion of Ginsburg J:

When an employer changes an employment practice in an effort to comply with Title VII's disparate-impact provision, the Court reasons, it acts 'because of race'—something Title VII's disparate-treatment provision... generally forbids... This characterization of an employer's compliance-directed action shows little attention to Congress' design or to the Griggs line of cases Congress recognized as pathmarking.[115]

The aim of redressing past discrimination and removing hidden barriers, when fully realized, is clearly a good reason for taking affirmative action. At the same time, this formulation reveals its very limited impact. Most importantly, while preference policies may change the gender or racial composition of some higher paid occupations, they do not challenge the underlying structural and institutional forces leading to the discrimination. As Young argues,[116] because affirmative action diagnoses the problem as one of maldistribution of privileged positions, its objective is limited to the redistribution of such positions among under-represented groups. However, this narrow distributive definition of racial and gender justice leaves out the equally important issues of institutional organization and decision-making power. For fundamental change to occur, the structural and institutional causes of exclusion need to be changed, including the division of labour in the home, the interaction between work in the family and work in the paid labour force, education, and others. Indeed, this insight was recognized and articulated by Advocate General Tesauro in *Kalanke* when he said:

Formal numerical equality is an objective which may salve some consciences, but it will remain illusory... unless it goes together with measures which are genuinely destined to achieve equality... In the final analysis, that which is necessary above all is a substantial change in the economic, social and cultural model which is at the root of the inequalities.[117]

---

[114] Ibid at 2681.
[115] Ibid at 2699.
[116] I Young, *Justice and the Politics of Difference* (Princeton University Press, 1990), p 193.
[117] *Kalanke*, above n 35, at 665.

(b) Representation and perspective

A more dynamic way of justifying the use of affirmative action policies is to argue that the very presence of women or other disadvantaged groups in higher status positions will lead to structural changes. On this argument, women or minorities in such positions will be able to represent the needs and interests of their groups in decision-making, changing both the agenda of decision-making and their outcomes. Women will, for example, be in a position to argue for maternity leave, childcare, and family friendly policies, thus paving the way for more women to enter these positions. This representative function is important, on this view, for both formal decision-making institutions such as legislatures or trade union executive bodies, and for informal decision-making. Managers, civil servants, judges, professionals, and chief administrators make a host of decisions, all of which require that the interests of women or minorities be properly represented.

However, more support is needed to underpin the assumption that the mere presence of women will guarantee that women's interests will be articulated. As Phillips puts it, we generally reject a politics of presence in favour of a politics of ideas.

> The shift from direct to representative democracy has shifted the emphasis from *who* the politicians are to *what* (policies, preferences, ideas), they represent, and in doing so has made accountability to the electorate the pre-eminent radical concern.[118]

Two possible arguments could be mounted to justify the renewed emphasis on presence, but both turn out to be problematic. The first is to argue that any woman or member of a disadvantaged group will inevitably articulate the needs, interests, and concerns of other women or members of the group. Their presence is therefore all that is needed. However, although there is some evidence that women may have a different moral sense to men,[119] modern feminists are acutely aware of the range of differing interests among women, and indeed of the potential for conflict. Attempts to construct an 'essential woman' merely end up replicating the dominant ideology about women, obscuring crucial differences in class, race, sexual orientation, etc. This is equally true of minority groups: the assumption that black groups share common

---

[118] A Phillips, *The Politics of Presence* (Clarendon Press, 1995), p 4.
[119] See C Gilligan, *In a Different Voice: Psychological Theory and Women's Development* (Harvard University Press, 1982), esp ch 5.

interests merely veils deep differences based on religion, country of origin, or language.

A second way of justifying the representative function of affirmative action is to accept that the mere presence of women is not sufficient, but to argue instead that women beneficiaries of affirmative action are there as genuine representatives of other women. But this in turn requires some mechanism of accountability. The experience of the regime of British Prime Minister Margaret Thatcher demonstrated clearly that a woman in power is not necessarily a representative of women's interests. Indeed, she may have achieved power partly because she was able to conform to a male ethic and thereby suppress any belief in the importance of articulating women's concerns. There are no mechanisms for accountability in affirmative action plans in public or private employment, and even on decision-making bodies, including the legislature, women decision-makers are not cast as accountable to women constituents. The same is true for a related justification, namely that those who benefit from affirmative action will return to serve their communities. This goal, which has been rejected by the US Supreme Court,[120] places too great a burden on the beneficiaries of the measure, burdens which are not shared by those who are already privileged.

There is, however, a third and more promising way to justify the use of affirmative action policies to improve the extent to which women's concerns are addressed. This is to argue, as Young does, that decision-making is wrongly conceived of as a process of bargaining between interest groups, each of which represents a fixed set of interests, and whose representatives are mandated to further those interests and to compromise only as a quid pro quo.[121] Instead, it is argued, decision-making is a result of communication and discussion based on more than egotistical impulses, but on a desire to reach a fair and reasoned result.[122] Participants are prepared to recognize others' concerns and beliefs in their own right, not just in order to wrest return favours catering for their constituents' interests. In addition, this approach does not take an abstract, impartial view of rationality, but recognizes that the particular life experience of the decision maker is reflected in his or her view. Since gender and race remain such strong determinants of a person's life experience, the overwhelming predominance of one gender or race in decision-making fora make it unlikely that the

---

[120] *Regents of the University of California v Bakke*, above n 2.
[121] Young, above n 116, pp 118–19.
[122] Ibid, pp 92–4.

experience and perspectives of the excluded group will be articulated.[123] On this view, it is possible to characterize women's presence as functioning to open up new perspectives on decision-making, to cast light on assumptions that the dominant group perceives as universal, and to enhance the store of 'social knowledge'.

This approach makes sense of the notion that women or minorities may have distinct perspectives, which the very process of exclusion negates, and therefore which need to be guaranteed a place in deliberative decision-making. In addition, it demonstrates the necessity for a critical mass both to make the common interests more audible. Indeed, such an approach was endorsed by O'Connor J in the US Supreme Court in *Grutter*, when she stated:

Just as growing up in a particular region or having particular professional experiences is likely to affect an individual's views, so too is one's own, unique experience of being a racial minority in a society, like our own, in which race unfortunately still matters.[124]

At the same time, it is important to move beyond essentializing a status group, or regarding all members as sharing the same interests or perspectives. Young argues that groups are better understood, not as fixed categories with impermeable boundaries, but as a set of relationships between different people. Such a relational understanding moves beyond the notion that a group consists of members who all share the same fixed attributes and have nothing in common with members of other groups. Instead, a group is characterized as a social process of interaction in which some people have an affinity with each other. Assertion of affinity with a group may change with social context and with life changes; and members may have interests which differ from other members of the group but are similar to members of other groups.[125]

(c) Role models and diversity

A third and related justification for reverse discrimination is that it provides diversity in an educational institution or workplace; and that it facilitates the provision of role models. In *Bakke*,[126] Powell J justified affirmative action in university admissions thus:

---

[123] Phillips, above n 118, p 52.
[124] *Grutter v Bollinger* 539 US 306 (2003) at 333.
[125] Young, above n 116, pp 171–2.
[126] *Regents of the University of California v Bakke*, above n 2.

An otherwise qualified medical student with a particular background—whether it be ethnic, geographic, culturally advantaged or disadvantaged—may bring to a professional school of medicine, experiences, outlook, and ideas that enrich the training of its student body and better equip its graduates to render with understanding their vital service to humanity.[127]

In other words, where a group has been excluded from a particular setting, be it a workforce or an educational institution, the likelihood is that the perspectives and experiences of members of the excluded group, particularly those relating to its exclusion, will be undervalued, misunderstood, or ignored by the dominant group, making it impossible for the excluded group to change its disadvantaged position.

Diversity has now been recognized as one of two interests which could satisfy the requirements of the strict scrutiny test now prevailing in the US,[128] the other being that of remedying the effects of past intentional discrimination.[129] The most spirited defence of diversity is found in the Court's decision in *Grutter*,[130] upholding a race-conscious policy by the University of Michigan Law School which, by enrolling a '"critical mass" of [underrepresented] minority students', sought to 'ensur[e] their ability to make unique contributions to the character of the Law School'.[131] The Court accepted that the educational benefits that diversity is designed to produce were substantial. Such a policy can promote cross-racial understanding, help to break down racial stereotypes, and enable students to better understand persons of different races. It endorsed the District Court's finding that these benefits are 'important and laudable', because 'classroom discussion is livelier, more spirited, and simply more enlightening and interesting' when the students have 'the greatest possible variety of backgrounds'.[132]

The compelling interest in diversity has now been reinforced by Kennedy J, in his swing judgment in *Parents Involved in Community Schools v Seattle*. As was mentioned above, Kennedy J disagreed with the plurality finding that diversity could not constitute a compelling State interest outside higher education. Instead, he agreed with the dissent that 'diversity, depending on its meaning and definition, is a compelling educational goal a school district may pursue'.[133]

---

127 Ibid at 314, 2760.
128 Ibid at 328.   129 *Community Schools*, above n 86, at 2752.
130 *Grutter v Bollinger*, above n 124.   131 Ibid at 316.
132 Ibid at 330.   133 *Community Schools*, above n 86, at 783.

While diversity operates to change the perspectives of the dominant group, the provision of role models operates on the self-perception of excluded groups, piercing stereotypes and giving them the self-confidence to move into non-traditional positions. This has not been accepted in the US Supreme Court. In *Wygant*,[134] the defendant Board of Education argued, inter alia, that its policy of protecting newly hired minority teachers against lay-offs was justified by the State's duty to reduce racial discrimination by providing minority role models for minority students. This Powell J roundly rejected on the grounds that it would permit affirmative action long past the point of its remedial purpose.

However, this aim has been vigorously supported by the Supreme Court of Canada, in *Action Travail des Femmes v Canadian National Railway Co*.[135] As Chief Justice Dickson put it, the aim of an employment equity programme (in this case setting a quota of one woman in four new hirings until a goal of 13 per cent women in certain blue collar occupations was reached) is not to compensate past victims; but 'an attempt to ensure that future applicants and workers from the affected group will not face the same insidious barriers that blocked their forebears'.[136] He identified at least two ways in which such a programme is likely to be more effective than one which simply relies on equal opportunities or the proscription of intentional prejudice. First, the insistence that women be placed in non-traditional jobs allows them to prove that they really can do the job, thereby dispelling stereotypes about women's abilities. This was particularly evident in the case at hand, in which the quotas ordered by the tribunal concerned traditionally male jobs such as 'brakeman' or signaller at Canadian National Railways. Secondly, an employment equity programme helps to create a 'critical mass' of women in the workplace. Once a significant number of women are represented in a particular type of work, 'there is a significant chance for the continuing self-correction of the system'.[137] The critical mass overcomes the problem of tokenism, which would leave a few women isolated and vulnerable to sexual harassment or accusations of being imposters. It would also generate further employment of women, partly by means of the informal recruitment network and partly by reducing the stigma and anxiety associated with strange and unconventional work. Finally, a critical mass of women forces

---

[134] *Wygant*, above n 4.
[135] *Action Travail des Femmes v Canadian National Railway Co* [1987] 1 SCR 1114, 40 DLR (4th) 193.
[136] Ibid at 213.   [137] Ibid at 214.

management to give women's concerns their due weight and compels personnel offices to take female applications seriously. As the Chief Justice concluded:

> It is readily apparent that, in attempting to combat systemic discrimination, it is essential to look to the past patterns of discrimination and to destroy those patterns in order to prevent the same type of discrimination in the future.[138]

(II) STANDARD OF SCRUTINY

The legitimacy of the aims of affirmative action is only the first question. Equally important is the question of whether the means fit the ends. This question is overlaid by the need to take account of relative institutional competence. How much deference should judges be according law-makers and the executive in determining how best to further their legitimate aims?

Courts vary widely in their response to this question. As we have seen, the US courts have in recent years adopted a standard of 'strict scrutiny',[139] framing the proportionality analysis in the narrowest terms. The State must demonstrate a 'pressing social need' and the measure must be 'narrowly tailored' to that end. Nevertheless, this standard does not revert to a purely formal approach. As O'Connor J has emphasized, 'strict scrutiny' does not amount to 'fatal in fact'.[140] In *Grutter*, speaking for the Court, she elaborated on how this balance could be achieved. In an approach which is remarkably similar to that adopted by the ECJ in applying EU law, she held that it was not legitimate to impose inflexible quotas. Instead, to fulfil the test of strict scrutiny, a programme must be flexible enough to ensure that each applicant is evaluated as an individual and not in a way that makes race or ethnicity the defining feature of the application. Thus race or ethnicity may be considered, but only as a '"plus" in a particular applicant's file'.[141] At the same time, the Court rejected the argument that the Law School should have used race-neutral means to obtain the educational benefits of student-body diversity.

> Narrow tailoring does not require exhaustion of every conceivable race neutral alternative or mandate that a university choose between maintaining a reputation for excellence or fulfilling a commitment to provide educational opportunities to members of all racial groups.[142]

---

[138] Ibid at 215.
[140] Ibid at 237.
[139] *Adarand Constructors v Pena* 515 US 200 (1995).
[141] *Grutter*, above n 124, at 317.   [142] Ibid at 309.

Furthermore, since a core purpose of the Fourteenth Amendment is to do away with all governmentally imposed discrimination based on race, race-conscious policies cannot be permanent. The need for a sunset clause is aimed to 'assure[s] all citizens that the deviation from the norm of equal treatment of all racial and ethnic groups is a temporary matter, a measure taken in the service of the goal of equality itself'.[143]

The standard of strict scrutiny, even if not fatal, is premised on the notion that affirmative action is a narrow exception to the equal treatment principle. Under a substantive view of equality, affirmative action is a means to achieve equality, and therefore strict scrutiny should be unwarranted. Does this mean, however, that courts should entirely abdicate their supervisory function? The lightest touch review is found in the Supreme Court of Canada, which takes the view that review should be primarily directed to the genuineness of the government's stated ameliorative purpose.[144] As will be recalled, section 15(2) of the Canadian Charter states that a programme does not breach the equality guarantee if it has 'as its object the amelioration of conditions of disadvantaged individuals or groups'. In *R v Kapp*, the Court held that the focus should be on ameliorative purpose, rather than on whether the programme is likely to achieve its ameliorative goal. Judicial examination of the actual effect of the programme was inappropriate, since results might be unpredictable or difficult to evaluate. Indeed, governments should be actively encouraged to be innovative in their approach to affirmative action.[145]

A focus on purpose, however, runs the risk of giving governments carte blanche to characterize any programme as having an ameliorative objective, regardless of its actual effect. The Canadian Court dealt with this by holding that a bald declaration of ameliorative purpose would not be sufficient. To prevent programmes masquerading as ameliorative, while at the same time preserving a significant degree of deference to the government, it held, the Court would require a showing that there is a correlation between the programme and the purpose. By contrast with the US standard of strict scrutiny, this is not a searching standard. As the Court stated:

Analysing the means employed by the government can easily turn into assessing the effect of the program. As a result, to preserve an intent-based analysis, courts could be encouraged to frame the analysis as follows: Was it rational for

---

[143] *Richmond v JA Croson Co* 488 US 469 (1989) at 510.
[144] *R v Kapp*, above n 98.   [145] Ibid, para 47.

the state to conclude that the means chosen to reach its ameliorative goal would contribute to that purpose? For the distinction to be rational, there must be a correlation between the program and the disadvantage suffered by the target group. Such a standard permits significant deference to the legislature but allows judicial review where a program nominally seeks to serve the disadvantaged but in practice serves other, non-remedial objectives.[146]

There is force in the Canadian courts' concern with the purpose of a programme rather than its effects. The *Kapp* case concerned the federal government's strategy to enhance aboriginal involvement in commercial fishing. As part of the strategy, the government had issued a communal fishing licence to three aboriginal bands permitting only fishers desig- nated by the bands to fish for salmon in the mouth of the Fraser River for a period of 24 hours and to sell their catch. The appellants, commer- cial fishers, mainly non-aboriginal, were excluded from the fishery during this 24-hour period. They argued that the communal fishing licence discriminated against them on the basis of race. In particular, they argued that the programme did not offer a benefit that effectively tackled the problems faced by these bands. The Court was rightly reluctant to adjudicate on the effectiveness of the programme in this sense. As it stated,

If the sincere purpose is to promote equality by ameliorating the conditions of a disadvantaged group, the government should be given some leeway to adopt innovative programs, even though some may ultimately prove to be unsuccess- ful. The government may learn from such failures and revise equality enhancing programs to make them more effective.[147]

Nevertheless, the Court was alive to the fact that courts have regarded a programme as ameliorative in surprising circumstances. Particularly worrying are measures which place restrictions on individuals which the government claims to be in their best interests.[148] Thus the Court drew a careful line between deference to the judgment of the executive, and appropriate judicial supervision.

The meaning of 'amelioration' deserves careful attention in evaluating programs under s. 15(2). We would suggest that laws designed to restrict or punish behaviour [of the target class] would not qualify for s. 15(2) protection. Nor, as already discussed, should the focus be on the effect of the law. This said, the fact that a law has no plausible or predictable ameliorative effect may render suspect the state's ameliorative purpose. Governments, as discussed

---

[146] Ibid, para 49.   [147] Ibid, para 47.   [148] Ibid, para 53.

above, are not permitted to protect discriminatory programs on colourable pretexts.[149]

The South African Constitutional Court, while rejecting the strictness of 'narrow tailoring', has nevertheless retained for itself a role which goes beyond checking only for genuine ameliorative purpose. Instead, it requires a measure to meet the standard of reasonableness. Although the constitutional text also talks of measures 'designed to protect and advance', in *van Heerden*, Moseneke J stated that the remedial measures must be 'reasonably capable of attaining the desired outcome', namely to protect or advance individuals or categories of persons who have been disadvantaged by unfair discrimination. This excludes measures which are arbitrary, capricious, or display naked preference, or are not reasonably likely to achieve the end of advancing or benefiting the interests of those who have been disadvantaged by unfair discrimination.[150] Importantly, he emphasized that the Constitution did not

postulate a standard of necessity between the legislative choice and the governmental objective. The text requires only that the means should be designed to protect or advance. It is sufficient if the measure carries a reasonable likelihood of meeting the end.[151]

This can be contrasted with the standard of scrutiny applied by the ECJ, which continues to regard affirmative action as a derogation from the principle of equality, and therefore to be construed strictly. According to the ECJ:

In determining the scope of any derogation from an individual right such as the equal treatment of men and women laid down by the Directive, due regard must be had to the principle of proportionality, which requires that derogations must remain within the limits of what is appropriate and necessary in order to achieve the aim in view and that the principle of equal treatment be reconciled as far as possible with the requirements of the aim thus pursued.[152]

Ultimately, the role of the court should be to further substantive equality, and therefore to support government measures which aim to achieve substantive equality. There is no equivalence between classification which perpetuates disadvantage or causes detriment, and measures which use status in order to achieve substantive equality. However,

---

[149] Ibid, para 54.
[150] *Minister of Justice v Van Heerden*, above n 95, paras 38–40.
[151] Ibid, para 41.
[152] *Briheche*, above n 36, at 24; *Lommers v Minister Van Landbouw, Natuurbeheer En Visserij*, above n 58, at [39]; de Kok, above n 58, at paras 37–43.

judicial support for affirmative action which furthers substantive equality should not be confused with deference to governmental decisions. Courts should still require governments to demonstrate that the aim of the measure is indeed to further substantive equality and to justify their choice of means. Justification need not amount to proof that there were no suitable alternatives, nor should the State have to demonstrate that the programme is effective. This preserves the space for innovation, as emphasized by the Canadian Court. But justification does require that the State demonstrate that its measures are not based on assumptions, generalizations, or stereotypes.

(III) DEMARCATING BENEFICIARIES

A further challenging question concerns how the group of beneficiaries of a preference policy should be determined. It is clear that, on a substantive approach, the class need not consist only of proven victims. But does this mean that all members of a disadvantaged group should benefit, simply because they share the same protected characteristic? Should middle class blacks or women benefit even though they no longer experience the socio-economic disadvantage or other detriment attached to their race or gender? This requires further thought to be given to the relationship between redistribution and recognition, or socio-economic disadvantage and status inequality.

Both the Canadian and South African courts have addressed this question. In *Kapp*, the question arose as to whether the three Indian bands denoted as beneficiaries of the exclusive fishing benefit were an 'identifiable disadvantaged group' for the purposes of section 15(2) which, it will be recalled, permits ameliorative measures the object of which is 'the amelioration of conditions of disadvantaged individuals or groups including those that are disadvantaged because of race, national or ethnic origin, colour, religion, sex, age or mental or physical disability'. The Supreme Court of Canada held that 'disadvantaged' in this case connoted 'vulnerability, prejudice and negative social characterization'.[153] It drew a bright line between programmes targeting the conditions of a specific and identifiable disadvantaged group, which were protected by section 15(2), and broad societal legislation. In determining whether the programme at issue targeted a 'disadvantaged group identified by' race, it referred to both status disadvantage—'the legacy of stereotyping and prejudice against Aboriginal peoples'—and

---

[153] *R v Kapp*, above n 98, para 55.

socio-economic disadvantage: 'the evidence shows in this case that the bands granted the benefit were in fact disadvantaged in terms of income, education and a host of other measures'. However, it did not require the proof that each individual member suffered such disadvantage. 'The fact that some individual members of the bands may not experience personal disadvantage does not negate the group disadvantage suffered by band members.'[154]

In the South African case of *Van Heerden*, a similar question was faced. It will be recalled that in this case a special measure was put in place in relation to the pensions of MPs elected in the first democratic elections, in order to bring them up to the level of those who had been collecting pension benefits because they had been MPs in the apartheid government. The aim of the measure was to compensate those who had been excluded from Parliament by the apartheid laws. However, although an overwhelming majority of the new MPs had in fact been prejudiced by past disadvantage and unfair exclusion, this was not true of all new parliamentarians. Moseneke and Mokgoro JJ took a different approach to the mismatch between the victims and the beneficiaries. Moseneke J took the view that it would often be

difficult, impractical or undesirable to devise a legislative scheme with 'pure' differentiation demarcating precisely the affected classes. Within each class, favoured or otherwise, there may indeed be exceptional or 'hard cases' or windfall beneficiaries.[155]

He thus held that the measure should be judged by 'whether an overwhelming majority of members of the favoured class are persons designated as disadvantaged by unfair exclusion.'[156] Like the Canadian Court, he regarded the validity of the remedial measures as unaffected by the existence of a tiny minority of MPs who were not unfairly discriminated against, but who benefited from the measure.

This can be contrasted with the decision of Mokgoro J, who held that a more exact fit was necessary. This was because a much lower standard of scrutiny was required in relation to a measure falling within the permission for affirmative action in section 9(2). Whereas under the standard provision prohibiting unfair discrimination, the State must prove that a distinction on a proscribed ground is fair, in the case of an affirmative action measure falling within section 9(2), the State is relieved of this burden. Mokgoro J therefore held that if the class of

---

[154] Ibid, para 59.   [155] *Van Heerden*, above n 95, para 39.
[156] Ibid, para 40.

beneficiaries could not be precisely delineated, then the measure should have to reach the high standards of fairness required in relation to an ordinary discrimination claim. This did not mean that the programme was unlawful. It simply meant that the State had to prove that it was not unfair, which in this case it had done. Thus the difference between Moseneke and Mokgoro JJ reflects an underlying principle about the role of judicial scrutiny. Requiring a higher level of scrutiny does not in itself mean that affirmative action programmes will be struck down as a breach of equality. It simply means that more care is taken to ensure that there is a sufficient match between the delineated class and the aim of redressing disadvantage.

(IV) RECOGNITION AND REDISTRIBUTION

As well as the problem of over-inclusiveness, an even more difficult question concerns the criteria for demarcating beneficiaries. Is it enough to define the beneficiary group according to their common experience of prejudice (recognition ills)? Or should it be necessary to show, in addition, that they have suffered socio-economic disadvantage (redistributive ills)? This raises deep questions as to the function of affirmative action and the relationship between status and socio-economic disadvantage. By requiring individuals to manifest both recognition and redistributive ills, it is assumed that the function of affirmative action is only in relation to the socio-economic dimension of status wrongs. Pure socio-economic disadvantage without status wrongs and pure status wrongs without socio-economic disadvantage both fall outside the affirmative action purview. On one argument, affirmative action is an inappropriate remedy in cases in which recognition wrongs need to be addressed but socio-economic disadvantage is no longer an issue. On this view, recognition wrongs are better addressed through other measures, such as prohibitions on discrimination and harassment. Indeed, to continue to use affirmative action for purely status wrongs could, on this view, simply reinforce stereotypes. However, this would ignore the extent to which the two issues are related. The aims identified above, including creating role models, increasing representation, remedying a history of discrimination, and enhancing diversity, all presuppose a deep linkage between recognition and redistribution, which should not be ignored in framing affirmative action measures.

The relationship between redistribution and recognition need not require much attention when there is a substantial overlap, as in the case of the First Nation tribes in *Kapp*. However, as affirmative action measures become more effective, and some members of the status group begin to prosper, questions arise as to whether the latter should continue to benefit from the measure in question. One response is to overlay status with socio-economic disadvantage in demarcating the group of beneficiaries. To qualify for the benefit, the individual must show socio-economic disadvantage as well as membership of the status group. This can be seen in both India and the US.

The Indian Constitution permits special provision to be made for two categories of disadvantaged groups. The first are known as 'Scheduled Castes and Scheduled Tribes' (SC/ST) and are specified by the President.[157] The second are referred to as 'socially and educationally backward classes of citizens'[158] or other 'backward classes' (OBCs).[159] The latter are specified in a list drawn up by the National Commission for Backward Classes.[160] The equality guarantee in the Indian Constitution provides that special provisions, known as reservations, may be made for the advancement of any these categories.[161] Reservations are now widespread in higher education and public service jobs. But in recent decades, the question has arisen as to whether they should continue to be available to the 'creamy layer', or those members of the certified groups who are in fact no longer socially or educationally disadvantaged.

In two of the foremost cases, the Indian Supreme Court has held emphatically that, at least in the case of OBCs, the creamy layer should be excluded. Justice Jeevan Reddy stated in *Indra Sawhney*'s case, 'In our opinion, it is not a question of permissibility or desirability of such test but one of proper and more appropriate identification of a class as a backward class.'[162] Similarly, the Chief Justice in *Ashoka Kumar* stated: 'To fulfil the conditions and to find out truly what is socially and educationally backward class, the exclusion of "creamy layer" is essential.'[163] In other words, the definition of the beneficiary class must correspond with the purpose of the provision, namely to advance those who are disadvantaged. However, the requirement that a group display both recognition and redistributive ills is only imperfectly

---

[157] Constitution of India, arts 341(1), 342(2). Available at: ⟨http://lawmin.nic.in/coi/coiason29julyo8.pdf.

[158] Ibid, art 15(4).

[159] See ibid, art 16(4).

[160] See ibid, article 340(1); the list can be found at: ⟨http://ncbc.nic.in/backward-classes/index.html.

[161] Art 15(4).

[162] *Indra Sawhney v Union of India*, AIR 1993 SC 447 at 724.

[163] *Ashoka Kumar v Union of India and Others*, IA No 13 In Writ Petition (Civil) No 265 OF 2006—(With WP (Civil) Nos 269/2006, 598/2006, 35/2007, and 29/2007), para 149.

executed. On the one hand, there is no creamy layer exclusion for the SC/STs. On the other hand, there is no provision for reservation in favour of disadvantaged Muslims.

A similar attempt to create a closer fit between status and socio-economic disadvantage is found in US affirmative action programmes, particularly in respect of set-aside programmes authorizing preferential treatment in the award of government contracts. In order to comply with the strict scrutiny test set out in *Adarand*, federal legislation mandating set-asides for status groups now also includes a requirement of evidence of socio-economic disadvantage. To participate in what has become known as a 'section 8(a) program',[164] a business must be 51 per cent owned by individuals who qualify as 'socially and economically disad-vantaged'.[165] The relevant legislation defines 'socially disadvantaged individuals' as 'those who have been subjected to racial or ethnic prejudice or cultural bias because of their identity as a member of a group without regard to their individual qualities'.[166] It defines 'eco-nomically disadvantaged individuals' as

those socially disadvantaged individuals whose ability to compete in the free enterprise system has been impaired due to diminished capital and credit opportunities as compared to others in the same business area who are not socially disadvantaged.[167]

There is a rebuttable presumption that members of certain groups are socially disadvantaged, including Black Americans, Hispanic Ameri-cans, Native Americans, Asian Pacific Americans, Subcontinent Asian Americans, and members of other groups designated from time to time by the Small Business Administration (SBA).[168] The presumption of social disadvantage may be overcome with 'credible evidence to the contrary', which can be submitted by third parties.[169] An individual who is not a member of a listed group can also be included if she or he can 'establish individual social disadvantage by a preponderance of the evidence'.[170] The presumption does not apply to economic disadvan-tage: each participant to must prove such disadvantage.[171] The result is to exclude businesses which, regardless of race, are not in fact socially or economically disadvantaged, a similar effect to that achieved by the Indian 'creamy layer' provisions above. Amendments adopted in 1994

---

[164] Small Business Act (SBA)15 USC §§ 631 et seq, sec. 8(a).
[165] As defined in 13 CFR § 124.105.
[166] 15 USC § 637(a)(5).   [167] Ibid, § 637(a)(6)(A).
[168] 13 CFR § 124.103(b).   [169] Ibid, § 124.103(b)(3).
[170] Ibid, § 124.103(c).   [171] Ibid, § 124.104.

specifically included 'small business concerns owned and controlled by women' in addition to 'socially and economically disadvantaged individuals'.

Also of importance has been the Transportation Equity Act for the 21st Century (known as TEA-21),[172] which authorizes the use of race- and sex-based preferences in federally funded transportation contracts. As in the SBA regulations, the TEA-21 regulations presume that Black Americans, Hispanic Americans, Native Americans, Asian-Pacific Americans, Subcontinent Asian Americans, and women are socially and economically disadvantaged.[173] However, this presumption is rebutted where the individual has a personal net worth of more than $750,000 or a preponderance of the evidence demonstrates that the individual is not in fact socially and economically disadvantaged.[174] Conversely, firms owned and controlled by someone who is not presumed to be disadvantaged (ie, a white male) can qualify for Disadvantaged Business Enterprise (DBE) status if the individual can demonstrate that he is in fact socially and economically disadvantaged.[175]

IV CONCLUSION

It has been seen above that there are strong arguments to support an understanding of reverse discrimination or affirmative action as a means to achieve equality, rather than as a breach or derogation. At the same time, it is important to stress the limitations of affirmative action as a strategy. The introduction of new perspectives, while an important goal, can only have a limited impact: entrenched structures are often resilient and indeed have powerful conformist pressures. Women, blacks, or minorities may find themselves forced to hide their views and ignore their own needs and interests in order to ensure that their continued participation is viable. Even if they do articulate their perspectives, the process of recognition and affirmation is halting and erratic. Thus affirmative action needs to be only one part of a broad-based and radical strategy, which does more than redistribute privileged positions but refashions the institutions which continue to perpetuate exclusion.

---

[172] TEA-21, extended through fiscal year 2009 by Public Law 109-59, signed into law during the 109th Congress.
[173] § 26.67(a).   [174] § 26.67(b).   [175] § 26.67(d).

6

Rights and Remedies:
The Limits of the Law

As we have seen, discrimination and equality law have become increasingly sophisticated in recent decades. However, while initial successes fuelled early optimism, deeper structures of discrimination have proved remarkably resilient. This raises doubts about the role of law in effecting social change. Is law inevitably limited? Or can we refashion legal tools in such a way as to play a major part in achieving substantive equality? In order to answer these questions, it is necessary to examine not just the conceptual apparatus of equality law, but also the enforcement mechanisms.

The primary means of enforcing anti-discrimination laws in the UK has been by means of individual claims to courts or tribunals. More recently, however, attempts have been made to fashion a new approach to enforcement, which goes beyond the individualized and backward-looking nature of tribunal claims. These positive duties require more than just a change in enforcement measures. They also require a reformulation of the aim of the law. Rather than simply penalizing individual acts of unlawful discrimination and compensating individual victims, the aim is to promote equality through structural change. This in turn involves striking a delicate balance between individual responsibility and legal incentives, be they positive or negative. It also involves weighing up different types of costs: not just the quantifiable and concrete costs to employers or the State, but also the price paid by individuals who suffer from institutional discrimination and by society more generally. Through all of this, of course, the less visible but equally important educational role of the law should not be ignored. It is important that the law conveys the right messages. Anti-discrimination legislation which relies wholly on individual claims to tribunals might well signal to employers, State agents, and other major actors that the function of the law extends no further. As long as they can avoid tribunal claims, and pay out compensation where necessary, the problem of discrimination has been dealt with. This chapter begins by considering existing structures of adjudication and compensation, and then turns to examine the role and nature of positive duties.

I ADVERSARIALISM:
THE NARROW REACH OF ADJUDICATION

The primary channel for enforcement of anti-discrimination law in the employment field in Britain is by individual complaint to an employment tribunal. Claims which relate to education or the provision of goods and services lie to the county court or the sheriff court in Scotland, but such cases have been a small minority of the total. Since the coming into force of the Human Rights Act 1998 (HRA), there has also been the possibility of judicial review to the High Court. Particularly influential has been the reference procedure to the European Court of Justice (ECJ), according to which tribunals and courts may refer questions of EU law for a definitive answer. Below, I consider first the nature of claims to tribunals, and then turn briefly to other types of court.

(I) TRIBUNALS

The tribunal system was deliberately structured to provide an accessible, cheap, and speedy alternative to the existing court process. Tribunals are more informal and accessible than courts: there are no complicated pleadings and tribunals are not bound by strict rules of evidence. Representatives do not need to be lawyers and applicants can represent themselves. This means that tribunal cases are potentially less expensive than court cases. Tribunals are also intended to be more sensitive than ordinary courts to employment-related concerns. Hence, tribunals were designed to be tripartite in structure. Decisions are made by a legal chair and two lay members with industrial experience, one appointed after consultation with trade unions, the other after consultation with employers' organizations. In race discrimination cases, it is the normal practice to appoint one lay member from a panel designated on appointment as having special knowledge and experience of race relations. The Employment Appeal Tribunal (EAT), to which appeals from employment tribunals lie, is similarly tripartite in structure, with a judge in the chair. Tribunals are also somewhat quicker than courts, due to the large numbers of tribunals throughout the country.

However, the record of tribunals in discrimination cases has been disappointing. Compared to the scale of discrimination in society, the number of complaints to tribunals is small, and the amount of successes minuscule.[1] In 2009–10, only 340 sex discrimination claims were successful at tribunal, a mere 2 per cent of the 17,500 sex discrimination cases disposed of during that year. This figure was even smaller for other grounds: 130 race discrimination cases were successful at tribunal (3 per cent of the total disposed); 170 disability discrimination cases (3 per cent); 95 age discrimination cases (2 per cent); and only 19 (2 per cent) on religion or belief and 27 (5 per cent) on sexual orientation discrimination. This is a remarkably similar outcome to previous years, the equivalent figures for 2008–9 being 341 sex discrimination cases (3 per cent); 129 race discrimination cases (3 per cent); and 177 disability cases (3 per cent). There were 53 (2 per cent) successful age discrimination cases, 13 sexual orientation (2 per cent), and 19 (3 per cent) on grounds of religion and belief. Equal pay has been particularly problematic. In recent years large, multiple, equal pay claims have been brought to tribunals, leading to soaring numbers of applications. However, the rate of success before a tribunal has been derisory. In 2008–9, as many as 20,148 equal pay claims were disposed of by tribunals, but only 36 were successful before a tribunal, a success rate of 0.2 per cent. In 2009–10, this figure rose negligibly, to 200 out of 20,100 claims (1 per cent). The pattern across all the grounds is little better than earlier decades.[2]

It is true, of course, that these figures leave out of account those cases that might have settled before a hearing. Thus in 2009–10, about 20 per cent of sex discrimination cases, 38 per cent of race discrimination cases, and 45 per cent of disability cases (but only 10 per cent of equal pay cases) were settled through the auspices of the Advisory, Conciliation and Arbitration Service (ACAS). Many other cases were withdrawn,

---

[1] Figures in this paragraph are taken from Ministry of Justice Tribunals Service, *Employment Tribunal and EAT Statistics 2009–10*; Ministry of Justice Tribunals Service, *Employment Tribunal and EAT Statistics 2008–9* available at: <http://www.tribunals.gov.uk/Tribunals/Publications/publications.htm>.

[2] (1999) 88 EOR 43. In 1993–4, 1,900 sex discrimination cases were completed, rising to 4,052 in 1994–5. 780 equal pay cases were completed in 1993–4, but only 418 in 1994–5. In 1994–5, over 80 per cent of sex discrimination cases were conciliated, withdrawn, or disposed of otherwise without the need for a tribunal hearing. In the same year, 70 per cent of equal pay cases were withdrawn and a further 23 per cent conciliated. For the handful, success rates are poor. About one-third of the SDA cases which reached a tribunal in 1993–4, and one-half in 1994–5, were successful, with compensation being awarded in only 58 and 134 cases, respectively. The success rate is even more discouraging. In 1994–5, applicants under the Equal Pay Act 1970 were successful in a mere one-third of the 25 cases heard by tribunals: (1996) 69 EOR 26.

although it is not clear how many of these were settled privately. Thus as many as 71 per cent of equal pay cases were withdrawn in 2009–10. Removing these cases from the picture yields a somewhat more optimistic success rate before tribunals: for example, although only 7 per cent of sex discrimination cases actually reached the hearing stage, about 29 per cent were successful. Nevertheless, the fact remains that fewer than 800 cases across all the discrimination grounds were successful at tribunal in 2009–10.

As well as the low success rate, tribunals have not lived up to the expectation of a quick and affordable procedure. The length of the process has been described by the EAT as 'scandalous' and 'a denial of justice to women through the judicial process'.[3] This is particularly problematic in relation to equal pay, where time taken to determine an equal value claim can range from eight to ten years,[4] up from an average of 18 months in 1992. Some cases, such as that of 1,280 women against British Coal ran for the extraordinary period of 15 years. The speech therapists' claim was finally concluded after 14 years.[5] A case might go all the way to the UK Supreme Court on a preliminary point, only to be remitted to the tribunal. Although a new procedure for dealing with equal value claims was introduced in 2004, research has shown that, far from improving matters, this has greatly lengthened the procedure, with some cases delayed by several years.[6]

The system has come under particular strain in the public sector. Slow progress in implementing the far-reaching job re-evaluation in local government precipitated numerous individual claims to employment tribunals. Whereas there were fewer than 8,500 equal pay claims in 2004–5, this figure soared to a high point of 62,700 in 2007–8. Although the number of claims dropped to 37,500 in 2009–10, such large cohorts of individual claims have brought the system close to breaking point. Thus equal pay remains a central demonstration of the limitations of individual enforcement.[7]

There is also a risk that the tripartite structure of tribunals is being undermined. In a growing number of situations, employment judges are permitted to sit alone, breaching the fundamental principle of an

---

[3] *Aldridge v British Telecommunications plc* [1990] IRLR 10 (EAT) at 14.

[4] K Godwin, 'Equal Value: justice denied?' EOR 186 (March 2009).

[5] Figures in this part are taken from B Hepple, M Coussey, and T Choudhury, *Equality: A New Framework*, Report of the Independent Review of the Enforcement of UK Anti-Discrimination Legislation (Hart Publishing, 2000), paras 4.28 and 4.29.

[6] Godwin, above n 4, p 16.

[7] Ministry of Justice Tribunal Service, *Employment Tribunal and EAT Statistics 2009–10*.

adjudicative panel which includes lay expertise from both sides of the industry. This is only partially compensated for by the growth in diversity of those appointed as employment judges or lay members. Although there has been some increase in the selection of women and people with disabilities, significant obstacles remain, particularly for black and minority ethnic candidates.[8]

Several factors have contributed to the discouraging performance of tribunals in the discrimination arena. First, like the ordinary courts, the tribunals depend wholly on the individual plaintiff to initiate the case, bring the evidence, and make the legal arguments. Not only is such a procedure premised on the assumption that discrimination complaints are purely individual, it also places an excessive burden on an individual victim of discrimination who must muster the courage to face an employer or ex-employer with a discrimination claim, as well as finding the personal and financial resources to pursue it. Moreover, each party bears his or her own expenses[9] and compensation levels are low, so that even a successful applicant could well be out of pocket. This creates a powerful disincentive on individuals to enforce the law through tribunals. The second and related difficulty concerns the obstacles to obtaining evidence. Direct discrimination is particularly difficult to prove, since most relevant evidence is in the hands of the respondent. Indirect discrimination and equal pay claims have their own difficulties, requiring complex compilation of statistics.

The third difficulty arises from the uneasy combination of a procedure which aims to be informal, simple, and accessible, with a set of legal provisions which are extremely complex, not least because of the interaction of anti-discrimination statutes with EU law and that of the HRA. This has prompted any party who can afford it to resort to legal representation. Research has repeatedly shown that a legally represented applicant in a discrimination case is more likely to be successful at a hearing than one who appears in person. Respondents are also more likely to be successful if they are legally represented.[10] Although the tribunal is meant to assist an unrepresented party, this role creates an

---

[8] Bob Hepple, *Equality: The New Framework* (Hart Publishing, 2011), ch 7; Judicial Appointments Commission, *Official Statistics Bulletin* (February 2010); Tribunals Service, *Statistics of the Employment Tribunals: Members Selections and Recommendations for Appointment Exercise showing Diversity held across Great Britain from August 2009 to February 2010* (2010).

[9] Unless one party acts unreasonably: Industrial Tribunals (Constitution and Rules of Procedure) Regulations 1993, Sch 1 para 12 (SI 1993/2687).

[10] Hepple, Coussey, and Choudhury, above n 5, para 4.34.

awkward tension with its adjudicative function. As a result, the number of claimants with legal representation before an employment tribunal has grown exponentially in recent years.[11] Yet legal aid is not available before tribunals, and legal costs are not awarded to the successful party, except where one of the parties has acted unreasonably. Moreover, the increasing role of lawyers in tribunal hearings has meant that some of the speed, informality, and inexpensiveness of the tribunal system are inevitably sacrificed.

The fourth factor contributing to the limited impact of the tribunal system is that, again like the courts, the procedure is essentially adversarial, processing the case as a bipolar dispute between two individuals, diametrically opposed, to be resolved on a winner-takes-all basis.[12] This all-or-nothing response leaves no room for compromise or synthesis. It is only outside the court process, in settlements, that compromise may be reached; indeed parties are encouraged to do so by the statutory provision for conciliation on request or on the initiative of an ACAS conciliation officer.[13] However, while the process of settlement may be more flexible than a full hearing, settlement is more intensely individualist. As Dickens shows, the primary aim of the ACAS conciliation process is to reach a compromise, rather than to eliminate discrimination or enforce individual entitlements. Indeed, ACAS has consistently resisted the suggestion that is should prioritize legal results, preferring to characterize its role as one of problem-solving.[14] Settlements reached through ACAS conciliation are a matter for the parties themselves and are not publicized. No precedents are created, nor guiding principles for society as a whole. The tension between private compromise and public adversarialism is particularly problematic in test cases.

There are several ways in which these difficulties could be overcome. First, wider standing rules can significantly ameliorate the burden on individual complainants by permitting institutional litigators, non-governmental organizations (NGO), and trade unions to bring proceedings. Such rules entail a recognition that discrimination is not

---

[11] eg, the number of legally represented claimants. leapt from 67,442 in 2005–6 to 161,900 in 2009–10. (This figure includes claimants for unfair dismissal and other rights covered by employment tribunals.) Figures in this paragraph are taken from Ministry of Justice Tribunals Service, *Employment Tribunal and EAT Statistics 2009–10*.

[12] A Chayes, 'The Role of the Judge in Public Law Litigation' (1976) 89 Harv L Rev 1281.

[13] Employment Tribunals Act 1996, s 18.

[14] L Dickens, 'The Road is Long: Thirty Years of Employment Discrimination Legislation in Britain' (2007) 45 British Journal of Industrial Relations 463–94 at 480.

just a question of individual justice. Social discrimination necessarily affects a group of individuals, and there should be legal mechanisms to permit remedial action to be taken on the part of the whole group. Particularly significant would be a provision which took the burden off the complainant entirely. Some progress has been made by giving the Equality and Human Rights Commission (EHRC) the power to bring proceedings in its own right.[15] However, the Commission's limited resources mean that this power will only be used strategically. This is discussed further below.

A second possibility is the representative action. This would give the power to a trade union or NGO to bring an action on behalf of a class of persons, all of whom would benefit from the litigation of common issues. However, existing powers to bring such a procedure into force have not been utilized.[16] One step further would be a fully fledged class action. Class actions aim to assist plaintiffs in cases in which an injury simultaneously affects many individuals, and involves law so complex that for any one individual to sue entails disproportionate expense.[17] The class suit is a particularly flexible type of joint action because any member of the injured group may sue on behalf of the whole group. There is no need to organize all the victims before the trial or to prove that the spokesperson is representative. Instead, participation of all plaintiffs is deferred until after the trial: all members of the group are entitled to participate in the end result and, by the same token, all share the burden of expenses on a *quantum meruit* basis. Trade unions and NGOs argued forcefully for the inclusion of representative or class actions into the EA 2010, especially for equal pay claims, but this was opposed by the Confederation of British Industries (CBI). Neither procedure was in the event incorporated in the Act.

All the solutions canvassed thus far are premised on finding an individual victim. However, given the institutional nature of discrimination, it is particularly important to be in a position to challenge a discriminatory rule even if it is not possible to identify a specific victim. For example, women and ethnic minorities may be deterred from applying for certain types of jobs because of indirect discrimination; yet such practices should still be open to challenge.[18] It is thus of great importance that the ECJ has recognized that discrimination can be

---

[15] EA 2006, s 30.
[16] Employment Tribunals Act 1996.
[17] H Kalven and M Rosenfield, 'The Contemporary Function of the Class Suit' (1940) 8 University of Chicago L Rev 684.
[18] See Hepple, Coussey, and Choudhury, above n 5, para 4.24.

committed even if no victim has been identified. In *Firma Feryn,*[19] an employer publicly let it be known that, under its recruitment policy, it would not recruit any employees of a certain ethnic or racial origin. The Court recognized that a public declaration of this type would dissuade members of these groups from applying in the first place, hindering their access to the labour market. A central aim of the Race Directive, namely 'to foster conditions for a socially inclusive labour market',[20] would be hard to achieve if the scope of the Directive were to be limited to cases in which an unsuccessful candidate for a post brought legal proceedings against the employer. Reflecting this principle, the Equality Act (EA) 2010 has now extended the powers of the EHRC to use its enforcement powers whether or not it knows or suspects that a person has been or may be affected by an unlawful act. Significantly, an unlawful act includes both direct and indirect discrimination, and also applies to arrangements to act in a way which would be a contravention if applied to an individual.[21]

A further problem with tribunals identified above was the difficulty of obtaining evidence. In a small gesture towards alleviating this difficulty, the statute permits the complainant to serve a statutory questionnaire on the respondent prior to institution of proceedings.[22] However, its effect is limited. Although the answers are admissible in evidence, the employer is under little pressure to respond. At most, a court or tribunal may draw an inference from an evasive or equivocal answer or a failure to respond within eight weeks.

A more helpful approach has been to shift the burden of proof to the respondent once the applicant has made out a prima facie case of discrimination. Such a principle, first developed by the ECJ, was initially given statutory endorsement in relation to sex discrimination,[23] and then extended to race for the purposes of the Race Directive,[24] and to sexual orientation, disability, age, and religion and belief for the purposes of the Employment Directive.[25] They are now consolidated in the

---

[19] Case C-54/07 *Centrum voor Gelijkheid van Kansen en voor Racismebestrijding v Firma Feryn NV* [2008] ICR 1390 (ECJ).

[20] Recital 8, preamble to Directive 2000/43.

[21] EA 2010, Sch 26 para 13 inserting EA 2006, s 24A(4).

[22] EA 2010, s 138. See previously SDA, s 74; RRA, s 65; Disability Discrimination Act 1995 (DDA), s 56; and see also Fair Employment and Treatment (Northern Ireland) Order 1998, art 44.

[23] Directive 97/80 [1997] OJ L14/6, extended to the UK by Directive 98/52 [1998] L205/66.

[24] Council Directive 2000/43/EC, Art 8.

[25] Council Directive 2000/78/EC, Art 10.

EA 2010 and apply to all claims of direct discrimination, indirect discrimination, harassment, and victimization. According to section 136 of the Act, 'if there are facts from which the court could decide, in the absence of any other explanation, that a person (A) contravened the provision concerned, the court must hold that the contravention occurred' unless 'A shows that A did not contravene the provision'. Also problematic, as we have seen, is the absence of legal aid to bring proceedings before a tribunal. This has been somewhat mitigated by the power of the EHRC to give assistance to complainants, including the funding of legal representation.[26] The former Commissions took different views of the function of their powers. Both the Equal Opportunities Commission (EOC) and the Disability Rights Commission (DRC) used their powers strategically, providing support in the interests of clarifying the law. By contrast, the Commission for Racial Equality (CRE) attempted to assist anyone who had an arguable case, only resorting to the test case strategy in the last years of its existence.[27] The EHRC has followed the route of strategic litigation. Cases which qualify for support include those which clarify an important point of law or would have a significant impact on a particular sector. Support for a case might also be forthcoming if it challenges multiple discrimination, or challenges a policy known to cause significant disadvantage.[28] However, the budgetary constraints on the Commission, like its predecessors, make it inevitable that only a small number of complainants receive financial assistance. Thus most individual litigants must rely on their own resources or support from trade unions or other voluntary bodies.[29]

(II) COUNTY COURTS, THE HIGH COURT, AND THE ECJ

Despite their limitations, tribunals still retain an advantage in terms of informality, cost, and speed over the county[30] and sheriff courts,[31] which have jurisdiction over discrimination cases involving education, public functions, premises, associations, and the provision of goods, services, and facilities to the public.[32] Of all the procedures, this one

---

[26] EA 2006, s 28. This power was previously held by the EOC (SDA, s 75(1)); CRE (RRA, s 66); and DRC (Disability Rights Commission Act 1999, s 12).

[27] B Hepple, *The Equality Act* (Hart Publishing, 2010), ch 7.

[28] EHRC Legal Strategy 2008–9. Available at: <http://www.equalityhumanrights.com/legal-and-policy/legal-strategy-consultations/>.

[29] Hepple, above n 27, ch 7.   [30] England and Wales.

[31] Scotland.   [32] EA 2010, s 114.

has been the object of most widespread dissatisfaction.[33] Only a handful of cases come before the county courts each year, a reflection of the formality, cost, and protracted nature of the county court process. The greater expense of this avenue of adjudication is in part accounted for by the fact that applicants have to pay court fees and may face an order for costs or expenses if unsuccessful. In addition, county court judges have little knowledge or experience of discrimination claims. It has therefore been suggested that all discrimination claims whether or not they involve employment should be commenced in employment tribunals, with the possibility of transfer to a county court if appropriate or if the parties so request.[34] However, this suggestion was not taken up in the EA 2010. Instead, a small gesture has been made in the direction of improving county court expertise in the field, by making provision requiring a judge or sheriff to appoint an assessor unless satisfied that there are good reasons for not doing so.[35] This is particularly important in the light of the likely increase in the workload of county courts resulting from the extension of protection in non-employment areas to cover more protected characteristics than previously.

More effective is the application for judicial review to the High Court. This procedure departs in significant ways from the traditional adversarial mould. Most importantly, public law remedies have effects well beyond the individual litigant. By striking down the discriminatory decision rather than focusing on the effect on an individual, judicial review can potentially change a discriminatory practice to the benefit of a whole class of present and future victims. The case of *R v Secretary of State, ex p EOC*[36] is the most dramatic example of the potential of this procedure. In that case, the requirement that part-time workers work continuously for five years in order to qualify for employment protection rights was struck down on the grounds that it breached the Equal Treatment Directive. In one fell swoop, all part-time workers were able to benefit. Also of great significance was the decision of the House of Lords that the EOC had standing to initiate judicial review proceedings. This opened up an important arena for public interest litigation spearheaded by the Commissions. The EHRC now has statutory standing to pursue judicial review cases.[37]

---

[33] Hepple, Coussey, and Choudhury, above n 5, para 4.13.
[34] Ibid, paras 4.13 and 4.14.   [35] EA 2010, s 114(7), (8).
[36] [1995] 1 AC 1 (HL).   [37] EA 2006, s 30.

Forays of this type into the public law arena are limited to cases characterized as public by the courts.[38] Nevertheless, the coming into force of the HRA has opened up a new avenue for judicial review. Under the HRA, all courts and tribunals have the duty to subject any executive decision, common law principle, or primary legislation to human rights scrutiny. Although only the High Court, Court of Appeal, and Supreme Court have jurisdiction to declare primary legislation incompatible with Convention rights, all courts must attempt to interpret legislation as compatible with Convention rights, ensure the common law develops consistently with human rights, and subject executive decision-making to human rights scrutiny. As we have seen, a number of landmark cases have come before the courts for judicial review on the grounds of breach of Article 14 of the European Convention on Human Rights (ECHR). Breach of the 'public sector duty' to promote equality is also subject to judicial review.

A further important adjudicative mechanism has been the ECJ. Under the special reference procedure, any tribunal or court may refer a question of EU law to the ECJ for definitive resolution. A number of seminal test cases have been litigated along this route, and this has increased with the extension of EU law to cover a wider range of protected grounds. There are several difficulties with this route, however. Unless a case is supported by the EHRC, it is a daunting project for an individual litigant to persist with litigation which could take years to complete. Moreover, the procedure before the ECJ itself is very different from that of the domestic courts. The emphasis is on written rather than oral presentations, and a central role is played by the Advocate General, who gives an influential opinion on each case. Finally, no dissenting judgments are given. The pretence at unanimity, or the even more basic notion that the law must be seen to produce only one answer, means that in practice a judgment is often a series of compromises, rather than a principled opinion.

(III) REMEDIES

Probably the most serious failing of the adjudication process has been in the nature of its remedies. As with the adversarial system as a whole, remedies are limited by their focus on the individual. Instead of engaging actively in forward-looking reform of the type essential to achieve comprehensive restructuring, the primary remedy available in

---

[38] *R v East Berkshire Health Authority, ex p Walsh* [1985] QB 152 (CA).

complaints to tribunals is in the form of monetary compensation. When employment tribunals (then known as industrial tribunals) were created, it was not thought appropriate to entrust them with an injunctive remedy. Nor do they have the power of ordering reinstatement or re-engagement in discrimination cases, despite having such power in unfair dismissal cases. Instead, tribunals are armed with the timid weapon of a recommendation, which requests the employer to take specified steps to obviate or reduce the adverse effects of the contravention.[39] An employer who fails to comply with the recommendation is treated gently in comparison with the vehemence of the sanction for contempt of an injunction. Failure to comply is not penalized if the respondent has a 'reasonable excuse'[40] and the standard of such justification is deliberately low.[41] If no such excuse is established, the sanction is mild: failure to comply with a recommendation is penalized merely by an increase in compensation,[42] in stark contrast with the hefty fine or even imprisonment which is the consequence of failure to comply with an injunction.

Until the EA 2010, even the recommendation was individualized: rather than reaching into structural causes of discrimination, the tribunal was merely empowered to recommend action to obviate or reduce the adverse effect on the complainant and then only if it appeared to the tribunal to be practicable.[43] There was therefore no power to make a recommendation that discriminatory practices be changed for the benefit of others.[44] The EA 2010 has now helpfully widened the scope of the recommendation, so that it can require action to be taken for the benefit of others. For example, the tribunal could recommend that the respondent should introduce an equal opportunities policy; retrain its staff; ensure its harassment policy is more effectively implemented; or set up a review panel to deal with equal opportunities and grievance procedures.[45] However, such a recommendation can be ignored with impunity: there is no power to award further compensation for failure to comply with a recommendation which is only aimed at obviating the adverse effect on others.[46] Recommendations are in any event conspicuous

---

[39] EA 2010, s 124(2)(c).
[40] EA 2010, s 124(7) (previously SDA, s 65(3); RRA, s 56(4); DDA, s 8(5)).
[41] *Nelson v Tyne and Wear Passenger Transport Executive* [1978] ICR 183 (EAT).
[42] EA 2010, s 124(7).
[43] SDA, s 65(1)(c); RRA, s 56(1)(c); DDA, s 8(1)(c).
[44] See eg *Noone v North West Thames Regional Health Authority (No 2)* [1988] IRLR 530 (CA), *British Gas v Sharma* [1999] IRLR 101 (EAT).
[45] EA 2010, s 124(3) explanatory notes para 414.
[46] Ibid, s 124(7).

by their absence in the repertoire of remedies generally used by tribunals. In 2009, recommendations were made in a mere seven cases, less than half the number in the previous two years.[47]

This may be contrasted with the mandatory injunction, used in the US in many of the important equal treatment cases. Unlike compensation, which is retrospective, individualized, and all-or-nothing, the mandatory injunction operates as a continuing constraint on future action. This challenges the adversarial system in several fundamental ways. First, the court is actively involved in balancing the interests not only of the parties before it but those of others who are inevitably affected. Secondly, because the focus shifts away from past conduct such as fault and intention, onto future consequences, the nature of the relevant evidence changes. Evidence on social facts is required, and wider interest representation necessitated. Thirdly, the prospective nature of the remedy creates the incentive for parties to reach a compromise. Finally, the judge is no longer a passive arbiter, but an active participant in the process.[48] Most importantly, the judge maintains a continuing role in mediating, supervising, and even managing the operation of the decree. The result is radical. Instead of litigation functioning as a private dispute settlement, it operates as a manner of carrying out a policy.[49] The use of mandatory injunctions in the US in this context has been far from uncontroversial, raising questions both about the suitability of judges in making policy decisions of this type, and the legitimacy and accuracy of social science information.[50] Nevertheless, it forms an important attempt to surmount the restrictions of the adversarial approach.

The substitute for dynamic and interactive remedies in Britain has been the almost exclusive reliance on compensation, which satisfies the law's neutrality and individualism by granting a one-off remedy to the individual alone. At the same time, there remains an intense ambivalence as to the function of compensation. Is it deterrent, or compensatory, or both? The legislation itself has always been partly based on an assumption that only if the party is at fault, can it be right to expect him or her to pay compensation. This was most floridly manifested in the Race Relations Act 1976 (RRA), which did not permit compensation to

---

[47] (2010) 201 EOR 12.

[48] O M Fiss, 'The Forms of Justice' (1979) 93 Harvard L Rev 1 at 16–28.

[49] Chayes, above n 12, at 1288–96.

[50] See the discussion in Chayes, above n 12, and Fiss, above n 48. See also M G Yudof, 'School Desegregation: Legal Realism and Social Sciences' in [1978] Law and Contemporary Problems 57.

be awarded for unintentional indirect discrimination.[51] A corresponding restriction in the Sex Discrimination Act 1975 (SDA) was finally removed in 1996, after a number of tribunals had held that it contravened the Equal Treatment Directive.[52] The principle still lingers, however. Under the EA 2010, there is still a difference in the remedial approach where unintentional indirect discrimination has been proved. In such a case, a tribunal should not award damages without first considering whether to make a declaration or recommendation instead; and a court should similarly consider whether to make any other disposal.[53]

At the same time, courts and tribunals have been unwilling to use damages in a punitive form. In principle, punitive damages are available for statutory tort cases, if compensation is insufficient to punish a defendant for oppressive and arbitrary conduct.[54] However, although tribunals have on occasion been prepared to impose an award of punitive damages, this has generally been overturned on appeal. The EAT[55] has emphatically ruled out the award of punitive damages in race discrimination cases. In another case, it refused to countenance the possibility of punitive damages against the Ministry of Defence for the dismissal of a servicewoman on grounds of her pregnancy.[56] This is despite the recommendation of the Law Commission that punitive damages should be awarded in any case, including a discrimination claim, where in committing a wrong or in conduct subsequent to the wrong, the defendant deliberately and outrageously disregarded the plaintiff's rights. There are clearly discrimination cases in which the tribunal or court should be able to set damages at a level which would both deter the discriminator, and express the strong disapproval of the court.[57] There is also a recognized principle that punitive damages may be awarded for oppressive acts by public bodies. It was under this jurisdiction that the Court of Appeal has on one occasion upheld the award of punitive damages against a local authority for discriminating on grounds of race and sex against a black woman.[58]

---

[51] RRA, s 57(3).
[52] Sex Discrimination and Equal Pay (Miscellaneous Amendments) Regulations 1996 (SI 1996/438), reg 2(4), repealing SDA, s 66(3).
[53] EA 2010, ss 119(5) and 124(4), (5).
[54] *Kuddus v Chief Constable of Leicestershire Police* [2001] UKHL 29, [2002] AC 122.
[55] *Deane v London Borough of Ealing* [1993] IRLR 209 (EAT).
[56] *Ministry of Defence v Meredith* [1995] IRLR 539 (EAT).
[57] See Hepple, Coussey, and Choudhury, above n 5, recommendation 50.
[58] *City of Bradford v Arora* [1991] 2 QB 507 (CA).

The primary aim of damages for unlawful discrimination therefore remains compensatory. The measure of damage is similar to that in tort claims, namely to put the victim into the position he or she would have been in had the wrong not occurred. Until November 1993,[59] compensation was subject to an upper limit, which frequently kept awards far below their real level. However, the path-breaking case of *Marshall (No 2)*[60] forced a repeal of the statutory limit on the grounds that it infringed the Equal Treatment Directive.[61] Most important was the ECJ's emphatic restatement of the principle that Member States must guarantee real and effective judicial protection of the right to equality of opportunity in a way that has a real deterrent effect on the employer. The removal of the statutory limit had an important impact, with compensation levels immediately moving steeply upwards.[62] While the highest awards in 1999 were over £180,000 in a sex discrimination case,[63] this figure leapt to nearly £442,500 in 2009.[64] Nevertheless, it is only in isolated cases that such high awards are achieved. The median award remains low. For the period 2006–9, this was less than £10,000 across all jurisdictions, with awards for race discrimination remaining well below £7,000.[65]

A similar pattern can be seen in relation to injury to feelings.[66] The Court of Appeal has set out three bands of award for injury to feelings:[67] a top band (£18,000–£30,000) for the most serious cases, such as a lengthy campaign of sexual harassment; a middle band (£6,000–£18,000) for serious cases not in the worst category; and a bottom band (£500–£6,000) for less serious cases or one-off occurrences. The court stressed that the bottom band should rarely be used since it suggests that the injury is trivial. However, in practice, awards for injury to feelings are predominantly in this category, with the median award in each year between 2007 and 2009 ranging between £4,500 and £4,800. It

---

[59]   Sex Discrimination and Equal Pay (Remedies) Regulations 1993 (SI 1993/2798).
[60]   Case C-271/91 *Marshall v Southampton and South West Hampshire Area Health Authority (No 2)* [1993] ECR I-4367.
[61]   Directive 76/207 [1976] OJ L39/40, Art 6.
[62]   (1994) 57 EOR 11–21.
[63]   (2000) 93 EOR 11–22.
[64]   *Scanlon v Redcar & Cleveland BC* (2010) EOR 10 or *Redcar and Cleveland Borough Council v Mrs P Scanlon* 2008 WL 2872520 (EAT), 20 May 2008.
[65]   Figures from (2009) 189 EOR 8–21; (2009) 190 EOR 19–26; (2010) 202 EOR 8–20; (2010) 201 EOR 7–21.
[66]   EA 2010, ss 119(4) and 124(6): previously SDA, s 66; RRA, s 57(4); DDA, s 8(4).
[67]   *Vento v Chief Constable of West Yorkshire Police (No 2)* [2003] IRLR 102 (CA); *Da'Bell v National Society for the Prevention of Cruelty to Children* [2010] IRLR 19.

is clear, therefore, that the levels of compensation awarded are far from adequate to discharge the State's entire remedial duty.

(IV) A CRITIQUE OF THE ADVERSARIAL STRUCTURE

It is arguable that discrimination law, by its nature, requires a departure from the traditional adversarial structure, even in the more informal setting of a tribunal. As Chayes demonstrates, legislation which explicitly modifies and regulates basic social and economic realities challenges the traditional adversarial model.[68] The bipolar structure is particularly inappropriate for public and private interactions which are not bilateral transactions between individuals, but have wide social implications. This in turn requires a transformation of the adjudicative structure from what Fiss calls a 'dispute resolution' model to a model of 'structural reform'.[69] In the dispute-resolution model, the victim, spokesperson, and beneficiary are automatically combined in one plaintiff. In the newer model, the victim is not an individual but a group; and the spokesperson is not necessarily one of the group. In addition, because a beneficiary need not prove individual damage, the class of beneficiaries may well be wider than the victims. Thus, all members of a particular racial group might benefit from the institution of prohibitions on racial harassment, even though not everyone has individually suffered from racial harassment. A similar analysis applies to the defendant. Whereas in the dispute-resolution model, the defendant is both the wrongdoer and the provider of a remedy, in the model of structural reform, the wrongdoer disappears, and instead the focus is on the body able to achieve reform. In the result, the individualism of the adversarial system is supplanted by a group-based model. Thus the individual no longer bears the burden of enforcing her own equality rights.

There are several elements which could be addressed within the existing structure in recognition of these insights. One is to retain the essentially dispute-oriented adjudicative method, but lift the burden off the plaintiff. We have seen that this can be facilitated by widening standing rules to permit public interest litigators, or representative or class actions. Another is to shift the burden of proof, and to permit litigation in relation to breaches without having to identify the victim. As we saw above, only limited steps in this direction have been taken. A further and even more radical step would be to move away from a dispute-resolution model altogether. Two possibilities are discussed

---

[68] Chayes, above n 12, p 1288.   [69] See Fiss, above n 48.

here. The first is enforcement by an agency, in this case the EHRC, and the second is the use of positive duties to promote equality.

II AGENCY ENFORCEMENT

Some of the weaknesses of an adjudicative structure have been addressed by the powers given to the EHRC[70] to initiate and conduct a 'formal investigation' into cases of suspected unlawful discrimination.[71] The formal investigation departs from adversarialism in several key respects. As a start, it is an active rather than passive process. The Commission has the power to initiate the investigation, thus inviting a strategic approach instead of an ad hoc series of actions. Moreover, it has strong information-gathering powers, including the ability to demand written or oral evidence and the production of documents. The formal investigation also deviates significantly from the individualism of the tribunal procedure. The power is specifically directed at a practice of discrimination rather than at a particular discriminatory act against an individual. Nor is the situation characterized as an all-or-nothing bipolar dispute. Instead, the investigation is intended to be an interactive process, during which the Commission aims to secure a change in discriminatory practices through discussion, negotiation, and conciliation. Its remedial powers are therefore essentially forward-looking. Thus the Commission has the power to issue an 'unlawful act notice', which can include a requirement that the respondent prepare and act on an action plan to avoid a repetition of the unlawful act. Judicial remedies are harnessed as a last resort: during the subsequent five-year period, the Commission can apply to court for an order requiring a person to act in accordance with the action plan. Failure to comply without reasonable excuse may be punishable with a fine.[72]

The formal investigation has the potential to stimulate significant change in structures of discrimination. In its early years, the CRE used its powers energetically, initiating 24 investigations beteen 1977 and 1982 alone. Its aim was not simply to enforce the law, but to uncover structural discrimination and trigger wider policy and procedural change.[73] However, the novelty of the procedure and the challenge it poses to deeply entrenched visions of adversarialism led to a reaction

---

[70] Originally the EOC, CRE, and DRC and now the EHRC.
[71] SDA, ss 57–61; RRA, ss 48–62.
[72] EA 2006, s 21.   [73] Dickens, above n 14, p 475.

against it by the courts. In a series of judicial review cases against the CRE, the formal investigation was trammelled with a chain of restrictive procedural requirements intended to protect the respondent against what was considered to be a harsh and inquisitorial procedure.[74] Lord Denning indeed went so far as to characterize the formal investigation as akin to the Spanish Inquisition.[75] Most damaging was the prohibition on the use of the power to investigate general evidence of structural inequality. In two cases in the 1980s, the House of Lords held that these powers could only be exercised if there was a reasonable suspicion that the named person had committed unlawful acts.[76] Given that there are unlikely to be monitoring records or other open evidence of discrimination, this is a significant obstacle. These procedural obstacles, combined with a shortage of resources and an absence of strategic use of the power by the Commissions,[77] meant that the impact of the formal investigation was disappointing. Indeed, between 1977 and 1995, the EOC conducted a mere 11 formal investigations, and none at all in the following decade.[78]

The opportunity to lift some of these restrictions presented itself with the creation of the EHRC in 2006. New energy could have been given to formal investigations by giving the Commission power to conduct 'equality audits', as its Irish counterpart can do, regardless of whether there is specific evidence of unlawful discrimination.[79] However, the restrictive jurisprudence of the courts was merely enshrined in statute. The Commission may only conduct a formal investigation against a named person if it suspects that the latter may have committed an unlawful act.[80] In addition, the power is hedged about with procedural protections for the respondent. This includes at least three opportunities to make representations: once about the terms of reference, once about the subject of the investigation, and once, with as much as 28 days' notice, about the final report.[81]

---

[74] *CRE v Prestige Group plc* [1984] 1 WLR 335 (HL), *London Borough of Hillingdon v CRE* [1982] AC 779 (HL); *R v Commission for Racial Equality, ex p Amari Plastics* [1982] QB 1194; and see generally G Appleby and E Ellis, 'Formal Investigations' [1984] PL 236.

[75] *Science Research Council v Nassé* [1979] 1 QB 144 (CA) at 172.

[76] *CRE v Prestige Group plc*, above n 74, *London Borough of Hillingdon v CRE*, above n 74.

[77] Appleby and Ellis, above n 74, at p 260.

[78] Hepple, above n 27, ch 7.

[79] C O'Cinneide, 'The Commission for Equality and Human Rights: A New Institution for New and Uncertain Times' [2007] 36 ILJ 141–62.

[80] EA 2006, s 20(2).

[81] Ibid, Sch 2 paras 3, 6–8, and s 20(4).

As well as the formal investigation, the EHRC inherits from its predecessors the power to undertake an inquiry, which is closer to a fact-finding exercise than an enforcement mechanism. The resulting report and recommendations are not binding: at most, a court or tribunal may have regard to the finding of an inquiry.[82] Although the inquiry may relate to one or more named persons, the Commission cannot use the mechanism of an inquiry to investigate whether a named person has committed an unlawful act. Nor may it state in its report that a named person has committed such an act. Nevertheless, the Commission's power to obtain information, documents, and oral evidence is strictly circumscribed and subject to judicial control. Its terms of reference must be publicized, with notice to any person specified therein, and it must send a draft of its report to any person who is the subject of adverse findings and give them 28 days to make representations.

The main power of the inquiry and the subsequent report is in their ability to publicize inequalities. If used strategically, an inquiry can uncover important areas of structural discrimination. The EHRC has indeed energetically pursued this possibility, conducting several well-targeted inquiries in its first years of operation. The inquiry into financial services was particularly illuminating, revealing an average pay gap of a shocking 55 per cent between the gross average annual salary of men and women in the sector. Further investigation showed that this was primarily due to the role of bonuses, with men receiving five times the performance pay of women. Nor was there any change in sight, with women in new jobs still earning well below their male counterparts.

However, the ability of the inquiry to generate change is doubtful. The recommendations in inquiry reports are 'light touch' and general. Because no particular organization or person can be named, they lack focus. For example, the inquiry into the financial sector encouraged 'organizations within the financial sector' to institute training on diversity, incorporate equality into organizational objectives, conduct and publicize equal pay audits, and ensure that parental support schemes are in place and effective. In addition, it recommended the appointment of a board member to 'set the tone, mainstream issues and drive change'. There is little incentive for organizations in the financial sector to respond to such encouragement; and even if they did, it is not certain

---

[82] Ibid, Sch 2 paras 2–5, 9–14, 17, and s 16.

that the pay gap would diminish as a result. The statute does permit the Commission to use evidence acquired in the course of the inquiry to launch a formal investigation;[83] and this might be a way of taking the findings forward in a more concrete way.

More effective would be a 'partnership' approach, which facilitated cooperation between the Commission and the employer or other relevant body, but with a background sanction acting as an incentive to agreement. This would entail giving the EHRC the power to enter into binding agreements with private or public sector bodies, according to which the latter undertake to formulate and implement an equality plan. A power of this sort was used systematically and strategically in Northern Ireland in order to achieve the statutory aim of fair participation of Protestants and Roman Catholics. Indeed, between 1997 and 1999 alone, the Fair Employment Commission entered into approximately 60 such agreements each year. While some of the agreements were binding, the majority were voluntary. McCrudden et al demonstrated that the existence and careful monitoring of these affirmative action agreements coincided with a trend towards more integrated workforces. Their research suggests that the Commission enjoyed some success in its attempts to achieve fair participation through the negotiation and monitoring of affirmative action agreements in the public and private sectors in Northern Ireland.[84] Heath et al also showed that it has been more effective to enter into agreements which aim at institutional change than to embark on lawsuits.[85]

A similar power has been included in the armoury of the EHRC. The Commission has the power to reach an agreement with a named person whereby the latter agrees to refrain from committing the unlawful act as well as to take the positive steps specified in the agreement.[86] Such steps could include the preparation of a plan aimed at avoiding unlawful acts. In return, the Commission must undertake not to use its enforcement powers (including conducting a formal investigation or issuing an 'unlawful act notice'). Failure to comply with the agreement can lead to proceedings in the county or sheriff courts, including, exceptionally,

---

[83] Ibid, Sch 2 paras 2–5, 9–14, 17, and s 16.

[84] C McCrudden, R Ford, and A Heath, 'Legal Regulation of Affirmative Action in Northern Ireland: An Empirical Assessment' [2004] 24 OJLS 363.

[85] A Heath, P Clifford, H Hamill, C McCrudden, and R Muttarak, 'The Impact of the Northern Ireland Affirmative Action Programme on Catholic and Protestant Employment' (Dondena, Centre for Research on Social Dynamics, Spring 2009).

[86] EA 2006, s 23.

the possibility of an order requiring the person to comply or take whatever steps the court specifies.[87] However, the Commission cannot enter into such an agreement unless it thinks the person concerned has committed an unlawful act.[88] This is likely to act as a severe constraint on the Commission's powers to enter into such agreements. Unlike its Northern Ireland counterpart, the Commission does not have the power to demand triennial reports from employers. This leaves little scope for the Commission to uncover unlawful acts, and therefore to embark on the process of reaching agreement.

III 'FOURTH GENERATION' EQUALITY: POSITIVE DUTIES

The most important response to the individualized, retrospective, and passive enforcement and remedial structure has taken the form of positive duties to promote equality. Positive duties are proactive rather than reactive. They aim to identify and redress unlawful discrimination even if there has been no complaint by an individual victim. But they go further. Proactive measures are also preventative. Duty-holders should consider the impact on equality of any new or established policies or legislation and adjust them accordingly. Equally importantly, proactive measures aim to promote equality, for example by introducing measures to facilitate the entry of under-represented groups or through family friendly measures.

Positive duties have the potential to overcome the central deficiencies of the complaints-led model identified above. Most importantly, the initiative lies with policy-makers and implementers, service providers, or employers. This relieves individual victims of the burden and expense of litigation: instead, the duty to bring about change lies with those with the power and capacity to do so. Secondly, change is systematic, instead of consisting in reactions to ad hoc claims brought by individuals. The institutional and structural causes of inequality can be diagnosed and addressed collectively and institutionally. This means that the right to equality is available to all, not just those who complain. Thirdly, there is no need to prove a breach of the law or find a named perpetrator. Rather than determining fault and punishing conduct, the focus is on systemic discrimination and the creation of institutional mechanisms for their

---

[87] Ibid, s 24(2), (3).   [88] Ibid, s 2(2).

elimination.[89] This also avoids the adversarial attitudes of the parties. Rather than viewing equality as a site of conflict and resistance, equality should be regarded as a common goal, to be achieved cooperatively.[90] Finally, proactive models ideally broaden the participatory role of civil society, both in norm-setting and in norm-enforcing. This participatory dimension fundamentally influences the nature of the norms themselves. Given that they are to be implemented programmatically over a period of time, proactive models tend to produce norms which are dynamic and renegotiable.

But at the same time, these very innovations carry with them substantial challenges, which need further attention.[91] The rest of this part considers some of these challenges, drawing on the experience of various jurisdictions. In order to do so, it is helpful to distinguish between different types of proactive approaches. All lie on the interface between law and politics and it is therefore useful to distinguish between them according to the extent to which they mobilize or interact with legal norms. The approach which is most policy-led is that of mainstreaming. Mainstreaming means that equality is not just an add-on or after-thought to policy, but is one of the factors taken into account in every policy and executive decision.[92] 'The reactive and negative approach of anti-discrimination is replaced by pro-active, anticipatory and integrative methods.'[93] It is a 'social justice-led approach to policy making in which equal opportunities principles, strategies and practices are integrated into the everyday work of government and other public bodies'.[94] Although these policies originate from equality norms, they are autonomous from them. At EU level, mainstreaming strategies have given a powerful boost to the effectiveness of sex equality legislation. Also of increasing importance is the role of the open method of

---

[89] Pay Equity Taskforce and Departments of Justice and Human Resources Development Canada, *Pay Equity: A New Approach to a Fundamental Right* (2004) (hereinafter 'Canadian Taskforce'), p 147.

[90] Ibid, p 98.

[91] This section draws substantially on S Fredman, 'Changing the Norm: Positive Duties in Equal Treatment Legislation' (2005) 12 Maastricht Journal of European and Comparative Law 369–98; S Fredman, 'Making Equality Effective: The Role of Proactive Measures' (European Commission, Brussels 2009).

[92] Commission Communication, *Incorporating Equal Opportunities for Women and Men into all Community Policies and Activities*, COM(96) final; see generally T Rees, *Mainstreaming Equality in the European Union: Education, Training and Labour Market Policies* (Routledge, 1998).

[93] Hepple, Coussey, and Choudhury, above n 5, para 3.8.

[94] F MacKay and K Bilton, *Learning From Experience: Lessons in Mainstreaming Equal Opportunities* (Scottish Executive Social Research, 2003), p 1.

coordination (OMC) which operates in the fields of employment, social inclusion, and pensions. The OMC moves deliberately away from the legal method and instead depends on reporting mechanisms and peer review under the coordinating auspices of the European Commission. Equality concerns are integrated or mainstreamed within the stated policy concerns. Proactive measures are also increasingly widespread in the EU, as a recent study of 27 Member States, together with Norway, Iceland, and Finland showed.[95]

At the other end of the spectrum are specific statutory duties, to take steps to achieve equality. Northern Ireland has been at the forefront of this approach. Pioneering legislation introduced in 1989 imposed a positive duty on employers to take measures to achieve fair participation of Protestant and Roman Catholic employees in their workforces.[96] Under this legislation, employers must periodically review the composition of the workforce and its employment practices to determine whether members of each of those two main communities are 'enjoying fair participation in employment in the concern'.[97] If this is not the case, then the employer is required to institute positive action in order to make progress towards fair participation. Similarly, in Canada, legislation in six provinces places a proactive duty on employers to achieve pay equity between men and women, the most innovative being that of Ontario.[98] In addition, the federal Employment Equity Act 1986 made it mandatory for federally regulated employers of 100 employees or more to produce employment equity plans, the aim being to produce a workforce which is representative of the labour market. Covering visible minorities, Aboriginal peoples, persons with disabilities, and women, the Act required employers to identify workplace barriers and to develop and implement equity plans for the four designated groups.

Between the policy-led notion of mainstreaming and the specific duties on employers lies a third approach, which is to place a statutory duty on public bodies to generate policy on equal opportunities, without prescribing what that should consist of. This was, again, pioneered in

---

[95] Fredman, 'Making Equality Effective', above n 91.

[96] Fair Employment Act 1989, now contained in the Fair Employment and Treatment (Northern Ireland) Order (FETO) 1998, Part VII; C McCrudden, 'Mainstreaming Equality in the Governance of Northern Ireland' (1999) 22:4 Fordham International LJ 1696.

[97] FETO, s 55.

[98] See eg Ontario Pay Equity Act, RSO 1990 c P7. This section also draws on the Canadian Taskforce Report (above n 89), which sums up the strengths and weaknesses of the models currently in use, and makes recommendations for future federal pay equity legislation. No legislation has yet been enacted.

Northern Ireland. Under section 75 of the Northern Ireland Act 1998, all public bodies have a duty in carrying out their functions to have due regard to the need to promote equality of opportunity between specified groups, including between men and women, between persons with dependants and those without, between persons with and without disabilities, and between persons of different religious belief, political opinion, racial group, age, marital status, or sexual orientation ('the section 75 duty').[99] British legislation soon followed suit. An amendment to the RRA, introduced in 2000, placed a positive duty on public bodies to have due regard to the need to promote equality of opportunity and good relations between people of different racial groups ('the race equality duty').[100] This was followed by a similar duty in respect of disability in 2005[101] and a gender duty a year later.[102] The EA 2010 consolidates and extends these to include all the protected characteristics (the 'public sector equality duty').[103] In a particularly innovative provision, a new duty in relation to socio-economic disadvantage is also introduced.[104] The implementation of the public sector duty has, however, been delayed until at least 2011; while the Coalition government in power since 2010 has stated its intention not to implement the socio-economic disadvantage duty at all.

The imposition of positive duties changes the whole landscape of discrimination law. The focus is no longer on the perpetrator of a discriminatory act. Instead, the spotlight is on the body in the best position to promote equality. Individual fault becomes irrelevant. One consequence of this is that the respondent is not identifiable simply from the definition of discrimination. Legislation must explicitly define and justify the choice of bodies upon whom to place the obligation. Similarly, the nature of the duty changes. Under the traditional model, individuals are required to refrain from discriminating. If they breach this duty, they are required to pay compensation to the victim. By contrast, the trigger for the duty to promote equality is not self-defining. Legislation must specify both when the duty arises, and its content. The following sections attempt to analyse positive duties under these headings. First, to whom does the duty apply? Secondly, what is the content of the duty? Thirdly, what are its aims? Fourthly, who is entitled to participate in the decision-making process, and finally, how are positive duties enforced?

---

[99] Northern Ireland Act 1998, s 75.   [100] RRA, s 71.
[101] DDA, ss 49A–D.   [102] SDA, ss 76A–C.
[103] EA 2010, s 149.   [104] Ibid, s 1.

(1) TO WHOM DOES THE DUTY APPLY?

The key to the advances represented by positive duties is that they fall not upon the perpetrator of a discriminatory act but upon the body in the best position to take action to address structural inequalities and to ensure that new policies promote equality rather than exacerbate inequalities. The question of who has such responsibility is therefore of central importance. There are a range of possible responsible bodies. It may be thought appropriate to confine the duties to public bodies, with a possible extension to private bodies with public functions. If the function is extended into the private sector, this might also include private employers, private service providers, and trade unions.

The recent survey of proactive duties among EU Member States demonstrated a wide variety of uses of such bodies. Public bodies had responsibility for taking proactive measures in 13 Member States. This might include members of the executive, from ministers, down to regional public authorities as well as public employers. In Belgium, for example, under the Gender Mainstreaming Act of 12 January 2007, the federal government as a whole and every one of its members individually are responsible for the implementation of the gender mainstreaming policy. In other cases, responsibility is general and therefore somewhat vague. Thus in Latvia, the Ministry of Welfare and the Ombudsman have very broad and indefinite obligations to take proactive measures, without any detailed obligations. Such a general allocation of responsibility runs the risk that everyone assumes that the responsibility will be carried out by someone else. It is therefore clearly more effective to specify the duty-bearer specifically. For example, in Austria, the public sector is covered by a network of institutions and responsible persons for the enforcement of equal treatment legislation: ombudspersons (up to seven in every ministry), working groups on equal treatment questions within the ministries and universities, as well as an inter-ministerial working group chaired by the Minister for Women's Affairs. The provision of a network of institutions tends to be the most effective at pinpointing responsibility. However, the risk remains that the apparatus of responsibility exists, but little action is taken in practice. As in other respects, much depends on political commitment and goodwill.[105]

In a significant number of Member States, responsibility for proactive measures also falls on trade unions. In some cases, this is limited to the

---

[105] Fredman, 'Making Equality Effective', above n 91.

duty to impart information to their members on the relevant equality
legislation, or to ensure that the collective agreements between employers and employees do not have provisions which create discrimination
on the ground of sex. In other countries it is more far-reaching. In
Iceland, the Gender Equality Act stipulates that trade unions must
deliberately work with employers to achieve equality for women and
men in the labour market. Sweden has a similar duty on trade unions to
cooperate with employers on active measures to bring about equal rights
and opportunities in working life regardless of sex, ethnicity, religion,
and belief. In Norway, trade unions and employers' organizations have a
duty to make active, targeted, and systematic efforts to promote gender
equality in their sphere of activity. Notably, however, in Germany any
suggestion of the imposition of proactive duties upon trade unions has
been rejected on the grounds that to do so would violate the freedom of
social partners (*Koalitionsfreiheit*).

Duties on trade unions are usually matched by duties on private
employers although in a handful of countries, private employers
might have duties even in the absence of duties on trade unions.[106]
In Northern Ireland, the fair employment legislation applies to public
and private employers. The Ontario pay equity legislation similarly
covers all private employers who employ more than ten employees as
well as all public employers.[107]

The British duties have always been regarded as appropriately confined to the public sector. However, in an important recognition of the
fact that a large number of functions are now contracted to private
bodies, the legislation also includes private bodies with public functions.
This means, in turn, that it is essential to draw a clear dividing line
between public and private, a distinction which remains contested. How
should the definition be drawn? Should it be left to the courts, with the
attendant uncertainty? Or should the legislation provide a list of bodies,
with the risk of rigidity? The list solution was chosen in relation to the
race equality duty, where a list of public bodies was provided in a
schedule to the Act.[108] For the gender and disability duties, by contrast,
the relevant statutory provision simply stated that a 'public authority'
includes any person who has functions of a public nature.[109] This left it
to the courts to define who was bound, following the example set by the
HRA.

---

[106] Ibid.   [107] Pay Equity Act, s 3(1).
[108] RRA, Sch 1A.   [109] SDA, s 76A; DDA, s 49B.

The EA 2010 has chosen a hybrid form. The 'list' approach is used to define public bodies. But the meaning of 'public functions' for the purposes of determining which functions of a private body are 'public', is the same as under the HRA.[110] However, courts in applying the HRA formula have taken a restrictive view of the meaning of 'public', thereby considerably narrowing the reach of human rights obligations.[111] This restrictive judicial interpretation is simply transplanted into the new legislation. While the list approach is clearly inappropriate for defining public functions, it is unfortunate that the opportunity was not taken to give a clearer statutory definition. The public body does, however, remain responsible for complying with the general duty even if it has contracted out some of its functions to private or voluntary organizations. Private bodies exercising purely private functions are not covered by the proactive duty under the EA 2010.

(II) THE NATURE OF THE DUTY

Traditional anti-discrimination legislation requires the victim to identify an act of discrimination in order to attract a compensatory remedy. Positive duties, by contrast, place the onus of identifying patterns of inequality on the body on whom the duty to promote equality lies. There are at least three levels at which proactive duties operate. The first is to provide more effective means of ensuring that existing anti-discrimination laws are fulfilled. Instead of responding only to individuals with the courage and resources to bring a complaint to a court or tribunal, the employer or public body should take the initiative in seeking out instances of unlawful discrimination and rectifying them. Moreover, rather than redressing unlawful discrimination only for the benefit of a particular individual, such an approach seeks to find collective solutions, covering all affected individuals. A second function of proactive measures is to look beyond existing anti-discrimination law and seek to promote equality. Examples might be the institution of quotas or family friendly measures. Thirdly, proactive measures aim to prevent inequality arising in the first place. This requires decision-makers to assess new policy or legislative measures to determine their impact on the protected characteristics and to adjust them if necessary ('impact assessment'). The EU report found that a significant number of Member States have instituted impact assessment of draft legislation

---

[110] EA 2010, s 150.
[111] *YL (by her litigation friend the Official Solicitor) v Birmingham CC* [2007] UKHL 27, [2007] 3 WLR 112.

and policy; and, in a few cases, impact assessment is also carried out by equality bodies or even private employers. However, few ensure that further action is taken once a negative impact has been identified, and even fewer review changes once instituted. Impact assessment might also be impeded by the shortage of resources, particularly where responsibility lies with the equality body.

Because proactive duties require the responsible body both to diagnose the problem and to set in place a process of addressing it, it is useful to isolate the elements of the duty. As a start, there should be a process of diagnosing the problem, through the collection of statistics, impact assessments, pay reviews, and other similar diagnostic devices. Arising from this diagnosis should be the formulation of a plan, optimally with full consultation of those affected. Implementation of the plan should be continually monitored and reviewed to assess whether a proactive measure is effective, to review its progress, and to readjust it if necessary. All these features are demonstrated well by legislation in Northern Ireland and Canada. As we have seen, Northern Ireland has two sets of duties: one on public bodies to pay due regard to the need to achieve equality of opportunity;[112] and one on employers in relation to fair representation of the Protestant and Roman Catholic communities. Both require an initial assessment of the scale of the problem, followed by a plan to bring about change. Thus the public duty in Northern Ireland requires public bodies to produce a scheme setting out its arrangements for assessing compliance; for assessing and consulting on the likely impact of policies on equality of opportunity; for monitoring any adverse impact of policies, for publishing results of the assessments, for training, and for ensuring and assessing public access to information and to service provided by the authority.[113] The Northern Ireland duty of fair representation in employment is more specific still. Employers must review the composition of their workforce every three years to establish whether there is fair participation of each of the two relevant communities. If they find there is not, then they must compile an affirmative action programme. Similarly, Canadian federal employment equity legislation requires employers first to identify equity issues in their workplace by doing a workforce analysis to determine whether the designated groups are under-represented compared to labour market availability. Under-representation triggers a further review to determine whether employment systems, policies, and practices pose barriers to designated

---

[112] Northern Ireland Act 1998, s 75.   [113] Ibid, Sch 9.

groups. Pay equity plans are even more specific: the Ontario pay equity legislation requires employers to determine female-dominated occupations and compare their pay to a male-dominated comparable group. Among EU Member States, the picture is mixed. There are now quite comprehensive duties to collect statistics. Alternatively, monitoring may be conducted through requiring regular reports from duty-bearers, to be assessed by a monitoring body such as the equality body or worker representatives at enterprise level. However, there is a danger that collection of data becomes an end in itself. The EU report found that although several Member States have instituted sophisticated structures for reviewing proactive measures and taking remedial steps in the light of the outcomes of monitoring, in some Member States this link was not made. One possible obstacle to monitoring might be that the collection of statistics might breach domestic confidentiality or data protection laws. In general, there are no such obstacles as long as individuals are not identified. However, the EU report found, a key source of difficulty arises in respect of equal pay where in many Member States wages are regarded as confidential. This makes it close to impossible to identify and monitor gender wage gaps at the enterprise level. A handful of Member States have dealt with this difficulty by permitting workers to disclose their wages.

The British approach has been far more deferent to public authorities' decision-making powers, preferring to leave the ultimate decision as to how to promote equality in the hands of the authority. The statutory standard is therefore a procedural one. The authority must 'pay due regard' to the need to promote equality of opportunity, but it is not expected to take particular steps in that direction. Ideally, the 'due regard' standard should introduce equality considerations into the decision-making process at an early stage, mainstreaming equality into the culture of decision-making itself. As Arden LJ put it in *Elias*:

[Legal] proceedings are not the only way of policing anti-discrimination legislation. Monitoring and self-assessment by public bodies in their decision making can also further the aims of such legislation . . . It is the clear purpose of [the race duty] to require public bodies to whom that provision applies to give advance consideration to issues of race discrimination before making any policy decision that may be affected by them. This is a salutary requirement, and this provision must be seen as an integral and important part of the mechanisms for ensuring the fulfilment of the aims of anti-discrimination legislation.[114]

---

[114] See *R (Elias) v Secretary of State for Defence* [2006] 1 WLR 3213 at para 274.

At the same time, the 'due regard' standard defers to public bodies' ultimate authority to decide how to prioritize various interests and in what ways to use their resources. This was summed up in the Code of Practice on the disability duty, which explained that

it will not always be possible for authorities to adopt the course of action which will best promote disability equality, but public authorities must ensure that they have due regard to the requirement to promote disability equality alongside other competing requirements.[115]

Ultimately, therefore, the duty is a deferent one. As Dyson LJ concluded in *Baker*, 'ultimately, how much weight [the planning officer] gave to the various factors was a matter for her... judgment'.[116]

What then does 'due regard' entail? In *Meany*, Davis J emphasized 'that public authorities must have not have "regard" but "due regard" to the matters specified. The word "due" must add something'.[117] The significance of 'due regard' as against simply 'regard' is highlighted in section 75 of the Northern Ireland Act 1998: while the public body must pay *due regard* to the need to promote equality of opportunity on a range of status grounds, it need only pay *regard* to the desirability of promoting good relations between persons of different religious belief, political opinion, or racial group. On one understanding, 'due regard' adds an element of proportionality to what would otherwise be a mere requirement to consider the relevance of equality to a particular decision. According to the Code of Practice on disability, 'due regard' entails both relevance and proportionality.

Proportionality requires greater consideration to be given to disability equality in relation to functions or policies that have the most effect on disabled people. Where changing a function or proposed policy would lead to significant benefits to disabled people, the need for such a change will carry added weight when balanced against other considerations.[118]

Similarly, the Guidance on the socio–economic disadvantage duty explains the duty as 'giving weight to a particular issue in proportion to its relevance'.[119]

---

[115] DRC, *The Duty to Promote Disability Equality: Statutory Code of Practice for England and Wales* (The Stationery Office, 2005), para 1.15.

[116] *R (on the application of Baker & Ors) v Secretary of State for Communities and Local Government, London Borough of Bromley* [2008] EWCA Civ 141, para 34.

[117] *R (on the application of Meany, Glynn, Sanders) v Harlow District Council* [2009] EWHC 559 (Admin), para 50.

[118] Disability Code of Practice, para 2.36.

[119] Guidance, p 15.

However, courts have generally preferred to use the terminology of balancing to reflect the standard. As Dyson LJ put it in *Baker*:

What is *due* regard? In my view, it is the regard that is appropriate in all the circumstances. These include on the one hand the importance of the areas of life of the members of the disadvantaged racial group that are affected by the inequality of opportunity and the extent of the inequality; and on the other hand, such countervailing factors as are relevant to the function which the decision-maker is performing.[120]

Under any reading, however, the duty is a light touch one. It is to 'pay due regard' to the specified issues, but not to take steps to achieve them. Dyson LJ stressed in *Baker* that the race equality duty

is not a duty to achieve a result, namely to eliminate unlawful racial discrimination or to promote equality of opportunity and good relations between persons of different racial groups. It is a duty to *have due regard to the need* to achieve these goals.[121]

Similarly, in *Brown*, the court emphasized that 'no duty is imposed to take steps themselves, or to achieve results'.[122] This can be contrasted with positive duties in other contexts. For example, the International Covenant on Social, Economic and Cultural Rights imposes a duty on the State to take '*take steps*, . . . to the maximum of its available resources, with a view to achieving progressively the full realization of the rights'.[123] Other duties are formulated as target duties, in the sense that they aim at specified outcomes and therefore require the public body to take steps to achieve that target rather than simply paying due regard to it. Thus in an unusually strong intervention, the Child Poverty Act 2010 places a duty on the Secretary of State to eliminate child poverty by meeting four UK-wide income poverty targets by 2020. In a slightly less robust version of such a target duty, the Warm Homes and Energy Conservation Act 2000 requires the Secretary of State to publish and implement a strategy for reducing fuel poverty which includes setting targets for the implementation of that strategy. The strategy must specify a target date (not more than 15 years from the publication of the strategy) for ensuring that 'as far as reasonably practicable persons do not live in fuel poverty'. Moreover, the appropriate authority 'shall

---

[120] *Baker*, above n 116, para 31.
[121] Ibid, para 31.
[122] *R (Brown) v Secretary of State for Work and Pensions* [2008] EWHC 3158 (Admin), para 84.
[123] ICESCR, Art 2 (emphasis added).

take such steps as are in its opinion necessary to implement the strategy'.[124]

The focus on 'due regard', rather than 'taking steps' in the equality duties has meant that, in practice, much of the activity under existing duties has been procedural. In its review of the effectiveness of section 75 in 2008, the Northern Ireland Equality Commission concluded that, while section 75 has been effective in key areas, particularly consultation, there is less evidence that the legislation has had the intended impacts. 'A shift in gear now needs to take place within public authorities, away from concentrating primarily on the process of implement Section 75 towards achieving outcomes.'[125] The duties in Britain have been particularly procedural. The government Consultation Paper in the run-up to the gender duty noted that the general view of the race duty was that it is 'overly bureaucratic, process-driven and resource intensive'.[126]

One way of making the duties more concrete was to complement the general duty in the statute with more specific duties on particular public bodies. This was the original scheme of the race, gender, and disability duties. In the race duty, for instance, a public body (if listed in the Act) was required to publish a race equality scheme showing how it intended to fulfil its general duty, including its arrangements for assessing the likely impact of its work to promote race equality, monitoring its policies, publishing the results, and training staff in connection with these duties. Even here, however, the duty was largely procedural. The requirement was to make arrangements, not to carry them out. Larger employers did have a duty to monitor their workforce. But where monitoring identified significant under-representation, the findings did not trigger a duty to take appropriate action.[127] The disability legislation went somewhat further. The specific duty under the disability regulations required public bodies to produce an action plan for each three-year period. More importantly, they were also obliged to demonstrate that they had taken the actions they committed themselves to and achieved the appropriate outcomes. Public authorities were also

---

[124] Warm Homes and Energy Conservation Act 2000, s 2.
[125] Equality Commission for Northern Ireland, *Section 75 Keeping it Effective*, Final Report (November 2008).
[126] Women and Equality Unit, 'Advancing Equality for Men and Women: Government Proposals to Introduce a Public Sector Duty to Promote Gender Equality' (DTI, October 2005), para 30.
[127] Race Relations Act 1976 (Statutory Duties) Order 2001 (SI 2001/3458); Race Relations Act 1976 (Statutory Duties) Order 2004 (SI 2004/3125), art 3.

required to involve disabled people in the development and implementation. A recent survey of the specific duties found that many organizations reported that they had seen improvements in the way that their organizations made decisions or allocated resources. At the same time, there was still a tendency to substitute bureaucratic 'form-filling' for taking action, especially in relation to impact assessment.[128]

The new Coalition Government, which came into power soon after the EA 2010 was passed, has very different ideas from its predecessors as to how to frame the specific duties. In line with its general anti-interventionist ideology, it has proposed a specific duty which leaves the public authority wide scope to make its own decisions. This is combined with a belief that it should be left to the local electorate or civil society to call public authorities to account, rather than through legal procedures. According to the consultation document issued in 2010:

We do not intend to prescribe how public bodies go about their business, but we will ensure that we put in place the right framework which empowers citizens to scrutinise the data and evidence on how their public services perform. We will do this by bringing data into the daylight—letting people see for themselves the information public bodies are using to make decisions and the data on their performance. Citizens will then be able to judge, challenge, applaud and hold to account the public bodies they ultimately pay for.[129]

Thus the draft regulations on the specific duties drastically reduce the obligations of public bodies. Instead, the emphasis is on publication of data. Public authorities are required to publish information each year relating to the performance of their public sector equality duty. This should include their assessments of the impact of their policies and practices on the furtherance of the objectives of eliminating discrimination, advancing equal opportunities, and fostering good relations as well as the information they took into account when making these assessments. If it employs 150 or more employees, the public authority should also publish information relating to the protected characteristics of its employees.[130] This change of approach contrasts strikingly with that of the Welsh Assembly government, which has chosen to retain

---

[128] Government Equality Office and Schneider Ross, *Equality Duties: Assessing the Cost & Cost Effectiveness of the Specific Race, Disability & Gender Equality Duties* (June 2009), p 13.

[129] 'Equality Act 2010—The Public Sector Equality Duty: Promoting Equality through Transparency—A Consultation' (Government Equalities Office, August 2010), p 5.

[130] Equality Act 2010 (Statutory Duties) Regulations 2011 (draft).

the requirement that a public body produce an equality plan, conduct impact assessments, and identify measurable targets.[131]

(III) AIMS AND OBJECTIVES

The radical nature of positive duties makes it tempting to view their introduction as an end in itself. Yet it is crucially important to consider what each strategy is aiming to achieve. In particular, which conception of equality is being utilized? The original race duty set out three objectives. A public authority was required to have due regard to the need to eliminate unlawful discrimination, advance equality of opportunity, and foster good relations. These aims have remained at the core of the public sector duty.[132] Indeed, with the elaboration of unlawful discrimination to include harassment, victimization, and other breaches of the Act, the EA 2010 retains these three basic objectives.[133]

However, the open-textured nature of these aims makes it difficult to formulate clear targets or objectives. While the elimination of unlawful discrimination can be referred back to the statutory prohibitions, 'equality of opportunity' is, as we have seen, open to a number of different interpretations. In the process of consultation leading up to the EA 2010, therefore, the current author and Sarah Spencer submitted that the objectives be elaborated to include the four dimensions of equality advocated in Chapter One.[134] These objectives were accepted by the Discrimination Law Review, established by the government to provide proposals for a consolidated Equality Bill.[135] Thus in the proposals put out for consultation, the Discrimination Law Review stated as follows:

---

[131] Welsh Assembly Government Consultation Document, *Equality Act 2010: Performance of the Public Sector Equality Duties in Wales: A consultation on the draft Equality Act 2010 (Statutory Duties) (Wales) Regulations 2011.*

[132] Some elaboration was provided in relation to disability, where the authority was in addition required to pay due regard to the need to promote positive attitudes towards disabled persons, to encourage their participation in public life, and to take account of disabled persons' disabilities, even if this involved treating them more favourably than others: DDA s 49A.

[133] EA 2010, s 149(1).

[134] S Fredman and S Spencer, 'Beyond Discrimination: It's Time for Enforceable Duties on Public Bodies to Promote Equality Outcomes' [2006] EHRLR 598–606; S Fredman and S Spencer, 'Equality: Towards an Outcome-Focused Duty' (2006) 156 EOR 14–19; S Fredman and S Spencer, 'Delivering Equality', Submission to the Cabinet Office Review (2006).

[135] *Discrimination Law Review—A Framework for Fairness: Proposals for a Single Equality Bill for Great Britain* (2007), paras 5.28–5.30; 'Equality Bill Government Response to the Consultation' (Cm 7454, July 2008), para 2.25.

If public authorities do not understand what promoting equality of opportunity actually means in practice, this reduces the effectiveness of the equality duties in achieving meaningful outcomes for disadvantaged groups. We therefore want a clearer articulation of the purpose of a single public sector equality duty.

In developing our proposals, we have had particular regard to the work by Sarah Spencer and Sandra Fredman on this subject and the general duty of the Commission for Equality and Human Rights. We have adapted the four 'dimensions of equality' as identified by Spencer and Fredman . . . (i) Addressing disadvantage—taking steps to counter the effects of disadvantage experienced by groups protected by discrimination law, so as to place people on an equal footing with others; (ii) Promoting respect for the equal worth of different groups, and fostering good relations within and between groups—taking steps to treat people with dignity and respect and to promote understanding of diversity and mutual respect between groups, which is a pre-requisite for strong, cohesive communities; (iii) Meeting different needs while promoting shared values—taking steps to meet the particular needs of different groups, while at the same time delivering functions in ways which emphasise shared values rather than difference and which provide opportunities for sustained interactions within and between groups; (iv) Promoting equal participation—taking steps to involve excluded or under-represented groups in employment and decision-making structures and processes and to promote equal citizenship.[136]

When finally enacted, the EA 2010 contained a distilled version of the four dimensions. Thus section 149(3) of the EA 2010 provides as follows:

Having due regard to the need to advance equality of opportunity . . . involves having due regard, in particular, to the need to—

(a) remove or minimise disadvantages suffered by persons who share a relevant protected characteristic that are connected to that characteristic;

(b) take steps to meet the needs of persons who share a relevant protected characteristic that are different from the needs of persons who do not share it;

(c) encourage persons who share a relevant protected characteristic to participate in public life or in any other activity in which participation by such persons is disproportionately low.[137]

The extra dimension, that of promoting equal respect for all, is less explicit, but is nevertheless implicit in the duty to foster good

---

[136] Ibid, paras 5.28–5.29.   [137] EA 2010, s 149(3).

relations.[138] However, while there is an acknowledgement that equality does not always mean identical treatment, these provisions hold back from fully endorsing asymmetrical treatment. This tension is manifested in section 149(6), which states that compliance with the duties may involve treating some people more favourably than others, but that this does not permit conduct which is otherwise prohibited by the Act. Thus these provisions do not go so far as to permit reverse discrimination.[139]

The specification of these dimensions of equality functions as an important counterweight to the increasing tendency within the justificatory rhetoric of positive duties to stress their role in improving efficiency of government. As we saw in Chapter One, this focus on economic efficiency is itself a reaction to the prevailing ideology of the 1980s and 1990s, which characterized State-imposed equal opportunity policies as a burden on business and a manifestation of over-regulation. In a powerful response to this approach, it began to be argued that in fact equal opportunities, properly focused, would improve efficiency. Cutting pay and equal opportunities would not yield a competitive advantage; instead the future lay in the development of a highly skilled, motivated, and integrated workforce. It was this approach which grounded the policy of the EU during the 1990s.[140] And since it was women who formed the majority of the economically inactive and unskilled potential labour force, the development of women's skills came to be regarded as highly significant in the overall economic policy aimed at creating a skilled workforce.[141] It was this objective which was the basis of many of the most important positive action programmes at EU level, such as the provision of funding to Member States to promote vocational training and employment for women. It was a major contributing factor to the commitment to mainstreaming at EU level.

This approach has played a central strategic role in countering neo-liberal ideology. However, the fact that equality is ultimately subservient to the market imperative means that it is inevitably limited. As soon as equality is considered to be too costly, it gives way to other priorities. For example, training programmes are resourced only to the extent that this is judged to produce efficiency gains. Many of the community initiatives

---

[138] Ibid, s 149(5).   [139] See Chapter Five.
[140] European Commission, *Growth, Competitiveness, Employment: The Challenges and Ways Forward into the 21st Century* (1994) Bulletin of the European Communities, Supplement 6/93.
[141] Rees, above n 92, p 63.

(such as NOW or new Opportunities for Women) were given only limited funding, and the proportion of the total budget of the EU which is spent on equality issues is tiny. Moreover, the 'economic prism' could well make it appear that there is a competitive conflict between different disadvantaged groups. Policies to absorb women may well entail fewer opportunities for migrant work, and a corresponding strengthening of immigration control.

A further strength of a multi-dimensional set of objectives is that it facilitates a holistic view. Focusing on one dimension to the exclusion of the others can limit the effectiveness of positive measures. This can be seen by considering the participative aim, which is now the third objective specified in the EA 2010, namely 'to encourage persons who share a relevant protected characteristic to participate in public life or in any other activity in which participation by such persons is disproportionately low'.[142] Increasing the participation of under-represented groups in employment or public office is the most readily measurable objective of a positive duty. Indeed, the explicit aim of the Northern Ireland provisions is to achieve proportionate participation of Roman Catholics and Protestants in all types and levels of employment. Employment equity schemes with similar aims have been introduced in several other countries, such as Canada, Australia, and South Africa. In addition, it was with the express aim of increasing the participation of women in the public sector that the reverse discrimination schemes described in the previous chapter in Germany and Sweden were introduced.[143] The aim of achieving fair participation extends too to representation in public office, including the judiciary, Parliament, and the other decision-making bodies.

This aim is attractive in that it is easily quantifiable. Targets can be set and achievement measured by properly structured monitoring. But its limitations should not be overlooked. In particular, it easily slips into a quantitative exercise, focusing only on results or outcomes. However, as was seen in Chapter One, results on their own can be misleading. Merely changing the colour, gender, or religious composition of a workforce may not achieve structural changes. Cultural change, crucial to a conducive working environment, may not be achieved. The result is either that targets remain stubbornly unattainable or that participation rates give an illusion of change. Moreover, the criteria of measurement of 'success' might themselves be contested. Indicators to measure progress

---

[142] EA 2010, s 149(3)(c).   [143] See Chapter Five.

are not, as Mackay and Bilton note, 'facts' which exist 'out there' for the policy-maker to use. Rather, they are created and 'validate particular world views and prioritise selected areas of knowledge'. For example, many traditional indicators assume that women and men experience the world in the same way. Alternatively, traditional indicators characterize families as single units, represented by the head of the household, who is defined as the male breadwinner. Internal relations within the family are therefore obscured and women are seen primarily as mothers or caregivers. The main indicators used at an international and national level, such as GDP (gross domestic product), ISH (Index of Social Health), and the HDI (Human Development Index) are all 'gender invisible'.[144] In a partial response to this problem, two gender-related indicators were introduced in the 1995 Human Development Report: the Gender-related Development Index (GDI) and the Gender Empowerment Measure. However, an evaluation of these measures after ten years of use came to the conclusion that the GDI did not meet the need for a measure of gender inequality, and should be replaced.[145]

It is for this reason that a multi-dimensional approach is valuable. As well as the participative dimension, it is necessary to consider the redistributive, transformative, and recognition dimensions. Thus the redistributive dimension entails addressing some of the root causes of under-representation, including equipping the under-represented to make use of the newly expanded opportunities. This too needs to be allied with the transformative dimension. Measures to redress disadvantage, while making an important contribution on the supply side, will only succeed if accompanied by corresponding changes on the demand side. As Rees puts it, there is a crucial difference between mainstreaming equality and transforming the mainstream.[146] Particularly at EU level, the model of full-time working, mobility, and job continuity continues to dominate policy formation; and ingrained assumptions about women's work and their marginal role in the workforce are deeply influential in shaping education and training. Within the European Employment Strategy, there is a particularly problematic tendency to focus on supply-side factors, such as training and flexibility for women, rather than insisting also on change in demand-side factors and

---

[144] MacKay and Bilton, above n 94, pp 46 ff.
[145] S Klasen, 'Guest Editor's Introduction' (2006) 7 Journal of Human Development and Capabilities 145–59.
[146] Rees, above n 92, p 69.

particularly from employers.[147] Instead of attempting to adapt members
of other under-represented groups better to fit in with the existing
framework, therefore, it is crucial to transform the existing framework
in order to reflect the norms of the excluded 'other'. For example,
training schemes which do not themselves adapt to women's needs for
flexible hours and childcare will have little impact. Long working hours
need to be adapted to achieve a better home–work balance, not just for
women, but for men too. The linkage of work-free days with the
Christian calendar needs to be severed and dress codes based on a
Christian tradition removed. Accommodation for disability needs to
extend to adaptation of premises and working places, and beyond that
to changes in transport systems, media images, and welfare payments.

Finally, the multi-dimensional approach requires a focus on the
recognition dimension, in particular the need to foster a culture of
respect for each individual. A central and pressing example is the need
to deal with homophobic bullying which, as we saw in Chapter Two, is
still endemic in schools across the country. It is notable that an important result of pay equity strategies in Canada has been the recognition of
the value of women's work, improving both women's own self-respect
and the respect accorded to them in the workplace.[148]

(IV) PROCESS OF DECISION-MAKING: PARTICIPATORY DEMOCRACY

The nature of the positive duty in the discrimination field is such that
the process of decision-making is as important as the outcome. One
approach is to institute a highly centralized scheme, with government or
a public agency dictating in detail the steps to be taken and enforcing
standards through legal proceedings. However, it has been shown that
the effectiveness of equality strategies depends on convincing those who
implement the plan of its appropriateness and value; and ultimately
changing the culture itself. More can be achieved by enlisting the self-
interest of employers and providers than through unilateral control.[149]
This has led to the evolution of mechanisms to facilitate a dialogue
between the relevant Equality Commission and those who are being
regulated. In the US, the powerful Office of Federal Contract Compliance Programs (OFCCP), for example, always attempts to reach a

---

[147] J Rubery, 'Gender Mainstreaming and Gender Equality in the EU: The Impact of the
EU Employment Strategy' (2002) 33 Industrial Relations Journal 500–22 at 503.
[148] Canadian Taskforce, above n 89, p 139.
[149] Hepple, Coussey, and Choudhury, above n 5, para 3.5.

formal conciliation agreement, or enlist binding undertakings, failing which there is negotiation and conciliation. It is only if all fails that the legal process is enlisted and the ultimate sanction of debarment invoked. It is in a sense a mark of the success of the OFCCP in enlisting the energies of employers that only a handful of contractors have been debarred since the scheme was instituted.

But harnessing the energies of the employer or provider is not sufficient. It has been shown that the quality of regulation improves significantly by incorporating those affected both into the decision-making process and its implementation. In this way participation to some extent fills the gap left by departing from reliance on victim initiative, preventing the process from being a top-down exercise imposed from above. As well as improving its effectiveness, the participatory dimension of proactive models arguably deepens the democratic legitimacy and reach of equality. Ideally this is done by incorporating civil society such as trade unions, community organizations, and public interest groups as well as relevant stakeholders into both the process of norm-setting and its implementation. At their most ambitious, proactive models aim to move beyond conflict and interest-based bargaining to a form of deliberative democracy, whereby interests are not taken as fixed or predetermined, but are themselves moulded by the process of decision-making to achieve a new public-regarding synthesis.[150] Norms are set in a dynamic and responsive way, and implementation and norm-setting interact.

The importance of this dimension is clearly evidenced by the experience of the operation of the Ontario Pay Equity Act. The Ontario scheme required recognized trade unions to be involved in the pay equity process; whereas in workplaces in which female job classes were not organized, employers were entitled to proceed alone. The results were striking. In workplaces without recognized trade unions, there was substantial employer manipulation in order to minimize the costs and impact of pay equity. This could be done because of the inevitably subjective nature of job evaluation, and the open-textured definitions of key terms such as the establishment within which pay equity was to be achieved, the definition of job classes, and the choice of appropriate comparators. McColgan notes that unions were in a position to resist such manipulation, for example by ensuring that the values assigned to job classes reflected a genuine and gender-neutral assessment; that the

---

[150] C R Sunstein, 'Beyond the Republican Revival' (1988) 97 Yale LJ 1539.

definition of 'establishment' was such as to include comparators for female job classes; and to influence the characterization of job classes as male or female.[151] Unions were even able to negotiate above the minimum required by the Act, using a combination of industrial muscle and threats to invoke the legal process to support their claims. Unions have played a particularly important role in negotiating plans to provide for pay equity in the traditionally low-paying female ghettoized service occupations such as hospitals, nursing homes, community services, shelters, and home support services.[152]

However, the participative dimension of proactive duties needs closer analysis. It is not always clear precisely what function participation performs. Is participation limited to the imparting of information? Alternatively, is the aim to glean information from those affected, the underlying aim being to improve the quality of decision-making? As the Canadian Taskforce stresses, those who are at the receiving end of discrimination are in the best position to detect it and to suggest change.[153] Or do participants have the right to co-decision-making? From the perspective of deliberative democracy, the process of decision-making should be a learning process, during which decision-makers are able to redefine their goals as a result of discussion and debate. Participation should facilitate the voice of groups which are excluded from traditional representative decision-making[154] with the aim of introducing new perspectives and refashioning outcomes. Finally, participation is part of effective implementation or delivery of the policy. Although the process of compliance is not driven by individuals, those affected are nevertheless in a good position to insist that duties are fulfilled.

Several EU Member States have created a durable consultative framework, some giving the function primarily to the equality body, and others involving members of the government, social partners, and other interested parties. Collective bargaining or works council structures also constitute an important arena for consultation at the enterprise level. It is clear, however, that the weight given to opinions of

---

[151] A McColgan, 'Equal Pay: Lessons from Ontario's Pay Equity Unit', Working Paper No 5 *Independent Review of the Enforcement of UK Anti-Discrimination Legislation* (November 1999), para 3.31.

[152] Equal Pay Coalition, available at: <http://www.equalpaycoalition.org/ontario.php>.

[153] Canadian Taskforce, above n 89, pp 160, 223.

[154] K A Armstrong, 'Tackling Social Exclusion Through OMC: Reshaping the Boundaries of EU Governance' in T Börzel and R Cichowski (eds), *State of the Union: Law, Politics and Society*, vol 6 (Oxford University Press, 2003), p 25.

consultees depends largely on the political culture, the goodwill of decision-makers, and the political or industrial strength and influence of consultees. An active and engaged civil society is thus crucial to the success of participative mechanisms. At the same time, it is important to ensure that marginalized groups are indeed represented in consultative mechanisms. There is a risk that participation favours the better organized:[155] for example, trade unions themselves might replicate structures of segregation within the workforce, with women-dominated sectors having less industrial muscle than those dominated by men.[156] Ensuring that participants are representative is even more complex outside the workplace. Finally, and most complex, is the question of how to ensure that those whose identity falls within more than one group and therefore suffer cumulative discrimination are properly represented. The Canadian Taskforce stresses the need to incorporate as a separate sector, visible minority women, indigenous women, and disabled women.[157] How these different perspectives are brought together is not as yet made clear.

The participatory dimension of the positive model therefore assumes a high degree of organization, commitment, and knowledge among potential participants. However, consultation can impose significant resource demands on already stretched NGOs or interest groups. The effect of this has been referred to as 'consultation fatigue'. One way forward is to incorporate capacity-building as part of the positive duty, making resources available for this purpose. Participants must have access to proper information, and training must be provided both to active participants and to all affected. For example, Status of Women Canada (SWC) is a federal government organization that promotes the full participation of women in the economic, social, and democratic life of Canada. As well as working with federal departments and agencies to ensure that the gender dimensions are taken into account in the development of policies and programmes, it also supports the work of women's and other Canadian organizations.[158] A similar role is performed by the European Social Fund, which earmarks funds for the promotion of equal opportunities for all in a variety of contexts, including specific measures to improve the access and active participation of women in the labour market. By contrast, among EU Member States,

---

[155] MacKay and Bilton, above n 94, p 71.
[156] Canadian Taskforce, above n 89, ch 5.
[157] Ibid, p 228.
[158] See: <http://www.swc-cfc.gc.ca/index-eng.html>.

support of this type is rare,[159] apart from the equality body itself, which is usually government-funded.

The democratic aspirations of the new model are therefore still in their infancy, requiring a deeper understanding and more focused analysis of the nature of the desired democracy and its mechanisms. Representative democracy might give way to deliberative democracy, but if sufficient care is not taken in its construction, there is a risk that it might be no more than a bureaucratic management device.[160] Particularly limited is the new approach in Britain to the public sector duty. As will be recalled, the current proposal is to move away from a fairly prescriptive set of specific duties. Instead, the proposal is simply to publicize the relevant information about steps taken to fulfil the duty. The hope is that if civil society or ordinary people wish to, they will use political and other channels to contest or support these steps.[161] The above discussion has, however, shown how limited this approach is. It is merely a duty to provide information. There is no established framework for gleaning the views of those affected nor taking them into account. There is no capacity-building for NGOs to perform this role, or any attempt to ensure that the least organized and most vulnerable are represented. Needless to say, there is no attempt to permit the views of those affected to influence the decision. This does not bode well for an effective mechanism.

(V) COMPLIANCE MECHANISMS

Departing from the traditional complaints-led mechanism raises many challenges for enforcement and regulation of positive strategies. Placing the onus of change on policy-makers, while a key strength of proactive models, is also problematic. This is particularly evident in respect of mainstreaming. A recent study demonstrated that political will is key to progress in most mainstreaming strategies.[162] But this also means that it is subject to the vagaries of policy-making. It is difficult to sustain positive action strategies without strong political and managerial support[163] and lack or loss of political will can turn mainstreaming into a mere gesture of even a pretext for inaction.[164] Similarly an assessment of

---

[159] Fredman, 'Making Equality Effective', above n 91.
[160] S Borras and B Greve, 'Concluding Remarks: New Method or Just Cheap Talk?' (2004) 11 Journal of European Public Policy 329–36 at 345.
[161] See the Equality Act 2010 (Statutory Duties) Regulations 2011 (draft).
[162] MacKay and Bilton, above n 94, p 97.
[163] Ibid, p 74.
[164] Ibid, p 143.

gender mainstreaming at EU level showed that its success depended very much on whether individual Directors General sympathized with its overall aims. Where gender mainstreaming has 'resonance' in a department, it flourished; where it did not, there was very little done to take it forward.[165] Paradoxically, positive action works best when there is high-level representation of women in the policy-making or implementation machinery. Yet this is precisely what it aims to achieve in the first place.

Thus the key challenge is to achieve compliance without undermining the proactive character of such models. Indeed, unless the impetus is found internally, in voluntary and motivated compliance, these models will not achieve their aim of ultimately transforming the organizational culture. Real change in organizational culture therefore depends on the interplay between the enlightened self-interest of public or private managers, on the one hand, and the drive and energy of affected participants, on the other.[166] However, it is well established that a system based entirely on self-regulation will have little effect.[167] Employers who consider that equal opportunities to advance their business needs will do so in any event; those who do not will safely ignore them. Moreover, the formal adoption of equal opportunities policy may simply be 'an excuse for complacency. Management . . . seems particularly prone to a conviction that equal opportunity "now exists".'[168] Nor is it sufficient for government to issue a code of practice without any enforcement mechanisms. Research has consistently demonstrated that, while it is important to harness the positive goodwill and energy of major actors, some enforcement mechanism must be available to keep all actors in line.[169]

Indeed, the Northern Ireland experience has demonstrated that voluntary action is much more likely when the possibility of sanctions exists as a default. Recognizing the deficiencies of the voluntary approach, the Northern Ireland legislation gives extensive powers to the Northern Ireland Equality Commission to function as the engine driving change both with respect to public bodies within its purview[170] and in relation

---

[165] M Pollack and E Hafner-Burton, 'Mainstreaming Gender in the European Union' [2000] 7 Journal of European Public Policy 432.

[166] Hepple, Coussey, and Choudhury, above n 5, p 57.

[167] Ibid, p 57; Canadian Taskforce, above n 89, p 395.

[168] J West and K Lyon, 'The Trouble with Equal Opportunities: The Case of Women Academics' (1995) 7 Gender and Education 51 at 60, cited in Rees, above n 92, at p 42.

[169] Hepple, Coussey, and Choudhury, above n 5, para 3.3; Rees, above n 92, p 36.

[170] Northern Ireland Act 1998, s 75 and Sch 9.

to all employers covered by the fair employment legislation. However, the Commission has had to make remarkably little use of its considerable investigatory powers, because employers have been willing to enter into voluntary affirmative action agreements. This is only the case, however, because those sanctions exist: the purely voluntary approach previously pursued yielded no such results.[171]

The ideal model in this context would be a pyramid of enforcement. The first tier is one of encouragement and support, to promote a cooperative rather than adversarial approach. Training and other support is given to responsible bodies to achieve compliance in ways which work best for the institution itself. The Canadian Taskforce stresses the need to promote and preserve long-term relationships and avoid an adversarial climate. At this stage, then, the regulatory body should assist with training and expert advice. For example, the diagnosis of discrimination may require complex decisions as to the appropriate pool of comparison.[172] Pay equity comparisons can be highly complex; in Canada, the specialist pay equity oversight body is envisaged as providing relevant statistical information and methodological guidance.[173] If compliance is not achieved voluntarily, the next tier would involve negotiation and discussion initiated by the regulatory body. If this is unsuccessful, the recalcitrant respondent could be subject to an order to comply issued by that body. Only if this further step fails do fines or other judicially enforced sanctions come into play.[174]

An important way of embedding proactive measures into the organizational culture is to make the duty as specific as possible. This is most effectively achieved through requiring an equality plan. This in turn raises the question of whether the regulatory body should be involved in scrutinizing such plans. The Northern Ireland section 75 duty requires advance approval of the plan by the Equality Commission.[175] This has been relatively successful: in their review of section 75 in 2003, the Commission stated that of 160 designated bodies, 156 had submitted reports and four had failed to do so. However, the Hepple report took the view, based on the Northern Ireland experience, that this could have the effect of externalizing the responsibility for implementing the plan,

---

[171] B Osborne and I Shuttleworth (eds), *Fair Employment in Northern Ireland: A Generation On* (Blackstaff Press, 2004), p 7.
[172] C McCrudden, R Ford, and A Heath, 'The Impact of Affirmative Action Agreements' in ibid, p 125.
[173] Canadian Taskforce, above n 89, pp 163, 406.
[174] Hepple, Coussey, and Choudhury, above n 5, p 59.
[175] Northern Ireland Act 1998, Sch 9.

rather than building up energy and resources from within.[176] In any event, the feasibility of such a requirement is largely determined by numbers. In Northern Ireland, the numbers are far more manageable than elsewhere: advance approval would simply not be feasible where a large number of bodies is involved.

Just as important as the equality scheme, is scrutiny of its implementation. The Northern Ireland Commission's review of the workings of section 75 found that

the effects of mainstreaming of equality of opportunity and good relations appear to stop at the policy development stage and are failing to 'trickle through' to implementation. Good compliance with the duties has not entirely led to good effect; in a number of instances, good practice has been followed in how decisions are made but not in how they are followed through.[177]

The final tier of compliance necessarily consists in the possibility of sanctions. Many of the proactive models stress that innovative remedies are required, remaining within the spirit of a proactive model and not regressing to an original fault-based approach. Considerable investigative and review powers can be vested in the Commission, leading to the issue of a compliance notice by the Commission itself, backed up by recourse to a court of law with injunctive powers to insist on compliance.[178] The Northern Ireland fair representation legislation leads to a possible legally enforceable affirmative action agreement.[179] Notably, the gender mainstreaming strategy lacks all these enforcement mechanisms.

The effectiveness of compliance mechanisms depends, of course, on which body is allocated regulatory responsibility. One possibility is to require regular reporting to Parliament, thereby relying on the political process to ensure that proactive measures are carried out. The practice of reporting to Parliament is widespread among EU Member States. The effectiveness of the reporting mechanism is, however, dependent on the seriousness with which it is regarded by Parliament or the relevant ministry and whether further action is taken. A second possibility is to give enforcement powers to equality bodies or other similar institutions. Such powers are given to the equality body in 11 EU Member States. Thirdly, regulatory functions could be added on to the powers of existing audit bodies, such as HM Revenue & Customs. The Hepple

---

[176] Hepple, Coussey, and Choudhury, above n 5, p 62.
[177] Equality Commission for Northern Ireland, above n 125.
[178] Canadian Taskforce, above n 89, pp 401, 406.
[179] FETO, art 13, see McCrudden, Ford, and Heath, above n 172, pp 122–50.

report recommended that instead of entrusting this function to a specialist regulatory agency, it should be built into existing performance management frameworks. Inspection and audit should be carried out by bodies with established inspection and audit functions, such as the Audit Commission, and the inspectorates of prisons, schools, and police.[180] Policy-makers already have a duty to produce a regulatory impact assessment of new statutory measures, which details the cost implications of such measures. Impact assessment could be built into these. A fourth possibility is to enforce legal obligations through collective bargaining structures. However, this depends heavily on a well-developed collective bargaining structure. Finally a range of judicial or quasi-judicial mechanisms could be used, including arbitral bodies and more traditional courts and tribunals. In fact, the regulatory machinery works best when it draws on all such institutional mechanisms, provided the functions are divided appropriately among them.

At the same time, it is important to decide whether the individual should have a continuing role. An individual claim for an immediate remedy could unravel the priorities set in the equality plan. Thus the key is to give the individual a role in enforcing the equality plan as a whole, rather than demanding immediate fulfilment of an individual entitlement. As was seen in Chapter Four, the solution in the EA 2010 in the context of equal pay has been to permit the individual to pursue her claim, but to allow employers to justify the pay differential on the grounds, for example, that a pay equity plan is in the process of being implemented. Thus section 69(3) of the EA 2010 provides that, in determining whether an employer can justify a pay differential, the long-term objective of reducing inequality between men's and women's terms of work is always to be regarded as a legitimate aim. This is, however, subject to a proportionality requirement: for example, the delay in affording the individual claimant her entitlement to equal pay must be shown to be proportional to this long-term objective. This is an important means by which a programme of phasing in equal pay for a group as a whole can be defended against individual claims for immediate entitlements. The difficulty with such an approach, however, is that if the defence is upheld, the employer simply wins the case. There is no ongoing requirement to put the programme into effect.

A more comprehensive solution is that of the Ontarian Pay Equity Act, which combines the functions of a regulatory Commission—the

---

[180] Hepple, Coussey, and Choudhury, above n 5, p 64.

Pay Equity Office—with a relatively robust individual complaints system, which, inter alia, gives employees and recognized trade unions the right to complain to a Pay Equity Hearings Tribunal on the grounds that a pay equity plan has not been implemented. The tribunal operates in some ways like a court: it is impartial, is independent of government, and must provide all parties with a fair hearing and fair process. However, it differs from a court in that decision-makers are appointed for their specialized expertise in labour law, compensation systems, and pay equity; and proceedings are expected to be less formal, less expensive, and more expeditious than court proceedings. Moreover, the tribunal does not replicate the passive structure of an ordinary court of law. Formal proceedings only take place after a review officer has investigated and attempted to settle the issues in dispute.[181] Finally, the tribunal's remedial powers extend well beyond individual compensation. For example, it can order a review officer to draw up a pay equity plan where none has been produced; it can order an employer to reinstate an employee who has been victimized; or it can order a pay adjustment for all women in an affected job class in order to achieve pay equity.[182]

The combination of Commission-led compliance with an individual complaints system appears to have worked relatively well in Ontario. The Pay Equity Office has also been relatively successful in intervening to prevent disputes from reaching the stage of legal proceedings. In addition, many issues were referred to the Pay Equity Hearings Tribunal, in order to establish the basic principles to guide other employers or stakeholders. The Tribunal played an important role in interpreting ambiguous provisions, which could then be applied in other cases. As the Taskforce commented: 'Although it took several years to resolve certain complex cases, the timeframes were much shorter on average than for cases dealt with under complaint-based models.'

Compliance mechanisms in the UK represent a hybrid of regulatory approaches. There is no cause of action at private law.[183] Instead, enforcement is either by judicial review through the ordinary courts, or by a Commission-initiated compliance procedure. As seen above, judicial review does not wholly replicate the deficiencies of the individual complaints model. Standing extends to anyone with 'sufficient interest', including a public-spirited citizen and the EHRC, and the remedy is not confined to the individual, but extends to all who are affected by the failure to comply with the duty.

---

[181] Pay Equity Act 1990, Part IV.   [182] Ibid, s 25(2).   [183] EA 2010, s 156.

Use of the judicial review procedure has been encouraging. There have been a number of claims for judicial review of failures by public bodies to comply with the race, gender, or disability duties, and courts have been more robust than might have been expected. Within the limits of the 'due regard' standard described above, and mindful of the deference built into that standard, courts have been willing to scrutinize public authorities' decisions closely to be sure that due regard was indeed paid to the equality goals mentioned in the statute. As we have seen, general awareness of the duty, or an *ex post facto* justification will not suffice: the duty must be fulfilled consciously and expressly at the time a policy is being considered. Nor can it simply be discharged by 'ticking boxes'. Instead, the requirements of the statutory duty should 'form in substance an integral part of the decision-making process'.[184] On this basis, both the High Court and the Court of Appeal have quashed decisions by public bodies in a number of important cases.[185]

At the same time, the judicial review procedure is expensive, time consuming, and potentially adversarial. At best, the outcome will be to require the authority in question to reconsider its decision. Judicial review should therefore be complemented by more targeted compliance powers to be exercised by the EHRC. This has been partially achieved by empowering the Commission to assess the extent to which a public body has complied with its duties.[186] Under the race, sex, and disability discrimination laws, the Commission had particular powers to enforce the 'specific duty'. The Commission could issue a compliance notice requiring the authority to comply with the duty and provide information to the Commission of steps taken to do so. If the compliance notice had not been complied with within three months, the Commission could apply to a county court for an order requiring the authority to do so. In 2009, for example, the Commission issued compliance notices to three NHS Trusts on the grounds that they had failed to put in place race equality schemes setting out their arrangements for meeting their duty.

---

[184] *R (on the application of Harris) v London Borough of Haringey* [2010] EWCA Civ 703; see also *Baker*, above n 116; *R (on the application of Gary Isaacs, Marilyn Isaacs) v Secretary of State for Communities and Local Government, South Somerset District Council* [2009] EWHC 557 (Admin).

[185] *R (on the application of Meany, Glynn, Sanders) v Harlow District Council*, above n 117; *R (Elias) v Secretary of State for Defence* [2006] 1 WLR 3213 (CA); *R (on the application of Harris) v London Borough of Haringey*, above n 184; *R (on the application of Juliana Boyejo) v Barnet London Borough Council* [2009] EWHC 3261 (Admin).

[186] EA 2006, s 31.

Each Trust had also failed to carry out equality impact assessments on their policies, and two of the Trusts had failed to fulfil their duty to monitor employees. The Commission asked the Trusts to address these deficiencies within three months or face legal proceedings. These powers, however, may well have been cut back significantly by the removal of specific duties to put an equality plan into place. If this is the case, the Commission's compliance powers will be limited to enforcing the general 'due regard' duty and the publicity requirements in the Act.

By contrast, Northern Ireland and Canada provide valuable demonstrations of how an enforcement pyramid might work in practice. Possibly the most effective compliance structure has been that in Northern Ireland. As we have seen, there are two sets of positive duties in Northern Ireland: the fair employment legislation and the 'section 75' duty to pay due regard. The fair employment legislation, introduced in 1989, imposed positive duties on employers to take measures to achieve fair participation in their workforces of Protestant and Roman Catholic employees.[187] The Northern Ireland Equality Commission plays a central role in ensuring compliance. Registered employers are required to send a monitoring return each year to the Commission including details of the number of existing employees who belong to each Community, the composition of applicants for employment; and in relevant cases, those ceasing to be employed. Criminal sanctions are available to enforce the obligation to serve a return. But the Commission also has a range of other sanctions at its disposal. It may make recommendations as to the affirmative action to be taken; it can serve directions on an employer who fails to give written undertakings where appropriate, and serve a notice about goals and timetables. Enforcement is complemented by recourse to the tribunal, for example to enforce a written undertaking. Particularly important is the Commission's power to have recourse to economic sanctions, such as the denial of government contracts.[188]

The enforcement structure has worked relatively well in Northern Ireland. We have already seen that the Commission (and its predecessors) used their powers to enter into binding agreements with great effect (see above). In its most recent annual report, the Commission reports that compliance with fair employment legislation remains high. In 2008, a total of 4,075 monitoring return forms were received from

---

[187] Fair Employment Act 1989, now contained in FETO, Part VII.
[188] FETO, arts 55–68.

employers and as many as 99 per cent of these were in compliance with the legal requirements.[189] Employers are also required to conduct a review every three years.[190] In addition, as we have seen, the Commission has the power to enter into binding affirmative action agreements with employers to undertake their duties. In 2008, 63 affirmative action agreements reached with employers were reviewed; and the Commission reported that in most cases good faith efforts were being made to address under-representation. The Commission also followed up 52 discrimination settlements; and evidence of improved equality practice was found as a result of 49 settlements. The Commission continues to work with employers to identify and address problem areas.[191]

The results have been encouraging. Although causation is always difficult to identify with certainty, the advent of fair employment legislation has certainly coincided with significant progress in improving the representation of the Roman Catholic community in previously under-represented areas.[192] By 2008, the Roman Catholic proportion of the monitored workforce had reached 45.2 per cent; an increase of 4.9 per cent compared to 2001 (the first year in which both full- and part-time employees were monitored).[193] Moreover, in 2007, the unemployment gap between Roman Catholics and Protestants was 2 per cent, compared to a high of 9 per cent in 1992. Nevertheless the higher rate of economic inactivity in the Roman Catholic community has persisted over time.[194] In addition, the effect of the recession has been somewhat more marked in relation to the Roman Catholic rather than the Protestant community, partly because of the younger age composition of the former.[195] There has also been progress in reducing segregation within most sectors. However, in security-related areas, generations of segregation have proved particularly tenacious. Although the Roman Catholic share of

---

[189] Equality Commission for Northern Ireland, *Tenth Annual Report and Accounts 2008–9* (Equality Commission, 2009).
[190] ILO, art 33.
[191] Equality Commission for Northern Ireland, above n 189, pp 29–31.
[192] Fair Employment Commission, 'Monitoring Report No 9' (1998).
[193] Equality Commission for Northern Ireland, 'Fair Employment Monitoring Report No 19' (2009). The Catholic share of the economically active working age population lies somewhere between 44.1 and 47.7 per cent.
[194] Office of the First Minister and Deputy First Minister, '2007 Labour Force Survey Report' (2009).
[195] R McQuaid, E Hollywood, and J Canduela, *Employment Inequalities in an Economic Downturn* (Equality Commission for Northern Ireland, 2010).

employment in security-related areas has increased, it still stood at only
19 per cent in 2008.[196]

Section 75, the duty to have due regard to the need to promote
equality of opportunity between specified groups,[197] presents different
challenges. The duty to 'pay due regard' is more amorphous and
difficult to pin down, risking responses which are bureaucratic without
being substantive. The Commission has always played a critical role in
ensuring the effectiveness of the legislation through advice, monitoring,
reporting on compliance, and investigating alleged breaches of schemes.
Its cooperative approach has meant that, in this area too, it has not had to
resort to its default sanction powers. However, in its 2008–9 annual
report, it recorded that for the first time, it made a formal referral to the
Secretary of State. This occurred when a recalcitrant district council
failed to comply with the finding of a Commission-initiated investigation that it should conduct an equality impact assessment. The Secretary of State directed the council to act in accordance with the
Commission's finding, which it duly did.

In its review of section 75 in 2007, the Commission reported that
section 75 had effected substantial change in the way in which policy
is made, towards a more informed and evidence-based approach. It
regarded effective consultation as a particular success. However, in
concluded,

there is less evidence that the legislation has had the intended impacts and
outcomes for individuals. A shift in gear now needs to take place within public
authorities; away from concentrating primarily on the process of implementing
Section 75, towards achieving outcomes.[198]

The scale and effectiveness of Commission-led compliance has, however, been difficult to replicate in other jurisdictions, especially where
there are larger numbers of employers to monitor, and a lower level of
political commitment. In particular, the possibility of Commission
enforcement on this scale is heavily dependent on proper resources.
This can be seen in Canada. Under the original Federal Employment
Equity Act, the employers' only obligation was to report annually to the
responsible minister on the representation of target groups within their
workforce. There were no other enforcement mechanisms in the Act.
Instead, the expectation was that employers would be encouraged to

---

[196] Equality Commission for Northern Ireland, '2008 Monitoring Report No 19'.
[197] Northern Ireland Act 1998, s 75.
[198] Equality Commission for Northern Ireland, above n 189, p 7.

implement employment equity based on public scrutiny of the reports and knowledge that the data could be used to file systemic discrimination complaints under the Canadian Human Rights Act. As Busby notes, this

focus on reporting rather than achieving was seen as a major weakness: failure to report was subject to a maximum fine of $50,000, but discrimination against the designated groups attracted no penalty.... The Minister for Employment and Immigration's response that the public disclosure of reports required under the Act would mean that those in breach of their obligations would 'have to answer to the people of Canada if they fail to achieve equality in employment' was received with derision.[199]

When a new Employment Equity Act was passed in 1995, it gave the Canadian Human Rights Commission (CHRC) the power to conduct on-site compliance reviews, and provided for final enforcement of the Act, where necessary, by an Employment Equity Review Tribunal, empowered to hear disputes and issue orders. One of the key initiatives in the 1996 Act was to provide the CHRC with the power to conduct compliance audits, negotiate undertakings, and issue directions. The Act specifies that non-compliance is to be resolved by focusing on persuasion, with directions to be issued as a last resort. In cases of non-compliance, an officer will negotiate a written undertaking from the employer to take specific remedial steps. If such an undertaking cannot be obtained, the Commission has the power to issue a direction to take specific action. If an employer fails to act on such direction, the matter can be referred to the Employment Equity Review Tribunal for an order.

Evaluation of the Commission's record in this respect has been mixed. Agocs and Osborne point out that 'the CHRC faces its task of reviewing employers' compliance... with little leverage and grossly inadequate resources'.[200] They note that only 11 per cent of the Commission's total budget for 2005–6 was devoted to employment equity audits. Instead, most of its resources were used to process individual complaints. The original compliance review process was lengthy and gave employers many opportunities to delay.[201] The review of the Act in

[199] N Busby, 'Affirmative Action in Women's Employment: Lessons from Canada' (2006) 33 Journal of Law and Society 42–58 at p 50.
[200] C Agocs and B Osborne, 'Comparing Equity Policies in Canada and Northern Ireland: Policy Learning in Two Directions?' (2009) 35 Canadian Public Policy 237–62 at 245.
[201] Ibid.

2001 was somewhat more optimistic, reporting that since the Commission commenced its audits in 1998, 87 per cent of the public sector and 61 per cent of the private sector workforce had been audited. Twenty directions had been issued but no case had been heard by the Employment Equity Review Tribunal. Of the employers audited, only eight were in compliance initially, but a further 62 had become compliant as a result of the intervention.[202] However, annual reports of the CHRC noted that most employers were poorly informed about their obligations, few began their compliance efforts until they were notified that a review was imminent, and were rarely compliant on the first or even the second visit. The resources of the CHRC could not meet this cumulative workload.[203]

A change of approach by the CHRC, towards a greater focus on educating employers on their obligations, as well as on targeting large employers, has yielded better results. Between 2003 and 2005, the Commission audited 205 of the 588 employers covered by the Act, and all were found to be in compliance. Nevertheless, only 37 per cent of promotion and hiring goals had been attained in private sector firms and 55 per cent in public sector organizations. Agocs and Osborne attribute this to a lack of meaningful sanctions. The

low-pressure and employer-friendly compliance review process was ostensibly designed to forestall employer resistance and win cooperation. . . . However, many employers continue in their previous pattern of . . . taking few steps towards compliance until the last possible moment. Once audited, many employers do not attain the goals they set for themselves.[204]

Certainly, recourse to Employment Equity Review Tribunals has been minimal. Only eight applications were made between 2000 and 2003, and none since then. In any event, sanctions are only available for failure to file or false reporting. There are no sanctions for failure to improve the representation of designated groups if the employer cites a plausible reason for lack of progress or failure to remove barriers. At the same time, the audit process seems to yield results, reflected in increased representation of women and visible in audited firms when compared to non-audited firms. The overall verdict, therefore, is that proactive

---

[202] Human Resources and Skills Development Canada, 'Employment Equity Act Review: A Report to the Standing Committee on Human Resources Development and the Status of Persons with Disabilities' (December 2001), para 4.5. Available at: <http://www.hrsdc.gc.ca/eng/lp/lo/lswe/we/review/report/toc.shtml>.

[203] Agocs and Osborne, above n 200, p 245.

[204] Ibid.

schemes can be effective provided clear obligations of result are imposed on employers, and compliance mechanisms are properly resourced with meaningful sanctions which can operate as both an incentive and a deterrent.

Demonstration of the importance of appropriate compliance mechanisms can also be found in Ontario, which, as we have seen, has one of the most progressive statutory requirements for proactive duties to achieve pay equity. However, it has been difficult to achieve compliance, particularly among small private sector employers. Although there are few up-to-date figures, early research demonstrated a significant lack of compliance. Thus Baker and Fortyn, who tracked the application of the legislation in the early 1990s, found substantial lapses in compliance among smaller firms where the majority of men and women worked.[205] Part of the reason for this is that, unlike the case in Northern Ireland, the Ontario legislation does not require employers to submit reports to the Pay Equity Office (PEO), which is responsible for implementing and auditing the Act. The PEO does have some powers to monitor the preparation and implementation of pay equity plans on its own initiative. However, due to limited resources, it has been unable to institute a thorough or comprehensive audit system, so that there has been no systematic means to identify organizations which fail to comply with the Act. Instead, the PEO randomly monitors particular sectors each year. For example, in 2008, it monitored the retail and hotel/motel sectors in the Peel Region for compliance with the Act. It has also directed much of its efforts towards developing information material, and establishing training tools and programmes. Its major success appears to be in this direction, although even here the PEO has been severely constrained by its budgetary limits.[206] Nevertheless, proactive measures, properly formulated and implemented, clearly have the potential to have a significant impact. Singh and Peng found that the Act has indeed contributed to narrowing the gender pay gap, where it was caused by gender discrimination, especially in the public sector.[207]

Possibly the most effective measure to achieve compliance in the private sector has been through the use of the State's considerable powers to award lucrative contracts.[208] Known as contract compliance,

[205] M Baker and N Fortin, 'Comparable Worth in a Decentralized Labour Market: The Case of Ontario' (2004) 37 Canadian Journal of Economics 850–78.
[206] P Singh and P Peng, 'Canada's Bold Experiment with Pay Equity' (2010) 25 Gender in Management: An International Journal 570–85.
[207] Ibid.
[208] C McCrudden, *Buying Social Justice* (Oxford University Press, 2007).

this approach has had particular traction in the US, where it was introduced in 1961 by President Kennedy. Contract compliance requires contractors of the federal government to increase the representation of racial minorities in their workforces as a condition for the award and the continuation of the contract.[209] Originally confined to race, these requirements have been extended to cover sex and religion,[210] and there are also schemes for persons with disabilities and disabled war veterans. Enforcement in race and gender cases lies with the powerful OFCCP, which has extensive investigatory powers, including routine compliance reviews; pre-award compliance reviews; individual complaint investigations; and class complaint investigations.[211] Most importantly, the threat to the economic well-being of private contractors by the sanction of withdrawal of lucrative federal contracts has been crucial in securing the effectiveness of positive duties. The OFCCP has a range of measures at its disposal to ensure compliance, culminating in the power to declare contractors ineligible to receive further contracts and to interrupt progress payments on existing contracts. In practice this power has rarely been used: both the threat of debarment and the risk of bad publicity have functioned as a sufficient deterrent. The importance of this deterrent is acknowledged by affected employers. Indeed, all the US employers interviewed in a recent study said that they would not have been able to sustain the significant increases in the representation of women and minorities which had taken place in their organizations without the compulsory affirmative action requirements.[212] The result is that this strategy, which applies to approximately 300,000 federal contractors, employing about 40 per cent of the working population, has had a significantly more powerful influence on employers than individual complaint-led litigation.

Also of great importance in the US have been measures which make the grant of federal or State funds or contracts conditional on participation by minority business enterprises, usually defined as businesses at least 50 per cent of which are owned by 'socially and economically disadvantaged individuals'.[213] Such policies, first established in 1969, generally make federal grants to State and local government entities for the purposes of local public works projects conditional on an assurance

---

[209] Executive Order 10925.   [210] Executive Order 11246.
[211] The facts in this paragraph are taken from Hepple, Coussey, and Choudhury, above n 5, paras 3.23–3.29.
[212] Ibid, paras 3.23–3.24, 3.29.
[213] Small Business Act 1953, s 4a; see Chapter Five.

that at least 10 per cent of the grant would be used for minority business enterprises. As we saw in Chapter Five, the major vehicle for present-day set-aside programmes is section 8(a) of the Small Business Act. The Act defines 'socially disadvantaged' individuals as 'those who have been subjected to racial or ethnic prejudice or cultural bias because of their identity as a member of a group without regard to their individual qualities'. There is a rebuttable presumption that members of certain groups are socially disadvantaged, including: Black Americans; Hispanic Americans; Native Americans; Asian Pacific Americans; and Subcontinent Asian Americans. The Small Business Act establishes as a goal that 5 per cent of the total value of all prime contract and subcontract awards each fiscal year should be awarded to small business concerns owned and controlled by socially and economically disadvantaged individuals, with a similar goal of 5 per cent for participation by similar concerns owned and controlled by women. Goals or set-asides have also been routinely part of federal funding measures of education, defence, transportation, and other activities over much of the last two decades.[214]

IV CONCLUSION

In surveying the limits of law through the prism of enforcement, we have come full circle conceptually. What does equality mean, and what are we hoping to achieve? The questions asked in Chapter One have received a range of different answers. Indeed, it is not just the answers, but also the questions, which have changed. As equality law faces new and increasingly complex challenges, so the conceptual apparatus has been adjusted and its legal manifestations re-examined. But the responses, although innovative, have often represented incomplete solutions; progress has been evident, but uneven. Those dedicated to equality still face an exacting, but ultimately deeply rewarding, task.

---

[214] Charles V Dale, 'Minority Contracting and Affirmative Action for Disadvantaged Small Businesses: Legal Issues', CRS Report for Congress Order Code RL33284 (24 February 2006), p 3; see eg Surface Transportation Assistance Act of 1982, Surface Transportation and Uniform Relocation Assistance Act of 1987, the Intermodal Surface Transportation Efficiency Act of 1991, and the Transportation Equity Act for the 21st Century (TEA-21), extended through fiscal year 2009 by Public Law 109-59, signed into law during the 109th Congress.

Index

Accommodation
  ethnic minorities 54
  gypsies and travellers, provision
    of sites 69–70
Adjudication
  adversarial structure, critique
    of 294–5
  county courts 280, 287–8
  European Court of Justice 289
  High Court 288–9
  human rights 289
  introduction 280
  remedies *see* Remedies
  sheriff courts 280, 287–8
  tribunals *see* Employment tribunals
Adverse effects discrimination
  154, 222
Affirmative action *see* **Reverse
  discrimination**
Age discrimination
  age-related benefits for older
    persons 102
  age-related public expenditure 103
  ageing population 102
  'ageism', justification 101
  classification on grounds of age 101
  default retirement age 106–7
  detrimental treatment of older
    persons 102
  direct discrimination,
    justification 198–202
  early retirement policies 102
  ethnic minorities 105
  EU Directive 105–6
  legislative developments 105–8
  negative discrimination 102
  older workers
    employment rates 102–3
    formal qualifications 104
    prejudice 104
    recruitment 104
    stigma and stereotyping 104
    training opportunities 104
    women 103
  pension ages 103
  pensioner poverty 105

  positive duties to promote
    equality 107–8
  retirement
    default age 106–7, 200–2
    early 102
    police officers 120
    tribunals, cases before 281
    young workers 107
Anti-discrimination law
  Civil Partnership Act 89–90
  disability 97–9
  enforcement
    adjudication *see* Adjudication
    Equality and Human Rights
      Commission *see* Equality and
      Human Rights Commission
      (EHRC)
    new duties of 279
    remedies *see* Remedies
    tribunals *see* Employment tribunals
  Equal Pay Act 42, 156
  Equality Act 7, 145
  equality, concepts of 153
  EU law *see* European Union
  grounds of discrimination
    see Discrimination
  historical background 6–7
  labour market, protection restricted
    to 144–5
  manifestations of equality, as response
    to 38
  private individuals/public bodies,
    bound by 148–52
  Race Relations Act 61–2
  scope 143–8
  Sex Discrimination Act 42
  sexual orientation 90–3
  States, bound by 148–52
  whom bound by 148–52
Armed forces
  discrimination in, sexual
    orientation 86–7
Asylum seekers
  backlog of cases 65
  detention 65
  hostility to 65

Asylum seekers (*cont.*)
human rights 66
screening 65
statistics 65
treatment of 65–6
welfare support 66
Autonomy
choice of grounds of
discrimination 131–4
dignity, link with 24–5

Bar
refusal of membership on citizenship
grounds 135
Belief *see* **Religion**

Canada
adverse effects discrimination 154, 222
Charter of Rights
affirmative action 257
grounds for discrimination 125, 128
positive duties to promote
equality 301
compliance mechanisms 323,
325–6, 330–3
decision-making process,
participation 318–20
reverse discrimination
beneficiaries, determination 273–4
strict scrutiny, standard of 270–2
'Capabilities' theory 27–8
Catholics
religious discrimination 76
Children
childcare role of women 45
citizenship 122–3
cultural diversity 67–8
custody
same-sex partnerships 87–8
sexual orientation 87–8
women 41
disabled 99
Citizenship
ethnic minorities 54
inclusive notion 54
'representation-reinforcing' theory 135
Civil partnerships 89–90
Civil rights 4
Civil Service
maximum age limit for new
entrants 181
women's pay 41
Classical society
principle of equality, not founded on 4

Collective bargaining
equal pay 159
Commission for Racial Equality
powers, function of 287
Comparators
dignity 22–3
direct discrimination
disability 171–4
introduction 168–9
pregnancy 12, 169–171
victimization 174–5
disability 171–4
equal pay 158–61
finding 10–1
group-based comparison, indirect
discrimination 183–9
hypothetical male comparator 161
indirect discrimination 183–9
EU 'particular disadvantage' test
187–8
statistics 184–7
sexual harassment 22
statistics, indirect discrimination
184–7
US 'four-fifths' rule 186–7
victimization 174–5
Compensation
injury to feelings 293–4
remedy of 291–2
statutory limit, removal 293
Contract
freedom of 5
County courts
cases before 280, 287–8
Cultural diversity
arranged marriages 67
children 67–8
combination of cultures 68
dress 66–7
family structure 67
households 67
inter-ethnic marriages 68
language 67
religion, importance of 67
single-parent families 67
social and cultural characteristics 67–8
Cumulative discrimination 112,
139–43

Damages
generally 293–4
punitive 292
Democracy
participative *see* **Participation**

Difference
accommodation and structural
change 30–1
detriment attached to 13
equality, relationship with 3
positive measures valuing 13
reconceptualization of notion of 112
substantial equality 30–1
treatment of 13
Dignity
autonomy, link with 24–5
choice of grounds of
discrimination 137–8
comparators 22–3
concept, interpretation 23
difficulties of 23
discrimination by association 229
discrimination by perception 229
equality as 227–30
EU Charter of Fundamental
Rights 20, 23
German Basic Law provisions 20
harassment 228
human rights 21–2
independent element in discrimination
law, as 23–4
individual liberty, link with 24–5
pension ages, equalization 21
primacy of 19
racism 229–30
recognition 28–30
sexual orientation 92
South African Constitution 20
substantive underpinning to equality
principle 21
Direct discrimination
aims of 176–7
comparator
disability 171–4
introduction 168–9
pregnancy 169–171
victimization 174–5
consistency, basis of 167–8
definition 166
generally 153
hypothetical comparison 168
intention, role in 203–14
introduction 166–7
justification 154, 190, 196–202
motive, role in 203–14
relative concept, as 166–7
symmetric concept, as 167, 175–6
Disability discrimination
characterization 95–7

comparators 171–4
conceptualization of disability 95
definition 214
duty of reasonable accommodation or
adjustment 98, 154, 214–21
justification 202
legislation 97–9
medical model of disability 95, 171–3
social model of disability 95, 172
tribunals, cases before 281
Disability Rights Commission
powers, function of 287
Disabled persons
benefits 100–1
children 99
current inequalities 99–101
discrimination *see* Disability
discrimination
employment 100
quota 97
statistics 99
statutory definition 97–8
stigma, prejudice and exclusion 95
UN Convention on the Rights of
Persons with Disabilities 98–9
Disadvantage
breaking the cycle of 26–8
ethnic minorities 54
history of, choice of grounds of
discrimination 138–9
redressing past, affirmative
action 260–3
Discrimination
adverse effects discrimination 154,
222
age *see* Age discrimination
association, by 229
cumulative discrimination 112,
139–143
defining grounds of
exhaustive list 113–8
fixed category approach 112–8
judges, decision of 118–25
introduction 112–3
non-exhaustive list 125–30
open-textured model 118–25
direct *see* Direct discrimination
disability *see* Disability discrimination
gender reassignment 93–5
grounds of
cumulative discrimination 112,
139–43
defining 112–30
determination 111

Discrimination (*cont.*)
difference, reconceptualization of
notion of 112
groups, identification 111–2
interaction between different
sources 111
intersectional 112
introduction 110–2
unifying principle, choice based
on 130–9
indirect *see* Indirect discrimination
intersectional 112, 139–43
justification
direct discrimination 196–202
indirect discrimination 190–6
introduction 190–1
law *see* Anti-discrimination law
perception, by 229
racial *see* Racial discrimination
reverse *see* Reverse discrimination
scope of law generally 109–10
sex *see* Sex discrimination
sexual orientation *see* Sexual
orientation
tribunals, record of 281
unifying principle, choice of grounds
based on
autonomy 131–4
dignity 137–8
history of disadvantage or
prejudice 138–9
immutability 131–4
individual choices 131–4
introduction 130
political process, access to
134–7
'representation-reinforcing'
theory 134–7
Diversity
reverse discrimination,
justification 266–7
Dress
cultural identity 66–7

Economic concerns
equality, relationship with 35–7
Education
ethnic minorities 56
reverse discrimination 252–5
Employment tribunals
ACAS 281, 284
adversarial procedure 284
appeals 280
burden of proof 286

claims to 279–80
discouraging performance,
contributory factors 283
Employment Appeal Tribunal
(EAT) 280
Equality and Human Rights
Commission
assistance to complainants 287
proceedings brought by 285
strategic litigation 287
evidence, obtaining 283, 286
individual, burden on 283
individual victim 285–6
legal aid, absence 287
length of process 282
members 280, 283
NGOs, actions brought by 284–5
pre-hearing settlements 281
public sector 282
race discrimination cases 280
record of discrimination cases 281
representative action 285
representatives 280, 283–4
success rate 281
system, structure of 280
trade unions, actions brought by 284–5
withdrawal of claims 282
Equal opportunities
generally 18–9
reverse discrimination 241–8
Equal Opportunities Commission
powers, function of 287
Equal pay
collective bargaining 159
comparators 158–61
consistency rather than substance 162
early policy of, striking down 40
equal treatment vs
proportionality 163
equal value 156–8
generally 9
introduction 156
justification for unequal pay for equal
work 163–6
regional differentiation 159
legislation 42, 156
lowering of men's pay to that of
women's 162
part-time women workers 46
pay gap 47–9
post-First World War 41
proportionality 163
statistics 45–9
treating like alike 9, 158–62

tribunals, claims before 281
  length of process 282
  public sector 282
Equality
  abstract view of justice, based on 2
  background 4–8
  business or market-oriented concerns,
    competing with 35–7
  choice between different conceptions
    of 2–3
  co-existence with domination 5
  comparator, finding 10–1
  concepts used in anti-discrimination
    law 153
  development 4–8
  difference *see* Difference
  dignity *see* Dignity
  disparate impact of equal
    treatment 154
  duty of reasonable accommodation and
    adjustment 154
  emancipation of all, arguments for 5–6
  emergence as organizing social
    principle 5
  Equality Act 2010 7
  equality before the law 153
  fairness as matter of consistency 14–7
  formulations of, different 2
  gender *see* Women
  ideal of 1
  individual fault, liability 13–4
  individualism 13–4
  legal form, capturing in 1
  legal formulations of 3–4
  legal impediments to, dismantling 6
  legal principle, phases of
    development 6
  levelling down 10
  liberty, competing value of 33–5
  'male norm' 11
  meaning of 1
  modern construct, as 4
  nine protected characteristics 7
  opportunity, of *see* Equal
    opportunities
  pensionable ages 108
  positive duties to promote *see* Positive
    duties to promote equality
  proportionality, as 221–6
  relative principle, as 9
  reverse discrimination and 233–6
  results, of 14–7, 180–1
  social values, conflict with 3
  substantive equality

difference, accommodation and
  structural change 30–1
disadvantage, breaking cycle of 26–8
four-dimensional concept 25–33
participative dimension 31–3
recognition dimension 28–30
redistributive dimension 26–8
respect and dignity 28–30
reverse discrimination and 235–6
social inclusion and political
  voice 31–3
transformative dimension 30–1
substantive view of justice, based on 2
treating likes alike 8–14, 153–4
unequal treatment necessary to
  achieve 2
'universal individual', assumption
  of 11
Equality and Human Rights
  Commission (EHRC)
action plan 295
agreements 298–9
employment tribunals
  assistance to complainants 287
  proceedings brought by 285–6
  strategic litigation 287
'equality audits' 296
formal investigations 295–6
inquiry 297
  report and recommendations
    from 297
obstacles and restrictions on
  predecessors 295–6
positive duties to promote equality,
  compliance powers 327–8
representations 296
unlawful act notice 295
Ethnic minorities
accommodation 54
African origin 54
age discrimination 105
Bangladeshis 57–9
Caribbean origin 53
child poverty 56
citizenship rights 54
culture *see* Cultural diversity
current inequalities 55–61
differences between 55–6
East African Indians 54
education 56
employment 54
  rates 56
harassment 59–60
historical background 53–5

Ethnic minorities (*cont.*)
income poverty 56
Indians 54
Jews *see* Jews
most disadvantaged groups 57
multiculturalism 52–3
Pakistani 57–9
police
Chief Constables from 59
lack of confidence in 60–1
prejudice against 59–60
racial prejudice 54
representation in public life 59
socio-economic classes 56
statistics 55
upward mobility 55–6
violence against 59–60
women, employment and pay 58–9
Ethnic origin
religion, and 83–4
Ethnicity *see* Cultural diversity;
Ethnic minorities; Racial
discrimination; Racism
EU Charter of Fundamental Rights
dignity 20, 23
grounds of discrimination 110
solidarity 33
European Convention on Human
Rights
affirmative action 258
approach to demarcating scope of
protection 146–8
cases before courts for review on
grounds of breach of 289
grounds of discrimination 7, 110
non-exhaustive list 125–8
primary guiding principle of
Article 14 155
religion 85
States bound by discrimination
law 148–9
European Court of Human Rights
same-sex partnerships, equality
87–8
European Court of Justice (ECJ)
cases before 289
referral to 280
reverse discrimination, standard of
scrutiny 272
European Union
age discrimination 105–6
Charter of Fundamental Rights
see EU Charter of
Fundamental Rights

citizens, free movement 64–5
equality and economic concerns,
relationship 35
grounds of discrimination 7
exhaustive list 113–6
harassment 228
indirect discrimination, 'particular
disadvantage' test 187–8
positive duties to promote
equality 307
proactive duties, survey 303–4
racial discrimination legislation 62–3,
144
religious discrimination 84
reverse discrimination, equal
opportunities 241–8
sexual orientation 91
States/individuals bound by
discrimination law 149–51
women's rights 42–3
Exclusion 5

Faith schools 83, 117–8, 207–10
Flexible working 45
Freedom of speech
equality in conflict with other social
values 3
racial comments and 3, 34

Gender equality *see* Women
Gender reassignment
discrimination on grounds of
93–5
marriage 93–5
Germany
Basic Law, dignity 20
Groups *see also* Ethnic
minorities; Prisoners;
Religious minorities;
Women
Canada, protection in 130
comparators *see* Comparators
identification 111–2
immutable characteristics 130
'out-groups' 26
subgroups 142
Gypsies and travellers
European policy 72
homelessness 70
human rights 71–2
population size 69
rights, claiming in court 71
Roma 72–3, 176–7, 204, 223
sites, provision of 69–70

Harassment
definition 228
dignity 228
ethnic minorities 59–60
sexual 22
sexual orientation 91
women 43
High Court
cases before 280, 288–9
Hindus
accommodation of religious
practices 220
religious discrimination 81–2
Homosexuals
criminal offence of homosexuality 86,
123–4
discrimination *see* Sexual orientation
promotion, prohibition 87
Human rights
asylum seekers 66
dignity 21–2
European Convention *see* European
Convention on Human Rights
gypsies and travellers 71–2
scrutiny of executive decisions,
common law principles and
primary legislation 289

Immigrants
asylum seekers *see* Asylum seekers
British colonies, from 53–5
controls on 55, 64–5
employers' checks 64
EU citizens 64–5
Immutability
choice of grounds of
discrimination 131–4
Indian Constitution
grounds of discrimination 129
special provisions for two categories of
disadvantaged groups 276–7
Indirect discrimination
aims 180–3
comparator, role of 183–9
concept, development 177–80
disparate impact element 178–9
justification 178–80
elements 154, 178–80
equal treatment element 178–9
equality of results 180–1
generally 154
intention, role in 203–14
justification defence 154, 182–3,
190–6

motive, role in 203–14
neutral rules, examination of 182
objectives 180–3
proportionality 190–1
statutory definition 179–80
Injunction
mandatory 291
Injury to feelings
award for 293–4
Institutional racism
definition 60
generally 60
Metropolitan police service 6–7, 60
Intersectional discrimination 112,
139–43

Jews
ethnic group, whether 115
faith schools 117–8, 207–10
religious discrimination 73, 76–9
Job segregation
women 40–1, 156
Judges
ethnic minorities 59
women 50
Judicial review
EHRC standing to pursue 288
European Convention on Human
Rights, breach 289
High Court 280, 288–9
positive duties to promote
equality 326–7
'representation-reinforcing' theory
of 32, 134–7

Language
cultural identity 67
Legal aid
employment tribunals 284, 287
Liberty
business or market-oriented
concerns 35–7
dignity, link with 24–5
equality, competing value of 33–5
interpretation 34
licence, interpretation as 34
speech, interpretation as 34

Marriage
arranged marriages 67
dismissal of women on 40
gender reassignment 93–4
inter-ethnic marriages 68
legal position of women in 38–9

Marriage (*cont.*)
  rape, in 39
  same-sex couples 89
  violence, in 39
  voting right, exclusion of married
    women 39
Maternity *see* **Pregnancy and
    maternity**
Mediaeval society
  principle of equality, not founded on 4
Members of Parliament
  ethnic minorities 59
  women 49–50
    all-women shortlists 239–40
Metropolitan police service
  institutional racism 6–7
Migration *see* **Immigrants**
Minorities *see* **Ethnic minorities;
    Religious minorities**
Multiculturalism *see also* **Cultural
    diversity**
  generally 52–3
Muslims
  accommodation of religious
    practices 195, 220
  cumulative discrimination 143
  ethnic group, whether 115
  religious discrimination 79–81

Neutrality
  State 235
Non-citizens
  denial of rights to 1
**Non-governmental organizations
    (NGOs)**
  employment tribunals, proceedings
    brought by 284–5
Northern Ireland
  Fair Employment Commission
    298
  positive equality duties 7, 301–2, 306,
    322–4, 328–30
  religious discrimination 73

Part-time workers
  women 45–6, 157, 164, 181–2
Participation
  political *see* Political participation
  positive duties to promote
    equality 317–21
  substantive equality 31–3
Paternity rights 44
Pensions
  ages 103, 168, 206

  equalization, dignity 21
  women's qualification for State 47
Police
  ethnic minorities
    Chief Constables from 59
    lack of confidence in 60–1
    persons stopped by 61
    institutional racism 6–7, 60
    Metropolitan police service,
      institutional racism 6–7, 60
  retirement age 120
  women's pay 41
Political participation
  access to political process 134–7
  ethnic minorities 59
  women
    all-women shortlists 239–40
    banned from 39
    Members of Parliament 49–50
    voting rights 39, 41
Political voice
  substantive equality 31–3
Positive duties to promote equality
  age 107–8
  aims and objectives 312–7
  approaches 300–2
  Canada 301, 306
  compliance mechanisms 321–35
    Canada 323, 325–6, 330–3
    contract compliance 333–4
    effectiveness 324
    EHRC powers 327–8
    individual, role 325
    judicial review procedure, use
      326–7
    Northern Ireland 322–4, 328–30
    private sector technique 333–4
  conclusion 335
  decision-making, process of 317–21
  'due regard' standard 307–10
  elements of duty 306
  generally 7, 230–1, 239
  impact assessment of legislation and
    policy 305–6
  initiative for 299
  introduction 299–302
  levels of operation 305–6
  mainstreaming 300
  nature of duty 305–12
  Northern Ireland 7, 301–2, 306
  open method of coordination 300–1
  plan, formulation and
    implementation 306
  public bodies 8

defining 304–5
responsibility of 303
statutory duties 301–2
publication of performance
information 311
statutory duties 301
trade unions, responsibility of 303–4
whom applying to 303–5
Pregnancy and maternity
comparators 12, 169–71
special treatment of women 176
women's rights, protection 43–4
Prisoners
ethnic minorities, statistics 61
racial segregation 9, 119–20
women with young children 23
Proactive measures *see* **Positive
duties to promote equality**
Proportionality
equal pay 163
equality as 221–6
generally 232
indirect discrimination 190–1
reverse discrimination 245–6
Public bodies
functions bound by anti-
discrimination law 151–2
positive duties to promote equality
see Positive duties to promote
equality
Public sector
equality duty 7–8

Race
concept 50–1
Race relations
institutionalized inequalities 50
Racial discrimination
EU legislation 62–3, 144
legislative developments 61–3
police, ethnic minorities stopped
by 61
tribunals, cases before 280–1
Racial segregation
prisoners 9
Racism
blackness, political concept of 51–2
dignity 229–30
institutional racism 6–7, 60
MacPherson Report 60
opposites, polarization 51
racially aggravated violence, offences
of 63
racially motivated incidents 59–60

racist comments, freedom of speech
and 3, 34
religious discrimination as form of 73
Rape
marriage, in 39
statistics 49
Rastafarians
accommodation of religious
practices 220
ethnic group, whether 115
Religion
discrimination on grounds of
see Religious discrimination
ethnic minorities, importance to 67
ethnicity, culture and community and,
relationship 74–5
faith schools 83, 117–8
reasonable accommodations of
religious needs of
employees 215, 219–22
reliance on religious belief to justify
other forms of discrimination 74
schools 82–3
Religious discrimination
absence of protection against 75
ethnic or cultural discrimination,
as 73
EU legislation 84
exception to prohibition 84–5
'faith-based communities' concept
of 75
historical background 75–83
human rights 85
institutionalized religious
privilege 75
legal developments 83–6
management of conflicting
equalities 84–5
political affiliation, close links with
discrimination based on 73
protection against, core value of
international human rights 73
racism, as form of 73
relationship with other grounds of
discrimination 73–4
religions discriminating against each
other 85
religiously motivated violence,
offences of 63
tribunals, cases before 281
Religious minorities
assimilationist tendency 12–3
Catholics 76
Hindus 81–2

Religious minorities (*cont.*)
    Jews 73, 76–9, 207–10
    Muslims 79–81
Remedies
    compensation 291–4
    damages 291–4
    injury to feelings 293–4
    mandatory injunctions 291
    nature of 289–90
    punitive damages 292
    recommendations 290–1
Representation
    affirmative action 264–6
Representative bodies
    equality of results 17
Respect
    sexual orientation 92
    substantive equality 28–30
Results
    equality of 14–7, 180–1
Retirement
    default ages 106–7, 200–2
    early 102
    police officers 120
Reverse discrimination
    aims and effectiveness
        affirmative action 260–9
        introduction 259
        standard of scrutiny 269–73
    approaches 237
    barriers, removal 260–3
    beneficiaries, determination 273–5
    conclusion 278
    derogation approach 241–8
    diversity 266–7
    education 252–5
    endorsement at international level 258
    equal opportunities 241–8
    formal approach 237–40
    formal equality, and 233–5
    innocent third party, discrimination
        against 249
    introduction 232–3
    limitations 278
    meaning of term 232
    past disadvantage, redressing 260–3
    policies 256–8
    proportionality 232, 245–6
    recognition and redistribution 275–8
    representation and perspective
        264–6
    role models 268–9
    scrutiny, standard of 249–50,
        269–73

    status and socio-economic
        disadvantage, relationship 275–8
    substantive approach 256–8
    substantive equality, and 235–6
    symmetrical approach 237–40
    US Supreme Court, approach of
        248–56
    voting rights 251–2
    women
        all-women shortlists 239–40
        decision-making, participation
            in 265–6
        protective legislation 246–8
        representation 264–5
Role models
    reverse discrimination 268–9

Safety
    accommodation of religious
        practices 220
Same-sex partnerships
    adoption 88
    children, custody 87–8
    Civil Partnership Act 89–90
    European Court of Human Rights,
        role 87–8
    marriage, right to refused 89
    recognition 87–90
    social security benefits 88
    tenancy rights 87
Schools
    faith schools 83, 117–8, 207–10
    homophobic bullying 92
    religion within 82–3
Sex discrimination *see also* **Women**
    equal pay *see* Equal pay
    gender reassignment 93–5
    harassment *see* Sexual harassment
    immigration rules, in 122–3
    legislation 42
    pregnancy and maternity
        see Pregnancy and maternity
    tribunal cases, statistics 281
    US Supreme Court, approach of 121
Sexual harassment
    comparators 22
    dignity 22, 228
    generally 43
Sexual orientation
    adoption 88
    age of consent 86
    anti-discrimination law 90–3
    bullying at school 92
    children, custody 87–8

dignity and equality, discrimination as
  denial of 86
dignity and respect 92
EU law 91
formal equality before the law 86–7
harassment 91
homophobia 92
military, exclusion from 86–7
same-sex partnerships,
  recognition 87–90
social security benefits 88
tenancy rights 87
tribunals, cases before 281
violence 92
Sexual violence
women, against 49
Sheriff Court
cases before 280, 287–8
Sikhs
accommodation of religious
  practices 220–1
ethnic group, whether 115
Slavery
abolition 53
eighteenth-century Britain 53
Social inclusion
substantive equality 31–3
Social justice
definition 26
Social security benefits
disabled persons 100–1
same-sex partnerships 88
Social values
equality in conflict with 3
Solidarity
participation 33
South Africa
affirmative action 256–7
dignity 20
grounds of discrimination 110, 125,
  129
reverse discrimination
  beneficiaries, determination
    274–5
  standard of scrutiny 272
Substantive equality *see* Equality

Terrorism
detention of suspects 10
Trade unions
employment tribunals, proceedings
  brought by 284–5
positive duties to promote
  equality 303–4

Transsexuals *see* Gender
  reassignment
Travellers *see* Gypsies and travellers
Tribunals *see* Employment tribunals

United States
affirmative action programmes, status
  and socio-economic
  disadvantage 277–8
Constitution, defining grounds of
  discrimination 118–25
'disparate impact' concept 154
First Americans, accommodation of
  religious practices 220
indirect discrimination
  concept 177–8
  'four-fifths' rule 186–7
mandatory injunction 291
positive duties to promote equality
  contract compliance 334
  minority business enterprises 334–5
reverse discrimination, strict standard
  of scrutiny 269–70

Victimization
comparators 174–5
Violence
ethnic minorities, against 59–60
racially aggravated, offences of 63
religiously motivated, offences of 63
sexual orientation 92
women, against 49
  marriage, in 39

Women
age discrimination 105
children
  childcare role 45, 181
  citizenship 122–3
  custody 41
cumulative discrimination 140–2
current inequalities 45–50
decision-making, participation
  in 265–6
employment and pay 6
equal pay *see* Equal pay
equal suffrage attaining 6, 39, 41
EU law 42–3
flexible working 45
harassment 43
job segregation 40–1, 156
judges 50
management, in 50
marriage *see* Marriage

Women (*cont.*)
  part-time workers 45–6, 157, 164,
      181–2
  pay 6
    equal *see* Equal pay
    ethnic minorities 58
  pension, qualification for State 47
  political participation, banned
      from 39
  post-First World War 41
  post-Second World War 41–2
  pregnancy and maternity
      see Pregnancy and maternity
  prisoners, with young children 23
  property rights, gaining 41

  representation, affirmative
      action 264–5
  sex discrimination *see* Sex
      discrimination
  sexual violence against 49
  'special' protection 168, 246–8
  subordination to men, legal 38–9
  teachers, dismissal on marriage 40
  under-representation of 49–50
  violence against 49
    marriage, in 39
  voting rights 39, 41
  workforce, disadvantages in 40–1

Young workers 107